THE IMAGINATION OF THE NEW LEFT

THE IMAGINATION OF THE NEW LEFT
A GLOBAL ANALYSIS OF 1968

BY
GEORGE KATSIAFICAS

SOUTH END PRESS BOSTON, MASSACHUSETTS

copyright © 1987 by George Katsiaficas

Cover design by Cynthia Peters
Produced by South End Press
Printed in the USA
First printing

Photo credits:
p. 63: Alan Copeland (ed.), *People's Park* (Ballantine Books, 1969), p. 70; p. 102 and cover: *Les inédit de Mai 68* (May 1978), p. 99 (from Agence Associated Press, May 22, 1968, Gare de Lyon; p. 121: J. Gregory Payne, *Mayday: Kent State* (Kendall/Hunt Publishing Company, 1981), p. 17; p. 149: *Ramparts* (April, 1970).

An earlier version of parts of this book appeared in *Monthly Review* as: "The Meaning of May '68" (May 1978) and "The Extraparliamentary Left in Europe" (September 1982). The author is grateful to the editors of *Monthly Review* for their permission to use these pages.

Library of Congress Cataloging-in-Publication Data

Katsiaficas, George N., 1949-
   The imagination of the New Left.

   Includes bibliographical references and index.
   1. Government, Resistance to--History--20th century.
2. Right and left (Political science)--History--20th century. 3. Dissenters--History--20th century.
I. Title.
JC328.3.K38 1987   322.4   87-2334
ISBN 0-896-8-228-8
ISBN 0-89608-227-X (pbk.)

South End Press   116 St. Botolph Street   Boston, MA   02115 for Herbert Marcuse, teacher and friend

TABLE
OF
CONTENTS

PHOTOGRAPHS, CHARTS, MAPS, AND TABLES

PREFACE

Unlike any year of the half century preceding it, 1968 will be remembered for the worldwide eruption of new social movements, ones which profoundly changed the world without seizing political power. From Paris to Chicago, and Prague to Mexico City, unexpectedly popular struggles erupted in a global challenge to the established order. What were these movements for? Where have they gone? What have been their effects? To answer these questions is the purpose of this book.

The literature on the New Left is already so vast that it would fill several libraries, yet there have been few attempts to answer the question: "What did the New Left want?" In part, the reactive nature of the movement—its appearance as the Great Refusal—accounts for this void. Indeed, what the movement aspired to create was scarcely known among many of its participants. Is it even possible to speak of a common vision?

I selected the general strike of May 1968 in France and the student strike of 1970 in the United States as the focus for this book because the actions of millions of people during these situations concretely demonstrated the New Left's vision of a qualitatively different society. By studying the spontaneously generated forms of dual power and the aspirations of millions of people during these periods of crisis, it became possible to discern the goals of the popular movement. In addition, the response of the established system to these crises reveals the powerful impact the New Left had on society, an impact obscured by the movement's decline amid apparent failure.

In these case studies, I emphasize the form and content of emergent forces during periods of social upheaval. Although there were many leaders, my analysis is focused on the praxis of *social actors*, millions of people who together generate a new dimension to reality by becoming a "class-for-itself." By focusing on these two general strikes, I hope to make clear the imagination of the New Left.

To deal with the May 1968 near-revolution in France involved reading dozens of analyses both in French and English, but when I turned to the May 1970 student strike in the United States, I could not find one book which analyzed these events as a whole. The student strike has been a neglected moment in an otherwise heavily studied social movement, and my chapter on May 1970 presents for the first time a comprehensive view of this history. For the most part, activists from the pre-1966 period of the movement have been its historians in the United States, and their writing of history has been an empirical endeavor based on their own experiences and perceptions. Furthermore, the post-1966 period of the New Left, when the movement spread to working-class students and inner-city ghettos, was one in which activists adopted "revolutionary" political ideas (in contrast to the reformism of the previous phase). The resulting situation is such that a great deal has been published on the experiences of the pre-1966 period of the movement and the ideology of the post-1966 period, leaving the events of 1968 to 1970 largely unrecorded, or at best, superficially analyzed.

The first part of this book provides a global analysis of the New Left because the international character of the movement was an essential dimension of its emergence and decline. More importantly, the various movements of 1968 developed a unified global focus for action, and their visions were international ones. Because these "new social movements" have generally been analyzed separately (in national, racial, gender, and organizational forms), the important dimension of their interconnectedness has been neglected. By introducing the notion of the "*eros* effect," I seek to universalize our understanding of the subjectivity of these movements within the framework of objective forces at work in the world system.

There exists a wealth of "data" about the New Left, and I was fortunate to be granted access to a diverse set of archives. These included the special collection of the Herbert Hoover Institution at Stanford University, the files of the *Zentralinstitut für Sozial Wissenschaftliche Forschung* in West Berlin, the archive at the *Otto-Suhr Institut* of the Free University of Berlin, and the personal archives of activists in France, West Germany, and the United States. The staff of the Central Library at the University of California, San Diego (where I completed an earlier draft of this book as my doctoral dissertation) procured materials from as far away as the library of the Pentagon in Washington, D.C. A Fulbright Grant made it possible for me to complete the research in Germany, and I conducted a number of interviews in France, West Germany, Holland, Czechoslovakia, Denmark, Hungary, East Germany, Jordan, Lebanon, Syria, Spain, Mexico, and the United States.

Peter Bohmer's comments have made this book appreciably better than it would have been. For their support during the years I have been working on this project, I wish to thank Carol Becker, James and Grace Boggs, Alan Cleeton, Jules and Martinne Chancel, Stew Albert, Judy Clavir-Albert, Alda Blanco and Rick Maxwell, Bertha and L.S. Stavrianos, Rosie Lynn, Paul Sweezy, Billy Nessen, Rudy Torres, Bernd Rabehl, Chrysoula, Nicholas, and Diane Katsiaficas, David Helvarg, Joseph Gusfield, and Doreen and André Gorz. I owe special and often unspoken gratitude to Dalal, Cassandra, and

Katherine Hanna. Cynthia Peters has been a tremendous help in navigating the manuscript through the editorial process.

As a researcher, I seek to make apparent dimensions of the New Left which have yet to be thematized, and as a participant in the movement, I have these same concerns close to my heart, a coincidence of interest which has been a key reason for my ability to complete the formidable project I began in 1977. Without the encouragement of Herbert Marcuse and the confidence with which he showered me, I would no doubt have abandoned this project. To him, I dedicate this book.

July 1987

Part I

A GLOBAL ANALYSIS OF 1968

Chapter 1

THE NEW LEFT
AS A
WORLD-
HISTORICAL
MOVEMENT

The nature of Spirit may be understood by a glance at its direct opposite—Matter. As the essence of Matter is Gravity, so, on the other hand, we may affirm that the substance, the essence of Spirit is Freedom.
—G.W.F. Hegel

The worldwide episodes of revolt in 1968 have generally been analyzed from within their own national context, but it is in reference to the global constellation of forces and to each other that these movements can be understood in theory as they occurred in practice. Particularly since World War II, it is increasingly difficult to analyze social movements from within the confines of a nation-state. The events which catalyze social movements today are often international ones. The 1970 nationwide student strike in the United States, for example, is remembered mainly because of the killings at Kent State and Jackson State Universities, but it was enacted in opposition to the U.S. invasion of Cambodia as well as the repression of the Black Panther Party at home.

The international connections between social movements in 1968 were often synchronic as television, radio, and newspapers relayed news of events throughout the world. In May 1968, for example, when a student revolt led to a general strike of nearly ten million workers in France, there were significant demonstrations of solidarity in Mexico City, Berlin, Tokyo, Buenos Aires, Berkeley, and Belgrade, and students and workers in both Spain and Uruguay attempted general strikes of their own. Massive student strikes in Italy forced Prime Minister Aldo Moro and his cabinet to resign; Germany experienced its worst political crisis since World War II; and a student strike at the University of Dakar, Senegal, led to a general strike of workers. These are instances of what sociologists have called "contagion effects" (and what I consider "*eros* effects"); they remain to this day understudied, a moment of neglect which stands in inverse proportion to their significance.

3

It was not by chance alone that the Tet offensive in Vietnam occurred in the same year as the Prague Spring, the May events in France, the student rebellion in West Germany, the assassination of Martin Luther King, the takeover of Columbia University, riots at the Democratic National Convention in Chicago, and the pre-Olympic massacre in Mexico City. These events were related to one another, and a synchronic analysis of the global movement of 1968 validates Hegel's proposition that world history moves from east to west. The global oppositional forces converged in a pattern of mutual amplification: "The whole world was watching," and with each act of the unfolding drama, whole new strata of social actors entered the arena of history, until finally a global contest was created.

Although there was a self-described "New Left" in France as early as 1957, and in 1971, there was a "New Left" insurrection in Sri Lanka, a climactic point was reached in the life of the New Left, a period of intense struggle between global uprisings and global reaction, a pivot around which protests appeared to lose momentum as "repressive tolerance" shed its tolerant appearance. This critical conjuncture in the world constellation of forces occurred in 1968, a year of world-historical importance. As one observer put it:

> History does not usually suit the convenience of people who like to divide it into neat periods, but there are times when it seems to have pity on them. The year 1968 almost looks as though it had been designed to serve as some sort of signpost. There is hardly any region of the world in which it is not marked by spectacular and dramatic events which were to have profound repercussions on the history of the country in which they occurred and, as often as not, globally. This is true of the developed and industrialized capitalist countries, of the socialist world, and of the so-called "third world"; of both the eastern and western, the northern and southern hemispheres.[1]

Prior to 1968, no one knew and few could have guessed what was in store for world history. Without warning, worldwide movements spontaneously erupted. At the beginning of the year, de Gaulle hailed France as an "infallible beacon for the world," but if he had known what kind of beacon France would be in 1968, he might never have delivered his New Year's Address. By the end of the year, President Lyndon Johnson summed it up in his Thanksgiving Proclamation: "Americans, looking back on 1968, may be more inclined to ask God's mercy and guidance than to offer him thanks for his blessings."[2] Without warning, the global turmoil of 1968 erupted and became directed against both capitalism and real-world socialism, against both authoritarian power and patriarchal authority.

Despite its apparent failure, the New Left regenerated the dormant traditions of self-government and international solidarity in Europe and the United States, and temporarily or not, the question of revolution was once again on the historical agenda. At the same time, the meaning of revolution was enlarged to include questions of power in everyday life as well as questions of power won by past revolutions, and the goal of revolution came to be the decentralization and self-management of power and resources.

If the idea of revolution in an industrialized society was inconceivable for three decades prior to the New Left, the *kind* of revolution prefigured in the emergent praxis of the movement was unlike ones of the century before it. By posing the historical possibility of a communalism based upon enlarged social autonomy and greater individual freedom (not their suppression), a new world society based on the international decentralization of political and economic institutions (not their national centralization), and a way of life based on a new harmony with Nature (not its accelerating exploitation), the New Left defined a unique stage in the aspirations of revolutionary movements. A new set of values was born in the movement's international and interracial solidarity, in its rejection of middle-class values like the accumulation of wealth and power, in its fight against stupefying routines and ingrained patterns of patriarchal domination, and in its attempt to reconstruct everyday life, not according to tradition or scientific rationality, but through a liberated sensibility. In crisis situations such as those of May 1968 in France and, to some extent, May 1970 in the United States, these values were momentarily realized in spontaneously generated forms of dual power.

Less than two decades since the New Left reached its high point, however, it is difficult to find obvious traces of that movement, particularly in the United States. The tempo of modern history has been so rapid that what was new twenty years ago seems to be as far away from the present as all the rest of history. Once we review some of the events of 1968, however, it should become clear that, far from evaporating into the stratosphere in failure, the New Left was diluted by its very success. The French May events rejuvenated the Socialist Party and brought it to power in 1981, and the crisis created by the student strike of May 1970 led to Watergate and an end to U.S. military involvement in Vietnam. The civil rights acts and equal rights initiatives indicate a broad shift in the status of minorities and women while anti-racist and feminist values of the New Left have spread throughout society, permeating even the most densely constructed protective membranes. In the early 1960s, the civil rights movement helped to desegregate schools, lunch counters, and buses and won the right for blacks to vote in the South. In the 1980s, Jesse Jackson's campaign for the presidency won millions of votes in the nation's primary elections. In the 1960s, only a few people in the industrialized countries supported the right of South African blacks to rule their country. Today, an end to apartheid is nearly universally desired.

In historical time, or "world time," as Theda Skocpol has named it,[3] it is still too early to fully account for the New Left. If there is one fact which has been established by the New Left, however, it is the renewed idea of revolution in the industrialized countries. Prior to the New Left, there was a widespread belief that industrialized societies were harmonious social systems which, internally at least, contained no major oppositional forces. The "end of ideology" was proclaimed in one form or another by Daniel Bell, Raymond Aron, and Seymour Martin Lipset. Since the New Left, however, a key question for social research has been the legitimation crisis of the system.

In the aftermath of 1968, it is widely recognized that social crises can arise unexpectedly and overnight reach proportions so immense that none of the participants (willing and unwilling ones) can be certain of their outcome. For some, social crises are moments of madness in which it seems that the social machine has broken down, that the driver's seat is empty, and that the passengers have become delirious. For others, these are moments when exhilarating new visions of life are created not by communication with God, not concocted through drugs, but developed here on earth in the midst of public life.[4] Though secular, such moments metaphorically resemble the religious transformation of the individual soul through the sacred baptism in the ocean of universal life and love. The integration of the sacred and the secular in such moments of "political *eros*" (a term used by Herbert Marcuse) is an indication of the true potentiality of the human species, the "real history" which remains repressed and distorted within the confines of "prehistoric" powers and taboos.

World-Historical Movements

Periods of crisis and turmoil *on a global scale* are relatively rare in history. Since the French and American revolutions, it is possible to identify only a handful of such periods of global eruptions: 1848-49, 1905-07, 1917-19, and 1967-70. In each of these periods, global upheavals were spontaneously generated. In a chain reaction of insurrections and revolts, new forms of power emerged in opposition to the established order, and new visions of the meaning of freedom were formulated in the actions of millions of people. Even when these movements were unsuccessful in seizing power, immense adjustments were necessitated both within and between nation-states, and the defeated movements offered revealing glimpses of the newly developed nature of society and the new kinds of class struggles which were to follow.

Throughout history, fresh outbreaks of revolution have been known to "conjure up the spirits of the past to their service and borrow from them names, battle cries, and costumes in order to present the new scene of world history in this time-honored disguise and this borrowed language."[5] The movements of 1968 were no exception: Activists self-consciously acted in the tradition of past revolutions. As one observer noted in discussing the general strike of May 1968 in France:

> In the Paris of May 1968, innumerable commentators, writing to celebrate or to deplore, proffered a vast range of mutually exclusive explanations and predictions. But for all of them, the sensibility of May triggered off a remembrance of things past. By way of Raymond Aron, himself in touch with Tocqueville, readers of *Le Figaro* remembered February 1848; by way of Henri Lefebvre, French students remembered the Proclamation of the commune in March 1871, as did those who read Edgar Morin in *Le Monde*; French workers listened to elder militants who spoke of the occupation of factories in June 1936; and most adults, whether or

not they had been in the Resistance, relived August 1944, the liberation of Paris.[6]

The historical parallels of the May events were recognized in the written statements of the strikers when they called on the tradition of 1789, 1848, the Paris Commune, and the Russian soviets of 1905 and 1917 to define their movement. Such periods of the *eros* effect witness the basic assumptions and values of a social order (nationalism, hierarchy, and specialization) being challenged in theory and practice by new human standards. The capacity of millions of people to see beyond the social reality of their day—to imagine a better world and fight for it—demonstrates a human characteristic (the *eros* effect) which may be said to transcend time and space.

The reality of Paris at the end of May 1968 conformed less to the categories of existence preceding May (whether the former political legitimacy of the government, management's control of the workplaces, or the isolation of the students from the "real world") than to the activated imaginations of the movement. Millions of people moved beyond a mere negation of the previous system by enacting new forms of social organization and new standards for the goal-determination of the whole system. Modes of thought, abolished in theory by empiricists and structuralists, emerged in a practical human effort to break out of antiquated categories of existence and establish non-fragmented modes of Being. Debate ceased as to whether human beings were capable of such universal notions as Justice, Liberty, or Freedom. Rather, these abstractions, concretized in the actions of millions of people, became the popularly redefined reality.

The May events, like the Commune and other moments of revolutionary upheaval, established however briefly a new type of social reality where *living human energy* and not *things* was predominant. From this perspective, the May events can be viewed as a taste of the joy of human life which will be permanently unleashed with the advent of a new world system qualitatively different than that in France or on either side of the "iron curtain." With the end of "pre-history" and the beginning of "human history," human imagination will be freed to take giant steps in constructing a better world. "All Power to the Imagination," written everywhere in May 1968, will become inscribed in the lives and institutions of future generations.[7]

Historically speaking, it has often been the case that a particular nation has experienced social upheavals at the same time as order reigned elsewhere. *Coups d'état,* putsches, and armed takeovers of power within the confines of a particular nation have become so commonplace in the modern world—particularly in the third world—that it is rare for a long period of time to pass *without* some change in national ruling elites. In the case of the New Left (and the movements of 1848 and 1905), there was no successful revolution or seizure of power despite the movement's global character, but the social convulsions of 1848, 1905, and 1968 were not contained within the boundaries of any particular country. The globalization of conflict in these periods and the massive proliferation of the movement's ideas and aspirations is a crucial aspect of their world-historical character.[8] World-historical movements emerge in a spontaneous chain reaction of uprisings, strikes, rebellions, and revolutionary movements. Around the world, the movement's strategy and aspirations become generalized, emerging here, then there, building up gradually in confined spaces, then erupting on a global level.

Some epochs of class struggle are world-historical and others are not, a distinction noted by Antonio Gramsci. He used the terms "organic" and "conjunctural" to describe this difference:

> It is necessary to distinguish organic movements (relatively permanent) from movements which may be termed "conjunctural" (and which appear as occasional, immediate, almost accidental). Conjunctural phenomena too depend on organic movements to be sure, but they do not have any very far-reaching historical significance; they give rise to political criticism of a minor, day-to-day character, which has as its subject top political leaders and personalities with direct governmental responsibilities. Organic phenomena on the other hand, give rise to socio-historical criticism, whose subject is wider social groupings beyond the public figures and beyond the top leaders. When an historical period comes to be studied, the great importance of this distinction becomes clear.[9]

The apparent climax and disappearance of the New Left, particularly in the core of the world system, have led many observers to conclude that these movements conform to what Gramsci called conjunctural, arising as a unique product of the post-World War II baby boom, the injustice of Jim Crow, or the prolonged intensity of the war in Vietnam. It is one of the purposes of this book to demonstrate the organic nature of the New Left by portraying its global impact.

World-historical movements define new epochs in the cultural, political, and economic dimensions of society. *Even in failure,* they present new ideas and values which become common sense as time passes. World-historical movements qualitatively reformulate the meaning of freedom for millions of human beings. The massive and unexpected strife and the international proliferation of new aspirations signal the beginning of a new historical epoch. During the dramatic outbreak of revolts and the reaction to them, new aspirations are passionately articulated and attacked, and progress occurs in weeks and months when previously it took decades and half centuries. History does not unfold in a linear direction or at an even pace. As Marcuse observed, "There is no even progress in the world: The appearance of every new condition involves a leap; the birth of the new is the death of the old."[10] He forgot to add that the birth of the new, after its period of celebration and youth, moves into maturity and then decays. In order to appreciate this, let us review what is meant by world history.

Hegel measured the development of world history through the emergence of individualized inward subjectivity.[11] Such a transposition of the individual for the species as the agent and outcome of world history thoroughly conformed to the ideology of the ascendant bourgeoisie.[12] The limitations of Hegel's outlook are apparent in his conclusion that history culminates in Germany[13] and in his legitimation of the Prussian state.

In contrast to Hegel, it is my view that history is nothing but the development of the human species and is not measured through the flowering of the individual in isolation from others (that is, bourgeois history) but in the unfolding of human collectivities and of an individuality which surpasses bourgeois individualism. Moreover, what for Hegel was a dialectic of *mind* is analyzed here as a dialectic of praxis, of the consciousness-in-action of millions of people.

The history of the modern world, from the struggle for national independence and democracy to the liberation of oppressed classes and managed masses, follows a logic similar to that uncovered by Hegel, a dialectical framework within which the potentiality of the human species as a species-being unfolds. The logic of world history carries an irony which "turns everything upside down," not only posing the new against the old, but simultaneously transforming what was once new and revolutionary into its opposite. In the past two hundred years, we see this in the history of the United States. From challenging and defeating the forces of "divine right," the world's first secular democratic state has long since degenerated, yesterday bloodily invading Vietnam and today arming *contras* in Central America while massively aiding one of the world's last states founded on a notion of "divine right," a religious state whose technological weapons of genocide are provided by the United States to forestall the realization of its own ideal foundation: a secular, democratic state for people of all religions, but this time in Palestine. So much for what can become of these world-historical leaps when left adrift in the world of the "survival of the fittest." Let us return to their moments of joyful infancy, to the attempts made by human beings to leap beyond the dead weight of the past.

In the modern world, the essential indication of these leaps, the signal for a whole epoch of class struggles, is the general strike. Such strikes are not cleverly orchestrated by a small group of conspirators or "world-historical individuals," but involve the spontaneous and conscious action of millions of people. As Rosa Luxemburg pointed out:

> Political and economic strikes, mass strikes and partial strikes, demonstrative strikes and fighting strikes, general strikes of individual branches of industry and general strikes in individual towns, peaceful wage struggles and street massacres, barricade fighting—all these run through one another, run side by side, cross one another, flow in and over one another—it is ceaselessly moving, a changing sea of phenomena...In a word, the mass strike...is not a crafty method discovered by subtle reasoning for the purpose of making the proletarian struggle more effective, *but the method of motion of the proletarian mass*, the phenomenal form of the proletarian struggle in the revolution.[14]

General strikes not only sum up new historical epochs of class struggle by revealing in utmost clarity the nature of the antagonists, they also indicate the future direction of the movement—its aspirations and goals, which, in the heat of historical struggle, emerge as popular wishes and intuitions. George Sorel described the general strike as:

...the *myth* in which Socialism is wholly comprised...Strikes have engendered in the proletariat the noblest, deepest, and most moving sentiments that they possess; the general strike groups them all in a co-ordinated picture, and by bringing them together, gives to each one of them its maximum of intensity; appealing to their painful memories of particular conflicts, it colors with an intense life all the details of the composition presented to consciousness. We thus obtain that intuition of Socialism which language cannot give us with perfect clearness—and we obtain it as a whole, perceived instantaneously.[15]

General strikes create a new reality, negating previous institutions, rupturing the hegemony of the existing order, and releasing seemingly boundless social energies which normally remain suppressed, repressed, and channeled into more "proper" outlets. The liberation of the life instincts in these moments creates unique qualities of social life. In 1848, 1905, and 1968, for example, anti-anti-Semitism was a recurrent public theme, and international solidarity momentarily outweighed patriotic sentiments.[16]

In contrast to what has become a commonplace alienation from politics, these moments are ones of the eroticization of politics, as portrayed by the May 1968 slogan, "The more I make revolution, the more I enjoy love."[17] Drudgery becomes play as imagination replaces practicality, and human competition and callousness are replaced by cooperation and dignity. During the Paris Commune of 1871, for example, the streets were safe for the first time in years, even with no police of any kind. As one Communard said, "We hear no longer of assassination, theft, and personal assault; it seems, indeed, as if the police had dragged along with it to Versailles all its conservative friends."[18]

The essential change which creates these leaps in human reality is the activation of whole strata of previously passive spectators, the millions of people who decide to participate in the conscious re-creation of their economic and political institutions and social life. Such spontaneous leaps may be, in part, a product of long-term social processes in which organized groups and conscious individuals prepare the groundwork, but when political struggle comes to involve millions of people, it is possible to glimpse a rare historical occurrence: the emergence of the *eros* effect, the massive awakening of the instinctual human need for justice and for freedom. When the *eros* effect occurs, it becomes clear that the fabric of the *status quo* has been torn, and the forms of social control have been ruptured. This rupture becomes clear when established patterns of interaction are negated, and new and better ones are created. In essence, general strikes (and revolutions) are the emergence of humans as a species-being, the negation of the age-old "survival of the fittest" through a process by which Nature becomes History (*Aufhebung der Naturwüchsigkeit*).[19]

Periods of revolutionary crisis bear little resemblance to crises produced by economic breakdowns. The latter have their roots in the irrational organization of the economy and the state (*Naturwuchs*), while general strikes and revolutions are essentially attempts to provide rational alternatives. A dialectical view of crisis includes both of these types, particularly since they commonly have a close relationship to each other. Traditional usage of the concept of crisis, however, generally denotes only economic dislocations like the Great Depression. Economic crises are one type of social crisis and differ from crises produced by the *eros* effect.

The global impact of revolutionary movements which have succeeded in seizing political power is widely recognized. Few observers would question the fact that the revolutions of 1776 in the United States, 1789 in France, and 1917 in Russia have had profound and long-lasting international repercussions. The ruptures of social order in 1848, 1905, and 1968 may not have toppled the dominant institutions, but even in "failure," they marked the emergence of new values, ideas, and aspirations which became consolidated as time passed. As I discuss below, these intense periods of class struggle were an important part of the self-formation of the human species. They were periods of action which dramatically changed the actors. As Rosa Luxemburg put it:

> The most precious, because lasting, thing in this rapid ebb and flow of the wave is its mental sediment: the intellectual, cultural growth of the proletariat which proceeds by fits and starts, and which offers an inviolable guarantee of their further irresistible progress in the economic as in the political struggle.[20]

The new reality created by the *eros* effect is not limited to a higher rationality among an elite, but contains popular dimensions as well. Thomas Jefferson observed this phenomenon in his analysis of the global impact of the American revolution:

> As yet that light (of liberty) has dawned on the middling classes only of the men of Europe. The Kings and the rabble, of equal importance, have not yet received its beams, but it continues to spread, and...it can no more recede than the sun return on his course. A first attempt to recover the right of self-government may fail, so may a second, a third, etc. But as a younger and more instructed race comes on, the sentiment becomes more and more intuitive, and a fourth, a fifth, or some subsequent one of the ever-renewed attempts will ultimately succeed.[21]

As Jefferson realized, the success (or failure) of a social movement in taking over political power is but one dimension of its impact. Even in failure, there remains a continuity in the needs and aspirations of millions of people, and the experiences accumulated from political praxis are a significant historical legacy. Whether in intuitive terms, directly intergenerational, or obtained from the study of history, human beings are changed by social movements, and the self-formation of the species remains the innermost meaning of history. If history teaches us anything, it reveals the process through which the human species becomes conscious of its own development, a consciousness which exists in concrete form during moments of the *eros* effect.

In retrospect, we can observe today that 1848, 1905, and 1968 marked the first acts of the emergence of new social classes on the stage of world history. Despite defeat in their first experiences in the class struggle, these "failed" movements had their moments of success—even if incomplete—in subsequent epochs. Within the context of the world system's escalating spiral of expansion, new social movements take up where previous ones leave off, an insight demonstrated below through an overview of the "failed" social movements of 1848, 1905, and 1968. This overview demonstrates the connections between the emergent subjectivity of millions of people over more than a century. Furthermore, the world-historical movements of the working class of 1848, the landless peasantry of 1905, and the new working class of 1968 provide a glimpse of the essential forces which have produced—and are products of—the movement of history.

Although each of these periods of upheaval revitalized social movements, differing economic conditions precipitated the storms. The revolutions of 1848 were preceded by the prolonged economic slump of 1825-48, and the movements of 1905 were also preceded by severe hardships following the worldwide slump of 1873-1896.[22] The two decades prior to 1968, however, were ones of immense global economic expansion. Although 1968 is usually seen as the beginning of the world economic downturn of the 1970s, the political and cultural storms preceded the economic slump.

Despite their differing precipitating conditions and historical epochs, the movements of 1848, 1905, and 1968 exhibit striking similarities, and parallels can be made between their cultural contestation of rules governing everyday life. As initially pointed out by Alexis de Tocqueville, the first revolution against boredom was in 1848. He makes it quite clear that in the established political life, "there reigned nothing but languor, impotence, immobility, boredom" and that "the nation was bored listening to them."[23] When he turned to the poet Lamartine, himself active then, Tocqueville concluded, "He is the only man, I believe, who always seemed to be ready to turn the world upside-down to divert himself." If 1848 was, at least partially, a revolution against boredom, the May events in France were even more so. As the Situationists put it: "We do not want to exchange a world in which it is possible to die of starvation for one in which it is possible to die from boredom." Shortly before May 1968, the front page of *Le Monde* ran the headline "*France s'ennuie!*" and Godard's film *Weekend* had expressed a similar message. In the United States, Abbie Hoffman's *Revolution for the Hell of It!* sold out as quickly as it was printed.

Leading up to the cataclysmic events of 1848 in Vienna, Jesuit priests were handed control of nearly all the high schools, and when they forbade the old and joyous custom of nude bathing in the river, the first sparks of student protest began to fly. From these small beginnings emerged the revolutionary student brigade that became the government in Vienna for months.[24] In 1968 at Nanterre University on the outskirts of Paris, a few men who had spent the night in the women's dormitory to protest sexual segregation and parietal hours were chased by police into a crowded lecture hall where scores of students were then mercilessly beaten. So began the escalating spiral of the May events.

Berlin in 1848 had a reputation of being gay in every way. Berliners adored picnics, bonfires, parades, and festivals, but one of the many prohibitions included a ban on workers' smoking in the public gardens, the Tiergarten. After the first round of barricade fighting in March, a crowd carried some of the 230 civilian dead to the palace, and someone called out loudly for the King to come and see the flower-covered corpses. His Majesty appeared on the balcony and took his hat off at the sight of the dead while the queen fainted. In this delicate moment, Prince Lichnowsky addressed the crowd, telling them their demands were granted. No one moved. Suddenly someone asked, "Smoking, too?" "Yes, smoking too." "Even in the Tiergarten?" "You may smoke in the Tiergarten, gentlemen." With that, the crowd dispersed. The fact that another Prussian, Prinz zu Hohenlohe Ingelfingen, questioned whether it was tobacco or some other concoction that workers were smoking, provides another aspect of cultural affinity between the movements of 1848 and 1968.

Such parallels might be regarded as trivial ones, but their significance should not be disregarded unless one refuses to contemplate the need of the established order to control leisure time and the aspirations of popular movements to transform everyday life. Precisely because these movements were rooted in the popular need to transform power structures in everyday life are they "world-historical." The birth of the women's movement in 1848, its revival after 1905, and its reemergence in 1968 are further indications of the "organic" awakening in these years. In order to appreciate their place in the development of the modern world, an overview of the social movements which emerged in 1848, 1905, and 1968 is provided below.

1848, 1905, 1968: An Historical Overview

These three world-historical movements emerged at different historical conjunctures, and they were comprised of differing social classes. Although many groups participated in the revolutions of 1848, these events marked the entrance of the working class on the stage of world history. On February 22-24, 1848, the workers of Paris rose up and toppled the monarchy, sending the King into exile and sparking a continent-wide movement for democratic rights, the end of the monarchies, and economic justice. In March, a bloody uprising in Vienna defeated the army and led to a new constitution. As the fighting spread to Berlin, Bavaria, Baden, and Saxony, the King of Prussia quickly formed a new government and promised a democratic constitution. In Sicily, the Bourbon dynasty was overthrown, and the revolt spread to Naples, Milan, Venice, and Piedmont. The Poles rose against their Prussian rulers, and two nights of bloody barricade fighting broke out in Prague. Altogether there were some fifty revolutions in Europe in 1848 (if one counts the small German and Italian States and Austrian provinces), and these movements converged in their demands for republics and in their tactic of building barricades for urban warfare.

In June 1848, a new round of insurrections began when the working class of Paris seized control of the city, and in four days of bloody fighting from behind barricades, thousands of people were killed. After the revolt, the army held more than 15,000 prisoners, and many of them were later executed.

Despite their defeat, the workers of Paris catalyzed a new wave of armed insurrections in Berlin, Vienna, and Frankfurt, and vast movements emerged among the peasantry. A revolutionary army appeared in Hungary, and the Pope fled Rome as the republican movement won control from the French army. If the Hungarian revolutionary army had been able to reach the insurgents in Vienna, a Europe-wide revolution might have consolidated. Instead, counterrevolution reigned as order was brutally restored. The Holy Alliance (fashioned by Metternich in the wake of Napoleon) may not have been shattered in 1848, but Metternich himself was forced to flee Vienna, and greater liberties were won within the confines of the existing state. Only after World War I would the Kaiser, the Czar, and the Hapsburgs be permanently dethroned, but after the storms of 1848, modern political parties, trade unions, and democratic rights emerged as bourgeois society was consolidated.

The defeats of the insurrectionary governments of 1848 throughout Europe led to a period of stagnation for revolutionary movements, and in the next twenty-five years, free enterprise experienced its most dynamic years. For the first time, industrialization took root in France, Austria, Hungary, Poland, and Russia, and Germany quickly developed into a major industrial country. The United States was conquered by new economic masters whose program of industrialization necessitated freeing the slaves. During this period, there was another wave of the global expansion of European powers: the Syrian expedition (1860); the Anglo-French war against China; the French conquest of Indochina (1863); Maximilian's dispatch to Mexico; and the conquest of Algeria and Senegal. There were also wars between the capitalist powers, notably those in the Crimea and the Franco-Prussian war (which precipitated the Paris Commune). Global expansionism after 1848 led to the accumulation of vast wealth in the industrialized nations, and the concomitant harnessing of science to production and new mass production techniques (that is, the Second Industrial Revolution) further intensified the system's tendency toward global expansion. The whole world became divided into oppressor and oppressed nations as "free trade" led to imperialist conquest.

Nearly seventy years after the emergence of the working class as a class-for-itself, the peasants and natives of the periphery, increasingly denied land and liberty by the expanding imperial system, emerged as a force in their own right. At the beginning of the twentieth century, the global networks of communication and transportation which accompanied the expanding world system were limited compared to our standards today, but nonetheless, they helped create a synchronized world movement unlike anything of the past. Beginning with Cuba (1895) and the Philippines (1897), uprisings and movements for national independence appeared throughout the world. From 1904 to 1907, significant social movements erupted in India, Indochina, Madagascar, Angola, Portuguese Guinea, Egypt, Crete, Albania, Serbia, Poland, Guatemala, and Peru. A protracted guerrilla war against German colonial rule in Namibia cost the lives of 100,000 Africans, and the Zulus in Natal rose against their British rulers.

The defeat in 1905 of Russia, a great European power, by Japan, a small

Asian kingdom, helped precipitate this global wave of revolutionary activity. At one end of Asia, Sun Yat-sen declared, "We regarded the Russian defeat by Japan as the defeat of the West by the East." Similarly, Jawaharlal Nehru described how "Japanese victories stirred up my enthusiasm...Nationalistic ideas filled my mind. I mused of Indian freedom."[25] At the other end of Asia, a British diplomat in Constantinople reported to London that the Japanese victory made every fiber in Turkish political life tingle with excitement. Three years later, the Young Turk revolt led to an insurrection in Saloniki, and a constitutional government was quickly won for the entire Ottoman empire. In China, the 1911 nationalist revolution led to the end of the Manchu dynasty and the emergence of modern Chinese political parties.

As the entire world convulsed in social upheavals, the Americas witnessed the Mexican revolution and heard Marcus Garvey's call, "Africa for the Africans!" In Asia, Korean insurgents rose against their Japanese rulers. Popular movements erupted among miners and railroad workers in Germany, England, France, and the United States, and among farm workers in Italy and Galicia. The praxis of the working-class movement from 1900 to 1905 was a demonstration of the historically new tactic of the general strike. In this period, there were general strikes in Russia, Bohemia, Spain, Sweden, and Italy, strikes which were modeled on the first general strike of 1877 in St. Louis, Missouri. Between 1900 and 1905, there were massive strikes by miners in Pennsylvania (1900), Colorado (1903-04), Austria (1900), and France (1902); a general strike of all production workers in Barcelona (1902); and strikes for universal voting rights in Sweden (1902), Belgium (1902), Prague (1905), Galicia (1905), and Austria (1905). Although no movement came to power, organizations of farm workers in Italy and Galicia were strengthened; the Wobblies (International Workers of the World) were launched in the United States; and in Belgium, Austria, and Sweden, universal suffrage was enacted.[26]

In Persia, general strikes and the emergence of soviets (organs of dual power or *anjomans*) precipitated a constitutional revolution which ultimately deposed the Qajar dynasty. In the course of these struggles, the Persian women's movement played an integral role. Organized into secret societies, masked women carried out armed actions while others published feminist newspapers and organized discussion groups. Although these actions achieved only minimal legal change in the status of women, there was a more significant transformation of the social attitude toward women, a change which established the cornerstone for future feminist movements there.[27]

Further to the north in Russia, the mighty Czar was nearly overthrown by his own subjects, another event of particular importance in the global movement. The massacre of hundreds of peaceful marchers in St. Petersburg on Bloody Sunday (in January 1905) precipitated a general strike coordinated by spontaneously formed soviets. Only after thousands of workers were killed in the course of months of strikes did the movement temporarily abate. The revolution of 1905 transformed Russian politics by illuminating the brutality of Czarist rule at the same time as it indicated the strength of the popular movement. As previously disenfranchised workers and humble peasants found themselves rallying the country to their cause, the women of Russia became activated:

> There had been no specifically feminist movement in Russia before this time, but there were obvious feminist implications in the idea of universal suffrage. And they encouraged the faint beginnings of a movement that now began to pick up a following.[28]

Although the movement did not seize power, the Czar was forced to grant limited democratic reforms, the *Duma* (Russian Parliament) was created, and Russian workers won a shorter working day and the right to organize.

The spontaneously generated movement of 1905 permanently changed the common sense of Russia, and over the next twelve years, there was a growing wave of strikes which culminated in the reappearance of the soviets and the overthrow of the Czar. Russia's defeat in World War I left a vacuum of power, and eight months later, the Bolsheviks seized power amidst an uprising they orchestrated. The Bolsheviks' success helped to catalyze council movements in Germany, Austria, and Hungary, movements of workers and peasants which led to the end of the Austrian and German empires, even though the insurgents were unable to remain in power. From the May 4 Movement in China to the massive strikes in the United States and Great Britain, the international repercussions of the Russian revolution were immediately felt.

In the decades following 1917, the working class and its peasant allies were successful in a host of countries as the locus of revolutionary movements shifted away from Europe to the periphery of the world system. Within industrialized societies, over-production led to a worldwide depression beginning in 1929, and the working-class movement was temporarily revived in the Popular Front government in France, the Spanish Republic, the San Francisco general strike, the battle of Minneapolis, and the great sit-in movements and factory occupations. Of course, the Comintern (or Third International) played an overdetermining role in many popular struggles of the 1930s. More often than not, it defused the vital energy of insurgent movements, and although the generation of the Abraham Lincoln Brigade demonstrated a remarkable source of proletarian internationalism, it was nearly extinguished in the struggle against fascism which filled the political void in the old Central European empires. In the United States and Western Europe, the struggles of the 1930s won trade unions new legitimacy, and the working class emerged from these struggles with a new sense of dignity. As one of the participants explained, he was "fortunate enough to be caught up in a great movement of millions of people, [which] literally changed not only the course of the workingman [sic] ...but also the nature of the relationship between the workingman [sic] and the boss, for all time."[29]

In the first half of the twentieth century, although social movements came to power in Russia and China, the global expansion of capitalism accelerated in the other half of the world. The origins of the world economy date well before the twentieth century, but in the latter half of this century, transnational corporations have centralized the world's productive capacity under their supervision. Monopoly production has moved from a national to an international level, and modern technology has revolutionized production through cybernetic control. In 1968, the Third Industrial Revolution announced itself with the publication of the *Double Helix*, (which revolutionized the knowledge of DNA), the marketing of the first microcomputer, and Apollo 8's rounding of the moon. The space-age production of the modern world, made possible by the global centralization of resources and modern technology, has engendered an increasing division of labor, and in 1968, new oppositional forces emerged in the most developed capitalist countries: the new working class (technicians, employed professionals, off-line office workers, service workers, and students). As the First Industrial Revolution produced the working class and the Second a landless peasantry, so the Third created the new working class. The rapid growth of universities necessitated by the Third Industrial Revolution, the increasing global division of labor, and the consolidation of the consumer society all converged in the creation of the new working class. In 1968, their aspirations for a decentralized and self-managed global society transcended the previous calls for liberty, equality, and fraternity in 1789; for jobs, trade unions, and employment security in 1848; and for land, peace, bread, and voting rights from 1905 to 1917.

As we will see, the New Left enriched the tradition of revolutionary organization and tactics: from the formation of insurrectionary parliaments and barricade fighting in 1848; to soviets and general strikes in 1905; to vanguard parties and insurrections in 1917; and finally to decentralized, self-managed councils and the popular contestation of public space in 1968. The New Left merger of culture and politics created situations in which the contestation of public space was neither an armed insurrection nor a military assault for control of territory. Moreover, the aspirations of the New Left in the advanced industrialized countries were decidedly not a dictatorship of the proletariat, but "Power to the People" and "All Power to the Imagination." In 1968, the issues raised by the movement, like racism and patriarchy, were species issues, and at the same time, a new "we" was concretely defined in the self-management which sprang up at the levels of campus, factory, and neighborhood. The chart on the next page summarizes the New Left's relationship to previous world-historical movements.

In order to further clarify the new meaning of freedom represented by the New Left, I turn to defining its fundamental dimensions.

The New Left: A Global Definition

Unlike the centrally organized Third International, the New Left's international political unity was not mandated from above but grew out of the needs and aspirations of popular movements around the world. That is why the New Left can simultaneously be called one social movement and many social movements. A global definition of the New Left does not correspond to the traditional understanding of it as the social movements in the industrialized West after World War II. Such definitions of the New Left obscure its global structure and functions, its international networks, and its universal intuition.

Chart 1

The Development of World-Historical Social Movements

	1776-1789	1848	1905	1917	1968
Ascendant Revolutionary Class(es)	Bourgeoisie	Urban Proletariat	Rural Proletariat	Urban and Rural Working Class	New Working Class
Emergent Organization	Representative Assemblies	Insurrectionary Parliaments and Political Parties	Soviets/Councils	Vanguard Party	Action Committees/Collectives
Vision/Aspirations	Formal Democracy; Liberty Equality Fraternity	Economic Democracy; Trade Unions; Democratic Constitutions	Universal Suffrage; Unions; Freedom from Empires	Socialism as the "Dictatorship of the Proletariat"; Land, Bread and Peace	Self-Management All Power to the People/ Imagination
Tactics	Revolutionary War	Popular Insurrections	General Strike	Organized Seizure of Power	Contestation of Public Space/ Everyday Life

By accepting uncritically the fragmentation of the world into two major power blocks (the "free world" and the "Communist bloc"), the traditional definition of the New Left identifies the movement in terms external to its identity and aspirations.

Despite attempts by some analysts to label the New Left a Communist movement, the New Left was globally opposed by the Communist Parties, and Soviet Marxists continue to defame it.[30] For its part, the New Left did not regard the Communist Parties as friends. As an observer in Italy put it:

> The fight of the New Left in Italy is taking place on two fronts: on one side against conservative forces and on the other against the traditional Left. One often gets the impression that the conflict with the Old Left is the predominant element in the choice of criteria for action by the New Left, since the target they set for themselves is to "unmask" the traditional Left as being "non-Left," as aiming at no more than an infiltration of the capitalist system in order to reform it; this they regard as a non-alternative, in fact as strictly organic and functional to the authoritarian and repressive system.[31]

It was not only the New Left in Italy that was independent of existing Left organizations. As a global movement, the New Left contested the structures of power on both sides of the "iron curtain." As I discuss in the next chapter, in 1968, movements erupted in Eastern Europe which displayed a remarkable affinity with their counterparts in the West in their opposition to ideological dogmatism, bureaucratic authority, and cultural conformity. In some cases, these movements self-consciously identified themselves as New Left,[32] and activists in the West spontaneously welcomed them as part of a larger international movement.

In the modern world system, nations and regions have complex relationships with one another, and they cannot be summed up by the terms "free world" and "Communist," nor by "core" and "periphery." Canada and Ireland are not third world countries, yet in Canada in 1968, radical students regarded the "co-opting of Canada into the American 'Great Society' as distorting our country's internal development in the broadest sense." One analyst took the matter even further when he said, "The Canadian student in his university is a colonial, even as the Canadian worker is within his enterprise, whether branchplant or not; and the Canadian economy, within the American empire."[33] In Ireland, massive marches and the founding of the People's Democracy party in October 1968 marked the renewal of the struggle for independence.

Despite their unity and similarity, however, it would be a mistake to equate the various social movements of 1968. Freedom from foreign domination and freedom from one's own government's attempts to dominate other nations may become the same struggle in the practicality of world events, but they are different freedoms, carrying within them different meanings of the word. More importantly, third world movements cannot become models for those in the core, because the movements in the economically advanced societies must deal with qualitatively different objective conditions, with different primary contradictions, and with different immediate goals than movements on the periphery of the world system.

Despite their obvious differences, however, it is clear today that the participants in the movements of 1968 did not act in isolation from one another. When the Yippies brought panic to the New York stock exchange by throwing money on the floor, when the Dutch *Provos* wreaked havoc on rush hour traffic in Amsterdam by releasing thousands of chickens into the streets, and when the Strasbourg Situationists issued their manifesto denouncing boredom, they were using methods obviously different than those of liberation fighters in Vietnam. Despite their tactical differences, however, all these groups enunciated similar goals—a decentralized world with genuine human self-determination—and they increasingly acted in unison. The practice of the New Left lends credence to the notion that despite the division of the modern world system into three "worlds" (the "free world," the "Communist bloc," and the "third world"), there remains the basic unity of the world as a system.

Of course, the uneven development of the world system conditioned the diverse composition of the New Left as a world-historical movement. In 1968, for example, Vietnam was fighting for national liberation and socialism. The United States had declared its independence in 1776, nearly 200 years earlier, and the Vietnamese modeled their struggle, at least in part, on that of the United States, even adopting word-for-word part of the U.S. Declaration of Independence. Similarly, their party organization was modeled on that of the Bolsheviks of 1917.

The global movement of 1968 was comprised of many components; there were newly emergent social actors as well as ones continuing unfinished struggles of previous epochs. The complete success of all these struggles would, of necessity, be a global revolution—the first truly world-historical revolution. Such a revolution would necessarily involve the radical transformation of the world system from within its core countries.[34] Successful twentieth century revolutions, however, have been confined to the periphery of the world system, a situation which resulted in the disappearance of the idea of a world-historical revolution, at least until the appearance of the New Left. My analysis of social movements focuses on the core of the world system to illuminate the possibility of such a world-historical revolution, a possibility which exists today more in the remembrance of the New Left than in the current world situation.

Taken as a whole, the New Left was a global movement which sought to decentralize and redistribute world resources and power at a time when their centralization had never been greater. Of course, the movement developed within the nation-state, not by its own choosing, but because of the national organization of political power. Around 1968, however, the growing feeling among social movements in Vietnam, Cuba, Latin America, Africa, and even in the United States and Europe was that they were all engaged in the same struggle. As Marcuse pointed out in that year:

> The theoretical framework of revolution and subversive action has become a world framework...Just as Vietnam is an integral part of the corporative capitalist system, so the national movements of liberation are an integral part of the potential socialist revolution. And the liberation movements in the Third World depend for their subversive power on the weakening of the capitalist metropolis.[35]

In the 1970s, international solidarity and coordination between radical movements in the core and periphery became even more intense than in 1968. Thousands of young Americans went to Cuba as part of the Venceremos Brigades, helping cut sugarcane during the harvests, building schools and houses, and planting trees. In February 1972, the Indochinese liberation movements hosted a world conference in Paris, and representatives of solidarity groups from eighty-four countries attended. A carefully prepared global action calendar was formulated, and on March 31, the same day that worldwide demonstrations had been called for, a major offensive was launched in Vietnam, one which included the surprising appearance of guerrilla tank columns and the temporary installation of a Provisional Revolutionary Government in Quang Tri. The international coordination of the world movement had never been as conscious or well-synchronized. Events such as these eloquently refute a strictly nationalistic reading of the New Left.

At the same time as the New Left's international character is revealed in these events, so is the impossibility of analyzing the movement in terms of its component parts. Although historians have treated the civil rights movement in the United States, the women's liberation movement, and the gay movement as separate phenomena, a global analysis of the New Left considers these movements as parts of the broadly defined New Left. To be sure, each of the above movements had its own autonomous organizations and beliefs, but as the empirical evidence in the following chapters reveals, there emerged an international movement from 1968 to 1970 which fused these seemingly separate social movements into a unified world-historical movement. The civil rights movement all but disappeared as the Black Power impetus emerged, and in 1970, autonomous women's and gay organizations worked as parts of an emergent internationalist revolutionary movement whose main domestic leadership was the Black Panther Party. The imagination and aspirations of this historical force went beyond the needs and beliefs of its various component constituencies. Of course, as the entire global impetus was dispersed and came to be contained within the existing structures of the world system, the civil rights movement, the women's movement, and the gay movement reassumed the specialized (and professionalized) forms in which they have continued to function as "new social movements."

Although the popular and academic understandings of the New Left tend to dissect the fused energies of the global movement, it was in the period marked by the *fusion* of the various national, ethnic, and gender movements into a world-historical movement that a vision of a qualitatively different world system (or non-system) emerged. Even the fondest dreams of an individual genius (or an official "Great Man" of history, as Martin Luther King is today identified by the mass media) fell far short of the imagination of the New Left when it became a world-historical movement. As eloquent and intelligent as Martin Luther King was, his individual dream concerned racially integrating the existing system. Although near the end of his life he began to discuss the connections between the struggle for civil rights and the war in Vietnam, he did so long after advocates of Black Power had already been persecuted for their anti-war stands. Like millions of other people, Martin Luther King was transformed by the global impetus of the 1960s, and in the months before his assassination, he even began to discuss the idea of qualitatively "restructuring the whole of American society."[36]

However revolutionary the Black Panthers may have considered themselves, their program never included self-management of the country's factories and universities (although it did call for community control of black neighborhoods). It was only when the Panthers convened the Revolutionary Peoples' Constitutional Convention, bringing together thousands of representatives of the popular upsurge of 1970, that they explicitly stated the need to radically transform the political and economic structures of the existing world system. (Documents from this convention are contained in an Appendix.)

Because the New Left's vision of a new society was never enunciated as eloquently as Martin Luther King's speeches or as clearly as the Panthers' platform, it has often been assumed that the New Left was simply a reactive social movement protesting the perceived injustices of the existing system— that it was a rebellious rather than a revolutionary social movement. As I discuss later, however, during the general strike of May 1968 in France and the student strike two years later in the United States, millions of people spontaneously joined together and not only imagined a new reality but *lived* one. Their day-to-day lives were based on international solidarity rather than nationalistic pride; on self-management of the factories, universities, and offices rather than top-down decision-making; and on cooperation, rather than competition. However briefly these moments existed, they offer a revealing glimpse of the possible future transformation of the existing world system.

In short, rather than defining the New Left nationalistically, organizationally, or ideologically, I locate it historically and practically—that is, in the praxis of millions of people in the post-World War II epoch. A global definition of the New Left cannot merely be based on organizational ideology, that is, that the "New Left" developed outside traditional organizations of the "Old Left" and therefore was a "New" Left. Nor can a global definition of the New Left identify the movement's imagination and vision solely in terms of specific organizations or theorists. The Student Non-Violent Coordinating Committee (SNCC), the Black Panther Party, the March 22 Movement in France, and Students for a Democratic Society (SDS) were all New Left organizations, and Martin Luther King, Malcolm X, and Herbert Marcuse were New Left theorists, but the movement extended beyond these organizations and theorists. They were all part of, but not equivalent to, the New Left.

The primary defining characteristics of the global New Left include:

(1) *Opposition to racial, political, and partriarchal domination as well as to economic exploitation.*

The New Left sought to overthrow the economic exploitation which the Old Left had opposed, but the anti-authoritarianism of the new radicals also opposed cultural and bureaucratic domination. Movements for national liberation and the civil rights of minorities, the primary basis of the global turmoil in 1968, insured that the racism of the society (and of radical movements) would be a central concern of the New Left. The women's liberation movement, itself reborn around 1968, challenged the sexism of the society (and the movement) and brought patriarchal domination into question.

There may be an analogy between the development of Christianity and that of secular liberation (as Frederick Engels insisted there was). From this perspective the New Left can be appreciated as having begun a re-interpretation of the scope of freedom in much the same way that the Protestant Reformation redefined the individual's relationship to God by taking out the middleman (the Pope) and affirming the sanctity of individual subjectivity. The universe of socialism spontaneously envisioned and practiced by the New Left included individual freedom within a framework of social justice. New Left activists were concerned not only with traditional economic and political issues, but also with domination in everyday life. Bureaucracy, the oppression of women, the repression of children, homophobia, racism—indeed, all aspects of the existing society—were called into question.

The sanctity of individual freedom and the primacy of social justice, values which were a moral underpinning of the New Left, represent a philosophical affirmation of the subjectivity which stands in opposition to the objectivistic materialism of Soviet Marxism. The attempts to transform everyday life and to politicize taken-for-granted patterns of interaction, particularly in the practice of the women's liberation movement, rest on a belief that economic and political structures are reproduced through the daily acceptance of predetermined patterns of life, a belief that stands in sharp contrast to the ideology of economic determinism. The inner reworking of the psyche and human needs—the cultural revolution—lays the groundwork for a new type of revolution, one which does not culminate in the political sphere, but which would move the realm of politics from the state to everyday life by transforming the notion of politics from administration from above to self-management. Through its universal realization in a new society, politics would cease to exist—as least as we know it today.

Nationalization of the economy and decision-making do not define the form of the free society envisioned by the New Left. New Left forms of freedom were the decentralization of decision-making, the international socialization of industry, worker and community self-management, and the extension of democracy to economic, cultural, and all aspects of life. In slogan form, the New Left's "All Power to the People"—not the "Dictatorship of the Proletariat"—stood as a political guide to such a free society.

All this should not be interpreted to mean that the New Left never reproduced the racist, patriarchal, bureaucratic, or exploitative characteristics of the system it opposed. Despite its many shortcomings, however, when taken as a whole, the New Left was profoundingly universalistic in its consciousness of oppression and its actions against its many forms.

(2) *Concept of freedom as not only freedom from material deprivation but also freedom to create new human beings.*

Compared with previous social movements, the New Left can be defined as *not* having developed primarily in response to conditions of *economic* hardship but to political and cultural/psychological oppression. The need to change daily life was evident in relation to Che Guevara's "new socialist person," and it applies equally well to Martin Luther King's "new Negro," the subsequent self-definition of Americans of African descent as blacks, and the new self-definitions of women, gay people, and students in the aftermath of 1968.

The New Left opposed "cultural imperialism" and "consumerism" at the same time as it sought to build people's culture: black culture, women's culture, Chicano culture, and youth culture (as the countercultures of the New Left became most widely known). These insurgent cultures were based on a new set of norms and values which were developed from a critique of generally accepted patterns of interaction.

In retrospect, cultural precursors of the movement stand out, aesthetic and philosophical qualities that found popular embodiment in the 1960s. Existentialism and Godard films in France, the Kafka revival in Czechoslovakia, jazz, blues, rock, pop art, and the theory of the Frankfurt School all contributed to the creation of a social soul which became manifest in political form with the New Left.[37] The massive fusion of culture and politics defined the New Left's uniqueness, and as a social movement, the New Left represented the political emergence of many of the same human values and aspirations which gave rise to modern art and philosophy. Spontaneity, individual autonomy amid community, and the subversion of bureaucratic as well as economic domination were all values and ideals shared by the New Left, Kafka, and Kirchner.

(3) *The extension of the democratic process and expansion of the rights of the individual, not their constraint.*

Within the movements, strict principles of democracy were the norm, and bottom-up participatory democracy defined the process of interaction from the largest general assemblies to the smallest action committees. Although the media often selected specific individuals to focus on, the movement generally avoided selecting leaders, and anyone with major responsibilities was often subject to immediate recall since positions of responsibility were rotated. Among the armed movements in the third world as well, an extension of the democratic process occurred. In Vietnam, for example, as often as possible, guerrilla units would meet before their attacks to discuss the tactics to be used. In some cases, full-scale models of the targets were constructed, and in simulated attacks, each member rotated from one specific task to another until each could function best. Commanding officers for the actual attack were then democratically elected. Once the real attack was launched, of course, orders had to be followed without hesitation.[38]

The democratic process of the New Left was manifested in its internal impetus toward self-management as represented in the consensus decision-making process at general assemblies involving hundreds of people; in the autonomy of the black and women's liberation movements; in the aspiration for self-determination for oppressed nations; and in the self-management of factories, schools, and cities during New Left strikes. In contrast to monolithic Old Left organizations, many tendencies co-existed within New Left organizations like SDS, from Maoism and feminism to anarchism and democratic socialism. Furthermore, in contrast to Stalinist methods of coercion, the New Left sought to win people's hearts and minds through persuasion.

(4) Enlarged base of revolution.

At the same time as the New Left sought to enlarge the scope of freedom, so too did its praxis demonstrate the enlarged constituency of liberation. The historical experiences of the New Left transcended a static model of class struggle developed from the previous practice of revolutionary movements. The legacy of the New Left is the enrichment of that tradition, a practical wealth often obscured by the metaphysics and orthodoxy of the "Left" and the "Right." Within the struggles for socialism and national liberation in the third world, oppositional forces emerged whose existence could not be contained within the existing typology of class struggle modeled upon previous occurrences in Europe.

At the same time as national liberation movements erupted in the periphery, within the industrialized countries, vast social movements were generated whose forms and constituency differed greatly from traditional types of class struggle. In 1968, it was not predominantly the working class and their parties which rose to challenge the existing social order, but groups normally considered marginal: students, young people, national minorities, women, and the lumpenproletariat. Within occupational categories, there were factory workers who helped lead workers' movements as part of the overall New Left (particularly in France, Czechoslovakia, and Italy), but the bulk of the opposition in the core was the urban underclass and the new working class. Particularly in France, the participation of the new working class (or middle strata) in the radical movement was an important defining contour of the New Left, perhaps as important as the hostilities of the Old Left Communist Party, the Social Democrats in Germany, and the Labour Party in England, all of whom were opposed to the new social movements. As the quantitative growth of the new working class has proceeded through the intensification of world industrialization, so *the practice of the New Left has demonstrated the "proletarian" aspect of these middle strata.*

Part of the reason for the inability of the Old Left (including the "new Old Left"—the myriad assortment of "Marxist-Leninist" and anarchist groups which emerged in the 1970s) to comprehend the meaning of the New Left lies in the differing roles played by the middle strata, students, and the lumpenproletariat in other times and places. In 1848, the lumpenproletariat of Paris was wined and dined by Louis Napoleon Bonaparte so that it would fight for him against the proletariat. Indeed it was Napoleon III's ability to use these gangsters, thugs, and hoodlums to maintain order which eventually won him the mandate needed to rule France. More recently, in places like Guinea-Bissau, Algeria, Angola,[39] and Greece, the lumpenproletariat has played reactionary roles as well. In the 1960s in the United States, however, when the civil rights movement entered its second phase by moving north, the black lumpenproletariat became the catalyst and leadership of the radical movement. Inspired by the example of Malcolm X, former criminals and drug addicts changed their lives, and rebelled *en masse* against the conditions of their existence. The middle strata formed the social basis for the Nazi regime and played a distinctly reactionary role in Allende's Chile, but in the core of the world system in the 1960s, middle-class people—particularly women and young adults—were among the progressive forces in these countries.

To be sure, there are economic reasons for the changing political role of these strata and for the enlarged base of revolution. In the post-World War II epoch of rapid technological change, new dimensions have been added to the class struggle. The peasants in the periphery are increasingly landless and proletarianized. Millions of office workers in the core are not directly involved in material production but are increasingly seen (and see themselves) as part of the working class. In the United States, 90 percent of the working population are employees as the logic of capitalism has reduced the possibilities of self-employment.[40] Furthermore, since World War II, the realization problem of capital has been heightened with the growing global surplus made possible by intensified exploitation and technological advances. The rise of "consumer society"—the necessary corollary of neo-colonialism—has meant that the realm of the cash nexus has been enlarged to include production *and* consumption, work *and* leisure.

Within the post-World War II global system, the universities have taken on an enlarged and more central role. When Clark Kerr compared the economic importance of the nation's universities in the last half of the twentieth century to that of automobiles in the early 1900s and to railroads in the late 1800s, he made, *if anything*, an understatement. In the 1960s, there were more students than farmers in the United States, more students than miners, and more people enrolled in formal studies than working in construction, transportation, or public utilities.[41] The new structural position of the universities within the modern world system gave rise to a student movement unlike ones of the past, a movement tied neither to "adult" nor "parent" organizations nor to the nation-state. Similarly, the urbanization of blacks and their central position after World War II in the inner cities, the military, and industry were conditions for the emergence of a new type of black liberation movement. Within the black movement in both the South and the North, students played a vital role, particularly in organizations like SNCC and the Black Panther Party.

(5) An emphasis on direct action.

Whether observed in the formation of the March 22 Movement at Nanterre or as early as the July 26 Movement in Cuba, the New Left was characterized by the belief that action—the initiation of confrontation—would create an unfolding process that would gradually bring in new supporters and, by its own logic, lead to larger confrontations which could eventually be won. Through the experiences of direct action, it was believed that the movement would become quantitatively larger and qualitatively stronger. The actionism of the New Left was not merely a reversion to pure and simple spontaneity but a new method for the integration of theory and practice. This was the case for New Left sit-ins and occupations, and even teach-ins can be seen as a form of the "actionization" of theory. The New Left's reliance on direct experience and the empirical evaluation of immediate events represented a negation of the Old Left's overemphasis on centralized organization and the primacy of the role of the "conscious element."

Although resulting in increased repression and growing armed struggle tendencies within the movement, the New Left's actionism did not culminate in attempted *coups d'etat* from above. The New Left continually maintained that society could be genuinely revolutionized only from the bottom up. Even the Guevarist strategy of inciting popular insurrection emphasized the need for the vast majority of people to be won over, and the movement in Guinea-Bissau actually delayed the seizure of state power in order to continue building popular power from below.[42] In the industrialized societies, New Left forms of action, from sit-ins to university takeovers and freeway blockades, were spontaneously developed in accordance with the military and political possibilities of 1968.

In the epoch after 1968, popular movements have internalized the New Left tactic of massive occupations of public space as a means of social transformation, and this tactic's international diffusion led to the downfall of the Shah, Duvalier, and Marcos. The pace of change in the modern world is so rapid that few observers are willing to predict what might happen in Europe and the United States with the intensification of the Third Industrial Revolution, the ongoing struggles in the third world, and the baby boom's own baby boom. As the political and economic integration of the world system continues to be strengthened as the twentieth century draws to an end, the significance of the *eros* effect and the importance of synchronized world-historical movements will only increase. In 1848 and 1905, there were limited communication and economic relationships between members of the world system, and the various movements of those times were relatively un-developed in terms of their spatial and historical integration. As I discuss in the next chapters, the movements of 1968 exhibited a remarkable international consciousness and interconnectedness, and their meteoric appearance and disintegration is a reflection of the rapid pace of change in the modern world.

If, as argued in this study, the New Left was a world-historical movement, it seems relatively clear that future social movements will quickly develop in unexpected explosions, as did the movements of 1968. Having sketched the world-historical nature of the New Left, I now turn to an empirical study of its emergence and impact.

Chapter 2

SOCIAL
MOVEMENTS
OF 1968

Those who cannot remember the past are condemned to repeat it.
—George Santayana

If anyone embodied the world-spirit of history in 1968, it was the people of Vietnam. From the American revolution of 1776, they inherited the Declaration of Independence, and from the Russian revolution of 1917, they borrowed their organizational form. During the 1960s, it was the resistance of the Vietnamese people to foreign domination which catalyzed the entire global movement. The prolonged intensity of their independence movement shattered the illusion of the democratic content of *pax Americana*, giving rise to movements in the industrialized societies aimed at transforming the structures of the world system. At the same time, their battlefield victories inspired anti-imperialist movements throughout the third world. As a global wave of new social movements occurred, even Eastern Europe was affected.

Significant social movements existed in nearly every country in 1968, but the focus of world attention was on Vietnam, and before the first month of that year ended, the Tet offensive made it clear that the national liberation movement had gained the upper hand. Half a million soldiers and billions of dollars of the world's most technologically advanced weapons were unable to defeat a tiny peasant nation's aspirations for independence. Because of the importance of the Tet offensive, it is there that any study of 1968 must begin.

The Significance of the Tet Offensive

On January 31, 1968, in the early morning of the third day of Tet (Vietnamese New Year), synchronized attacks were launched from within almost every major city and town in the southern part of Vietnam. Five of the six major cities, thirty-nine of forty-four provincial capitals, seventy-one district capitals, and nearly every U.S. base in Vietnam simultaneously became scenes of vicious fighting.[1] Over 500 Americans, and many more Vietnamese, lost their lives *each day* of the uprising, and in the two months of fighting from January 29 to March 31, 1968, at least 3,895 U.S. soldiers died.[2]

The offensive began when a squad of guerrillas penetrated the defenses of the newly constructed U.S. embassy in Saigon. A total of eleven battalions of the National Liberation Front (NLF) entered Saigon, captured the government radio station, and surrounded the Presidential palace. The capital was disrupted by fighting for a week, and the battle of Hue, the old imperial capital in central Vietnam and center of Buddhist/student revolts in 1963 and 1966, was even more intense. A unified revolutionary power was established there, and revolutionary Hue held out for over three weeks. It was only after bloody house-to-house fighting and massive bombing (which destroyed 18,000 of the city's 20,000 houses) that the NLF flag was no longer flying.[3]

After Hue was retaken, the Western media abounded with stories of the "bloodbath" supposedly perpetrated by the NLF against the people of Hue. A year and a half later, Douglas Pike was quoted in the *Los Angeles Times* of December 6, 1969 as having conducted an "intensive investigation" of events in Hue in which he concluded that the "Communists had slaughtered almost 6,000 civilians for political purposes." This figure was double all previous ones quoted in the mass media. I mention this because the "Hue massacre" was such a prominently used attack on the NLF, when, in fact, the vast majority of the civilian deaths were caused by U.S. aerial bombardments.[4] The mass graves found later had been dug by the NLF and were necessary because of the casualties caused by the air war.

The lies surrounding events in Hue were part of a campaign of deliberately perpetrated misinformation designed to intensify the war against Vietnam. From the fabrication of the Gulf of Tonkin incident to the continual promises of quick victory, U.S. generals systematically misled public opinion in order to expand their military adventure. In a move designed to counter the deceptions of the Pentagon, the Tet offensive was timed to coincide with the beginning of the election-year primaries in the United States, and the precision of the timing was such that the attack on the U.S. embassy came early enough in the day so that the network national news in the United States could carry coverage the same day. The fortress-like U.S. embassy had more of a symbolic than a military importance, particularly since it had little to do with the day-to-day direction of the war. The embassy of the United States was, however, a place which the American public could understand, unlike Khe Sanh or Hue. When the embassy came under attack, the public could summon a mind's-eye picture of the place and understand that the war was being lost. The massive offensive did not attack power stations, telephones, or telegraphs and the press was able to wire out reports more or less normally.[5] The Vietnamese were well aware that theirs was the world's first televised war (a hundred million television sets were in use in the United States in 1968, compared with ten million during the Korean War and only 10,000 at the time of Pearl Harbor), and the Tet offensive became the first televised superbattle.

To the Vietnamese people, the lunar new year was not only the most important holiday of the year, it also marked the anniversary of the 1789 surprise attack on Hanoi when Chinese invaders had been defeated by an army led by Quang Trung, an epic event in Vietnamese history analogous to George Washington's Christmas Eve crossing of the Delaware River in 1776. Five days before the 1968 Tet holiday began, the General Association of Students in Saigon University celebrated Quang Trung's 1789 victory by recreating it on stage. At an assembly attended by thousands of people, many of the songs and speeches carried anti-American overtones.

When the offensive finally seemed over, General William Westmoreland, the commander of U.S. forces in Vietnam, claimed a "major victory," asserting that the enemy had failed to achieve its goals. By March 9, however, as guerrilla attacks continued, he asked President Lyndon Johnson for 206,000 additional U.S. troops to protect the more than half a million already in Vietnam. The *New York Times* of March 10 headlined Westmoreland's request side-by-side with the story that thousands of U.S. troops had been cut off and surrounded for more than a month at remote Khe Sanh. The Pentagon was clearly worried that another Dien Bien Phu was in the offing, a defeat so large it could not be hidden, and in and around Khe Sanh the equivalent tonnage of five Hiroshima bombs (103,000 tons) was dropped to prevent an NLF attack. The use of tactical nuclear weapons came under consideration as well.[6] At the same time, as Noam Chomsky's reading of Pentagon documents revealed, one of the factors which concerned the Joint Chiefs of Staff was that if they sent more troops into Vietnam, they might not have enough for *domestic* control. They knew that sending more troops to Vietnam or invading northern Vietnam would cause even greater disruption at home.[7]

All at once, the bottom had fallen out of the U.S. attempt to control Vietnam. For nearly a year before the Tet offensive, Ambassador Ellsworth Bunker and General Westmoreland had insisted that the NLF was exhausted, played out, and all but finished off, but the intensity of the Tet attacks had quickly made it clear that the official reports were far from true. As Frank McGee put it on the NBC Sunday news of March 10:

> It is a new war in Vietnam. The enemy now has the initiative; he has dramatically enlarged the area of combat; he has newer, more sophisticated weapons; he has improved communications; he has changed his tactics. . . . In short, the war as the Administration has defined it is being lost.[8]

Two days later, on March 12, Eugene McCarthy, standing on an anti-war platform and aided by thousands of student volunteers who went "clean for Gene," polled 42 percent of the votes in the New Hampshire primary, only 7 percent behind Lyndon Johnson. In the same month, a Gallup Poll showed that for the first time, more Americans were against the war (40 percent) than were for it (26 percent). Finally, on March 31, Lyndon Johnson delivered his most famous speech, the one in which he announced a limitation on the bombing of northern Vietnam, eventual withdrawal of U.S. troops, and a promise not to run for re-election.

President Johnson's withdrawal from the elections was immediately hailed as a major political victory by the Vietnamese as well as by anti-war activists in the United States. The dramatic turnaround in U.S. public opinion concerning Vietnam after Tet was due both to the battlefield success of the Vietnamese and the firm articulation of anti-war sentiments at home, sentiments which quickly became a majority viewpoint. In the midst of the Tet offensive (on February 23, 1968), the National Council of Churches opposed the assertion that peace could be won by military might and the simplistic view of U.S. policy that the world is divided into two camps: the "Communist" and the "free world." Their resolution concluded:

> We believe that further intensification of the American military effort would be useless and would contribute to the destruction rather than the realization of American objectives.[9]

The February 11, 1968 meeting of Pax (an association of Catholics and non-Catholics founded in 1962) took a similar stand by adopting two resolutions addressed to the Catholic hierarchy. One called on the bishops to condemn the bombing of Vietnam, and the other requested a public statement affirming that it is morally questionable to participate in war or at least a statement endorsing every individual's right to decide the matter on one's own.[10]

The calls for "peace now" quickly caught on with the American public, but those who directed the U.S. war machine had little intention of surrendering. Instead, they clung to the same twisted logic exemplified in the words of an American officer who told an Associated Press reporter as they surveyed the ruins of the town of Ben Tre, "We had to destroy it in order to save it." After Tet, the whole of Indochina came under intensified attacks. On March 16, 1968, hundreds of women and children at My Lai were brutally murdered by the company under the command of William Calley. A twenty-month cover-up temporarily concealed this massacre from the American public, but an even bigger massacre—an automated air war—was already well underway. By the end of 1968, the United States had dropped more tonnage of bombs on Vietnam than it had used in all of World War II. Hundreds of thousands of innocent people were killed and wounded, and millions were made refugees as the killing became increasingly indiscriminate and genocidal. During the Tet offensive, the Vietnamese may have freed large parts of their country, but these liberated zones were then targeted for Agent Orange and cluster bombs. When the war finally ended, the total firepower used by the United States and its allies in Indochina had exceeded the total firepower used in all other wars in history combined;[11] the Pentagon would count 57,661 American dead and at least 300,000 wounded; a minimum of one million and possibly as many as three million Vietnamese were killed; and five million more were wounded or made into refugees.

The spirit of the Vietnamese resistance was not broken, however, by the brutality of the invaders. Despite heavy losses, the NLF moved from the strategic defensive to the strategic offensive after Tet. By the end of the year, 14,500 of the 550,000 U.S. troops in Vietnam were dead,[12] nearly as many as had died in all the previous years combined, and the total number of American planes shot down was in the thousands. With each day that the war continued, the polarization within the United States became more bitter and antagonistic.

At the same time as the circles of the anti-war movement widened, the black movement became more militant. Martin Luther King was one of those who became radicalized by the brutality of the Vietnam War—a radicalization evident in his call for the civil rights and the peace movement to unite and in his denunciation of "white colonialism:"

> We must unite our ardor for the civil rights movement with the peace movement. We must demonstrate, teach, preach, and organize until the very foundations of our nation are shaken...We are engaged in a war which is trying to turn back the tide of history by perpetuating white colonialism...In truth, the hopes of a great society have been killed on the battlefields of Vietnam...The bombs from Vietnam are exploding in our own country.[13]

Vietnam provided a clear dividing line between those who were "part of the problem" and those who were "part of the solution." The war dramatized the gap between the deeply ingrained notion that the United States is a free country and the all-too-evident reality that the U.S. government was committing the genocidal destruction of an entire nation. This moral contradiction broke apart families and churches, led to the disruption of higher education, and eventually even found its way into the highest ranks of the rich and powerful.

In the aftermath of the Tet offensive, tens of thousands of demonstrators regularly appeared in the streets of cities throughout the world, and U.S. embassies and information offices came under attack. The high visibility afforded radicals in the industrialized West encouraged their counterparts in the socialist East and vice-versa. The rising of Vietnam helped catalyze oppositional forces in the industrialized North, forces which in turn sparked new strata of rebellion in the South (the student movement in Mexico, for example, as I discuss below).

As the *eros* effect operated on a global level, so it did within each nation. In the United States, opposition to the war against Vietnam quickly became part of an emergent youth culture. The war crystallized a political dimension to the culture gap which already existed, and the cultural politics of the New Left intensified both opposition to the war and disgust with the politics and lifestyle of what became known as "Amerika." That word—and indeed much more—was contributed by the growing black liberation movement in the United States, a movement whose constituents had long opposed the war. In 1966, Julian Bond was denied his elected position in the Georgia legislature for his public opposition to the draft, and in 1967, Muhammed Ali was stripped of the world heavyweight boxing title for the same reason. By 1968, the combination of the Tet offensive and the Black Power movement had radicalized tens of thousands of black youth at the same time as campus protests mounted. The women's liberation movement re-emerged in 1968 as women articulated their need for autonomy from male militarism and sought to define their own lives and identities, thereby deepening the movement's scope and widening its public and private impact.

Altogether then, the energies of 1968 galavanized millions of Americans into a movement which came to challenge the existing structures of the world system (as I discuss in Chapter 4). The world-historical convergence of radical oppositional movements in 1968 was not entirely spontaneous and unconscious. A careful reading of the internal documents of the National Liberation Front of Vietnam reveals a high level of self-consciousness in relation to the potential worldwide effects of its planned offensive, particularly during an election year in the United States.[14] On the other side, many activists in the United States fully understood that their country was wrong and that they could not, in Camus's words, "love their country and freedom too." Theirs was not a passive understanding of freedom, but an active opposition to their country's government. As the gap widened between the official U.S. version of the war and its reality, hundreds of thousands of Americans even went over to the side of Ho Chi Minh and the NLF. The fact that so many Americans embraced their government's official "enemies" as friends and viewed their own government as the enemy is one of the clearest examples of the internationalism of the New Left and its break with established politics and culture.

The victorious resistance of the Vietnamese gave the international movement a basis for its unity. The militant demonstrators who marched in the streets of Paris, Prague, Chicago, and hundreds of other cities in 1968 were all carrying the same flags: not only the red flag of revolution and black flag of anarchism, but the red, yellow, and blue flag of the National Liberation Front of Southern Vietnam. In London (which had been relatively quiet in the 1960s), one observer described the situation this way:

> The reports of the Tet offensive had a powerful effect on British campuses where meetings called by local groups of the Vietnam Solidarity Campaign with national speakers could assemble 1,000 students within hours. The intense debate inevitably spilt onto the streets where, aside from dozens of local demonstrations, there were two significant mass demonstrations. On March 17, some 30,000 confronted police horses and drawn batons in Grosvenor Square in front of the fortress United States embassy. That night, 246 demonstrators were in police cells and 117 policemen in London hospitals.[15]

During Tet, 3,000 people attacked the U.S. embassy in Rome, and 10,000 people peacefully marched in West Berlin. Throughout the world, similar demonstrations occurred, and even the slogans were similar: "Ho, Ho, Ho Chi Minh, NLF is going to win!" and "Two, Three, Many Vietnams!"

The latter slogan was derived from a speech Che Guevara gave to the Organization of Latin American Solidarity (OLAS) shortly before he left for Bolivia to open another front. In his view, that was the best way to act in solidarity with the Vietnamese.[16] Although captured and murdered in 1967, Che's call had not gone unheeded. In Latin America, guerrilla movements in Venezuela, Colombia, Guatemala, Nicaragua, Bolivia, and Peru took up

Che's call to arms and, mistakenly or not, modeled their armed struggle on his "*foco* theory."[17] Guerrilla movements in Eritrea, Angola, Mozambique, Guinea-Bissau, the Philippines, Thailand, and many other nations intensified their actions in this period, and anti-imperialist military *coups* made their appearance. In Peru, a 1968 *coup* led to one of the most far-reaching agrarian reform programs ever directed from above, and the military government which came to power in Panama in 1968 continues to be bothersome to the United States.

In the Middle East, the defeat of the Arab regimes and the occupation of the West Bank and Gaza by Israel in 1967 led to the reorganization of the PLO and a new chairperson, Yasser Arafat. There was an upsurge of Palestine Liberation Organization (PLO) guerrilla attacks, the first jet hijacking, the defeat of Israeli troops at Karameh, and massive demonstrations—some led by women—against the Zionist occupation of Jerusalem. As the *eros* effect swept the Arab world, an Arab New Left was galvanized which identified with the Cuban and Vietnamese revolutions at the same time as it saw through the bankruptcy of the "progressive" Arab regimes and criticized the Soviet Union and Arab Communist Parties for their "rigid and fossilized" leadership. In more than ten Arab countries, a New Left developed, stressing popular struggle, and in some cases, "cultural revolution," the need for autonomy from world superpowers, and the significance of the upsurges in Poland, France, and Italy as well as the black revolt and student anti-war movement in the United States.[18] Nineteen sixty-eight was also the year in which Khomeini published a collection of essays on Islamic government; a republican government was won in South Yemen; and a July *coup* brought the Arab Socialist Baath Party to power in Iraq.

In short, the balance of world power shifted in 1968, a change obvious as early as January of that year when the *USS Pueblo* and its crew were captured by North Korea after the intelligence-gathering ship "wandered" into its waters. In the 1950s, the United States had been able to impose the division of Korea and install friendly governments in Iran and Guatemala, but in 1968, the Tet offensive signaled the end of the epoch in which the United States would be unchallenged in its role as world policeman.

As Vietnam inspired the global movement, the theories of Che Guevara helped direct its energies. His strategic outlook differed from that of the Communist Parties in several respects. These differences merit close attention since they provided a strategy for the New Left at the same time as they refute the conservative opinion that the New Left was directly linked to Moscow.

Che's "*Foco* Theory"

The call for armed struggle to be undertaken in the countryside by the "*foco*," a small and dedicated group of guerrillas, as a way of setting a popular movement in motion, constituted a strategic alternative to the Communist strategy of building an urban-based vanguard of the working class. If the Communists sought to build their base within the most advanced sectors of production, the guerrillas located themselves among the peasants as far as possible from the military-political-economic concentrations of the Establishment. If the Communist Parties sought to work whenever possible within the established political process and believed in the possibility of peaceful change, the guerrillas wanted only to smash the established state. In broad terms, the Communist Parties argued for a gradual transition to socialism by continually emphasizing that conditions favorable to revolution were not present, and the guerrillas sought to create these conditions by setting in motion "the big motor of the mass movement through the small motor of the *foco*."

Although the implementation of Che's *foco* theory was unsuccessful in Bolivia, Colombia, and Venezuela,[18] the *foco* theory proved of value to the Nicaraguan revolution. Attempts to duplicate the success of the Cuban revolution by adopting its strategy were not confined to Latin America or to the third world. The Weather Underground and Black Liberation Army in the United States, the Irish Republican Army, the Red Army Faction in West Germany, the Red Brigades in Italy, the *Front de Liberation Quebequois* (FLQ) in Canada, *Euzkadi Ta Askatasuna* (ETA) or Basque Land and Liberty in Spain, and the *Gauche Proletarian* in France all carefully studied Che and Debray (as well as Marighellia, Mao, and Giap) and—successfully or not—put the strategy of Cuba into practice in their own countries.

The success of the Cuban guerrillas led to the creation of a Guevarist wing within radical movements in both the core and periphery, sparking major splits between the radical Left and Soviet Communists. As early as 1961, Brazilian Communists had divided into pro-armed struggle and Soviet factions. Around the same time, similar divisions occurred in the movements in Bolivia, Venezuela, Peru, Chile, and Colombia. Years later, the same splits occurred in the Black Panther Party and SDS in both Germany and the United States, although the Communist position was Maoist, not Soviet, and the pro-armed struggle factions included Marxists.

Besides the difference over strategy and tactics, there was another dimension to the gap between Soviet Communism and the new radicalism, a difference summed up in Che's call for the transformation of human beings—for the "creation of a new socialist human." Soviet Marxism has long regarded the transformation of the basic structures of society as inevitably and automatically leading to cultural and social transformation. The new radicalism demanded a simultaneous transformation of politics, economy, and culture, of social structure and individual subject. Abstractly, the refusal to passively accept non-revolutionary objective conditions as unmodifiable is analogous to the new radicalism's refusal to accept the position that the transformation of everyday life must be delayed until "after the revolution."

In their call for direct action and cultural-political revolution (including the liberation of women), the guerrillas in the third world and radical movements in the core were intimately tied together in theory, and in practice, they forged a unity against a common enemy (U.S. "imperialism") and a common rival (Soviet-style "radicalism"). Although Cuba has developed increasing ties to the Soviet Union, its revolutionary movement was neither Communist-led nor tied to the Soviet Union until after the U.S. invasion and economic blockade, and Cuba provided a powerful impetus for the New Left. When the speeches of Fidel Castro were published in the United States, for example, their North American editor wrote:

> The example of Cuba gives the New Left inspiration; it is living proof that a determined people and strong leadership can defeat the most powerful military forces in the world. Fidel's speeches, with their emphasis on struggle and their vision of a new society and a "new man," speak not only to the Cuban people but also to the youth of America today.[19]

The same book's dedication was unabashedly optimistic in its understanding of the historical possibilities: "This book is dedicated to the Cuban and the Vietnamese people who have given North Americans the possibility of making a revolution and to the young North Americans who have taken advantage of that possibility."

The Student Movement of 1968

If 1968 was anyone's year, it was the year of the students. From Peking to Prague and Paris to Berkeley, students sparked the movements which marked 1968, and more than any other group, it was their international practice (partially illustrated by the map on the next pages) which made the New Left a global movement. In conjunction with the movements for national liberation, particularly with Vietnam, the student movement became a force in international relations, compelling world policymakers to modify—and in some cases to cancel altogether—their grandiose plans. Soon after Richard Nixon was elected to his first term as President, for example, he threatened the Vietnamese with the use of nuclear weapons on Hanoi if they did not immediately surrender. It was the hundreds of thousands of predominantly student demonstrators who marched in cities across the United States in October and November 1969 that caused him to modify his choice of weapons.[20] Six months later, the 1970 nationwide student strike compelled Nixon to limit the U.S. invasion of Cambodia and helped provide the Black Panther Party with some protection from police and FBI attacks.

Within movements for national liberation, students have long played a significant role both in sparking popular mobilizations and in the initial formation of revolutionary organizations. In Cuba, it was the student movement (organized as the *Directorio Estudiantil Universitario*) and the army which overthrew the Machado regime in 1933. When Batista and the army overthrew the constitutional government in 1952, it was again students who

Map 1

Major Student Disruptions, 1968-1969

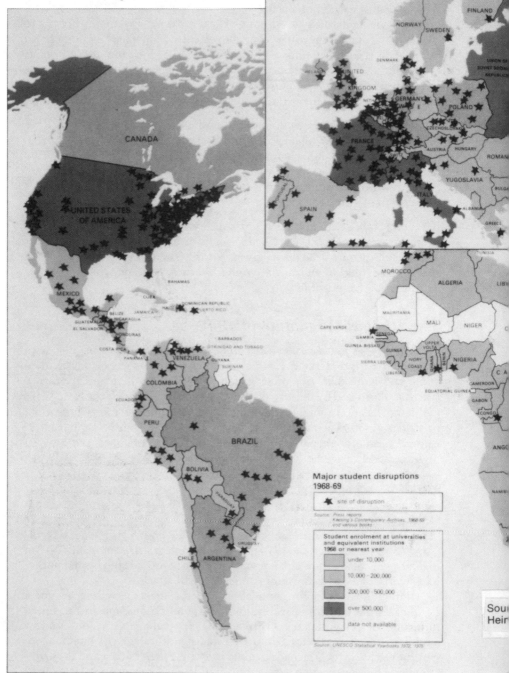

Major student disruptions
1968-69

★ site of disruption

Source: Press reports
Keesing's Contemporary Archives, 1968-69
and various books

Student enrolment at universities
and equivalent institutions
1968 or nearest year

under 10,000

10,000 - 200,000

200,000 - 500,000

over 500,000

data not available

Source: UNESCO Statistical Yearbooks 1972, 1973

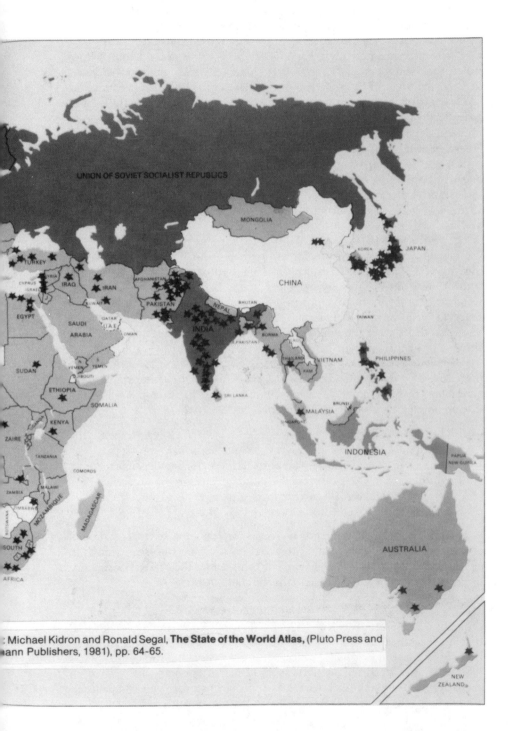

: Michael Kidron and Ronald Segal, **The State of the World Atlas,** (Pluto Press and ann Publishers, 1981), pp. 64-65.

initiated the armed struggle against Batista and who maintained opposition to his regime in the brutally suppressed national student strike of 1955-56.[21] In Vietnam, students played an important role in sparking oppositional movements in the cities. As early as 1949, they began to demonstrate against U.S. involvement in their country,[22] and in the early 1960s, their actions helped isolate the Diem regime. In January 1965, together with organized Buddhists, the student movement appealed for a general strike in Hue, and once the strike broke out there, it quickly spread to Danang among the workers at the U.S. air base. As the situation grew more desperate, police fired on demonstrators in Hue and Dalat, wounding four students.[23] Thirty more people were wounded by police and paratroopers in Saigon a few days later. As the disturbances continued, the military staged a *coup d'état*, and ten days later, the United States began its bombing of northern Vietnam. Students in Vietnam continued their opposition to foreign domination through general strikes from March to May 1966, and again in the spring of 1970, when more than 60,000 students participated.

As early as 1960, C. Wright Mills noted the new role of students.[24] The signs were clear enough: Students in South Korea caused the downfall of Syngman Rhee; in Turkey, student riots led to a military *coup d'etat*; massive student riots against the Japan-United States Security Treaty forced the resignation of the Kishi government and compelled President Eisenhower to cancel his visit there; in Taiwan and Okinawa, Great Britain and the United States, students were showing signs of becoming, as Mills put it, "real live agencies of historic change."

The international connections among these student movements were forged as they heard of one another's existence. In describing the origins of the awakening of black students in the United States, for example, Clayborn Carson noted the influence of African movements:

> The African independence movement, led by college-trained activists, also affected black youths...Students who later took part in the sit-in movements heard reports of the African independence struggle...a few weeks before the initial Greensboro sit-in...even the most unintellectual black students were envious of the African independence movement and vaguely moved by it.[25]

If, in 1960, the signs of awakening were present, few expected that by the end of the decade, the actions of students would precipitate a near-revolution in France (discussed in the next chapter) or bring about the greatest crisis since the Civil War in the United States (the topic of Chapter 4). Inspired by Vietnam and activated by the global *eros* effect, anti-imperialist student movements erupted throughout the world in 1968. In Ethiopia, Ecuador, India, Thailand, Peru, Puerto Rico, Uruguay, Venezuela, Brazil, Argentina, Indonesia, Pakistan, Greece, Turkey, Panama, Mexico, Italy, Spain, Japan, Belgium, France, West Germany, and the United States (to make only a partial list), these movements spontaneously acted in solidarity with one another. Even the most casual observers were compelled to acknowledge the international character of the movement:

The turbulence of student radicalism now has the appearance of being worldwide. Alongside the formal international federations of students that appear to be of scant significance for the more dramatic activities of the student radicals, there is a spontaneous and unorganized, or at best an informal, unity of sympathy of the student movement which forms a bridge across national boundaries. In 1968, student radical movements seemed to be synchronized among different countries and uniform in content and technique.[26]

Or as Seymour Martin Lipset, a specialist in the study of student movements, observed in 1968:

Anyone who attempts to interpret the revival of student activism in recent years must face the fact that he is dealing with a worldwide phenomenon. Wherever one looks—at stagnant underdeveloped countries like Indonesia, at rapidly expanding, economically successful ones like Japan, at right-wing dictatorships like Spain, at Communist systems such as Czechoslovakia and Poland, and at such Western democracies as Germany, France, Italy, and the United States—one finds aggressive student movements that challenge their governments for not living up to different sets of social ideals.[27]

The international character of the student movement has long been one of its defining contours, providing a reference point within which its theory and practice were articulated. In 1968, however, television, radio, and travelling spokespersons spread the movement around the world as never before, synchronizing its actions and making the political generation of 1968 a truly international one. It is quite apparent that the chain reaction of protests (or *eros* effect) operated on a global level because so many of the significant outbursts of student protest were related to one another. In February 1968, for example, students in France were heard chanting "Solidarity with SDS," the New Left organization in Germany which was under attack. The next month, 400 German SDS members formed a prominent contingent at a demonstration in London. After the French students erupted in May, police battled 5,000 students in Rome who gathered to burn de Gaulle in effigy. In June and July, there were four days of street fighting in Berkeley when police attacked demonstrations in solidarity with the striking workers and students of France. On June 15, 10,000 Japanese students blockaded the center of Tokyo to show their solidarity with French students. In Santiago, Chile, thousands of students attacked the U.S. Embassy on October 4 in support of students in Mexico and Uruguay, who themselves identified with the May 1968 student-led revolt in France.

What is striking about the 1968 student movements is the degree to which their actions became political. Seldom in history has such a general will been formulated in spontaneously generated moments of confrontation. The day-to-day story of class struggle seems to be much more concerned with immediate material gains or losses. The transformation of economic struggles into political ones was (and is) a central turning point in the life of social movements. This transformation of self-interest into universal interest— another dimension of *eros* effect—was what occurred in 1968 and was obvious for all to see. In Scandinavia, for example, what had been student politics "characterized by an extraordinary tranquility and a virtual absence of mass activism" in 1967 suddenly became remarkably militant and internationally focused activism in 1968.[28] In Turkey, there were suddenly sit-ins, boycotts, and militant confrontations again in 1968, although between 1960 and 1968, press statements, meetings, and occasional demonstrations had been the norm.[29] In Africa, there were major student demonstrations in at least seventeen countries in 1968. In Nigeria, a student movement emerged in May 1968 demanding the right of assembly. The university was closed for three weeks, and only when high school students joined the revolt did the government give in.[30] On May 29, 1968, students occupying the University of Dakar (Senegal) as a protest against scholarship reductions were attacked by police, and in the days of street fighting which ensued, one student was killed, twenty-five wounded, and 900 arrested. When the trade unions went on strike to support the students (as well as for higher wages and price controls), the President closed the university and imposed a nationwide state of emergency.[31]

The table on pages 44-45, tabulated by counting the articles in *Le Monde* dealing with student protests, statistically demonstrates the incredible extent to which students became mobilized in 1968, particularly in the period from May 3 to June 18 (when the general strike paralyzed France). It should be remembered that these numbers refer only to student protests which were reported in the pages of *Le Monde*. The actual numbers are much higher.

If the actions of students in 1968 were directly political, the impact of their actions was felt on other levels as well. By questioning the assumptions of everyday life—the cultural conformity of consumerism, the oppression of women, discrimination against minorities, and the segregation of youth—the student movement helped stimulate a worldwide cultural awakening which accompanied and outlasted the global political revolt. In both the core and periphery, the East and the West, the student movement spontaneously generated coherent global aspirations which stood in sharp contrast to the established reality. From France to Tunisia and Yugoslavia to Mexico, students broke with traditional political parties of the Left and the Right and developed new forms of organization and practice. Their unified actions and emergent aspirations were a product of centuries of centralization of the world economic system, but at the same time, they helped define new dimensions to the global culture. New values for international and interpersonal social relationships quickly spread as a result of these movements, values which went beyond what was previously considered possible or acceptable. In many countries, the student movement built a cultural base outside the universities and established semi-liberated territories in places like San Francisco's Haight-Ashbury; in Berkeley, Madison, and Cambridge; in Amsterdam in the period of the *Provos, Kabouters,* and the Orange Free State; in Berlin's Kreuzberg; in

Nanterre and other parts of Paris; and in London's Notting Hill. Free schools, food co-ops, radical bookstores, communes, and collective coffeehouses were established as focal points of this emergent counterculture, and many of the values built within these communities could not be extinguished after the political turmoil has subsided. In Zurich, 10,000 people demonstrated for an autonomous youth center on June 29 and 30, 1968, and the police mercilessly attacked the marchers (hospitalizing 200 people and severely beating 2,500 more who were arrested). Twelve years later, in 1980, a new generation successfully used tactics like nude marches and "roller skate commando" demonstrations and temporarily won an autonomous youth center.

In some cases, student revolts in 1968, such as those that occurred in Canada, Ghana, and Finland, were limited to issues involving educational reform. In Belgium, Flemish students at the Roman Catholic University in Louvain rioted for three weeks in January after the French-speaking faculty announced that they planned to remain at the university. Even in a case such as this, when the focus was purely educational, the student movement had *political* repercussions; tensions over the Louvain University disturbance contributed to the collapse of the government of Premier Paul Vanden Boeynants in February.

In other countries, students responded to issues which originated outside the universities. In February 1968, Egyptian students rioted over the military defeats in the 1967 war and closed five universities. Later in the year, at Mansura, demonstrations over a university regulation spread to Alexandria and Cairo, where the unrest became more political in character. In the ensuing confrontations, sixteen people were killed in Alexandria on November 25 as police battled 5,000 students with clubs, tear gas, and gunfire.

As a general pattern in the twentieth century, students and youth have been in the forefront of those who would end wars and establish a new system of international cooperation. From the May 4 Movement in China to the May events in France, students have been a blasting cap capable of detonating upheavals throughout society. Although there have been important exceptions—notably the fascist students of Hitler, Tojo, and Mussolini—students have generally been pro-liberty and anti-war. They have marched peacefully, demonstrated militantly, and formed their own international associations. In terms of massive upheavals, however, the student generation of 1968 was the first since 1848 to erupt globally with such numbers and enthusiasm.[32]

How do we account for the new role played by students around the world in 1968? There are many factors underlying their activism: their youthfulness (which leaves them free from many of the responsibilities which immobilize their elders); their segregation on the campuses (which creates a "critical mass"); the relatively free nature of the universities in terms of both the exchange of ideas and the leisure time afforded its members (both of which contrast sharply to "adult" institutions); and last, but not least, the fact that students are *supposed* to study social issues (a demand which brings them face-to-face with some of the obvious problems of the existing world system). While the above factors may account for student activism, they do not

Table 1

Incidents of Student Protest as Reported in Le Monde

	1967 4th Qtr.	1st Qtr.	1968 Total	2nd Quarter 4/1-5/2	5/3-6/18	6/18-30
France	30	79	1205	41	971	193
Austria	—	—	6	—	6	—
Belgium	—	2	19	1	14	4
Czechoslovakia	4	16	12	7	4	1
Denmark	—	—	1	—	1	—
East Germany	—	1	1	—	—	1
Great Britain	1	3	26	3	20	3
Greece	2	4	4	1	3	—
Ireland	—	—	1	—	1	—
Italy	2	24	34	6	22	6
Luxemburg	—	—	3	—	3	—
Netherlands	1	1	7	—	5	2
Poland	—	33	17	12	4	1
Portugal	1	1	1	—	1	—
Spain	18	49	34	13	19	2
Sweden	1	1	4	—	4	—
Switzerland	—	—	11	—	9	2
Turkey	1	—	10	1	5	4
U.S.S.R.	1	6	4	2	1	1
Vatican	1	—	1	—	—	1
West Germany	6	13	63	33	25	5
(West Berlin)	—	—	23	6	14	3
Yugoslavia	—	—	14	—	12	2
EUROPE—Total	39	154	296	85	173	38
Algeria	2	21	5	1	4	—
Comores	—	3	—	—	—	—
Congo	—	1	—	—	—	—
Dahomey	1	—	—	—	—	—
Egypt	1	4	2	—	2	—
Ethiopia	—	—	2	2	—	—
Morocco	—	2	2	—	1	1
Mauritania	—	—	2	—	2	—
Rep. Central Africa	—	—	1	1	—	—
Senegal	—	—	16	—	16	—
Tunisia	—	8	12	6	3	3
AFRICA—Total	4	39	42	10	28	4

	1967 4th Qtr.	1st Qtr.	1968 2nd Quarter			
			Total	4/1-5/2	5/3-6/18	6/18-30
Argentina	—	2	21	2	10	9
Bolivia	—	—	2	1	—	1
Brazil	5	2	24	8	7	9
Canada	—	1	1	—	1	—
Chile	—	—	6	—	6	—
Colombia	—	1	3	1	1	1
Cuba	1	—	—	—	—	—
Ecuador	2	2	—	—	—	—
Guadelupe	1	—	1	—	1	—
Guyana	—	—	1	—	1	—
Haiti	—	1	2	—	2	—
Mexico	—	—	1	1	—	—
Nicaragua	—	—	2	1	—	1
Peru	—	2	4	—	3	1
Santo Domingo	—	3	2	—	—	2
United States	11	12	21	7	12	2
Uruguay	—	—	11	—	4	7
Venezuela	—	2	2	1	1	—
AMERICAS—Total	20	28	104	22	49	33
Afghanistan	—	—	1	—	1	—
China	2	2	12	1	8	3
India	6	—	1	—	1	—
Indonesia	—	2	2	—	2	—
Israel	—	3	3	1	2	—
Japan	3	6	9	3	3	3
Lebanon	—	1	2	2	—	—
Palestine	2	—	2	1	1	—
South Korea	—	1	—	—	—	—
South Vietnam	1	1	—	—	—	—
Syria	—	—	1	1	—	—
Thailand	—	—	1	—	—	1
ASIA—Total	14	16	34	9	18	7
Australia	2	—	—	—	—	—
Philippines	—	1	—	—	—	—
PACIFIC—Total	2	1	—	—	—	—
Africa	4	39	42	10	28	4
Americas	20	39	104	22	49	32
Asia	14	16	34	7	18	7
Europe	39	154	296	85	173	38
France	30	79	1205	41	971	193
Pacific	2	1	—	—	—	—
General Total	109	328	1681	165	1239	274

Source: J. Jousellin, **Les Rèvoltes des Jeunes** (Paris: Les Editions Ouvrières, 1968), pp. 13-15.

explain why international events catalyzed the eruptions on campuses in 1968 or why the vision and demands of the students were international ones. In order to understand this central dimension of the student revolt, its context in the Third Industrial Revolution and the globalization of production needs to be considered. The modern world system increasingly depends upon its universities for technical research as well as for the education of its technicians. After World War II, the quantitative expansion of the universities and the increasing interpenetration of national economies in a world economy occurred at a dizzying rate, creating the preconditions for the emergence of the student movement of 1968. Far from remaining marginal institutions reserved for the training of new elites, the universities were moved to the center of the global system of production. The tens of millions of college students in 1968 represented the ascendent new working class upon whom the functioning of the global system increasingly depends. Not only were (and are) students in a central position in a global system undergoing rapid technological changes, they were also one of the "weakest links" in such a system. As Ernest Mandel put it in 1968:

> A new social group has emerged from the very vitals of capitalism, from all that it considered its essential "achievement": the higher standard of living, the advances in technology and the mass media, and the requirements of automation. There are six million university students in the United States, two and a half million in Western Europe, and over a million in Japan. And it proved impossible to integrate these groupings into the capitalist system as it functions in any of these territories... What the student revolt represents on a much broader social and historic scale is the colossal transformation of the productive forces...the reintegration of intellectual labor into productive labor.[33]

If, as Clark Kerr observed, the universities stood in relation to the latter half of the twentieth century as the railroads did to the end of the nineteenth, then the student movement of 1968 stands historically in line with the militant railroad workers of 1905 whose strikes and struggles met with apparent defeat, but whose goals of an eight-hour working day, universal suffrage, and trade unions were realized decades later. Fortunately, the students of 1968 did not have to wait for decades before reforms were made. Within a few years, the war against Indochina was ended, archaic campus procedures were liberalized, the voting age was lowered, and "human rights" became the avowed priority of the world's most powerful nation-state.

What was significant in 1968 was not only that students were in the forefront of the New Left, nor merely that their numbers were so swelled that they were in themselves an important social force. What was most significant was that the particular interests of the student movements became identified with the needs of the most oppressed members of the world system and that a general will was articulated which negated the accepted values of nationalism, hierarchy, and the global division of labor. In May 1968 and May 1970, the general strikes sparked by students transcended the existing system of values and simultaneously sought to transform the structures of the world system and the everyday routines conditioned by those structures.

From the start, it was at the level of everyday life that the New Left sought to transform society, an aspiration which explains why the movement built its own communities and attempted to define a new process of politics. At the same moment, however, an essential dimension of the movement's identity was its international connectedness, a phenomenon understood by both the CIA and the KGB (who organized their own international student associations in an attempt to gain control of the movement).[34] In Santo Domingo in 1967, the CIA went as far as organizing an entire "Counter-University."[35] Coupled as it was with a diffuse cultural revolt, however, the student movement was controlled neither by outsiders, nor by its own hastily organized groupings. Perhaps this is clearest in the case of Mexico, where the 1968 student movement endured its bloodiest days during preparations for one of the world's premier events: the Olympic Games.

In order to further document the international character of the movement of 1968, I will review events in Mexico and Latin America, West Germany, Italy, Spain, Pakistan, England, Japan, and Eastern Europe.

Mexico and Latin America

In the summer of 1968, the spectacle of the coming Olympics became a stage upon which Mexican students hoped to win social reforms. By threatening to force postponement or cancellation of the Olympics, the student movement sought freedom for political prisoners, dismissal of the police chief in Mexico City, and the allocation of public monies on domestic needs rather than the Olympic Games. In 1967, a student strike in Hermosillo had been suppressed when the police violated the traditional autonomy of the university and bloodily dispersed the strikers. Because that police action quickly became so notorious, few people expected increased violence to be used against students.

In the summer of 1968, although demonstrations had called for the release of an imprisoned railroad union leader, the students were internally divided. On July 23, however, when rival student groups from two secondary schools in Mexico City were attacked by the riot police, the divisions among students were temporarily set aside. Three days later, not coincidentally the anniversary of the 1953 attack on the Moncada army barracks in Cuba, thousands of students took to the streets to protest police brutality, and they were again attacked by the riot squads. This time seven people were killed, 500 wounded, and hundreds arrested. On July 29, all schools in Mexico City were ordered closed after more than 150,000 students began a general strike. When the students continued to occupy their classrooms, the police used a bazooka to enter a junior college in Mexico City. By the end of the month, anti-police demonstrations and street fighting had spread from Mexico City to Veracruz, Tabasco, and as far north as Sonora.

On the first of August, 100,000 students marched from the National

University on the far outskirts of Mexico City to the center of the city. Four days later, 150,000 students gathered at the Polytechnic Institute and by the end of the month, twice that number were marching behind revolutionary banners, chanting Che Guevara's slogan, "Create Two, Three, Many Vietnams." A strike council drew up a multi-point petition which had little to do with the problems of students alone: repeal of the laws under which "subversives" could legally be arrested; disbanding of the Corps of Grenadiers, as the riot police who brutally suppressed the 1957 railroad strike are known; aid for the "victims of police aggression"; and a role for the public in determining which officials were responsible for the police attacks on the universities.[36]

In response to these demands, police occupied both the National University and the Polytechnic Institute on September 18. This new violation of the university's autonomy provided the impetus for students throughout Mexico to renew their strike. A National Strike Council representing 128 schools was quickly formed in the hopes of negotiating a peaceful settlement to the burgeoning national crisis. Strike Council delegates were chosen by "combat committees" at the local level, and a National Coordinating Committee of 600 students was the final decision-making body. When President Gustavo Diaz Ordaz refused to make the negotiations with the Strike Council public, a rally was called for October 2 at the Plaza of Three Cultures in the Tlatelolco housing project in downtown Mexico City.

Without warning, soldiers and police viciously attacked the rally, shooting hundreds of people. In many cases they followed the wounded into the hospitals and killed them there. To this day, no one knows for sure how many people were killed at Tlatelolco. At the time, government reports estimated about 100 deaths, but it is common knowledge that there were over 400 deaths in one of the most violent confrontations between a government and students in history. October 2, 1968, now known as the "Night of Sorrow," is still remembered as a peak of unrest in Mexico, and it has continued to have political repercussions. In February 1969, the police chief in Mexico City quietly resigned, and in 1977, when former president Diaz Ordaz was appointed ambassador to Spain, Carlos Fuentes resigned as ambassador to France to protest against the man held responsible for the Tlatelolco massacre.

Elsewhere in Latin America, the pattern of brutality was similar. Although the student movements in Latin America reached their culmination in 1968, their roots predate the global eruptions of that year. In the 1950s, Colombian students sparked a popular revolution which overthrew the Rojas dictatorship, and in Venezuela, it was a militant student uprising which led to the ouster of Perez Jimenez. When the military threatened a *coup* against the new government, armed student militias guarded the autonomy of the universities and the capital from the threatened attacks by reactionary sectors of the army.[37] In 1966, thousands of paratroopers finally invaded the Central University of Venezuela in Caracas, forcibly clearing the dormitories and searching the entire university. Tanks, infantry, and police occupied the university for over three months. In the same year in Ecuador, the military junta fell as a result of actions by university students which led to a general strike. In Argentina, Brazil, Colombia, and Mexico, troops were called out against students who were protesting educational policies, and the protests turned into serious political problems. In Panama, Nicaragua, and Uruguay, student protests caused severe unrest in 1966.[38]

Coupled with the global upheavals of 1968, these continuing student movements led to major crises throughout Latin America. In Rio de Janeiro, the death of a student at the hands of the police on March 29, 1968, sparked two weeks of riots which culminated in the deaths of three more students, the closing of schools, and the occupation of the city by the army. Riots continued through June as the student movement demanded an end to President Costa de Silva's government as well as reforms in the educational system. Over 800 students were arrested on June 21 when students at the Federal University protested the government's failure to give enough aid to Brazil's forty-one universities. When the unrest spread to other cities, a ban on demonstrations was enacted, and only the arrest of 1,240 students near Sao Paulo in October temporarily quieted the revolt.[39]

In Uruguay, a month of fighting between students and police was joined by strikes called by the country's unions in early July. To head off the potentially explosive situation, the government imposed martial law on July 14. Nevertheless, student unrest continued through the fall, and finally, on September 22, following a week of particularly violent clashes in Montevideo, the government ordered all universities and high schools closed for a month.

In Argentina, 23 students were shot dead in May 1968, and 400 students occupied the University of La Plata in Buenos Aires on June 12 in protest of the government's repression. Exactly three months later, a student strike in the capital erupted into a bloody clash with police.[40] As only became known in the 1980s, the Argentine student movement was brutally liquidated in the 1970s by tens of thousands of "disappearances" and deaths.

West Germany

The German New Left was among the most theoretically inclined and internationally conscious members of the global movement. German students demonstrated against the President of Senegal when he arrived at the Frankfurt book fair because he had suppressed the student movement at home; they protested the arrival of Moise Tshombe for his role in the murder of Patrice Lumumba; and they mobilized against the Korean secret service for its treatment of dissidents. The internationalism of the German *Sozialistischer Deutscher Studentenbund* (SDS) defined that organization's identity from its inception, leading it to break away from its parent organization, the German Social Democratic Party. As the Social Democrats formed a Grand Coalition to govern Germany, SDS became increasingly extraparliamentary, using "sit-ins," "go-ins," and demonstrations as a means of precipitating parliamentary action.[41]

Although SDS in Germany and the United States shared the same initials and grew out of similar social democratic labor groups, the two organizations were not formally connected. German SDS was explicitly "socialist," while SDS in the United States contained a more diverse and theoretically underdeveloped membership. Nonetheless, the two groups were intuitively tied together. Although their actions were quite similar (German SDS adopted the "sit-in"—both the word and the practice—from the United States), the German New Left was never able to synthesize a cultural politics like the U.S. countercultures. Nonetheless, the German New Left was the first massive opposition to the Cold War consensus which took up the long-abandoned revolutionary tradition of the German working class, a heritage betrayed by the opportunism of Social Democracy and nearly destroyed by the Nazis' slaughter and Stalinist purges.

More than any other New Left organization, the roots of German SDS were in the dynamics of European political discourse. Its first president was Helmut Schmidt (later a chancellor of West Germany), and some of SDS's initial campaigns protested the presence of former Nazis in the administration of the universities and the government. As the organization grew, its membership became a unique combination of exiles from East Germany, radical Christians, and libertarian socialists. Divided Germany became a focal point for many of the international problems of the post-war era, and the German New Left became increasingly oriented to global issues.

When the Shah of Iran hoped to attend the opera in West Berlin on June 2, 1967, he was greeted by several thousand demonstrators, whose presence made them the targets of vicious attacks by both the Berlin police and the Shah's secret police (SAVAK). One student, Benno Ohnesorg, was shot in the head and killed, an incident which had profound repercussions for the German movement. A few days later, 20,000 people formed a miles-long funeral procession which was allowed to pass uninterrupted through East Germany despite the usual time-consuming checks. After Ohnesorg's funeral, the German New Left convened in Hannover.

Although the Hannover Congress should have been a time for unity, it marked the beginning of the end for the German New Left. It was there that Jürgen Habermas first raised the problem of "Left fascism" for discussion, and the acrimony which ensued eventually led to sit-ins at the Frankfurt Institute for Social Research (where Habermas, Adorno, and Horkheimer taught). Two decades after the Hannover Congress, the Frankfurt School continues to be poorly regarded by German activists, while the *Bewegung der 2 Juni* (a guerrilla group which took its name from the day of Ohnesorg's death) are regarded as folk heroes. In Teheran, there now exists a Benno Ohnesorg street.

By the fall of 1967, much of German society opposed SDS, but the movement had entrenched itself on the campuses, particularly in West Berlin where thousands of people voted to reconstitute the Free University as a "Critical University": a self-managed institution oriented toward changing society and governed by university-wide plebiscites. Of course, university administrators refused to accept the results of the vote reconstituting the university, but there was little they could do to stop the growing involvement of thousands of students in an extraparliamentary opposition (APO).

At the beginning of 1968, German SDS hosted an international gathering in Berlin to discuss solidarity actions with Vietnam. Significantly, many participants in the subsequent student revolt in France participated in the Berlin conference. Before the delegates took to the streets for one of the largest anti-imperialist demonstrations in German history, they issued a call to the world movement:

> We call on the anti-imperialist resistance movement...to continue to build unified mass demonstrations against U.S. imperialism and its helpers in Western Europe. In the course of this unified struggle, political and organizational working unity between the revolutionary movements in Western Europe must be intensified and a United Front must be built.[42]

Of the many diverse groups which constituted the APO, the largest umbrella organization sponsored an annual Easter March for disarmament. Unlike the Campaign for Nuclear Disarmament in Great Britain (whose membership and base of support began to erode in the early 1960s), the German anti-nuclear impetus saw its numbers swell: from 100,000 marchers in 1966 to 150,000 in 1967.[43] By Easter of 1968, more than 300,000 Germans marched for peace in the midst of a violent upheaval caused by the attempted assassination of Rudi Dutschke, one of the principal spokespersons of SDS.

On March 11, the Thursday before Easter, a Munich house painter carrying a pistol and a newspaper clipping of Martin Luther King's assassination a week earlier, fired three shots at "Red Rudi." Although one shot hit him in the head, Dutschke survived, at least until 1980, when he died from the epilepsy caused by the bullet. The fact that Dutschke's attacker carried a clipping of King's assassination confirmed many people's suspicions that the German media's campaign against SDS had helped cause the attack, and throughout Germany, the APO attacked and attempted to stop the distribution of publications of the Springer Press, a newspaper monopoly which controls over 80 percent of German daily newspapers. Axel Springer had long used his control of German public opinion to incite his readers against the student movement. Not only did the APO blame Springer for Dutschke's fate, they also saw his monopoly of the media as a symbol of the problem of private ownership of social resources, a problem all too evident in Springer's sensationalist attacks on the New Left.

The anti-Springer campaign was not confined to Germany. In London, the march of March 17 on the U.S. embassy at Grosvenor Square prominently included anti-Springer posters carried by at least sixty members of Berlin and Frankfurt SDS, and in Paris, two days after Dutschke was shot, more than 1,000 people demonstrated in front of the German embassy. Significantly, that demonstration was the first time that a coalition of all the New Left groups in France worked together. On March 19, several thousand people again converged on the German embassy, but this time, issues relating to France were also raised.[44] Three days later, the administration building at Nanterre University was occupied to protest the U.S. war against Vietnam, an action which led to the formation of the March 22 Movement, the group generally credited with sparking the general strike in France.

After Dutschke was shot and the Springer Press was under attack throughout Germany, the stage was set for the German *Bundestag* (or Parliament) to impose the *Notstandsgesetze*, emergency laws aimed at social control, measures that had long been desired by the German Right but which had not been politically possible until the eruption of the APO and the near-revolution across the Rhine. In a concerted campaign to stop the new laws from being passed, the APO mobilized tens of thousands of Germans. Students in high schools and colleges boycotted lectures. In Berlin, a "permanent" teach-in of several thousand students was convened, and on May 20, hundreds of students occupied the Free University. In Bochum, a coordinating center was set up, and a call was sent out for a general strike on May 29 (a strike which some believed would match the one of 10 million workers which had brought France to a standstill that same month). The strike was quickly endorsed by representatives of 50,000 *IG Metall* workers in Munich and 120,000 unionists in Cologne, while in Frankfurt, 10,000 workers downed tools in a brief warning strike. By May 27, the APO staged go-ins during theater performances in Berlin, Munich, Bremen, Bonn, and Stuttgart, and the entrances to universities were barricaded in Bochum, Frankfurt, Hamburg, Göttingen, and Aachen. The actors on the stage of the Frankfurt Theater stopped their production and called on the audience to oppose the emergency laws. The Cabaret group *Floh de Cologne* called on all cabaret workers and artists to work against the legislation. Hundreds of steel workers in Bochum went on a wildcat strike, as did 200 chemical workers and hundreds of Ford workers in Cologne. Massive demonstrations continued as the *Bundestag* debated the bill. Finally, on May 20, the date the legislation passed, the APO blocked traffic in downtown Berlin, Cologne, Hamburg, and Hannover. In Munich, the tracks in the central train station were blockaded by thousands of people. In Bonn, 100,000 people marched, while 20,000 trade unionists mobilized in Dortmund.[45]

The conservative political climate in Germany, however, was such that the German *Bundestag* overwhelmingly approved the emergency legislation, thereby enabling the government to curtail individual rights during declared "national emergencies." At the same time, the intensity of the movement and the attacks on it led to the formation of adventurist guerrilla groups and dogmatic Maoist tendencies within SDS, and internal sexism and splits helped destroy the organization. In the late 1960s, the German New Left discovered rock n' roll at the same time as the Kreuzberg Hash Rebels came into existence. As guerrilla groups like the Red Army Faction and the June 2 Movement began their armed attacks and bombings, their marginalization as "terrorists" helped depoliticize the mass movement and signalled the end of the APO. Despite its quick demise, the New Left permanently altered the political landscape of West Germany, setting the stage for the emergence of a new APO and the Green Party ten years later.[46]

Italy

Beginning in the fall of 1967, Italy witnessed the eruption of a protest movement which built up on the campuses until the spring of 1968, when the revolt spilled over to the whole society. In 1968, nearly all Italian universities were taken over by popular movements which governed them by a type of democracy by assembly. Traditional hierarchies within academia were overthrown, as was the segregation of students from society. The protests began over academic issues like inadequate classroom facilities and archaic standards of excellence, but by November of 1967, Turin University was occupied by students opposing the university's authoritarian power. In huge assemblies, students debated the meaning of their revolt, and it was there that the radical demand for self-management was first proposed and massively embraced. As opposed to co-management, which called for professors and administrators to appoint a few students to serve on joint committees, students in Turin demanded nothing less than full control over the curriculum, classrooms, and life of the university.[47] The University of Urbino had established co-management in the Faculty of Economics in 1966, but student protesters soon objected to these joint student-faculty groups on the grounds that they were a form of co-optation. When students occupied the University of Turin on November 27, 1967, they refused to negotiate because they felt they couldn't express their demands until an open general assembly of students could freely discuss their needs. After a month of democratic discussions, the students united around the demand that all university decisions be made at open general assemblies of students. When the administration finally called the police into Turin, the disruption of classes had been the norm for months throughout Italy.

By the spring of 1968, the center of protests had moved to Rome University, where over 400 people were arrested and hundreds injured in February and March. The university was twice ordered closed, and in May, as events in France unfolded, the strikes and sit-ins spread to campuses in Florence, Turin, Pisa, Venice, Milan, Naples, Padua, Palermo, Bologna, and Bari,[48] touching off a political crisis which forced Prime Minister Aldo Moro and his cabinet to resign. In Italy, as around the world in 1968, the sheer *quantity* of protests produced a qualitative break:

> Almost everything that happened in the Spring of 1968 had happened before, but this time it happened all over Italy, involving tens, perhaps hundreds of thousands of students, in the space of less than nine months. It was as if the isolated actions of the preceding five years had been compressed into one year and multiplied by the participation of thousands of new people. In 1968, for the first time, neither the issues nor the actions were isolated.[49]

By the end of 1968, the qualitative break was revealed by the ties to the workers that had been developed, ties indicated by a peaceful twenty-four hour joint strike for educational reform on November 14, 1968.

In the next year, the student movement transformed itself as all the groups of the New Left joined the workers' struggle, hoping to help spark an explosion of the "French May" type and seize the leadership of the workers' movement from the unions.[50] In the fall of 1969, two million workers went on strike and forms of dual power emerged (notably in the Montecatini-Edison factories in Venice and the Fiat plants in Turin), but the established trade unions were able to lead the way out of the "Hot Autumn" by negotiating a settlement which, at least on paper, granted the workers significant wage increases as well as better working conditions.

With the unions firmly in control of the workers' movement, the numerous New Left parties and groups (*Potere Operaio, Lotta Continua*, and the group which published *Il Manifesto*) were increasingly active in the world outside the factories, particularly in working-class communities. "Let us seize the city" was a slogan put forth by *Lotta Continua* in the hope of persuading workers to occupy vacant housing. Despite their failure to capture the leadership of the working class from the trade unions, the new generation of radicals deepened the political crisis of Italy[51] and created the preconditions for a vast cultural revolt. By 1977, a new generation of youth was once again on the offensive on campuses in Italy, and violent attacks against both conservatives and Communists occurred. Off the campuses, the "Metropolitan Indians" shot at police in the midst of mass demonstrations.[52] Under the slogan, "1968 has returned," the movement of the late 1970s in Italy exploded in a merger of culture and politics which the first phase of the New Left there had never attained. By then, however, the worldwide cultural revolt had been depoliticized, and the Italian youth revolt of the late 1970s quietly suffered the same fate.

Spain

In Spain as in Italy, the student movement erupted in 1967 and was able to forge significant links with the working class. Although a general strike of workers and students quickly developed, it was not on the scale of the May events in France. The escalating spiral of confrontation in Spain began on January 27, 1967. After two weeks of student protests and police attacks, over 100,000 workers in Madrid answered the students' call for a national demonstration in support of independent student and worker unions and an end to the Franco dictatorship. It was business-as-usual as that demonstration was viciously attacked and hundreds arrested. The next day, as students attempted to regroup, the cafeteria at the University of Madrid was attacked by police, and throughout the country, hundreds more students were arrested. Rafael Moreno, an activist in Madrid, was murdered by police in his family's home, and when student delegates from all of Spain arrived in Valencia to found the *Sindicato Democrático de Estudiantes* (Democratic Student Union), they were systematically arrested and beaten. In response, 60,000 factory workers and thousands of railroad workers went out on strike on January 30.[53] The next day, the University of Madrid was closed, and a week later, thousands of workers joined a general strike among the students. Over 20,000 students were quickly expelled from Spanish universities, but when the revolt continued to spread and street fighting broke out in all the major cities, the army was called upon to control the country.

Although the movement's activists suffered incredibly, their spirit remained strong, and they did not give in. By October 1967, teach-ins on Vietnam led to refrains of "Ho, Ho, Ho Chi Minh," and at least 20,000 people became members of illegal student groups in Madrid alone. On October 27, a general strike called by students received the support of the Workers Commissions, but it was averted when 400 delegates of the Workers Commissions were arrested. The next week, as a renewed spiral of rebellion and repression occurred, the students of Spain overwhelmingly elected delegates to the illegal student union, the *Sindicato Democrático de Estudiantes*. The delegates were promptly arrested and the students' vote voided, but over 100,000 students (out of a total of 147,000 in all of Spain)[54] went on strike, and some went as far as setting fires in the University of Madrid. This time the police response was even more brutal than it had been in January. Another activist, Enrique Ruano, died while in police custody, and a virtual state of siege was declared to combat the "subversion of the universities."

Although heavily repressed, the Spanish students maintained the integrity of their vision. Their union, which they had fought for since 1956, continued to be organized along absolutely horizontal lines. In January of 1968, the students concluded that the actions of the government precluded reforms, adding that "we know that it will be possible to destroy it only through violence."[55] From March 28 to May 6, 1968, Madrid University remained closed. It was not until the government finally allowed reforms in the university at the end of May that the violence subsided. By November, the University of Madrid was again closed when students refused to submit to new repressive measures.

These two years of intense struggles both on and off the campuses in Spain gave new energy to movements for regional autonomy, particularly in the Basque country. In 1968, *ETA* (acronym for Basque Land and Liberty) began its armed struggle and numerous other guerrilla groups emerged to fight the Franco dictatorship. With the transition to a corporate democracy ten years after the renewed upsurge of 1967, the movements for regional autonomy intensified, as did the impetus toward socialism. In 1982, five decades after their bloody civil war, a Socialist government was democratically elected.

Pakistan

The isolated actions of students led to general strikes by workers in Pakistan as well. In October 1968, a student revolt broke out to protest government restrictions on student political activity. For two months, the students fought for reforms in the universities even though the parties of the Left did not support them. On November 6, riots broke out in all of West Pakistan's major cities. In response, the government ordered all schools closed and arrested (and later executed) its former Foreign Minister, Zulfikar Ali Bhutto, on charges of inciting students. Five days of demonstrations were held to protest government repression, and in December, the students called for a general strike in the major cities. When they received the immediate support of workers in many cities, the upsurge spread throughout the country (including what was then East Pakistan and is now Bangladesh). Workers and students successfully fought the police and army for control of the factories. For a week, civil authority broke down in Dacca, the main city of East Pakistan which by then had become the center of the revolt. Faced with the spontaneously generated unrest, on the one hand, and the offer by the organized opposition parties for negotiation on the other, President Ayub Khan agreed to meet several student demands and was able to remain in power for a few more months.

When the revolt broke out again less than a year later, the Pakistani army took control and invaded Bangladesh. Hundreds of thousands of people were murdered by the invading troops, including at least 500 students at the University of Dacca on the first night of the fighting. After a midnight raid by a tank battalion, the *London Times* reported: "Outside the university buildings, there was a fresh mass grave. Inside blood streamed from every room."[56]

England

In England, university students are particularly elite, and the thrust of the movement at schools like the Royal College of Art and Cambridge, Oxford, and Hull Universities was largely confined to issues of educational reform. In 1968, there were several significant upsurges of political activity: Over 100,000 people marched peacefully against U.S. intervention in Vietnam; 30,000 demonstrators confronted the police at the U.S. embassy in Grosvenor Square; and there was an occupation of the London School of Economics to protest the war. As the movement spread, there were direct actions at one-third of Britain's universities in 1970 following disclosures that secret political files were being assembled on teachers and students who were involved in the movement. At Cambridge University, there was a militant demonstration against supporters of the Greek junta, and in the subsequent trial of fifteen activists, six received prison terms ranging from nine to eighteen months.

The working class in Britain became activated with the world economic downturn beginning in 1968, and between 1968 and 1972, there was a record number of strikes, prompting Tony Benn to remark that "we can speak of Labour's own New Left as a force to be reckoned with." Although the movement in Great Britain never reached the proportions of its counterparts in Germany, France, or the United States, the New Left created the preconditions for the radicalization of the Labour Party, and since 1968, a significant generation of new political activists has emerged.[57]

Japan

The case of Japan is quite significant. A militant but controlled use of violence, a great deal of it appearing as play, was initially coupled with a rejection of ideologies from Europe and Asia. The Japanese student movement was the first massive student movement to reject both capitalism and Communism, and as they denounced both the United States and the Soviet Union, they were in turn vehemently criticized by pro-American, pro-Soviet, and even by pro-Peking observers.

The Japanese movement was partially created by the rapid expansion of higher education. In 1940, there were only 47 universities in Japan, but by 1960, there were 236 four-year universities and an additional 274 colleges. In 1948, representatives of over 300,000 students from 145 universities created the All Japan Federation of Student Self-Government Associations, or *Zengakuren*, as it became widely known. One of the first spokespersons of the *Zengakuren* declared that both capitalist and Communist governments were "enemies of peace, democracy, and student freedom" and asserted that if not for the world superpowers, "the innate good sense of ordinary people would make it possible to have minimum control by the government."[58] Despite their hostility to Moscow, the *Zengakuren* cooperated with the Japanese Communists in 1960, and massive demonstrations forced President Eisenhower to abandon his plans to visit Japan.

As the movement deepened both in the experience of its activists and its impact on Japanese society, the theory and practice of the worldwide movement was embraced. A few months after the Free Speech Movement in Berkeley, 12,000 students at the University of Keio in Tokyo unanimously voted to strike for "the democratization of the campus." The Commune of Keio, as the movement became known, won student power, temporarily quieting the nation's campuses. By the fall of 1966, the Chinese Cultural Revolution had electrified the Japanese Left, and with the escalation of the U.S. war against Vietnam in 1967, students again mobilized. They attacked U.S. bases in Japan and confronted Prime Minister Sato when he attempted to board a plane to Saigon and again when he went to the United States.[59] Trade unions quickly joined the anti-military movement, although workers and students were unable to unite at some critical moments.

By June of 1968, a giant poster of Mao complete with his words, "It is right to rebel," adorned the entrance to Todai University. The medical school there is the most prestigious in Japan, but it was also one of the most authoritarian and feudalistic. At the same time, according to one observer, the writings of Herbert Marcuse were more popular in Japan than in Europe.[60] When a strike at the medical school finally broke out in August, it was to "dislocate the imperialist university of Tokyo," and students called on their peers to become "proletarian intellectuals," not "slaves of the technocratic-industrial complex." The Japanese movement had long been militant and well organized, but the months-long occupation of the medical school proved to be one of its most violent and tenacious struggles. It was only ended seven months later in (January 1969) after a massive and bloody three-day battle involving thousands of police.[61] Although the Japanese movement quickly became depoliticized (either through the withdrawal of some activists or the armed attacks of a few), the struggle for Narita airport which began in 1968 lasted over ten years and remains one of the longest fought single battles of the global movement of 1968.

New Left vs. Old Left

In each of the above cases, a militant student movement developed outside traditional organization of the Left. In Spain, Pakistan, and Italy, students were notably successful in building links with the working class and creating wide circles of activity outside the campuses. Elsewhere—particularly in Sri Lanka and India—New Left movements that were self-consciously autonomous of the traditional Left emerged from a broad base that included students as well as many others.

In Sri Lanka, the New Left exploded in an insurrection in 1971 which left 1,200 persons dead and more than 10,000 (mostly youths) in jail. Rohana Wijeweera, one of the insurrection's arrested leaders, took the opportunity of his trial to explain why a New Left had developed:

> It was because the old Left Movement had no capacity to take the path to socialism, had gone bankrupt and deteriorated to the position of propping up the capitalist class and had no capacity to protect the rights and needs of the proletariat any longer, that we realized the necessity of a New Left movement.[62]

The Naxalite movement in India, the most significant social movement since independence, erupted in 1967, and as its participants assassinated landlords and organized popular power on a local level, vast areas were liberated. By 1968, at least 50,000 peasants had become members of revolutionary organizations which coordinated self-defense committees to defend and manage their newly liberated villages.[63] The tea workers of Darjeeling observed three general strikes in support of the Naxalites, and a student movement in the cities emerged in support as well. Amid brutal repression, the Naxalite movement disintegrated internally, although the popular revolt in Northeast India continued until 1972. Looking back at the movement years later, one observer noted the Naxalites' relation to the global movement of 1968, particularly its rejection of Soviet Marxism:

> The Naxalbari movement was a part of this contemporary, worldwide impulse among radicals to return to the roots of revolutionary idealism...Its stress on the peasants' spontaneous self-assertion, its plan of decentralization through "area-wide seizure of power" and the setting up of village soviets, its rejection of the safe path of parliamentary opposition...posed a challenge to the ideological sclerosis of the parliamentary Left in India.[64]

Similarly, new opposition movements in Latin America developed outside (and in some cases against) the parties of the Soviet Left. In 1968, the Sandino National Liberation Front, an organization which had adopted Che's *foco* theory, was written off as "petit-bourgeois" by the Communist Party of Nicaragua.

The tension between the Soviet Left and newly emergent popular movements has a long and tragic history. In 1935, the Communist International accused Augusto César Sandino of having gone over to the side of the United States and the counterrevolution,[65] and in that same period, a popular movement in Spain was similarly misinterpreted by Marxists faithful to the Soviet Union. After World War II, an insurgent movement in Greece liberated the vast majority of the countryside, but it was tragically betrayed by Greek Soviet Communists.[66] All of these examples help clarify the historical limitations of Soviet Marxism, particularly in its relationship to newly emergent social movements. They also explain why the New Left was autonomous of and relatively unattached to existent Left parties in general. In some cases in 1968, New Left organizations could not begin the process of enunciating their own positions or consolidating their memberships until after they had severed their ties with parties of the traditional Left.

Moreover, New Left social movements also developed in "socialist" societies in 1968, and their practice makes even more apparent the autonomy of the New Left. Whether or not it is appropriate to label the movements in Czechoslovakia, Yugoslavia, and Poland as New Left, it is clear that the *eros* effect of 1968 penetrated Eastern Europe. In Hungary, students of Lukács began to call themselves New Leftists.[67] In the Soviet Union, words coined by the New Left found their way into the Russian language: *kontrkultura, khippi, kampus, marginalnost, kheppening, ekolog, tich-in, stsientism.*[68] In order to make apparent both the political autonomy of the New Left and its world-historical character, I now turn to events in Eastern Europe.

Czechoslovakia

The movement in Czechoslovakia, rooted as it was in the working class, sectors of the Communist Party, and the government, could hardly be classified as a student movement. Students and intellectuals did play a catalyzing role, both in the Kafka revival beginning in 1963[69] and in the agitation for an autonomous student union, an issue first raised in the stormy days of May 1956, after Khruschev had denounced the Stalinist purges, and movements had risen up in Poland and Hungary. For nearly a decade, students in Czechoslovakia continued to demand an autonomous union, and at a national conference in December 1965, students proclaimed their right to criticize the society publicly and even asked to be represented in the Parliament. As the students organized themselves, they "influenced the growing awareness in other parts of the awakening infrastructure that artificial organizational unity was a restrictive factor and a barrier to assertion of group interests."[70] By November 25, 1966, those favoring an autonomous union were in the majority at a national student conference. When one of their key activists was expelled from school and drafted into the army, it was clear that autonomy was not yet in the realm of possibilities. Czechoslovak youth have long been Nature-lovers and spontaneous and have never responded well to governmental attempts to control them. It was no surprise that they had nothing but derision and scorn for the authorities who tried to control the student union, banned rock music, and arrested musicians like the Plastic People.

The opposition movement in Czechoslovakia has long defined itself within larger domains than that of politics alone. Beginning in 1956, a number of non-conformist cultural journals appeared, and although somewhat censored, these journals prepared the groundwork for the more direct political criticisms of the 1960s. Film, mime, theater, variety shows, and music became an increasing source of anti-bureaucratic values. One observer noted:

> A typical line of thought, quite popular in Czechoslovakia after 1956 in connection with the inimitable and by now legendary atmosphere of the Reduta Jazz Club, attributed a symbolic importance precisely to jazz. . . . Take a jazz band, people used to say, with its freedom of improvisation, spontaneity and joy of free expression. Is it not the exact contrary of what the regime wants us to do?[71]

As the agitation continued for an autonomous student union, what had been a cultural gap and political squabble were greatly intensified by the events of Halloween 1967. On that night, the lights went out in the Charles University dormitories in Strahov as they had done many times before, but this time, hundreds of students poured into the streets and began marching into Prague shouting, "We Want Light!" When they arrived at the bottom of the hill entering the city, police greeted them with clubs and were heard to say, "Here's your light!" as they beat the students. Although the students were beaten that night, meetings were quickly organized to protest the "unhealthy situation in the country." Students forged links with dissidents within the Writers' Congress, and even the National Assembly denounced the police and demanded an investigation. It was the first time that a majority of the Assembly had supported any anti-regime activity.[72]

Events moved rapidly in this period. The right-wing of the Party immediately charged the students with trying to "return capitalism, unemployment, hunger and poverty to Czechoslovakia," but with Novotný's resignation as Party Chairman and the ascension of the reformist leadership of Alexander Dubček in January 1968, the political struggle which was opened by students spread to the whole society. On March 12, 1968, when there were significant forces within the government, the Party, and the working class moving to liberalize state control of society, the students went ahead and reconstructed their organization on the basis of "socialist humanism" and "self-management."[73]

A notable influence on this movement was the March student revolt in Poland. Prague press and radio carried detailed coverage of these events and publicized the dismissal of students and faculty there. Two Polish professors, Leszek Kolakowski and Bronislaw Baczko, were later invited to speak at Charles University in Prague, and the Czechoslovak Academy of Sciences sent a letter protesting their firings to the Polish embassy.[74]

Students in Czechoslovakia may have served to catalyze other forces, but the impact of their actions was streamlined by the new Dubček Party leadership which instituted a technocratic reform program. Despite the co-optive thrust of the Dubček leadership, the openings provided by the Party's attempts at reform lent credibility to non-conformist thinkers. In May 1968, one journalist had the boldness to recall that the Party Central Committee had not even discussed foreign policy for over twelve years.[75] Even though fresh thinking had entered Czechoslovak political discourse, the Action Program of the Party (which was adopted on April 10, 1968) was a moderate one, and it continually called for expert management and equated material wealth and science with socialism. It was not a revolutionary program, merely a streamlining (a word the program itself used on many occasions) of the system as it existed. Although it had the distinction of reformulating Rosa Luxemburg's insistence on the need to expand democracy, worker self-management was not a part of the program nor was it culturally subversive of technocratic values. Indeed, technocratic values were precisely the values which the reform program called for, since they were considered necessary to lift the country from the outgrown bureaucratic centralization of the epoch of industrialization into the epoch of the "scientific-technological revolution." Although the slogans of "self-government" and "councils" modeled on Yugoslavia were raised and discussed, these proposals were considered too far-reaching.[76]

Even such a technocratic reform program proved unacceptable to the leadership of the Soviet Union and the Eastern bloc Communist Parties,[77] and on the night of August 20, 1968, over half a million Soviet-bloc troops invaded the country. Popular resistance was massive: At least twenty people died in Prague alone, and the overwhelming majority of the people refused to cooperate with the invaders. In Prague, rebels quickly removed the street signs, and it took over a week for the Soviets to find the post office. In a secret post-invasion meeting, a thousand Czechoslovak Party delegates were smuggled into a Prague steel factory under the noses of Soviet guards, but the Dubček-led Party decided to passively resist in order to avoid precipitating bloodshed on the scale of Hungary in 1956.

The Soviet invasion did bring calls for armed resistance, notably from novelist Ludvík Vaculík, whose "2,000 words" had already gotten him expelled from the Party. In a remarkable change in style, the gentleness of his remarks at the Writers' Congress in June 1967, that "politics are subordinate to ethics," became a confrontational call for defense "with weapons if necessary."[78] Nonetheless, the main form of resistance was passive and spontaneous. As reported in the *Sunday Telegraph* of August 24: "People are using Hippie methods—sticking flowers into the helmets or into the gun barrels. For the Russians it is absolutely weird...It is very peculiar and sometimes even rather gay." Free speech and assembly, first won in the post-January reforms, intensified under the barrels of tanks as people staged sit-ins, organized vigils, and demonstrated against the occupation. Underground radio broadcasts and newspapers abounded, and graffiti was everywhere. A sign in Russian in Prague's Wenceslas Square read: "Moscow—1800 kilometers." Another said: "Lenin wake up—Brezhnev has gone mad." Two days after the invasion, there was a one-hour general strike, and for days, railroad workers stopped trains bringing in equipment from the Soviet Union.

Although the leadership of the Czechoslovak Party did not actively oppose the Soviet invasion, workers, students, and intellectuals continued to intensify their resistance. At the beginning of October, workers threatened to strike if there was any attempt "to return to the pre-January (pre-reform) position."[79] What was described as a "typically Schweikian form of resistance to the Russians," that is, passive non-compliance, occurred throughout the country. Finally on October 16, a joint treaty was signed which permitted the "temporary" stationing of Soviet troops in Czechoslovakia.

A new wave of student demonstrations greeted the announcement, and students renewed attempts to forge an alliance with the working class. There was a total university strike in November, and action committees modeled on those that had been so prominent during the general strike in France in May 1968 were set up. In December, a meeting between the Student Commission for Cooperation with Workers and the Congress of Czechoslovak Metal Workers (representing 90,000 workers) reached a political accord. All industrial unions in Bohemia and Moravia concluded similar agreements with student unions there, and worker-student action committees were established throughout the country. Workers' councils were elected, and people were mobilized to defend civil liberties.

It quickly became clear, however, that the Soviet Union was not about to let Czechoslovakia break free of its sphere of influence. In a desperate act, Jan Palach, a philosophy student, burned himself to death in Wenceslas Square on January 16, 1969, calling for a general strike in support of three demands: abolition of censorship, a ban on *Zprávy* (the publication of Soviet troops in Czechoslovakia), and the resignation of Czechoslovak collaborators. The oppositional movement intensified, and in his inaugural speech in April 1969, new Party Chairman Husák declared:

> Some people go into the factories and stir up anti-Party tendencies, on every occasion there appear slogans such as "Students and Workers Together," or "Students, Intelligentsia, Workers Unite." We all know that this platform is contradictory to the policy of our Party . . . We consider similar concepts and activities as illegal.[80]

He continued: "We received information that a conference of students and workers in Prague is being held without the knowledge of the appropriate organs. What are they up to? Planning strikes perhaps?"[81]

The popular resistance in Czechoslovakia, however, could in no way match the severe repression suffered by dissident elements.[82] As its situation deteriorated year after year, the opposition movement reorganized itself in 1977 as "Charter '77," but activists suffered even worse controls and arrest after joining Charter '77, controls which seemed to mimic the kinds of grotesque bureaucratic domination portrayed in the faction of Kafka.[83]

Whether or not the movement in Czechoslovakia should be labelled "New Left," there certainly was much similarity to other movements of 1968, and the global movement intuitively identified with Czechoslovakia. The week after the invasion of 1968, demonstrators brutalized by police in Chicago at the Democratic National Convention carried placards reading "Welcome to Czechago," and in the battle for People's Park in Berkeley, "Welcome to Prague" was spray-painted on the streets (as portrayed in the photo on page 63). In France and Germany (as throughout Europe), there were massive shows of support. In East Germany, 4,000 people gathered in

Photo 1
Berkeley: People's Park, 1969

Eisenach on August 24, 1968 at a protest rally, and there were smaller rallies and protests by writers in Moscow and Leningrad.[84]

There were also people and groups within Czechoslovakia who deliberately identified with the New Left. According to Vladimir Kusin: "A certain affinity with the 'New Left' was expressed...within the reformist theories of the Party, but was never accepted as a program for action."[85] Karel Bartošek, a historian, although professing adherence to "authentic Marxism," called for the formation of a Czechoslovak "New Left" in June 1969. He summed up the opportunities available to the defeated reformers as follows:

> In the immediate future the following should be the aims of the forces of the New Left:
> a) To work out a coherent programme of a revolutionary transformation of our society, primarily arising from the theoretical analysis of the specific experience of 1968.
> b) To combat defeatism and despondency which are "normal" features of every period of defeat and which are spreading in our country...
> c) To make use of all legal organizations to project a new programme, to unmask the bureaucratic system and to establish the nuclei of new political organizations of the future. If the New Left is to be historically new, it must direct its entire activity at encouraging the formation of several, not just one, political organizations of the working class and the working population, and to pave the way for their public activity...Utopianism has been an impediment only when it has suppressed critical reflection on reality and on itself, and when it has transformed a potential will for a change of reality into an illusion about such will and reality.[86]

Yugoslavia

In Yugoslavia, the student movement first acted in solidarity with the emergent movements in Poland, West Germany, and France. As one observer described the repercussions of the global movement:

> What is completely new and extremely important in the new revolutionary movement of the Paris students—but also of German, Italian, and U.S. students—is that the movement was possible only because it was independent of all existing political organizations. All of these organizations, including the Communist Party, have become part of the system; they have become integrated into the rules of the daily parliamentary game; they have hardly been willing to risk the positions they've already reached to throw themselves into this insanely courageous and at first glance hopeless operation.[87]

While drawing inspiration from the New Left in other countries, the Yugoslav movement self-consciously attempted to create a New Left for themselves. In

May 1968, there was a discussion organized at the Faculty of Law under the title "Students and Politics." The "theme which set up the discussion" was:

> ...the possibility for human engagement in the "New Left" movement which, in the words of Dr. S. Stojanovic, opposes the mythology of the "welfare state" with its classical bourgeois democracy, and also the classical left parties—the social democratic parties which have succeeded by all possible means in blunting revolutionary goals in developed Western societies, as well as the communist parties which often discredited the original ideas for which they fought, frequently losing them altogether in remarkably bureaucratic deformations.[88]

On June 2, the student movement exploded when a controversial theater performance which was to be held outdoors was rescheduled for a room too small to fit everyone. Those who could not get in began to protest, and their ranks spontaneously swelled to several thousand outside the student dorms in New Belgrade. As they marched toward the downtown government buildings, police riot batons and arrests greeted them, setting in motion an earnest political struggle. The next day, general assemblies convened at the Karl Marx Red University (as the University of Belgrade was renamed). In the streets of New Belgrade, students met outside their classrooms, and animated discussions ensued. In the large assemblies, students emphasized the gross social stratification and differentiation within Yugoslav society, the problem of unemployment, the increase of the private wealth of a few, and the impoverished condition of a large section of the working class. The talks were interrupted by loud applause and calls like "Students with Workers," "We're sons of working people," "Down with the Socialist Bourgeoisie," and "Freedom of the Press and Freedom to Demonstrate!"

The next issue of the newspaper, *Student* (on June 4, 1968), was banned by the state, but this ban only served to expose the regime's attempts to isolate and muzzle the student movement. The government attempted to portray the students as only interested in their own material well-being or as under the influence of "foreign elements"—as Tito put it in a speech on June 10. For their part, the week before Tito's speech, the Yugoslav Student Federation proclaimed a "Political Action Program" emphasizing larger social issues, and the Belgrade Youth Federation journal declared:

> The revolutionary role of Yugoslav students, in our opinion, lies in their engagement to deal with general social problems and contradictions... Special student problems, no matter how drastic, cannot be solved in isolation, separate from general social problems: the material situation of the students cannot be separated from the economic situation of the society: student self-government cannot be separated from the social problem of self-government: the situation of the University from the situation of society...[89]

Soon thereafter, Tito had a change of heart and the movement was co-opted by the regime's consideration of its Political Action Program. One commentator, M. Krleža, put it well within the Situationists' domain when he described the events as "not only a conflict between production and creation, but in a larger sense—and here I have in mind the West as well as the East—between routine and adventure."[90]

Poland

The events of the 1980s in Poland far outshadow the student revolt of 1968 which was limited to Warsaw and a few big cities. The Polish working class largely ignored the revolt of 1968 when it occurred, yet that step in the development of the workers' movement was not forgotten. In the midst of the 1970 uprising in Gdańsk, some of the workers marching on the local Party headquarters entered the Polytechnic School chanting, "We apologize for March 1968." A decade later, Solidarność's exhibition of Polish history had displays focused on the workers' revolts of 1956, 1970, and 1976 as well as one on the student movement of 1968 as the background to the crisis which shook Polish society in the early 1980s. Just as the student revolt did not find massive support from the workers in 1968, neither was the 1970 working-class uprising supported by many Polish students. It is not an understatement, however, to say that the embryonic movements of 1968 and 1970 prepared the groundwork for the overwhelming popular support and unity of the movement of the 1980s.

The 1968 demands of the students and intelligentsia for an end to cultural censorship stand in stark contrast to the 1970 worker rebellion for affordable food prices. In both cases, these revolts occurred as *reactions* to unpopular measures by the authorities: the suppression in January 1968 of an Adam Mickiewicz play (written in 1831 after the defeat of the Polish uprising but applauded by audiences for the continuing political relevance of its anti-Russian passages) and the 1970 decision of the regime to raise the price of basic groceries. As much as the movement of the 1980s combined both aspirations (cultural and political autonomy as well as a greater degree of economic equality), it was itself a *subject* of changes in vision and policy as prior movements were *objects* of the excesses of the regime. In order to comprehend this dramatic change in initiative and momentum, it is helpful to review several episodes of political struggle.

As early as 1962, students had organized informal discussion clubs, each with a distinctive name like "Contradiction Seekers."[91] During 1963 and 1964, the Gomulka regime (which came to power as a result of the revolt of 1956) shut down independent literary magazines and dissolved the main discussion club at the University of Warsaw, beginning an escalating spiral of repression and dissent, a spiral in which Kuron and Modzelewski's "Open Letter" and subsequent three-year jail sentences were but one example. The tenth anniversary of the 1956 "Polish October" was ignored by the regime but celebrated by the Socialist Youth Organization at the University of Warsaw, and Kolakowski was the main speaker. The next day he was expelled from the Party, and six of the student organizers were suspended from classes.[92]

The revolt of 1968 was precipitated when the regime banned Mickie-wicz's play and *Dziady*, an independent magazine. The first demonstrations were allowed to transpire, but as the winter relented and public support grew, so did the violence of the specialists in crowd control. On March 2, in its first special meeting, the Warsaw Writers' Union voted to condemn the regime's censorship, and the Actors' Union soon took a similar stand. In defiance of a ban on demonstrations, over 1,500 people assembled at the University of Warsaw on March 8 to protest the arrest of students who had led the fight against the regime's censorship. Shouts of "Long Live the Writers!" and "Long Live Czechoslovakia!" were heard at the same time as workers passing by were pelted with coins and snowballs for siding with authorities. Brutal attacks by groups of club-carrying "Party activists" soon incited the students, bringing tens of thousands of them into the street fighting. On March 11, some workers joined the students, and together they fought the police for eight hours as the protestors tried to reach Party headquarters. The next day, there was renewed fighting at the University of Warsaw, where students held an American-inspired "sit-in"; fighting broke out in Poznań, Kraków, and Katowice; and protest meetings were held in Lublin, Gliwice, Gdańsk, Lodz, Szczecin, and Wroclaw. On March 13, a national call went out from Warsaw for a general strike. Thirteen demands were formulated (including freedom of speech, press, and assembly, as well as against both anti-semitism and Zionism), but even though thousands of students acted, the working class did not. Many working-class women brought bundles of blankets and food to students occupying the universities, but without the massive participation of the workers, the regime was able to arrest thousands of students and dismiss thousands more from the universities, thereby bringing the movement under control by May.

What began in Poland in March of 1968 was a student movement, but the aspirations of the activists pertained to the whole society. In their 1968 "Theses of the Program of the Young Generation," they wrote:

> The principal objective of our action, that which gives meaning and value to our struggle, is the total and real liberation of humans, the abolition of all forms of human slavery (economic, political, cultural, etc.) from all elements of human life that prevent progress and make being pitiful. We struggle for humanism in practice.[93]

Two years later, the working class in Poland initiated the next phase of class struggle, and this time the response of the regime was bloody: Official reports today confirm forty-six deaths in Gdańsk, and it is rumored that as many as 300 people were killed.[94] Beginning in November 1970, workers in and around Gdańsk went on strike to protest the regime's new system of "economic incentives" which caused lower wages, higher prices, and a scarcity of food. When radio and TV announced on December 13 that price adjustments would cause a 30 percent increase in food prices, two sections of the striking Gdańsk shipyard workers immediately elected delegates to go to the Party headquarters for discussions. All of the delegates were promptly arrested.[95]

These arrests marked the beginning of an insurrection, since they transformed a strike for wages into a political confrontation. The next day thousands of workers marched from an assembly at a Gdańsk factory toward the Party's regional headquarters. On the way, the procession more than doubled in size as sailors, workers, women, and youth joined in. They unsuccessfully tried to force their way into the northern shipyards and then changed direction for the Polytechnic (where only a few students joined them despite the crowd's apology for their passivity in 1968). Another column of several thousand workers left the shipyards and headed for the city, but divided one another and frustrated by the lack of support from the students, the workers soon withdrew.

On the afternoon of the next day, however, the fighting began in earnest. In Gdańsk, the Party headquarters was momentarily set on fire as were numerous stores, cars, and even a fire engine. Tear gas and gun shots could not stop the attackers. Demonstrators attacked police cars to obtain arms and loudspeakers. At least thirty-five people were wounded, and hundreds were arrested. The next day, when the prison where the arrested demonstrators were being held was attacked, it was bloodily defended by the army. The local Party headquarters was completely burned, and "shoot on sight" orders were issued from Warsaw. That day alone, local authorities admit that six people died and 300 were wounded.[96] According to even the most conservative figures, the fight for Gdańsk claimed the lives of 45 workers and resulted in 19 buildings and 220 shops being set on fire.[97]

Although the army won control of Gdańsk, the fighting spread to Gdynia, where workers took managers hostage, and crowds attacked the city hall seven times. In Szczecin, workers assembled and drew up a list of demands including independent unions, reduction of food prices, a 30 percent wage increase, release of all those currently arrested, limitation of salaries of Party and state employees, better housing, and a meeting with members of the Parliament. Once again their delegation to the Party was arrested, and renewed fighting broke out. The assembled workers marched to the city singing the *Internationale* and were joined by students, workers, women, and schoolchildren:

> The crowd set fire to the Party building. . . they first brought out, in a remarkably orderly and calm fashion, the furniture, documents and supplies which were in the building. "All the archives were methodically piled in the street along with the luxury provisions (champagne, sausages, caviar) prepared for the Party's New Year's celebration." The villa of Walaszek, local Party secretary, was also burned. On the walls of the city you could see: "We are workers, not hoodlums."[98]

A Central Strike Committee in Szczecin became the epicenter of the whole revolt. Of its thirty-eight members, seven were members of the Party, one was a shipyard director, and the rest were workers, the majority of whom were under twenty-five. They organized production, food subsidies, and communications:

The city was transformed into a veritable workers' republic where all power was held by the strike committee. A strike committee was set up which took over all authority in the city, all activities of the Party organs and the city government. The general strike did not end until the strike committee had been guaranteed complete immunity for everyone.[99]

In the midst of the crisis, on December 20, Edward Gierek replaced Wladyslaw Gomulka as first secretary of the United Polish Workers' Party. Gierek admitted the revolts were not against socialist ideals, and he moved to alleviate the "crisis of confidence." Special concessions of 450 *zloty* were allotted to each of the Szczecin shipyard workers at the same time as activists were fired in Gdańsk and Gdynia.[100] In January, after Gierek refused to meet with workers in Gdańsk and went to Moscow instead, strikes again broke out in Gdańsk (although workers maintained gas, electricity, and water services), and the Central Strike Committee in Szczecin sent messengers to factories throughout the country. Scattered strikes broke out among transport workers, and the official unions came under heavy attack. From this point on, the state changed its approach and began to encourage the idea of workers' councils; Gierek met with delegations from the workers; he announced he was taking legal steps to restore Church property and launched negotiations with the clergy; and numerous high Party and union officials were fired.

Nonetheless, workers in both Gdańsk and Sczecin continued to strike. They demanded an accurate list of those who had died, the release of those jailed, democratization of the unions, better economic conditions, and that Gierek come to the shipyards for discussions. In their meetings, the workers debated such issues as the role of the workers' councils and the choice between investments for production and investments for other human needs. Gierek met with their delegations, and after the newspapers contained long denunciations of the "*enragés*" (the same word used in France to defame militant students) who sought to lead the majority of honest workers astray, Gierek humbled himself in front of television cameras by meeting with assemblies of workers in both Gdańsk and Sczecin. If this, his final effort to placate the workers, had failed, few observers doubt that the bloodshed would have been even greater than in December, since the army was in position to rescue Gierek if he had been detained.

His homage to the power of the workers, however, helped to end the second phase of their struggle: the January phase in the factories which had been created by the December actions in the streets. Although he did not suspend the price increases, he did concede retroactive pay raises for 40 percent of Poland's ten million workers, better retirement and child allowances, discontinuation of the system of economic incentives, free elections of delegates to workers' councils, dismissal of the head of the unions, and reorganization of the Party in Sczcecin. Even when women textile workers in Lodz went on strike in February, the government quickly gave in, cancelling price increases and ignoring the fact that the authorities (including the Prime Minister) who had come to Lodz for discussions had been held hostage by the striking women. At a Lodz meeting of delegates from factories and workers' councils, a union official stressed "the fundamental importance of restoring the authority of trade unions and of gaining the confidence of large numbers of people."[101] Such reforms were considered necessary for the regime to prove capable of harnessing the benefits of the "scientific-technological revolution" and the energy of the workers. In saving the regime from crisis, the stage was then set for the emergence of Solidarity and the next phase of the class struggle.

It may be appropriate to label the movement in Poland as New Left, but, at the same time, it is clear in the language of the rulers—their use of *"enragé"*— that the French May events were a direct historical antecedent to the Polish uprising of 1970-71. As in Paris, the Polish students of 1968 helped to detonate the explosive struggles of the working class, although the fuse took much longer to burn in Poland than the two weeks it had taken in France. Furthermore, the forms of the uprisings closely resembled one another. In both countries, the contests were social, political, and economic in nature— occurring in the streets, Party headquarters, and the factories. In both cases, essential services like gas and electricity continued amid general strikes because of the workers' own initiative and their concern for the vast majority of the citizens. The responsibility of the workers is one of the noteworthy aspects of these movements, although it is a double-edged sword, as evidenced by their return to work and docility in the face of Gierek at the shipyards of Sczcecin.

As the "maturity" of working-class movements in France and Poland functioned in some ways to undermine their effectiveness, so the very youthfulness of the student movements of 1968 prevented them from going beyond the first phase of their struggle (the contestation of power) to the second phase (the reconstruction of life according to more humane values).

China

We can observe this contrast between workers and students most clearly in the case of China, where the unrestrained rebelliousness of the students seriously clashed with the reserve and discipline of the working class. Beginning in 1966, the Cultural Revolution strove to accomplish some of the same goals articulated by the New Left: the abolition of the superiority of mental over manual work, consideration of the political implications of purely "technical" questions; the overthrow of bureaucratic domination; and greater democracy.

The creation of public debate on these political issues in China began innocently enough when students initiated a poster campaign denouncing teachers and the admissions policy which favored the children of the Communist Party and the well-to-do. When Mao called on the students to "turn the fire on headquarters," he signalled the beginning of a series of social convulsions which erupted in violent class struggles. The violence between factions of the Red Guards was halted once by the army in the fall of 1967, but by March of 1968, rival Red Guards fought pitched battles involving thousands of armed students. One faction disrupted the railroad line carrying supplies to Vietnam and armed peasants loyal to it as major battles broke out in Southern China.

Although the student movement had been initially encouraged by Mao, its actions were soon controlled by no one, particularly at the center of the revolt in Tsinghua University. Rival student groups battled for control of that campus using homemade cannons, tanks, hand grenades, spears, and Molotov cocktails. Even when thousands of well organized workers marched from their factories to the campus gates and demanded that all violence cease, the students would not relent. They attacked the disciplined throng of workers with spears, grenades, pistols, and knives, killing 5 of them, wounding 731, and capturing 143.[102] For days, 30,000 workers stood their ground surrounding the campus as they attempted to convince the students to lay down their arms. (Some estimates placed the number of workers who surrounded the campus at over 100,000.) It was only after Mao's personal intervention that the barricaded students finally relented.

For some observers, the Cultural Revolution (particularly the events at Tsinghua University) defined the essential failure of the New Left by demonstrating its purely nihilistic nature. Of course, in the birth of any world-historical movement, there are many currents, some of which have little to do with the essential character of the movement. The anti-colonial impetus which began with the American revolution of 1776, for example, can scarcely be held accountable for the nationalist dictatorship of Idi Amin—no matter how much he cloaked his rule in the language of national independence. Similarly, the excesses of the Cultural Revolution in China cannot be attributed to an essential part of the New Left's character. Neither can the New Left be held accountable for any similarity to groups whose symbols and language may be borrowed from the movements of 1968 but whose fundamental nature is radically different. The Jewish Defense League, for example, uses the clenched fist for its banner, but it is a neo-fascist organization whose hatred of Semites has resulted in violence on several continents.

If there was a shortcoming of the New Left, it was its global inability to move from the contestation of power to the reconstruction of a better society, an inability which helps account for the rapid rise and decline of the movement. Nonetheless, the New Left was able to ignite sources of energy which were able to continue to impact the social consciousness of an emergent world society long after the *eros* effect of 1968 had ceased to function. As its world-historical energy included China and Eastern Europe, it also found its way into the Catholic Church.

The Theology of Liberation

Coinciding with the Tet offensive of February 1968 was the first Latin American meeting of Christian revolutionaries in Montevideo, Uruguay. A certain number of priests, the best known being Camilo Torres, had already joined guerrilla movements in Peru, Venezuela, Colombia, and Guatemala, but 1968 marked a massive shift in the ranks of the church. On March 9, a group of priests in Peru publicly denounced the "economic exploitation of the country's resources" and called on priests and laymen to fulfill their mission as prophets of justice.[103] Another letter, this one signed by the Latin American provincial superiors of the Jesuits at their meeting in Rio de Janeiro in 1968, opened with the acknowledgement that the majority of Latin Americans live in destitute conditions "which cry to heaven for vengeance."[104] There were many similar religious appeals in this period, including those of Pope Paul VI during his visit to Bogota in 1968, when he said, "In the vast continent of Latin America, development has been unequal...while it has favored those who originally began the process, it has neglected the great masses of the native population."[105] There was the letter signed by 900 Latin American priests, addressed to the Medellin Conference of 1968, an international meeting of the Catholic hierarchy which embraced the theology of liberation.

> Because the privileged few use their power of repression to block this process of liberation, many see the use of force as the only solution open to the people...one cannot condemn oppressed people when they feel obliged to use force for their own liberation; to do so would be to commit a new injustice.[106]

The concluding statement of the Medellin conference condemned "the tremendous social injustices that exist in Latin America. These injustices keep the majority of our peoples in woeful poverty, which in most cases goes so far as to be inhuman misery."[107] The Medellin conference's strong denunciation of injustice motivated priests and bishops in many countries to gather and discuss social problems. In Peru, for example, the 36th Assembly of Bishops took an even stronger stand than that of Medellin:

> This situation of injustice...is the result of a process that has worldwide dimensions. It is characterized by the concentration and economic power of a few and by the international imperialism of money, which operates in league with the Peruvian oligarchy.[108]

As the injustices of poverty were obvious throughout the third world, so the radicalization of the Church was not confined to Latin America. In 1968, a group of Christians in South Africa publicly accused Prime Minister Vorster of an "attitude analogous to that of Hitler toward German Christians."[109] Years earlier in Rhodesia (now Zimbabwe), the Catholic Church had integrated its colleges in Salisbury, a move which brought the settler-state to cut off these colleges from all government subsidies for education.[110] Priests who sided with the liberation movements in the Portuguese colonies of Angola and Mozambique (or those who refused to explicitly support the regimes there) suffered long imprisonments and exile. As the brutality of repression mounted, the expulsion of missionaries and state intervention in the Church became more frequent. In 1968, the major seminary in Mozambique was taken out of the hands of its staff and entrusted to the conservative Portuguese Jesuits. Two-thirds of the seminarians refused to continue teaching, and a number of them joined revolutionary groups.[111] Pressure on the Pope was brought to bear by the priests, and on July 1, 1970, Pope Paul granted a Vatican audience to leaders of the national liberation movements in the Portuguese colonies of Angola, Mozambique, and Guinea.

To be sure, the Vatican was not the center of a New Left organization. It contains within it *Opus Dei* and some of the most conservative members of the modern world, but nonetheless, the global insurgency of 1968 swept into the Church, fracturing traditional clerical support for the forces of order. In 1968, the Vatican momentarily came to recognize the needs of the impoverished millions in the third world, but it also maintained its opposition to feminism, cracking down on the more than 100 U.S. theologians who publicly voiced their disapproval of the Pope's ban on birth control.

On the whole, however, there was more than a superficial affinity between the new radicalism within the church and New Left ideas,[112] and the gradual elaboration of this new symbolism within Christianity was part of the worldwide eruption of 1968. Like the movements of 1968 as a whole, the clerical liberation movement drew inspiration from a global membership. Beginning in 1968, Dom Helder Camera modeled his movement for peace and justice in Latin America on Martin Luther King and the activism of black theologists in the United States.[113] On Easter Sunday 1970, he published a joint appeal with the Reverend Ralph Abernathy, Martin Luther King's successor as head of the Southern Christian Leadership Conference, for a "non-violent protest against the political, economic, and social structures of the world which subject so many to destitution or the constant threat of war."

Revolt and Counterrevolution in the United States

With the global awakening of 1968, no country or institution could defend its borders from the infiltration of the *eros* effect. Even the center of the modern world system, the United States, soon found itself embroiled in bitter domestic conflict. At first, the highest circles of power could do little but watch with horror as the war against Vietnam came home. As subsequent events made clear, however, the enemies of the New Left were far from defeated. Whether it was the "preventive" measures employed in industrialized countries or the brutal repression typical in the third world counterrevolutionary violence became prevalent in 1968. In short, that year marked both the end of U.S. world hegemony and the reorganization of *pax Americana*; formal political independence would be tolerated in the third world so that economic penetration could continue. The year in which the United States experienced its first major military defeat in 200 years, the Tet offensive, was also the year in which Richard Nixon and Henry Kissinger, arrogant power-brokers schooled in the cheap tricks of anti-communism and the "elegance" of order, ascended to the highest positions of world power.

The integrity of the New Left's vision and the high hopes of movement participants were some of its chief strengths, but with the assassination of Martin Luther King, the failure of the near-revolution in France, the Soviet invasion of Czechoslovakia, the pre-Olympic massacre of hundreds of students in Mexico City, and the election of Richard Nixon, the hopes of the New Left were dashed against the hard rocks of reality. Although these events marked a clear turning point, there were earlier signals of the coming counterrevolution. On April 27, 1967, a fascist clique of Israeli-trained and U.S.-armed colonels activated a NATO plan and seized power in Greece.[114] Che Guevara was captured and murdered in Bolivia. In the United States, the 1967 uprisings in Detroit, Newark, Atlanta, and Cincinnati were brutally suppressed by the National Guard, and hundreds of people were killed. In Detroit alone, forty-five people were dead and over 2,000 wounded before order was restored; the Newark riots lasted six days, and twenty-three people were killed there.[115]

However bloody they were, the murders in Detroit and Newark were but appetizers for the colossal apparatus of repression which became unleashed on the American people, a counter-offensive which ultimately was only stopped by the Watergate affair. Detroit and Newark were symbols of government violence, but they also marked a new phase in the development of the movement in the United States, one which went beyond Black Power but fell short of its stated aim: revolution.

In 1965, the Student Non-Violent Coordinating Committee (SNCC) abandoned the pacifist teachings of Martin Luther King and embraced the ideas of Frantz Fanon and Malcolm X. The next year, they expelled all their white members, arguing that whites should organize among themselves and try to break down the racism of white communities. Around the same time, SNCC took a strong anti-draft and anti-war position, a stance which drew wide criticism from its liberal supporters and brought increasing attacks from conservatives. An integral part of SNCC's new Black Power consciousness were its programs for black autonomy through the formation of institutions like co-ops, credit unions, and independent political parties.

The radicalization of SNCC coincided with the rise of the Black Panther Party ("the heirs of Malcolm X"). Founded in Oakland, California in 1966, the Panthers quickly developed a nationwide membership and program. In the month of June 1968 alone, the Panthers recruited nearly 800 members in New York City, and by 1969, they had chapters in forty-five cities. Although they did not allow white members, the Panthers worked closely with white activists, particularly in forming defense committees for their leadership, nearly all of whom were assassinated, arrested, or forced into exile. The Black Panther Party supported black self-determination and called for the United Nations to sponsor a plebiscite of blacks to decide whether or not a separate black nation should be formed in the United States. On February 18, 1968, SNCC formally merged with the Black Panther Party, a merger which quickly fell apart, but one which indicated the growing shift to a new radicalism within the black movement.

In March 1968, the Republic of New Africa held its founding convention at the Shrine of the Black Madonna in Detroit. Nearly 200 delegates signed a declaration of independence making all blacks "forever free and independent of the jurisdiction of the United States," and they initiated an organization advocating the establishment of a black nation in what consists today of the states of South Carolina, Georgia, Alabama, Mississippi, and Louisiana. Followers of Malcolm X, this group—like many others—staunchly rejected the reformist goals of Martin Luther King and the civil rights movement. In the major industrial cities, particularly in Detroit, militant black unions emerged, and in Philadelphia, Boston, Denver, Los Angeles, and Washington D.C., Black United Fronts emerged in the struggle for community control of business and police.

There was a material basis for the rise of Black Power and the rejection of the goal of integration by the black liberation movement. The urbanization of blacks following World War II, their integration into the armed forces and the bottom of the labor market, and the continuing segregation and discrimination they suffered within these arenas outlined a powerful contradiction. For those who were unaware of it, the blue-ribbon Kerner Commission—the National Advisory Commission on Civil Disorders formed to study the rebellions of 1967—made the society's racism all too apparent when it released its report to President Johnson on February 29, 1968: "Our Nation is moving toward two societies—one black and one white—separate and unequal."[116] These words shocked the American public, not because many had not suspected as much, but because it set the official tone for determining "the causes and prevention" of the violence of 1967. In order to avert what the Commission considered likely—future racial violence—their report listed several necessary federal reforms: the creation of two million jobs in three years; the elimination of *de facto* segregation in both the North and the South—a call which brought forth the busing of the 1970s; federal funding for on-the-job training, later concretized in the Comprehensive Employment and Training Act (CETA); a federal open housing law; and the building of six million units of low income housing in five years.

The Commission's report consistently treated the various Black Power groups as having been marginalized from the hundreds of thousands of riot participants. Similarly, they regarded the growing radicalism among blacks as unique.[117] If they had taken the time to conduct their polls among a broader cross-section of Americans, however, they would have found that the appearance of Black Power was no isolated occurrence. Mexican-Americans formed the Brown Berets (a group similar to the Black Panther Party), and Puerto Ricans, Asian-Americans, Filipinos, and other minorities whose cultural roots are in the third world also became radicalized and mobilized in this period.[118]

One of the most spectacular indications of the awakening of Mexican-Americans came on June 5, 1967, when Reies Tijerina and the *Alianza Federal de Pueblos Libres* seized the county courthouse in Tierra Amarilla, New Mexico. They freed eleven prisoners who were being held because they were part of a movement aimed at using the treaty of Guadalupe Hidalgo to legally reclaim the Southwest United States. Although Tijerina was acquitted of all charges stemming from this incident, he was later sentenced to two years imprisonment for burning a U.S. National Forest sign, and the movement he is part of has come to exert a significant cultural hegemony among the native peoples of the Southwest.[119] As the *eros* effect activated Chicanos, a militant student movement emerged in high schools and colleges, and a self-conscious Chicano culture was born, transforming the identities and aspirations of Mexican-Americans.[120]

There was a rebirth of resistance among Native Americans as well, an opposition which has been continuous for hundreds of years, but one which was intensified by the global upheavals of 1968. The American Indian Movement (AIM) was founded in 1968, as was a national newspaper, *Akwesasne Notes*, and in 1969 the occupation of Alcatraz symbolized the intensification of revolutionary consciousness among Native Americans in the aftermath of 1968.

Among Puerto Ricans, their independence movement, which has maintained a following since before the beginning of this century, was joined by a new generation of activists. Puerto Rican street gangs organized the Young Lords, developed ties with the Black Panther Party, and played an important role in the Rainbow Coalition brought together by Panther leader Fred Hampton in Chicago. The Puerto Rican Socialist Party was revitalized and took an active role in demonstrations against the war in Vietnam.

The radicalization of the civil rights movement and its transformation into the Black Power movement not only led to the galvanization of other minorities, but the new militancy affected the nation's campuses as well. By 1968, student protests became the rule, rather than the exception. Black students at Howard University were the first to raise the issue of self-management when they staged a four day sit-in on March 19. By June, the newly elected leaders of Students for a Democratic Society (SDS) were "revolutionary communists" committed to violent confrontation, and as the radical mood spread among white students, the number of campus confrontations continued to escalate. By conservative estimates there were 136 in the academic year 1967-68; 272 in 1968-69; 388 from September 1969 to April 1970; and finally the student movement reached its peak during the nationwide strike of May 1970 (see Chapter 4), when there were at least 508 violent confrontations in a one-month period on the campuses.[121] During the entire school year of 1969-70, the FBI listed 1,785 student demonstrations, including the occupation of 313 buildings.

Nineteen sixty-eight was also a year in which the women's liberation movement re-emerged. Although the media made events like the anti-Miss America demonstrations in Atlantic City and the wounding of Andy Warhol seem all important to the women's movement, there was an unreported grassroots emergence of women's consciousness-raising and action groups in every major city in the United States as well as in many smaller cities and towns. By 1970, New York City alone had over 200 such groups.[122] Autonomous women's groups had been formed as early as 1967, and by 1968 there were numerous feminist journals being published.

The women's movement developed from many sources: The decline of the nuclear family after World War II was such that less than 20 percent of all American households in 1968 contained a father, mother, and children. The new independence of women was reflected in the fact that nearly one out of four women chose not to marry, a possibility premised on women's increasing participation in the labor force. Modern feminism was crystallized as the silently endured personal pain of women became a public topic in consciousness-raising groups. As the feminist group Redstockings explained: "If all women share the same problem, how can it be personal? Women's pain is not personal, it's political."[123] Although women strongly articulated the need for the integration of feminism within SDS and SNCC, their efforts were initially greeted with silence or heckling at these groups' conventions.

By 1968, the autonomous women's groups which had formed began to develop a national focus. Hundreds of women invaded Atlantic City on September 7 to protest the Miss America pageant's commercial exploitation of the female body, and two months later, the first national women's liberation convention was held in Chicago. Although formed in October 1966, the National Organization for Women (NOW) had little to do with the cultural-political universe of The Feminists, SCUM (Society for Cutting up Men, whose founder, Valerie Solanas, shot Andy Warhol), and the New York Radical Feminists. The reformist program of NOW (its focus on birth control and equal rights) represented the needs of women who had moved from being housewives and entered the labor force, where they had to fight for legislative changes and constitutionally guaranteed rights. Radical feminism, on the other hand, developed more from women's collision with sexism in the movement, and this younger generation of women developed a program directed at building women's culture and alternative institutions (like women's health clinics and rape crisis centers) as part of a militant and confrontational movement aimed at the revolutionary transformation of society.

Women's liberation became central to the idea of a qualitatively new social order as the feminist movement grew, and New Left organizations like the Black Panther Party were ultimately changed from within, widening their base and enlarging their goals. At the same time as thousands of autonomous women's groups formed in the United States, the women's movement rapidly became an international phenomenon.

By 1968, it was evident that there was such a global awakening of radical social movements that only a global counterrevolution could manage the crisis, and this counterrevolution soon emerged with a vengeance. Domestically, the "generation gap" in the United States had been widely discussed before the Tet offensive in Vietnam, but after Tet, the U.S. government abandoned policies of discussion and appeasement at home and embarked on a program of systematic domestic repression. A week after Tet began, on February 8, 1968, three black students were shot dead and thirty-four wounded at a peaceful demonstration in Orangeburg, South Carolina. The Orangeburg murders led to renewed questioning of the legitimacy of non-violence and integration as the means and ends of the civil rights movement—means and ends which already had been heavily eroded by the riots of 1967 and the emergence of Black Power. In late March 1968, advocates of Black Power in Memphis, taking their cue from Adam Clayton Powell's words that "the day of Martin Luther King has come to an end," broke away from a march led by "de lawd" (as they called King) and began breaking windows. The rioting spread, and when the police response was over, one demonstrator had been killed and sixty wounded, and the National Guard patrolled the city. Tensions continued to mount between King and more militant blacks right up to April 4, when Martin Luther King was assassinated in Memphis.

The public outrage at the assassination of this man of peace has few precedents in the history of the United States. In over 168 cities, the ghettos rioted, and flames reached to within six blocks of the White House. For the first time since the Civil War, federal troops were called in to protect federal buildings, and machine guns were mounted on the Capitol balcony and the White House lawn. The combined forces of the police, army, and National Guard occupied the ghettos, and, as had happened a year before, the forces of law and order ruthlessly suppressed the uprisings. By the time a cease-fire was established, at least forty-six people lay dead, over 21,000 had been injured, and another 20,000 were in jail. In Washington, D.C. alone, more than 7,600 people were arrested, over 13,500 federal troops were needed to restore order, and more damage was done to the city than had been inflicted by the British during the War of 1812. All told, over 50,000 federal troops (more than were used in any single battle in Vietnam) had been necessary to restore order, and property damage was estimated at over $130 million.[124]

White backlash quickly set in. In one day, President Johnson established a riot control center in the Pentagon and an Urban Institute to monitor the inner-cities. On the same day that 150,000 people attended King's funeral in Atlanta, Congress was busy cutting anti-poverty funds, and the *New York Times* editorialized against "black criminals." A little over a week later, the FBI publicly claimed that King "was closely associated with Communists and sex deviates. His program for America was an unadulterated Communist program."

The national and international repercussions of events in this period are easy to underestimate. The day that King was assassinated, black students at Cornell University held the chairperson of the Economics Department hostage for six hours to struggle with his racism.[125] At Tuskegee, 250 students held twelve trustees captive for twelve hours on April 7 to demand an end to ROTC and changes in campus curfews.[126]

Seven days after the assassination of Martin Luther King, as mentioned earlier, there was an attempt to kill Rudi Dutschke, one of the key figures in German SDS, and movements throughout Europe renewed their actions. Nineteen days after King's murder, students at Columbia University began their now famous occupation of five university buildings. They temporarily took a dean prisoner and lived in the offices of Grayson Kirk, president of Columbia. Their reasons included opposition to the war against Vietnam and racism, the latter symbolized by plans for a new gymnasium for Columbia students but not for the residents of the neighboring ghetto, many of whose houses would be demolished to make room for the gym. The police waited a week, and then they:

> . . . simply ran wild. Those who tried to say they were innocent bystanders or faculty were given the same flailing treatment as the students. For most of the students it was their first encounter with brutality and blood, and they responded in fear and anger. The next day almost the entire campus responded to a call for a student strike. In a few hours, thanks to the New York City Police Department, a large part of the Columbia campus had become radicalized.[127]

The police rampage lasted only a few hours, but over 150 people were seriously injured and 700 arrested before it ended.

The occupation at Columbia was one of the most famous spectacles of the student movement, and it was afforded wide coverage by the mass media as the subject of numerous retrospective books, television shows, and even a full-length Hollywood production, "The Strawberry Statement." Columbia quickly became a model for similar university takeovers in the months after it, not only in the United States (as at Ohio State University were students held two vice-presidents and four staff members hostage), but throughout the world.[128] Tom Hayden, himself one of the participants at Columbia, borrowed a slogan from the walls of Columbia to find a title for his article: "Two, Three, Many Columbias." Writing in *Ramparts* on June 15, 1968, Hayden called for "raids on the offices of professors during weapons research," noting that:

> Columbia opened a new tactical stage in the resistance movement which began last fall; from the overnight occupation of buildings to permanent occupation; from mill-ins to the creation of revolutionary committees; from symbolic civil disobedience to barricaded resistance. Not only are these tactics already being duplicated on other campuses, but they are sure to be surpassed by even more militant tactics.[129]

The violence and male aggressiveness of the leaders at Columbia, however, made it all too clear to feminists that the old values of the movement were also under attack. As Sara Evans noted twelve years later:

> The New Left had begun by raising the "feminine" values of cooperation, equality, community and love, but as the war escalated, FBI harassment increased, and ghettos exploded, the New Left turned more and more to a kind of macho stridency and militarist fantasy.[130]

In 1968, the escalating spiral of violent confrontations drew millions of people into it, and as the base of the movement broadened, internal divisions mounted between blacks and whites and men and women. There were no individual leaders capable of giving the movement a coherent direction or providing unity for its massive base. The assassination of Malcolm X had already deprived the movement of a visionary and charismatic leader, and the assassination of Martin Luther King again deprived the bourgeoning movement of an articulate (although more moderate) leader, further escalating the intensity of confrontation at a time when the internal fragmentation of the New Left was beginning. The increasing attacks on the movement served to heighten these tensions as disagreements mounted over what direction the movement should take. The arguments became polarized into what might have been two illogical extremes: the complete rejection of confrontation, on the one hand, and the glorification of it, on the other.

For the student radicals, the question of violence may have been the focus of intense debate, but off the campuses, whether in the ghettos or in Indochina, the level of political violence was such that, of necessity, the student movement was drawn into its ever widening circle. Even Resurrection City II, a peaceful encampment near the White House of 3,000 followers of Martin Luther King's Poor People's Campaign, was cleared out by the government, further intensifying the atmosphere of confrontation. When Robert Kennedy was killed because of his support of Israel, it seemed that Malcolm X had correctly predicted that "the chickens would come home to roost" (that the violence exported by the United States would come home to haunt it).

Whether or not the student New Left in the United States unanimously approved the new militancy, there were forces at other wavelengths on the political spectrum which were on a collision course with the movement. On August 8, six blacks were killed during riots which coincided with the Republican National Convention in Miami. The two-day battle for Liberty City left over 100 people wounded and hundreds more arrested, and it was finally over only when thousands of National Guard patrolled the streets. At that time, however, the media granted the Liberty City insurrection only scant coverage. Censorship across the nation became more overt, even beeping out a line in the 1968 Smothers Brothers show: "Ronald Reagan is a known heterosexual." There was a "silent majority" which was said to have nodded their heads in agreement.

On August 28 came the spectacle of the Democratic National Convention and a nationally televised police riot. The events of Chicago revealed how far the new hard-line within the Establishment had reached. Non-violent sitting protesters were mercilessly and bloodily clubbed in front of television cameras, and even network anchorpeople were not immune from what was later characterized as a "police riot" by the official Walker Commission report.[131] At least sixty-five newspeople were arrested, maced, or beaten, and one was attacked and carried out of the convention while broadcasting. Chicago's Mayor Richard Daley had carefully waited for the demonstrators, assembling more than 20,000 law enforcement officials (12,000 police, 5,000-6,000 National Guard, and 6,000-7,000 Army troops complete with rifles, bazookas, and flame throwers).[132]

The events in Chicago had an immense impact both on the New Left and on the Establishment, particularly since the police violence was carried *inside* the Convention. Eugene McCarthy's bid for the Presidential nomination may have been doomed to fail, but when his supporters were mercilessly attacked by the Chicago police, it appeared as an assault on the "democratic" process and the "free" press. Even before the Convention, there were signals that all was not going smoothly, as, for example, when forty-three black G.I.'s of the First Armored Division, all decorated Vietnam veterans, refused to leave Fort Hood, Texas for riot duty in Chicago.

The spectacle in Chicago was orchestrated in full view of the public, but there were even more sinister forms of repression being organized and implemented. The FBI's COINTELPRO operation (directed against the New Left in the United States) went into full operation on a national basis on May 10, 1968, and in the same period, the CIA's Operation CHAOS began its illegal activities inside the United States. The offices of the Black Panther

Party, the organization which was thrust into the leadership of the burgeoning movement, were attacked across the country, and in these shootouts, as many as twenty-eight Panthers were killed. The Omnibus Crime Bill passed both houses of Congress, a measure deemed necessary by the "rising crime rates," but clearly a measure aimed at the New Left. In the first applications of this new law, the Chicago 8 (including Bobby Seale, chair of the Black Panther Party) were indicted for conspiring to cause the riots in Chicago; H. Rap Brown, another leader of the black liberation movement, was arrested for violating provisions of the new law and received a sentence of five years in prison; and thirteen Chicano activists in Los Angeles were indicted and jailed. The Federal Law Enforcement Assistance Administration was started up to better arm and organize local police departments.

At the same time as the forces of order resorted to violent repression, the movement was made into a television spectacle by the mass media. The coverage of the demonstrations at the Miss America pageant gave wide circulation to the notion that the women's liberation movement burned bras. In fact, no bras were burned there.[133] For its part, the media greeted the movement's shocking displays of nudity, the love-ins, be-ins, and rock n' roll by turning them into profitable commodities. In 1968, *Hair* opened on Broadway, and Yves St. Laurent quickly produced an evening see-through blouse and a similarly styled full-length dress, great sellers in the fashion world. That the emergent counterculture proved both pleasing and useful to high society was evident by the Chicago Convention: *Esquire* sent both Jean Genet and William Borroughs to report on it. The Doors were offered five million dollars by Universal Studios to appear in a motion picture, and groups like the Jefferson Airplane and the Grateful Dead became millionaires. In the face of their new celebrity status, is it any wonder that Jim Morrison, Janis Joplin, and Jimi Hendrix chose to exit from rather than sing for the society which raised *The Money Game* to number one on the 1968 Best Seller List; or any wonder that in 1968, LSD gave way to heroin in Haight-Ashbury and to speed in the East Village?

A whole epoch ended in 1968. One observes it in the effects of the violent restoration of order on the national cultures of affected countries. In France, it appears that the epoch of their great novelists has ended.[134] In Germany, the post-war "economic miracle" and new democracy have turned into crisis. In the United States, as John Hersey pointed out, we appear to have lost our last heroes:

> One of the lessons of 1968 surely should have been that America cannot do without heroes, that the old human need for larger-than-life models, for striking examples of courage and compassion and admiration still persists in our country, fashionable though it may have become for neo-Freudians, revisionist historians, and investigative journalists to remind us that heroism often has a dark and shabby side. We lost our last heroes in '68—either through glimpses of failure of nerve such as those given us, in very different ways, by Lloyd Bucher of the Pueblo, Grayson Kirk of Columbia, by Lyndon Johnson, by Hubert Humphrey, by the plastic-masked

policemen of Chicago, or through a refrain of violent removal
which led us to feel that all our paragons must die by the gun, as
Martin Luther King and Bobby Kennedy did.[135]

Even the most advanced technological achievements of industrial society
were marred by their political and human inadequacy. When Apollo 8
rounded the moon in December 1968 (the first time human eyes focused on
the dark side), the message beamed to the astronauts from the earth was that
the U.S. spy-ship Pueblo had finally been released by North Korea. The
patriotic spirit had already been dampened when American athletes at the
1968 Olympics in Mexico City raised their fists in a Black Power salute before
they received their medals.

Hersey may be right that the culture of the West has lost its last heroes,
but he failed to comprehend how many people adopted the heroes of the third
world like Ho Chi Minh and Che Guevara. It may be true that 1968 marked
the end of an epoch, but at the same time, it may be possible that it marked the
first act of an unfolding *species-consciousness*—the initial emergence of a new
global culture—a global "we" which both negates Western individualism and
preserves it at a higher level. In 1968, *national* heroes and culture may have
been transcended, but *global* ones were created.

The New Left may have been labelled a movement of pure negativity,
but in its practice, it contained the rebirth of new forms like self-management
and internationalism, and the New Left helped create a global culture which
was born as an international political culture.[136] Centuries of the centralization
of the world system and unending technological breakthroughs set the stage
for this world culture. To focus on the emergence of this political culture, I
turn to the strikes of May 1968 in France and May 1970 in the United States.

Part II

NEW LEFT
GENERAL STRIKES

Chapter 3

THE
NEW LEFT
IN FRANCE:
MAY 1968

It is truly with confidence that I envisage, for the next twelve months, the existence of our country. . .in the midst of so many lands shaken by so many jolts, ours will continue to give the example of efficiency in the conduct of its affairs.

—Charles de Gaulle,
New Year's Broadcast, January 1, 1968

The May explosion came as a surprise not just to de Gaulle. No one planned it. Few expected it. In the apparent tranquility of a modern industrialized society, a student revolt precipitated a general strike in France. Although the May events were but one of the many uprisings which shook the world in 1968, they were a significant one, shattering the myth of "the end of ideology" and raising anew the spectre of socialist revolution for the "post-capitalist" countries.

The events of May demonstrated a unity between generations of people who came to consciousness along different roads. There were the main forces of the explosion: workers and students who had not known material scarcity at any time in their lives. There were also those who had lived through the Great Depression and the Nazi occupation, and despite the appearance of affluence in post-World War II France, fought for a new type of social order.

Throughout France in May and June of 1968, millions of people refused to continue their normal day-to-day activities. Students closed their universities and high schools, many demanding a new mode of education. Workers occupied their factories and offices, frequently calling for a new mode of production. Some cities established new forms of government, as in Nantes, where a Central Strike Committee representing autonomous unions of workers, peasants, and students took over the town hall for six days and even issued their own currency.[1]

The dimensions of the 1968 explosion are difficult to comprehend. In less than thirty days, business-as-usual in France was brought to a halt. Nearly ten million workers were on strike, and tens of thousands of people were rioting in Paris, battling with the police for control of the city. The uprising threatened to transform not only the previous modes of production, education, and government, but the entire mode of existence in all its social manifestations. What began as springtime student protests against U.S. involvement in Vietnam and sexual segregation in university dormitories was rapidly transformed into a potentially revolutionary situation.

The tactics of the government contributed to the escalation of this conflict. In the first eleven days of May, various ministers closed the universities and called on the police to suppress the student revolt. When the police entered the campuses, it was for the first time in the twentieth century (with the lone exception of the Nazi occupation) that the autonomy of the university in France had been violated. As hundreds were arrested and many more injured, thousands of people took to the streets, building barricades against the police onslaught and refusing to submit. People all over Paris witnessed the savagery of the police and were sickened by the system's dependence on force to maintain order. On May 8, after nearly a week of riots, the French public opinion poll, IFOP, reported that four-fifths of the people of Paris were sympathetic to the rebellious students.[2]

By Saturday, May 11, the day following the "night of the barricades," the government abandoned its strategy to repress the students and attempted, instead, to defuse their revolt. The police were withdrawn from the universities and the streets of Paris, amnesty was granted to all those who had been arrested, and it was promised that the closed universities would be reopened on Monday. These measures, seen as government capitulation to students' demands, brought legitimacy to those who had fought the police and gave them a renewed feeling of strength. The day after the government declared its new posture, the University of Strasbourg was occupied, declaring it autonomy from the National Ministry of Education, and the Censier annex of the University of Paris Faculty of Letters (Sorbonne) was taken over. These actions catalyzed new motion among workers and students throughout France.[3]

On Monday the 13th, 800,000 workers and students took to the streets of Paris and marched in solidarity with the student revolt.[4] At the end of the march, the Sorbonne was seized and a student soviet declared. Over the next month, the occupied Sorbonne served as a meeting place for students and workers where questions of strategy and tactics were openly discussed and democratically decided. As factory after factory was occupied, the fighting in Paris intensified and spread throughout France.

The massive popularity of the occupations made it impossible for the state to use its army to intervene. Moreover, there were many within the government who feared that the soldiers would fight side-by-side with the workers and students, not against them. Fearing the radicalization of the military, the government called up all reservists and kept military personnel on the bases and out of touch with the outside world, even with state-run radio and television. For a time, the strikers themselves were able to close down the mass media, making it even more difficult for the centers of power to function and precipitating intensified discussions in the streets, cafes, and neighborhoods.

In an attempt to buy off the workers, Prime Minister Pompidou organized a weekend of negotiations with all major trade unions at the Rue de Grenelle in Paris. The agreed upon reforms were modeled after the Matignon agreements of 1936, when the working class was guaranteed a minimum of rights such as collective bargaining, unionization, and election of shop stewards. The 1968 Grenelle settlement was even more stupendous: a 35 percent increase in the minimum wage (agricultural workers received a 56 percent raise, and, in some industries, wages were increased by as much as 72 percent); a shorter work week; a lower retirement age; more family and elderly people's allowances; and more union rights. To top it off, the strikers were to be paid at half their normal rate for the days of the occupations.[5]

Surprisingly, the striking workers rejected the results of the negotiations. When Georges Séguy, secretary-general of the largest trade union in France, the Communist-dominated *Confédération Générale du Travail* (CGT), and Bénoît Frachon, CGT president and a signatory of the Matignon agreement, drove directly from the concluded negotiations to the huge Renault plant at Boulogne-Billancourt to address 25,000 workers assembled there, their speeches were met with boos and catcalls. Shop stewards from around the country telephoned and telegraphed CGT headquarters turning down the agreements.

The workers continued to occupy their factories and offices, and at this point, revolution seemed to be the order of the day. De Gaulle left Paris, and according to his own admission, he was tempted to resign. There was a vacuum of power in France on Monday, May 29. For over six hours, no one even knew where to find the President. Later, it became known that he spent these mysterious hours in Baden-Baden, Germany, where, in close collaboration with top French Army generals, he was plotting his comeback. The release a few weeks later of General Raoul Salan, former head of the paramilitary right-wing Secret Army Organization (whose actions included an attempted assassination of de Gaulle in 1961), prompted many to wonder what deals and/or promises had been made to the paramilitary Right.

It is not my intention to offer a detailed chronology of the May explosion and June containment. Having briefly indicated the dimensions of these events, I will analyze their roots, the aspirations of the participants, and their effects on France.

Global Connections

French political life during the 1950s and 1960s was intimately connected with the successful anti-colonial movements in Vietnam and Algeria. It was within the national liberation support movements in France that many activists gained their first experiences in extraparliamentary political praxis.[6] The refusal of the *Parti Communiste Français* (PCF) to support the *Front de la Libération Nationale* (FLN) in the early 1960s caused many people to leave the PCF and its affiliates, leading to the creation of independent *"groupuscules,"* the small, ideological groups generally credited with sparking the May events.

French students have long acted in solidarity with movements in other countries. As discussed in Chapter 2, hundreds of activists from France went to an international conference in Berlin in February 1968 to help organize pan-European actions against U.S. involvement in Vietnam. The next month, the various *"groupuscules"* in Paris united for the first time to demonstrate against the Springer Press's sensationalist attacks on German SDS. And it was the arrest of three students protesting the U.S. war against Vietnam which precipitated the occupation of the administration building at Nanterre University on March 22, bringing into existence the March 22 Movement. Although prior to the May events, the membership in all the New Left groups and organizations in France was miniscule, numbering at most 2,000, these activists comprised a political force of great importance, one which detonated the entire society.[7]

One might ask whether the May explosion could have enjoyed such massive participation before the Comintern's influence over the PCF had waned or before NATO troops had been asked to leave France. While the post-World War II period witnessed an increasing interdependence of European economies, it also saw each Western European nation experience relative military autonomy. In the immediate aftermath of May 1968, André Glucksmann summed up this dimension of the situation:

> At present, everything at stake in France is decided in a neutralized military space; no foreign power can act physically to alter a relation of forces decided within the national frontiers. For the first time for more than a century, Marx's formula is true again for Western Europe, and the revolutionary struggle may be national in form (not nationalist in content): "The proletariat of each country must, of course, first of all settle matters with its own bourgeoisie."[8]

Of course, it is never certain that foreign powers will refrain from intervening during another nation's moments of crisis. There are many methods of intervention in the modern world: covert and overt, economic, political, and military. The power of transnational corporations and their U.S. protectors was demonstrated in 1973 by their subversion of the democratically elected Allende government in Chile. A minimum of outside military strength was necessary to destabilize Allende, and even in the 1980s, the U.S. government has continued to deny its role in the military *coup* there.

At the same time that the French movement was the *product* of global forces, it also acted as a *producer* of the worldwide turmoil of 1968. The May events were internationally significant since the vast majority of the working class in France, unlike their peers in other industrialized countries, joined with the students and nearly made a revolution. As in 1848, the revolutionary movement of 1968 in France revealed a new epoch of class struggles at a more intense and advanced level than in other economically advanced countries. Of course, it is a coincidence that the Paris peace talks between the United States and Vietnam began in the first part of May 1968, but this correspondence in time and space may illustrate some of the social forces of 1968 that affected

France. Is it a mere coincidence that the spectre of socialism reappeared in Europe as the American Empire, the last Western colonial empire, reached its limit in Vietnam?

That the French explosion came exactly in May was as much an accident as it was a product of the specific socio-historical developments inside and outside of France. As mentioned, government mistakes played a role in the rapid escalation of the student revolt. What seems clear after the crisis is that a host of forces converged in 1968, and the totality of French society convulsed in a near revolution.

Roots of the May Events

The industrial revolution originated in Western Europe, but for many reasons, France was not in the center of it. Not until after World War II did French industry develop parity with neighboring Germany or England. Industrial production in France increased by 75 percent from 1948 to 1957. From 1953 to the first quarter of 1958, the increase was 57 percent (compared to 53 percent in West Germany and 33 percent for Western Europe as a whole.)[9]

It was not simply the quantity of industrial production which changed dramatically. There was a vast movement from the countryside to the cities as agriculture was intensely industrialized. From nine million French people working on the land in 1921, to seven and a half million in 1946, there were only three million in 1968.[10] There were a host of business mergers, and the state took on a larger role in the functioning of the economy.

The French state is one of the most centralized and bureaucratic political instruments ever created. A series of popular uprisings and near-revolutions in the nineteenth century, as Marx said, "perfected this machine instead of smashing it." Bonapartism, characterized by strong and unlimited state authority, urbanization, and the preponderance of the army, had already accelerated the centralization of power in Paris. As in all industrialized societies, the modern French state has taken on more power in the national and international coordination of the economy.

The role of college training is increasingly important for the functioning of industrialized societies. Large-scale industry needs more technicians within its offices to coordinate space-age production, more managers to administer it, more psychologists to find ways of keeping employees working, advertising specialists to market the goods of the new consumer society, and sociologists to maintain the system's overall capacity to function.[11] As the bureaucratic organization of industry and politics developed after World War II, the educational sector was expanded in response. In 1946, there were 123,000 college students in France; in 1961, 202,000; and in 1968, 514,000.[12] New universities were hurriedly constructed, including the Nanterre campus—a concrete jungle on the west end of Paris.

French education is almost entirely state-organized and run by the huge Ministry of National Education which employed more than 700,000 persons in 1968, making it the biggest employer in the country.[13] The rigidity of the

French educational system, its ultra-centralization and its adaptation to an earlier society enabled it to resist all attempts at serious reform for over 150 years. Paternalism toward students and neglect of their needs were part of the regular mode of operation, and the rapid expansion of French education exacerbated its nascent contradictions.

That there was a structural and human crisis in higher education was common knowledge long before the explosion of 1968. In November 1963, France's universities had been shut down by a national student strike called to protest their overcrowded conditions and lack of government foresight in accommodating the increased enrollments of the postwar baby boom. During the May events, however, many faculty and students questioned the entire organization of the university system, not just its inadequate management. In an interview during May 1968, Alain Geismar, general secretary of the *Syndicat National de l'Enseignement Supérieur* (National Union of Higher Education) said:

> We have been saying that there is a profound crisis in the universities for several years. It has various kinds of underlying causes, in particular the maladaptation of the university structure to its economic and social functions, in research as well as in education and hence in the training of the cadres . . . Our proof? Seventy percent of those who attend the French university fail to complete their courses, and even among those that do graduate, there is an absolutely astonishing number of unemployed. As for the internal organization of the university, it is completely inadequate in an advanced country, with its compartmentalization of the various disciplines, a hierarchy of disciplines dating from Auguste Comte and of faculty structures inherited from the Empire.[14]

In another May interview, Jacques Sauvageot, vice-president of the *Union Nationale des Étudiants de France,* reiterated some of the same thoughts.

> Students are expected to have a certain critical intelligence, while their studies are such that they are not allowed to exercise it. On the other hand, they realize that in a few years' time they will not be able to find a part to play in society that corresponds to their training. This dual phenomenon is, I believe, the basic cause of their revolution.[15]

Even those who managed French education recognized some of its shortcomings before May. The Fouchet plan of reforms had already proposed a two-year degree, seeking to modernize education and bring it more in harmony with the needs of industrialized France. Student opposition to this plan was widespread since it seemed designed to decrease the numbers of working-class people who would have access to a university education as well as to fundamentally reduce the traditional humanitarian content of university courses to a technocratic version.[16]

It is possible to define a central contradiction within the French universities: On the one hand, there was an archaic orientation to the training of elites and an authoritarian structure, and on the other hand, an enlarged need for college graduates and an increasing diversity among faculty and students. In an attempt to resolve this contradiction while remaining within the bounds of the existing socio-economic system, several programs were proposed. They included Fouchet's reforms as well as more radical visions of departmental reorganization, student and faculty power, and an end to archaic centralization. Students and faculty flocked to the banner of academic reform during May, and in the aftermath of the explosion, they saw many of these "radical" proposals implemented.

While many faculty and students conceived of the universities' problems as solvable through adjustments in the existing system, others were more skeptical because of the dependency of the universities on the social system as a whole. They raised questions about the nature of the entire society and the universities' role within it. Those involved in the May events who had less at stake in the university, who were less careerist in their life-orientation, or who were simply more visionary than their reformist friends brought the issue of the universities' role within an unfree and unjust society to the forefront of the student revolt. Following the pattern of general strikes of the past, specific grievances were translated into universalized insurgency. Demands and actions were formulated which focused on the whole society and included such issues as the need to abolish the privileged status of students, the nature of jobs which graduates might find, and the mystification of knowledge in the hands of experts.[17] During May, these visionaries opened the universities to all people ("a university without borders") in the hope of using their resources to overthrow the entire system.

Academic freedom, the traditional autonomy of academia from politics, was originally challenged not by these activists but by the development of advanced capitalism. In the modern era, science and technology have become one of the system's main productive forces, capable of drastically altering old methods of production (or warfare) in a short time. As scientific research, one of the essential functions of universities, has come to the center of the system's needs, higher education has increasingly become directed by the economic, political, military, and cultural needs of the entire society.[18] In this sense, the crisis of the French universities was part of the total crisis of that society. The contradiction within the universities simultaneously reflected and embodied a contradiction of the entire society: The incessantly expanding forces of production were contained within ancient social relationships. Productive forces are not simply constituted by dead objects—machines and raw materials—but include living human energy without which production is impossible. For the first time in history, space-age production was capable of providing the vast majority of people in industrialized countries with sufficient food, clothing, and shelter. With their socialization, the modern forces of production could bring such prosperity to the entire world. This global contradiction weighed heavily on the thoughts of activists[19] and helped to detonate an explosion in May 1968 which reaffirmed the possibility of a new world, one freed from the scarcity and exploitation of "pre-history."

The general strike which shut down France for nearly a month would never have occurred without the massive participation of the working class.

By itself, the student revolt would have remained utopian, unable to question in practice the entire society. The workers empathized with the brutality suffered by students at the hands of the police, especially since the most brutal of the police, the *Compagnies Républicaines de Sécurité* (CRS), were first organized after the workers' strikes of 1947. But there were also grievances within the working class which the students' struggle helped to crystallize.

The Workers

The long tradition of working-class militancy in France, often attributed as the primary reason for the unique juncture of worker and student movements in 1968, does not fully account for the workers' actions. Tradition is double-edged, providing a source of revolutionary inspiration in France, but also an inertia to maintain old patterns of social interaction. The PCF's tradition of Marxism within the industrial proletariat helps to explain why French factory workers were not as dominated by the ideology of capitalism as their counterparts in the United States, West Germany, or England *as well as* why the French May uprising gave way so easily to the restoration of order.

Although the French working class in 1968 was one of the lowest paid and had one of the longest work-weeks in Europe, they had seen a dramatic rise in their standard of living since the Nazi occupation. With the postwar economic expansion of 1945-1968 and the rise of a consumer society, French workers saw their standard of living improve, a fact which led many sociologists to believe that class struggle in its traditional forms had come to an end. Of course, theories which posited the impossibility of a qualitatively new social order were temporarily swept aside in May. What radical sociologists had not been able to accomplish in years of painstaking debate in the universities occurred almost overnight in the streets.

The growth of higher education in France and the open admissions policy common to continental systems gave an increasing number of the children of workers the opportunity for individual advancement. As the sons and daughters of the working class were seen to be rubbing elbows with the children of the rich, it was argued that the workers received the same cultural artifacts which are mass produced by consumer society: The same television programs, movies, and, it was argued, even theaters were "democratically" available. Although cars and refrigerators were less common among families of factory workers, "post-industrial" society has brought to many what previously had been the privilege of a few.

Official French estimates at the beginning of 1968 showed that 40 percent of wage and salary earners received less than $1,800 per year. Only one household in four simultaneously owned a refrigerator, washing machine, and television, while only one in five had all these and a car.[20] These figures may indicate poverty to some, but they serve to outline the level of comfort in a society where there is freedom from hunger and disease for the vast majority (in contrast to much of the third world).

Of course, not all economic problems had been solved in 1968. Unemployment hovered around the half-million mark, inflation began to eat away at disposable income, and a world economic crisis was beginning. But it would not be an understatement to say that in the ten years since de Gaulle had seized power on May 13, 1958, the French economy had prospered. The gross national product rose 63 percent, foreign trade tripled despite the shift from colonial to more competitive markets, and the once empty Bank of France was filled with $6 billion worth of gold and foreign currency.[21]

In 1968, workers in France did not go on strike simply for a greater share of the capitalist pie. Their overwhelming rejection of the Grenelle agreements, the many proposals for self-management, the effigies of capitalism found hanging outside many factories during the general strike, and the widespread discussions of expropriation are ample proof that they had a more radical agenda. The break with the usual short-term, goal-oriented activities of the working class can be explained, at least in part, by the new type of workers engendered by advanced capitalism and by the productive relationships common to all industrialized societies.

The New Working Class

With the advent of monopoly capitalism, the unity of ownership and control of the means of production has become more and more fragmented. Large-scale financial organizations, on the one hand, and corporate structures involving such people as managers and systems analysts, on the other, have taken over what had been the individual entrepreneur's functions of ownership and control. Greater numbers of employees have become supervisors and specialists, giving rise to a new division in the working class both in terms of levels of authority and functional fragmentation.[22]

Executives, along with an increasing number of bureaucrats who exercise authority, constitute the administrative apparatus of modern industrial, academic, military, and political organizations. At their command are manual workers as well as a growing number of white-collar workers like researchers, technicians, secretaries, and teachers. Expressed as either the proletarianization of the intellectuals or the mass-education of the proletariat, monopoly capitalism and large-scale bureaucratic organizations have created an increasing number of workers whose jobs defy traditional distinctions between manual and intellectual work.[23] As the proletariat was the ascendant social class in the period of the First Industrial Revolution, these technicians are growing in the period of the cybernetics revolution, or Third Industrial Revolution. As machinery is the accumulated labor-power of manual workers, computer memory and cybernetically controlled processes are the accumulated labor-power of the new working class.

The rapid expansion of this new section of the working class is a common feature of industrialized countries. In 1968, employment in health and education exceeded one and a-half million people in France, or about 7 percent of the total labor force. The number of technicians and scientists, excluding executives, rose from 457,000 in 1954 to 877,000 in 1968.[24] In the same year, the extractive and manufacturing industry employed only 41 percent of the workforce (33 percent in the United States, which was at a more advanced stage of economic development).

The industrial struggles of early capitalism were generally between skilled factory workers and owners. Over the decades, these conflicts have largely become institutionalized through negotiated settlements between trade unions and management. In modern times, a new level of conflict has developed within what was formerly the small and obedient staff of the supervisor: the conflict between technocrats who give orders and technicians who receive orders. As the general strike spread, the participation of the new workers was impressive. As Alain Touraine put it:

> The fact that most of the workers actively participated in the May-June strikes should not mislead us. Those who were responsible for the social movement character that these strikes often had were neither skilled workers nor the great organized labor groups such as the miners, the longshoremen, and the railroad workers. The leading role in the May movement was not played by the working class, but by those whom we can call professionals, whether they were actually practicing a profession or were still apprentices.[25]

An example of the conflict between technocrats and technicians during May was the popular strike by the government radio and television workers. Some 13,000 producers, journalists, and technicians stayed out longer than any other section of the working class, denying the government the capability to make significant use of the mass media during the general strike. Not on strike just for more money, these workers were motivated by a desire to no longer be obedient tools.[26] They launched a creative public campaign with slogans like, "The police on the screen means the police in your home."

Some journalists of large newspapers sought power over the orientation of their papers by demanding changes in the structure of their ownership. In a few cases, printers and journalists published newspapers but changed them, as in the case of *Le Figaro,* when the news it was supposed to carry misrepresented the aims of the student movement. At one point in the general strike, the technicians responsible for communication between the Ministry of Interior and police headquarters went on strike, disrupting a sensitive and important connection in what was by then the fragmented repressive forces of the French state.

Strikes among technicians marked the emergence of a new social movement for some observers. While the conflict between technocrats and technicians is peculiar to advanced capitalism,[27] the May movement consistently located itself in the socialist tradition of the nineteenth and twentieth centuries. What seems clear is that the rapid pace of change in the French economy in the postwar years helped precipitate the May movement, particularly among the new workers. The blind hand of change which rested solely on the internal developments of the economy (*Naturwuchs*) was slapped aside by attempts to rationally reorganize France. Whether we look at the new workers engendered by the system's inner logic or at the rapid rate of urbanization in the same period, we can see that the social conditions of existence of the people of France were rapidly transformed in the period leading up to 1968. Is it surprising that such rapid social change was accompanied by the rise of a vast social movement hoping to humanly decide the quality of the change?

While the differences between the classical proletariat and modern technicians are real, both groups experience similar oppression as workers. While some technicians may be elevated to executive status and some proletarians to roles of bureaucratic authority in their unions or companies, the vast majority of people in both categories hold jobs distant from the decision-making top. They both receive orders from technocrats and hold jobs with narrowing creative outlets and rewards, a common situation in the modern world.

Capitalist Relations of Production

In a capitalist system, the producer sells his or her labor power for the material rewards of wages and consumer goods. In exchange for human energy, the worker receives things. In this way, capitalist society tends to transform qualitative human factors into quantifiable commodities. The terms of the exchange are unequal on both the quantitative and qualitative levels.

Quantitatively, despite the vigorous and long-term efforts of trade unions, it remains true that workers' productivity is far greater than their wages. Surplus value continues to be extracted from their energy. No matter how vigorously the science of economics attempts to mask or apologize for this inequality by arguing that capitalists contribute to production and should be reimbursed, the fact remains that workers produce more than they are paid. Otherwise, how could profits be made? The participation of capitalists through the use of "their" machinery is a sham. Long ago, Marx demonstrated that the capital owned by the capitalist is nothing but stored labor-power ("dead labor") extracted from workers of the past. Dead and neutral property comes alive in this context.

Unions have traditionally fought only for a more "equal" and safer quantitative exchange between capitalists and workers. "Unions help workers *have* more, not *be* more. They serve to increase the quantity of goods the worker receives in exchange for his alienated labor; they do not serve to abolish alienated labor."[28] This analysis seems to be especially revealing in terms of the trade unions' role in the May events. In entering into the ill-fated Grenelle agreements, in trying to keep the student revolt separated from the working class, and in preventing whenever possible the formation of autonomous strike committees by the workers, the CGT continually attempted to channel the general strike toward reformist objectives.

Qualitatively, the exchange between capitalists and workers differs in kind: energy for things. The fact that workers might get higher wages does not alter this qualitative inequality. Industrialization and pressure from unions have resulted in more things being allocated to the workers, but the qualitative inequality of exchange continues. It is a structural backbone of the capitalist mode of production, and it was this backbone which was challenged and nearly broken in May.

The Cultural Poverty of Consumer Society

The roots of the May explosion can be found in the dynamic conflict between forces and relations of production and in the rapid changes in France in the decades immediately preceding 1968. A full investigation of the May events reveals broader human grievances which also contributed to the movement. I refer to the cultural fragmentation and unmet human needs glaringly obvious in France and in "affluent" countries generally.

For most people in the industrialized core of the world system, the drastic rise in the standard of living during modern times—the allocation of more things to the workers—has come at a high human cost. Energy at the workplace has become more automated and fragmented, and what was formerly leisure time has become increasingly objectified and controlled. Assembly line production, the basis for consumer society, has routinized jobs, reducing workers to mere appendages of machinery. Vast differentiations in the division of labor, necessary for assembly-line production, have caused workers to specialize in jobs which block the use of nearly all creativity. The increasing separation between decision-makers and executants has reinforced alienation and passivity. As space-age production has given human beings atomic weapons, for example, the decision to pull the trigger is beyond the power of the vast majority.

In the university classroom, military service, and virtually all the institutions of modern society, the role of the individual has been reduced to a passive cog in the social machinery. The transition from public to mass, to use C. Wright Mills's words, has been accompanied by the growth of one-way communication and the demise of dialogue and collective discussion.

In the realm of consumption, mass society reproduces the primacy of things, not people.[29] Instead of a person going to a cobbler, for example, and having a pair of shoes specially made, one now goes to a shoe store where a variety of styles and prices are available. Instead of the commodity being matched to the person, the person must match the commodity.

Service industries have risen in importance, providing for cash what used to be available in the family. From acts of intimacy and love to cooking and cleaning, mass society gains what the atomized individual has lost. The exchange of human energy for things and the proliferation of the cash nexus to nearly all aspects of life have combined in their effects on the human psyche. People tend to view themselves, not simply others, as objects—things to be sterilized by deodorants for various parts of the body much as cleaning aids are available for different parts of the house.

The strength of consumer society has been its ability to "deliver the goods" to a majority of people within the industrialized nations. Urbanization and the mass media have centralized consumer markets, and as disposable incomes have risen, new markets have been developed. Using a variety of advertising techniques, new ways of manipulating human consumption have been devised. Products hitherto unheard of have been invented, and the desire for them has been created through advertising. On a covert level, advertisers and experts in marketing have designed subliminal techniques for stimulating unconscious needs and desires in order to sell products. Thus, after establishing its capacity to profitably satisfy the physical needs of humans—food, clothing, and shelter—capitalism has moved on to new markets: the manipulation of cultural and psychological needs for profit.

The increasing importance of consumer markets for monopoly capitalism has created a new situation in the industrialized countries. In the words of Henri Lefebvre:

> Organizational capitalism now has its colonies in the metropolis, and it concentrates on the internal market in order to utilize it according to a colonial pattern. The double exploitation of producer and consumer carries the colonial experience into the midst of the erstwhile colonizing people.[30]

The coercion needed to maintain these internal colonies is predominantly psychological, in distinction to the third world where physical force is more common. The human regimentation and standardization which monopoly capital imposes on its subjects in the industrialized core are hidden behind the freedom to choose among gadgets, pretty politicians, and other goodies of the consumer society.

Is it surprising that the May explosion erupted in spontaneous actions that challenged the power of manipulation and regimentation? As the Situationists put it in their critique of the society of the spectacle: "We do not want to exchange a world in which the guarantee of no longer dying of hunger is exchanged for the risk of dying of boredom." The implicit message during May was "DO IT," not watch it. Leaflets called for the formation of autonomous action committees (ACs) in schools, workplaces, communities— wherever people would organize themselves. In contrast to the ultra-centralization of France, self-reliance and self-management were stressed as new means for social organization. As one leaflet said:

> If you are a group of comrades, form a committee, draw up your own leaflet, set a place for daily meetings, make dates for demonstrations. Contact the provisional coordination committee of the AC's and name a liaison delegate. If you are alone, contact the coordination committee.[31]

This call for self-organization did not go unheard. Within two weeks, hundreds of ACs were formed throughout France; more than 250 came into existence in Paris alone. A General Assembly of ACs was created, subject to instant recall and with no power beyond coordination. *Action*, the newspaper of the ACs, was an immediate success with a daily circulation of 30,000. In contrast to the rigid bureaucratic structure of the traditional Left, new forms for liberation and a new content of freedom were developed during May. The Freud-Che Guevara Action Committee called on the movement to unite "all those who are crushed or excluded by an inhumane system:"

> The struggle must have as its final objective the establishment of a socialist system in which, through the destruction of barriers, the creativity of each individual will be set free. This objective implies a revolution not only in the relations of production, but in the mode of life, in ways of thought, in human relations, and in the concept of the sexual life of all.[32]

It is difficult to overestimate the anti-bureaucratic thrust of the May insurgents. The pomp of officials, Communist or not, was everywhere held up for public ridicule. Rules, an essential ingredient of rational-legal forms of authority, were flaunted according to the slogan: "It is forbidden to forbid." Economic and bureaucratic domination were simultaneously challenged: "Mankind will not be free until the last capitalist has been hanged by the entrails of the last bureaucrat."

In word and deed, May marked the merging of the social movement for economic liberation with a vast cultural revolt. Romanticism of the non-fragmented life of the past was combined with a modern awareness of the possibilities opened by space-age production. Science was not totally rejected, yet material progress was made secondary to human needs.

Some observers, like Alfred Willener, viewed cultural concerns as a prime cause for the May explosion. An example of a cultural struggle occurred early in February 1968, when the government removed Henri Langlois from his position as the head of the *Paris Cinémathèque*, an internationally prominent archive and theater. Organized protests succeeded in restoring Langlois to his position in an episode of activism which helped set the stage for May.[33] In a social-psychological study of the May events, Willener stated:

> Whatever the situation was in 1968, there was no question of Gaullist France being in ruins; nor did the economy show any major signs of crisis, such as widespread poverty or unemployment, at least for the overwhelming mass of opinion. On the other hand, the extent of the cultural ruin was steadily increasing: although the perfectly functioning, automatic, and now almost immediate tactic of absorption soon unprimed Dada and its radical negation, adopted and reapplied the most refined Surrealist techniques of subversion, and took over all later experiments of a similar kind so successfully that so many of them now seem to have conformed from their very inception, it is true nonetheless that every attack, whether in the form of a gradual disintegration or a sudden explosion, has had its effect and that bourgeois or post-bourgeois values as such now seem well and truly dead. A whole civilization, which no one will call "Western" and "Christian," survives only as a skeleton.[34]

The cultural roots of the May events can be found in Dada, Surrealism, free jazz, the Living Theatre, and Godard's films. All share a desire to return to a "natural state" as far as possible from established structures, and they create a space where the free play of the imagination and the work of the hands and mind can find new unity. Far from being atypical of industrialized societies, the May 1968 explosion was a social manifestation of the same human values and needs contained within these modern forms of art. The surrealist ethic of living for one's fantasies was matched by the popular May slogan: "I take my desires for reality, for I believe in the reality of my desires." Another May slogan, "As long as we have not destroyed everything, there will remain ruins," was reminiscent of Dada's attempts to destroy dead art in order to create a living one. The perception of cultural injustices and attempts to overturn them during May demonstrated the non-reducibility of the actions of human beings to economic factors.

A strong impulse in May, especially among the more youthful participants, was the conscious reshaping of themselves to become different kinds of people than those the mass system produced. Everyday life became a topic for politics. The personal values of yesterday were held up for collective re-evaluation. One sociologist, who happened to be with members of the March 22 Movement as they were waking up one afternoon, was amazed as they evaluated their previous night in the streets:

> The astonishing thing was that what interested them were the little incidents that arose from their own practice, their relations with each other in the gang (sic)—and as boys and girls (sic) for sexual problems were not divorced from politics, even during the night of the barricades . . . either we're at the antipodes of politics, or it's a new way of seeing politics.[35]

In contrast to the human fragmentation engendered by mass society, the May events and the vision for the future which emerged called for a new integration of the individual in a different kind of society. The totality of life under the previous mode of existence came into question in theory and practice as new possibilities for the future were developed. Norman Birnbaum viewed this concern with integration and fragmentation as an essential one:

> The (admittedly precarious) co-existence since the French Revolution of bourgeois routine and bohemian cultural innovation, of bourgeois domination and working-class challenge, of Catholicism and laicism, has proven so fruitful in the sphere of culture precisely because of a common language. The continuation into an industrial epoch of these conceptions, combined with the absurdly backward aspects of much of French social organization, in May of 1968 provoked a convulsion. Typically, French debate about the convulsion has been concerned to a considerable extent with restoring the fragmented unity of the cultural community.[36]

The social fragmentation of French culture was answered with the call by activists for the transformation of relationships between human beings and with Nature. "The forest precedes man, the desert follows," said one inscription. The notion of the unlimited interrelation of all life was present within the spontaneous and dramatic nature of the protests and in the appearance of love at the barricades. If the May insurgents challenged the cultural hegemony of the middle class, they affirmed new values for life, not ones having to do with the domination of Nature but ones based on a playful and loving interaction with it.[37] From this source flowed such demands as the liberation of the Luxembourg Gardens and freedom for the animals in the zoos.

The May critique of the impoverished culture of contemporary society is an important contribution to the continuing development of revolutionary aspirations. It was the fusion of cultural and political revolt within a vast social movement which gave the May events a new character within the long tradition of socialist insurrections. At one point, de Gaulle said that the situation was *"insaisissable,"* impossible to grasp or control. The universities and workplaces were not held by armed force but through the massive participation of their members, and their demands were incomprehensible to those in power. The insurgents were not concerned with traditional political power, and they envisaged their victory through the transformation of the general strike into an "active strike:"

> ...the workers would set their factories back into motion on their own account. Then with the economy beginning to turn again, but for the workers and not for their former bosses, the state would succumb in impotence and be ripe for overthrow. A parallel power would arise in each town and village as workers coordinated their efforts with each other and the farmers. Socialism would be initiated from below as self-management and not handed down from above in nationalizations.[38]

Such a strike made it difficult for the state to intervene. When the occupied buildings were retaken by the government, there was considerable bloodshed, but not of the scope that followed the Commune. In this sense, the fusion of the forces of production and culture in May presented a new method and new goals for the transformation of society. The imagination of May opened the possibilities for the construction of a qualitatively new future, one where not only the material needs but also the cultural needs of human beings would be of prime concern, where liberation would not be decreed from above but achieved by an activated population.

The Political Meaning of May 1968: Internationalism and Self-Management

The May insurgents did not act with an already developed model for a new society. The spontaneous escalation of the student struggle necessitated the improvisation of strategy and tactics and brought new forms of social organization into existence. A vision for the future where nations, hierarchies of domination, boredom, toil, and human fragmentation no longer would exist came to light during the general strike. A brief investigation of some of the aspects of this vision will be undertaken to demonstrate its qualitative difference from the *status quo*.

Photo 2
Paris: May 1968, Love at the Barricades

Patriotism and Internationalism

The vision which was fought for in May knew no national boundaries. "To hell with borders" expressed a popular feeling. Through leaflets and posters ("*Frontiers = Repression*"), a systematic campaign against petty nationalism was conducted, a campaign which immediately made it possible for students from many parts of the world who were studying in France to participate in the May events. As the student revolt intensified, foreign students' residence halls in Paris were occupied by their more radical members. Democratic reorganization of the residences and support for liberation movements at home and in France were called for. (Of course, there were exceptions, notably the Brazilians who literally closed their doors to the movement in May.) A Tri-Continental Committee was established in Paris which proclaimed that "to contest capitalist structures within a national framework is also to contest the international relations set up by these structures."[39]

Bilingual posters urged such seemingly antagonistic groups as Arabs and Jews to "turn against your common enemy: imperialism and capitalism." One of the episodes of May concerned a demonstration in support of Daniel Cohn-Bendit, the German-born Jew who was expelled from France after he and the March 22 Movement helped spark the explosion. As the support demonstration unfolded, 50,000 people, including a prominent contingent of Arabs, chanted: "We are all German Jews."

Foreign workers in France, traditionally considered a threat to the jobs of French workers and subject to racist attacks, were received as comrades during May. Immigrants from nearby countries have long been compelled to find work in French industry, even though they are hired for the worst jobs at the lowest pay. For the most part unable to speak French, these workers were often used by management to break strikes, or in periods of relative calm, to disrupt communication and organization among the workers at the point of production. Working at the grueling pace of an assembly line provides little time or space for discussion, especially if there is a Yugoslav on your left and an Algerian on your right. Moreover, foreign workers in France generally live in company-owned houses where they are purposely assigned roommates who speak a different language.

The general strike temporarily transformed the divided workers. Multilingual worker-student action committees very successfully canvassed the housing projects where foreign workers lived. Not only was management unable to mobilize strike-breakers, but the vast majority of foreign workers joined in the general strike.

In early June, the General Assembly of Worker-Student Action Committees passed a resolution "For Abolition of the Status of Foreigner in France." Invoking the example of the Paris Commune, where a Hungarian was the Minister of Labor and a Polish worker the military chief, the resolution went on to call for an end to residence cards, work cards, and deportations:

> These foreigners come under an oppressive special statute which subjects them to almost permanent special police checks and threats, which we, Frenchmen, avoid simply because of our

nationality. This concept of "nationality" is profoundly reactionary. People work, are exploited, dream, and fight for their freedom
in a specific geographic and social context; there they have every
right.[40]

In contrast to the internationalism of the insurgents, the government sealed off
French borders to the many young people from Germany and Italy who
attempted to get to Paris. Deportations were used to rid France of foreign
activists. In response, an Action Committee for the Abolition of Borders was
formed in Paris and urged Europeans to spread the revolution throughout the
continent. Their call to action did not go unheard, particularly in Germany
and Italy.[41]

Traditional French ethnocentrism was swept aside by unleashed imaginations during May. The Gaullist counteroffensive in June, of course, played
heavily on the myth of foreigners who had caused the disruptions and riots.
What may surprise some, however, was the nationalism of the French Communist Party, an organization originally committed to proletarian internationalism. On June 10, Waldeck-Rochet, the Party's secretary-general, publicly said:

We Communists have always fought and shall continue to fight
remorselessly the lack of national feeling that certain anarchist
elements vaunt as a sign of their revolutionary ardor. We, for our
part, are proud to have restored to the working class what Aragon
so nobly called "the colors of France."[42]

The nation-state as a rational form for social organization was questioned by
the activists of May, but national sovereignty had already been undermined
long before 1968. Modern transnational corporations, which today account
for over one-third of the world's total production, are capitalist forms of global
organization which transcend national boundaries. Is it so surprising that the
New Left's vision for the future included a world without borders?

Authoritarianism and Self-Management

With the rise of large-scale modern industry and the fragmentation of
production, managers of all varieties have become a necessary part of the
productive apparatus. Are they really? The May events indicated not. Many
factory occupations exposed managers as essential to a profit-oriented economy, but also as superfluous, if not destructive, to a human-oriented system.

In the first days of the general strike, many managers found themselves
prisoners in their offices at the mercy of occupying workers. The first two
factories to be taken over by workers who then detained their managers were
Sud-Aviation in Nantes and Renault at Cléon. This caused an uproar in the
government as well as in the largest trade union in France, the Communist-
dominated General Workers Confederation (CGT). Georges Séguy, secretary-general of the CGT, broadcast an appeal to the workers in Nantes to
release the management team, and he even sent a delegation by private plane to

intervene. Alarmed by the workers' drastic actions, the CGT issued a public statement praising the "responsibility" of its membership and guaranteeing safety for management and the means of production.[43]

It should be noted that during the same period, some managers expressed sympathy for the aims of the strikers, and a few even contributed money to the movement. At Orly Airport, for example, the Air France staff donated 10,000 francs at the start of the strike, and the vast majority of management helped the strike committee in negotiations and upkeep of the 90-odd planes grounded during the strike.

In general, however, workers' actions against management revealed a fundamental aspiration of the general strike: *autogestion* (or self-management). The main thrust of the vision of self-management was to abolish hierarchical authority, but this kind of authority was only one of many permeating France. As scientific innovations in production progressed, so did the need for experts with technical qualifications to develop and implement them, and knowledge became even more a means for power over others. The self-managed institutions of 1968 aimed to socialize such specialized knowledge.

Because participation in the general strike included large numbers of professionals, technicians, and off-line office and service personnel (the new workers), the united working class was able to synthesize what had been a fragmented and partial view of production. The compartmentalization of knowledge and concomitant need for privileged experts and managers were refuted not only in desire, but often in reality.

In some factories, the workers continued production without the "help" of management. Utility workers, for example, insured regular supplies of gas and electricity for the community. At the electricity plant in Cheviré, workers refused to readmit managers to the plant despite an offered increase in monthly wages averaging 150 francs. As one worker said: "The managing staff has been away for two weeks, and everything is going fine. We can carry on production without them."[44] At the Atomic Energy Center in Saclay, the Central Action Committee, the organ of dual power, organized production to such an extent that when gasoline was running low in the area, 30,000 liters were delivered with the compliments of the Finac strikers in Nanterre. In Vitry at the Rhône-Poulenc factories, the workers established direct exchange with nearby farmers and made contact with various chemical workers in Western Europe, hoping to develop similar relationships.

These examples indicate a profound aspiration of French workers for control over their jobs and lives, not simply for more things in exchange for obedience to superiors. The absence of specific demands for the first ten days of the workers' occupation at the Atlantic shipyards in St. Nazaire, even though under pressure from their union, is a spectacular demonstration of the workers' disdain for management, whether capitalist or "Communist." As the advances of capitalism in the days of Marx relegated the capitalist to an unnecessary component of the productive process, so it seems that modern capitalism has carried managers to the abyss of irrelevancy. Indeed, in 1976, 45,000 professional and managerial personnel were unable to find work in France, compared to only 14,000 in 1971.[45]

The concept of self-management did not originate in the workplaces during May, but in the universities. Nonetheless, it quickly became a general aspiration of the May explosion, a spontaneously created form for dual power. The student soviet at the Sorbonne developed a comprehensive plan for restructuring the goals and methods of the university system. The occupied Sorbonne was managed by a general assembly which had final decision-making power. Medical services, food, space allocations, and all other functions within the liberated Sorbonne were taken care of by the occupiers. In Nantes, food and gasoline distribution, traffic control, and other activities in the life of the city were conducted by a democratically elected Central Strike Committee. This committee even developed its own currency.[46]

The occupied high schools, universities, offices, and cities which succeeded in establishing direct control were the concrete realizations of a new vision for society, a vision which existed among nearly all sectors of the population of France in May. An eloquent articulation of this vision came on May 28 from a student-worker action committee:

> Self-management as an economic and social system has as its goal fully to achieve free participation in production and consumption through individual and collective responsibility. This is therefore a system created above all for human beings, to serve them and not to oppress them.
>
> Practically, for working-class comrades, self-management consists in having their factories . . . doing away with the hierarchies of salaries as well as the idea of employees and employers . . . setting up workers' councils elected by themselves to carry out the decisions of everyone together. These councils should be in close relationship with the councils of other companies on regional, national, and international levels. The members of these workers' councils are elected for a determinate period and tasks are to be rotated. We must in fact avoid the re-creation of a bureaucracy which would tend to set up a leadership and thus re-create a repressive power.
>
> We must show that worker-management in business is the power to do better for everybody what the capitalists were scandalously doing for a few.[47]

As a universal aspiration of the May explosion, self-management affected not only the occupied institutions, but also, as mentioned, the unions which controlled large parts of the working class. Many of the younger workers struggled against the CGT from within, and others left that structure entirely. In the Wonder Batteries factory at Saint-Ouen, the workers elected their own strike committee and refused to let CGT officials inside the occupied plant. (The vast majority of the takeovers, however, were controlled by the CGT, which encouraged occupations, but not dual power.)

In contrast to the ultra-centralization and authoritarianism of France, self-management provided a realistic alternative based on autonomy and direct participation. In contrast to the passivity of the consumer society, self-

management demanded active involvement. In contrast to the compartmentalization of knowledge, self-management required collectivity and pooling of
individual skills. In short, self-management implied a social reality qualitatively different from that which existed prior to May.

The Limits of Spontaneity

The elements of the May movement which at first glance appeared to be
its strengths were also its weaknesses. Spontaneity, a refusal to accept any
form of hierarchy or leadership, and initiative solely from the base cannot be
permanently maintained in a new social formation except within a framework
of political power. The centralized organization of monopoly capitalism
necessitates the organization of the seeds of the new society—the revolutionary culture and organizations—prior to the overthrow of the system. (See
Chapter 5.)

The May insurrection developed outside the traditional parties on the
Left for good reasons. The bureaucratization of the PCF made that organization incapable of comprehending the totalized impulse for liberation which
emerged in May, and the Socialist Party was virtually non-existent at that
time. The inability of the May insurgents to advance the political crisis (except
to the extent that the cultural revolt and social movement precipitated it) had
its corollary in a rebellion against traditional organizations of the Left. There
was not a transcendence of obsolete organizations, no development of a
political form for the creation of socialism. What Lenin once said in another
context could be said about May, that "anarchism was often a sort of punishment for the opportunist sins of the working class movement. The two...
were mutually complementary."[48]

In the aftermath of 1968, many of the insurgents (like André Gorz)
envisioned the construction of a new kind of party. Besides destroying the
traditional state, such a revolutionary party would need to be capable of fusing
the partial concerns of the subjects of social transformation—the students,
factory workers, new workers, the ecology and women's liberation movements—into a totalized vision of the future. Without the unifying effects of
such organization, the fragmented consciousness of monopoly capitalism
would in time insidiously reassert itself in the generation of specialized self-
interest issues and concerns.

Analyzed in isolation, each sector of the May movement was incapable of
conceptualizing and implementing a new society. The student movement was
able to detonate a larger social explosion. Despite the modern-day entrance of
academia into the "real world," the limits of the student movement were
marked by the confines of its environment. Students embodied a particular
expression of the general contradiction between capitalist relations of production and the productive forces. Only their momentary integration into a larger
movement in 1968, i.e., the abolition of a purely student movement, allowed
the student revolt to trigger such a vast upheaval.

By themselves, the new workers tend toward the modernization solution.
As educated executives, they tend to look for a better way to do this, a less

painful way to implement that. The immense birth pains involved in creating a new society make it easier for the new workers to adopt technical solutions to human problems. Generally speaking, the new workers are relatively better paid than other sectors of the working class. This relative privilege cut the other way in May 1968, however, as the new workers, more often than others, stressed qualitative demands and were relatively unconcerned with pay raises. In the climate of the explosion, the majority of these new workers allied themselves with students and factory workers. Together they constituted a united force which, if it could have been maintained, might have served as a basis to abolish different categories of existence while establishing a new mode of life.

The student revolt would not have become much more than the now usual springtime festivities had it not been for the general strike. In their rejection of the Grenelle agreements and the examples of dual power created during the strike, French factory workers momentarily demonstrated aspirations to transform the entire society. By themselves, however, the factory workers neither initiated nor successfully concluded the general strike. It was only after two weeks of the student revolt and the fighting in Paris that the working class acted. What the students had proposed—a new social formation—the workers were in a social position to implement. Unfortunately, when all was said and done, the working class by itself proved incapable of carrying through what many regard as its historic task.

Neither the absence of a revolutionary party nor the reformism of the PCF totally accounts for the limitations of the May movement. The questions must be asked: Why did the workers ultimately remain obedient to their unions and return to work? Why did the students obey the commands of CGT officials to leave the factories, as on May 16 when over 1,000 students marched from the Sorbonne to the huge Renault plant at Boulogne-Billancourt? The next day an even larger march was not admitted inside the factory by CGT officials. Even when some chemical workers went to the Sorbonne and invited students to their factory occupation, few went and many opposed the idea, using the "revolutionary" argument that "we would be substituting ourselves for the workers."[48]

Some of the answers to these questions can be found in the social conditions of modern capitalism, a system which has consolidated its hold over half the earth while fragmenting people's needs, desires, and relationships to the whole. As Marcuse said:

> In the domain of corporate capitalism, the two historical factors of transformation, the subjective and objective, do not coincide: they are prevalent in different and even antagonistic groups. The objective factor, i.e., the human base of the process of production which reproduces the established society, exists in the industrial working class, the human source and reservoir of exploitation; the subjective factor, i.e., the political consciousness, exists among the nonconformist young intelligentsia...The two historical factors do coincide in large areas of the Third World.[49]

During May, it was the momentary merging in action of the subjective and objective forces of transformation which brought France to the edge of revolution. The June containment necessitated their separation. But even from the start, the PCF and CGT militantly struggled to isolate the student revolt, calling students the "children of the big bourgeoisie" in the Party's paper, describing their leaders as agents of Gaullism, and keeping students out of the occupied factories. The student revolt challenged the influence which the PCF and CGT held over the French proletariat, a legacy from the trade-union struggles of the past. Feeling its power threatened, the CGT did its utmost to split students and workers. In early May, one of its statements said: "Some petty bourgeois with feverish brains slander the workers' movement and pretend to teach the workers a lesson. The working class rejects these stupidities; it has come of age a long time ago; it needs no tutelage."[50]

"Workerism" was common during May, accepting as it did a fundamental social category of capitalism. To have overcome it, a vision for a new society transcending the fragmented realities of modern capitalism would have been needed. In such a society, property would be socialized, and the vast majority, not simply a fraction of the population, would view the modern productive forces as their responsibility. On the other hand, Marcuse's notion of a "psychic Thermidor," an internally conditioned impetus to return to the *status quo ante*, applies to the workers as well. At Saclay and elsewhere in May 1968, some workers showed how they viewed the long-term prospects of their strike by punching their time clocks in the usual fashion. Even at Saclay, the well-organized workers did not question the propriety of nuclear power.

A transcendent vision could only have been practically conceptualized in the heat of May by the prior existence both of human beings who had taken on the responsibility of changing themselves—their needs, aspirations, and ideas—and of a revolutionary party which refused to define itself simply in terms of the social divisions brought into existence by capitalism.

The May events came by surprise. Perhaps the privilege of historical hindsight allows mistakes to be made transparent, but it is the future which the legacy of May should serve. It is difficult to assess the long-run effects of the taste of freedom in May. People will not simply forget the explosion, nor will the social contradictions that were then manifested disappear of their own accord. Mistakes made and victories won through the courage of those who rose up are a guide for the future. In shoving aside a social order and a conditioning aimed to pacify them, the people of France reaffirmed the dignity of human beings, legacy enough for them and people all over the world.

Some Implications of May

Between the direct participation of self-management and a new international reality freed from the fetters of borders lay the power of the French state. The inability of the May insurgents to come to terms with national political power can be defined as their major shortcoming—the primary explanation for the collapse of the May impetus to establish a new society and the apparent return in June to the inertia of the established order. Whether or not the French state could have been overthrown in the heat of the May explosion will never be known. That there was no organized force which could have led such an undertaking is also debatable. In the aftermath of 1968, everyone became a general capable of offering strategic and tactical alternatives which could have led to revolution (or, as some insisted, to disaster). Perhaps it was a blessing in disguise that the May movement did not culminate in a seizure of power. The disorganization of the Left could have produced a monstrosity weighing heavily on future revolutionary movements, once again disillusioning people about the possibilities of socialism.

But such considerations ignore an important legacy of 1968: the *possibility* of revolution in an industrialized country. In the five decades since the demise of the Second International, the prospect of socialism did not realistically appear until the May explosion. Socialist revolution in France, practically inconceivable in the decades before 1968, appeared to be back on the historical agenda. If May succeeded in nothing else, it was not a total loss.

Yet there were other results. On April 27, 1969, the French electorate (by over a million votes) said *"non"* for the first time to a Gaullist referendum, sending the General into permanent retirement. His power and prestige were shattered in May, making it only a question of time before he would fall. Even before the end of the crisis, three hard-line Gaullist ministers had been replaced, and the new Minister of Justice, although himself a Gaullist, resigned his seat in the National Assembly in May 1968 to protest the government's repressive measures. Fouchet, the hated Minister of Education, was forced out in favor of Edgar Faure, who in his first appearance before the newly elected Assembly admitted to the government what French common sense had known all along: The grievances of the students rightfully pointed to much needed educational reforms.[51]

Moreover, following 1968, a host of reforms was inaugurated in France which streamlined authority structures and gave a semblance of participation to students and workers. The thrust of most of these reforms has been to provide temporary relief to an incurable patient. Increased government planning of the job market and university curricula has helped reduce the number of workers and college graduates without jobs. In classrooms and factories, the stuffiness and formalism of pre-1968 France have been replaced by a more casual approach. University problems are now considered by councils which include students. The entire university system has been reorganized into a "co-governing" one with a more multidisciplinary focus for each school. An experimental university at Vincennes was created in response to student demands of 1968, and academic disciplines within other universities were redefined and transformed.[52]

While the system's rhetoric may have come to include student power, the reality of a student power transcending the borders of the university remains a dream. Student power of the contemporary kind is little more than an attempt to legitimate the administration. Modernization in France has hidden behind the progressive rhetoric of its time, much as the ascendant bourgeoisie temporarily adopted the slogan *"liberté, egalité, fraternité"* following the struggle of 1848. Accordingly, self-management was made into co-management, a profitable venture where more initiative from workers may replace some of their supervisors, thereby lowering the company payroll and helping to reduce the "alienation" of workers. While co-management may help bring the "little people" closer to the decision-making centers, it does not aim, nor will it serve, to abolish the hierarchy of domination.

Co-management and other reforms institutionalized after 1968 have served the authority of the top. Archaic structures inherited from the days of Napoleon were altered according to the modern needs of monopoly capitalism, not revolutionized to meet human needs. Such modernization did not call into question the fundamental assumption of the present system—the top-down organization of production and consumption for private profit—but merely attempted to make the system more efficient. These reforms were designed to keep protests scattered and ineffective while devising technical solutions for social problems.

A popular conjugation of May indicated a high degree of consciousness about co-management and co-optation:

je participe (I participate)
tu participes (you participate)
il participe (she, he, it participates)
nous participons (we participate)
vous participez (you participate)
ils **profitent** (they **profit**)

The internationalism of May also had a use for those who wished to streamline the present system. A top manager of IBM, Jacques Maisonrouge, some of whose children participated in the May events, was heard to mimic them when he said: "Down with borders." After all, transnational corporations are bodies whose wealth and influence transcend any particular country. The global corporation, so he says, increasingly views the world as "one economic unit," a unity which leads to "a need to plan, organize, and manage on a global scale."[53]

But the global vision of transnational corporations is the internationalism of profit-making and domination, not of an anti-authoritarian socialism. Here, as elsewhere, the modernization thesis rests on two assumptions. First, that what is needed are new people with better ideas to manage the same structures of society. It fails to conceive of a new type of system, one in which people themselves would govern their lives and institutions. Second, modernists conceive of social problems as technical ones which can be solved through science and technology. The need for change in the human structures of society is neglected. This neglect causes science and technology, originally great forces for the liberation of human beings from material scarcity, to turn into their opposite. Under the modern capitalist system, science and technology increasingly become means for domination, not liberation.

In the aftermath of 1968, the groundswell of popular aspirations for a better society was also channeled into parliamentary action by the established political parties. As electoral strategies for "socialism" gathered momentum, the Communist Party was temporarily swelled with new, younger, and more radical members. More importantly, the Socialist Party (practically non-existent in 1968) was juvenated by hundreds of thousands of new members and millions of supporters, and in 1981, the legacy of May 1968 brought the Socialists to power. Even with the election of François Mitterrand and the formation of his Socialist government, however, the aspirations of the popular forces which converged in the May explosion were not satisfied. The contradiction between the *possible* (given modern technology's ability to meet world needs) and the *real* (hierarchical organization for warfare, nuclear power, and the domination of Nature) only grew more pregnant. The vision of a self-managed international order remained frustrated because the nation-state defined the limits of Mitterrand's reforms, and the middle class defined his cultural model for the future of France.

To be sure, the Socialist government produced some significant results: In its first four days, the new administration announced the cancellation of the highly-contested nuclear power plant at Plogoff in Brittany; an end to attempts by the military to expand their training grounds in Larzac; and better conditions for immigrant workers. The official program of the Socialist government was not the usual reformism. It included a thirty-five hour work-week; the nationalization of all banks, insurance companies, steel producers, and the defense, aircraft, and nuclear industries; reform of abortion laws; an end to discrimination against homosexuals; an end to the death penalty; an end to nuclear testing; atomic disarmament; and voting rights in local elections for foreigners who have worked for more than five years in France. The new administration immediately hired 200,000 unemployed people and raised unemployment benefits to the most needy. Five of France's largest industrial groups (including the country's largest banks and steel producers) were nationalized in February 1982, bringing more than 650,0000 workers onto the state's payrolls.

Immediately after Mitterrand's election, there were spontaneous festivities, but subsequent events have caused the celebrations to subside. Even though they were limited, the nationalizations satisfied neither private industry nor the trade unions, and the Socialist decentralization plan, which sought to dismantle prefecture powers created in 1793 by Napoleon, also drew wide opposition. Moreover, as time passed, the Socialists were unable or unwilling to fulfill their campaign promises. They did halt work on twenty-five nuclear power sites two months after their 1981 electoral victory, but the construction ban was later lifted on six sites, and a $4 billion expansion of reprocessing plants like that at La Hague was approved despite continuing anti-nuclear protests. In another reversal of policy, the Socialist government decided to launch a major arms export drive. More than 16 percent of the world arms market is controlled by France (worth over $10 billion a year), and it is apparently needed for the stability of the national economy and for the maintenance of the traditional national defense system.

Furthermore, Mitterrand's environmentalist supporters were disappointed by his refusal to stop nuclear tests in the South Pacific, particularly since islanders' children have high rates of birth defects, and the union representing French workers there claimed that a storm caused severe contamination in the

Mangareva Atoll. According to Greenpeace, the ecology organization formed in 1970, the forty-seven explosions on the atoll since 1975 have produced a crack, half a mile long and a foot wide, in the base of the atoll from which radioactivity is seeping into the ocean.[54] Greenpeace's continuing exposés led to the Mitterrand government's involvement in the bombing and sinking of a Greenpeace ship in Australia and the murder of a photographer who was on board, and the ensuing scandal rocked the Socialist administration at the same time as it made all too apparent the limitations of the parliamentary victory of the Left.

Less well known to the world was the fact that Mitterrand adopted a more belligerent posture toward the Soviet Union than that of Giscard d'Estaing. The Socialists raised expenditures for the French nuclear strike force nearly 25 percent and did not reduce them as promised. Events such as these made it appear that French *national* interests dominated the Socialist government more than that of international financier Giscard d'Estaing, whose attempt in 1977 at a quiet re-integration of French units into the NATO alliance had alarmed his old Gaullist supporters. As a result, it was estimated that half of the junior officers in the military voted for Mitterrand in the 1974 presidential elections.[55] Even Régis Debray, the companion of Che Guevara in Bolivia who accepted a job in Mitterrand's government, used the occasion of the tenth anniversary of May 1968 to celebrate the nation-state as eternal. According to Debray, May 1968 marked the Americanization of France: the influx of systems analysis and unfettered technocracy needed to modernize archaic France. The activists accomplished the opposite of what they intended. May 1968 only served to stabilize France since genuine revolution there has been and remains out of the question; the best that can be done is to lend a hand "to the 'barbarians' struggling outside the walls [i.e., in the third world] against our sophisticated barbarism."[56]

Debray may be right that the system has been able to use the energy of May 1968 for its own purposes, but that is nothing new. As early as 1852, it was pointed out in reference to the French state that: "All revolutions perfected this machine instead of smashing it. The parties that contended in turn for domination regarded the possession of this huge edifice as the principal spoils of the victor."[57] In 1963, M. Crozier pointed out that crises are the main adaptive mechanisms of French bureaucratic culture.[58]

Debray, like Mitterrand, failed to comprehend the specificity of the political-cultural contradictions which exploded in 1968, contradictions which, if anything, have only deepened. In 1978, for example, it was discovered that only 1 percent of French youth "would give their life for France," compared with 20 percent in 1968.[59] The feminist movement has grown by leaps and bounds since 1968,[60] as has the ecology movement. Another indication of the popular awakening has been the radicalization of the French stage and the emergence of a popular theater movement.[61] All in all, it appears that the French people were transformed more profoundly by the events of 1968 than were French political parties.

The Mitterrand government's failure to take seriously the aspirations of its base of support led to popular disenchantment with the new government, a sentiment which even existed within the Socialist Party, many of whose members felt that their party's government was not implementing its program of workplace self-management and foreign assistance aid aimed at lessening the economic disparities between France and its former colonies. The legitimation crisis of the Socialist government led to an electoral defeat in 1986, and the new Prime Minister, Jacques Chirac, quickly unleashed a counter-offensive aimed at reversing many of the reforms implemented by the Socialists. Although Mitterrand remained the President (in an unstable power-sharing arrangement called *cohabitation*), Chirac moved to make the educational system more "selective" and introduced a "merit-based" pay scale for public employees. Less than a year after its election, the new conservative government was faced with massive social unrest, greater than anything seen in France since 1968. Student strikes and sit-ins in November and December of 1986 compelled the government to retract its plans to raise university tuition and tighten admission standards. As in 1968, the student movement catalyzed a strike, this time among public sector employees, particularly railroad and subway workers. At scores of railroad stations, police battled picketers, and the resulting work stoppage ended only after Chirac agreed to suspend the merit system proposal.

Whether frustrations like these will explode in yet another upheaval like that of 1968 remains to be seen. The fact that the Socialists were able to capture the French state through elections did not satisfy enthusiasts of the May events, an historical event which again verifies the insight drawn from the Paris Commune of 1871: A genuine revolution necessitates smashing the bourgeois state, not simply taking hold of that apparatus in its inherited form. Can a qualitatively new society be built as long as the centralized, authoritarian state exists? In organizing its "legitimate" role as the present government, the Socialists, like any other traditional party, were required to conform to the existing political-economic and cultural structures of the global system. As the editors of *Monthly Review* said in analyzing the role of the Communist Party during the May events:

> No mass party which is organized to work within the framework of bourgeois institutions can also be revolutionary. If it accepts these institutions and adapts itself to them—even if it thinks it is doing so only provisionally and temporarily—it is bound to acquire vested interests in the existing social order which would not merely be jeopardized but actually wiped out by a genuine revolution.[62]

A socialism worthy of the name in the industrialized countries presupposes the destruction of the centralized hierarchical state by an activated population. Such destruction is required of those who would construct a qualitatively new society, a socialism which would have little in common with the bureaucratic "socialisms" of today.

Of course, the disappointing results of the Socialists' five years of power also served to disillusion its popular base. Moreover, by restabilizing the French political system, Mitterrand may have helped to legitimate a political system in which parties come and go, but the state (i.e. the Fifth Republic) remains intact, a normal occurrence in the United States, but not in France (where the heads of government have periodically reconstituted new republics in accordance with new historical conjunctures).

A further problem encountered by those whose aspirations resemble the values which emerged in May 1968 (self-management and international cooperation) is the strong showing made by the National Front in the elections of 1986. Their 10 percent of the vote (roughly the same as that received by the Communists) indicates that a significant number of people share the Front's anti-immigrant and militaristic sentiments. Whether or not the National Front's share of votes increases in coming elections, there will remain the ethnocentric dimension of French culture, a dimension which even parties of the Left—like the Communists—have yet to free themselves from.

Without a popular movement mobilized to transform everyday patterns of interaction, even if a Socialist government is again mandated to rule France, such a government would, at best, provide nothing more than a more humane means of modernizing archaic social relations in France while preserving the existing structural imperatives of profit and domination. At worst, a new Socialist government would merely be tolerated by the electorate as a means of checking the far Right. The five years of experience generated by the Socialists' tenure from 1981 to 1986 provide ample evidence of their qualitative similarity to other political parties. The Socialists' nationalizations can even be seen as following in the tradition of Louis XIV (the "sun king" under whom classical French culture reached its high point, and the absolute monarchy was consolidated). Louis XIV's finance minister created many state-owned industries, as did de Gaulle, who nationalized Renault and other major industries after World War II. Nationalization, in contrast to socialization, leaves everyday life ensnared in an increasingly administered (rather than self-determined) social reality, and the possibility of more freedom is frustrated by the growth ·of the state.

Rather than seeking to stimulate the emergence of a popular mobilization aimed at transforming France, Mitterrand's reforms—particularly his concessions at Plogoff and Larzac—were designed to quiet well organized and widely supported grassroots movements, not to empower them. Is it surprising that Mitterrand and the Socialists, like any other political party, sought to avoid another period of generalized insurgency?

For anyone to think that a repetition of the May events is out of the question would be a grave mistake. Given the intensification of some of the same cultural contradictions which exploded in 1968, such a scenario may be realistic, but in the absence of organizations and leadership prepared to provide a framework for the transformation of the French state, a new explosion would be unable to translate popular aspirations into reality. Indeed, the ensuing political crisis might even be resolved in a regressive direction. History might repeat itself, but *not* as has been said before: the first time as tragedy, the second as farce. Rather, it might well become: the first time as *eros*, the second as *chaos*.

Chapter 4

THE
NEW LEFT
IN THE
UNITED STATES:
MAY 1970

The crisis on American campuses has no parallel in this history of the nation. This crisis has roots in divisions of American society as deep as any since the Civil War. The divisions are reflected in violent acts and harsh rhetoric, and in the enmity of those Americans who see themselves as occupying opposing camps. Campus unrest reflects and increases a more profound crisis in the nation as a whole....We fear new violence and growing enmity...If this trend continues, if this crisis of understanding endures, the very survival of the nation will be threatened.
　　　　　　　—The President's Commission on Campus Unrest,
　　　　　　　　　　　　　　　September 1970

Two years after the French May, the United States experienced what is today regarded as its worst political crisis since the Civil War, a crisis precipitated by the U.S. invasion of Cambodia. The first general strike of students in the history of the United States was not the usual springtime festivities: At Kent State and Jackson State Universities, six students were shot dead, and throughout the nation, confrontation and violence became commonplace. The nationwide student strike of May 1970 was the high point in the development of the student New Left in the United States and, as such, reflected both its limitations and strengths.[1] The crisis of 1970 was created by the more than four million college and high school students who went on strike and the many faculty members who joined them, but as the *eros* effect was felt, the rank and file of military combat units refused to fight, the militant black liberation movement intensified, workers went on strike, the feminist movement grew stronger, and a whole array of rural Southerners and middle Americans became activated.

I will examine the contours of the events of May 1970 in order to help uncover the essential nature of the society and the social forces that were in motion during this period. The intensity of these events provides historical clarity, not only of the New Left, but also of the society which produced it. In contrast to prevailing norms and values, the millions of people who were involved in the nationwide strike acted according to principles of international solidarity and self-management. Like the French events of 1968, the movement emerged abruptly, reached proportions of historical importance overnight, and necessitated a series of reforms designed to maintain the stability of the existing system.

The Black Panther Party at Yale University _____

In 1970, the student movement had no national leadership. Nearly a year before the student strike (in the summer of 1969), Students for a Democratic Society (SDS) had self-destructed by splitting into factions which were united in their denial of the political importance of student activism but differed over whether it was the working class or the third world who was the "vanguard of world revolution." For the most part, the old guard of the New Left's early college days was no longer active, since the movement had developed far beyond their wildest fantasies. Less than a month before the invasion of Cambodia, the National Mobilization Committee to End the War in Vietnam had closed its office a few blocks from the White House, under the impression that the anti-war movement had already run its course and that President Nixon's April 20 television announcement of the withdrawal of 150,000 additional U.S. troops from Vietnam meant the war was winding down.

The Black Panther Party was the only national New Left organization which continued to grow in this period, but it was under intense attack from the state: More than twenty-five Panthers had been killed by police; Huey Newton was in jail; Bobby Seale was on trial for murder; and Eldridge Cleaver was in exile. The only national leader of the Panthers not dead, incarcerated, or in exile was David Hilliard, and he was jailed briefly in April following a speech he gave at the spring Anti-War Moratorium in San Francisco in which he allegedly threatened Nixon's life.

The New Haven trial of Bobby Seale, Erica Huggins, and other members of the Party for the alleged murder of a police informant brought Panthers and their supporters to Yale University, where the majority of students soon swung over to their side. A national mobilization to free Bobby Seale and his co-defendants was scheduled for the weekend of May 1 in New Haven, and on April 15, the Bobby Seale Brigade rioted at Harvard Square in Cambridge, Massachusetts, in an action designed as a build-up to May Day.

By Wednesday, April 22, most of Yale College was striking in support of the Panthers. The next day, more than a thousand people gathered on the lawn at the house of the university's president, Kingman Brewster, to listen to speeches by members of the Panthers. Within forty-eight hours, Brewster surprised a faculty meeting with his statement: "I am appalled and ashamed that things should have come to such a pass that I am skeptical of the ability of black revolutionaries to achieve a fair trial anywhere in the United States."[2] Brewster's last minute change of heart had the effect of imposing a mandate on the Panthers to control the volatile assortment of radicals they had organized to come to New Haven.

When the arrival of the first groups of the 15,000 demonstrators coincided with Nixon's announcement of the invasion of Cambodia on April 30, it appeared that a confrontation at Yale was unavoidable. But there were only scattered incidents that night, probably due to both the orders from the Panthers not to take to the streets and the presence of 4,000 Marines and 8,000 National Guardsmen in New Haven. The next night, rioting broke out, but not on the scale feared by the Yale administration.

Although Brewster's "skepticism" had succeeded in helping to avoid a confrontation at Yale, the pacification of the demonstrators created a space within which the movement came together to formulate plans for a national student strike against domestic racism and the war in Indochina. Between the two planned rallies, there was a spontaneously assembled meeting of almost 2,000 people at Yale University's Dwight Hall. This free-flowing meeting was one of those rare moments of optimism and solidarity when imaginations ran wild. Speaker after speaker rose to call for greater resistance and to spread the movement. One activist called for a national student strike. A few minutes later someone called for a general strike. By the end of the meeting, all agreed to organize a national student strike beginning Tuesday, May 5 (coincidentally Karl Marx's birthday).

The three strike demands formulated at this meeting and accepted throughout the country were:

> 1. that the United States government cease its escalation of the Vietnam War into Cambodia and Laos; that it unilaterally and immediately withdraw all forces from Southeast Asia;

> 2. that the United States government end its systematic oppression of political dissidents and release all political prisoners, particularly Bobby Seale and other members of the Black Panther Party;

> 3. that the universities end their complicity with the United States war machine by the immediate end to defense research, the Reserve Officer Training Corps (ROTC), counterinsurgency research, and all other such programs.

Without the accidental coincidence of the New Haven rally and the invasion of Cambodia, the focus for the nationwide strike (particularly the demand relating to political prisoners in the United States) would no doubt have been more diffuse. The attacks on the Black Panther Party had the effect of bringing together a spontaneously generated political avant-garde which was able to provide a vision and program for the movement which erupted.

The Campuses Erupt

Students demonstrated a remarkable capability for self-organization and apparently leaderless actions as the strike unfolded. Within forty-five minutes of Nixon's televised announcement of the invasion of Cambodia, students at Princeton had organized a protest. That same night, students at Oberlin College occupied the administration building and demanded that the faculty meet to discuss the invasion. During the first six days after the invasion of Cambodia, there was an average of twenty new campuses going on strike every day, and in the days after the slaughter at Kent State on May 4, one hundred more colleges joined each day.[3] By mid-May, as the *eros* effect swept the nation, more than 500 colleges and universities were on strike, and by the end of the month, at least one-third of the nation's 2,827 institutions of higher education were on strike. More than 80 percent of all universities and colleges in the United States experienced protests, and about half of the country's eight million students and 350,000 faculty actively participated in the strike.[4]

The scale and intensity of the protests during May was new to the student movement in the United States. In the first week of that month, thirty ROTC buildings were burned or bombed.[5] At the University of Wisconsin in Madison alone, there were over twenty-seven firebombings, and across the country there were more incidents of arson and bombing (at least 169, 95 alone on the campuses) than in any single month in which government records have been kept. A $6 million computer, owned by the Atomic Energy Commission and used by New York University, was captured by a racially mixed group of sixty students and held for $100,000 ransom early in May. The protesters demanded the money be used for bail for a jailed member of the Black Panther Party in New York. After twenty-four hours of futile negotiations, the protesters left gasoline bombs to destroy the computer, but the quick action of faculty successfully defused the explosives.[6] At Fresno State College in California, a firebomb destroyed a million dollar computer center.

During May, over 100 people were killed or wounded by the guns of the forces of law and order. Besides the four murdered and ten wounded at Kent State on May 4 and the two people murdered and twelve wounded at Jackson State on May 14, six black people were murdered and twenty were wounded in Augusta, Georgia; eleven students were bayonetted at the University of New Mexico; twenty people suffered shotgun wounds at Ohio State; and twelve students were wounded by birdshot in Buffalo.

Nearly 2,000 people were arrested in the first two weeks of May for political reasons. The governors of Ohio, Kentucky, Michigan, and South Carolina declared all campuses in a state of emergency. The National Guard was activated on twenty-four occasions at twenty-one universities in sixteen different states. Between April 15 and May 19, more than 35,000 Guardsmen were involved in domestic duty, and for the first time, the nation's universities were occupied at gunpoint.[7]

A national strike information center was quickly established at Brandeis University and functioned as both a coordinator of local protest activities and an information center for the national strike. On May 11, over 500 delegates attended a National Student Strike Conference in San Jose, California. On almost every campus, a strike coordinating committee was spontaneously formed and linked up with the newly created national centers. At Berkeley, over 2,000 activists democratically participated in one meeting of their strike

Photo 3
Kent State University: May 1970

committee after which "action groups" were formed. There was the general feeling that "if a person can't find a place to plug in, he can create his own niche."[8]

During May, more than 11,000 draft cards were returned to the Selective Service. A Union of National Draft Opposition was set up at Princeton immediately after the invasion of Cambodia (the day before the deaths at Kent State). By the middle of June, chapters had been established at twenty campuses who together hoped to return 100,000 draft cards. When they tried to give the Selective Service 5,000 more cards on June 10, they were turned away without the cards being accepted.[9] The impact of draft resistance was admitted by the Selective Service when, for the first time, they filled less than 80 percent of their national quota. Soon thereafter, they began to investigate the sudden increases in failures to report, particularly in Rochester, New York, and northern Alabama.

On less than a week's notice, there was a demonstration of over 100,000 people in the nation's capital.[10] The speakers represented not only the striking students, but also organizations of black people and workers. From the podium, the American people were called upon to go on a general strike to end the war, and the recent strikes by post office workers, truck drivers, and workers at General Electric were all interpreted as responses to inflation caused by the war. Although at least 400 people were arrested after the rally, the popular surge toward massive civil disobedience was successfully defused from above by the hastily reconstituted New Mobilization Committee, a broad coalition of anti-war forces including pacifists and clergy as well as Communists and Trotskyites. One of the leaders of the "New Mobe" believes "to this day" that the committee suffered "an untimely failure of nerve"[11] on May 9. Of course, a confrontation then would have made the May 4 massacre at Kent State seem small by comparison, since over 25,000 police and soldiers were standing by.[12]

From the outside, the movement may have appeared as a threat to national security, but the high water mark had passed. Two days later, George Winne, a student at the University of California in San Diego, died of self-immolation, a desperate act of protest that reflected the national decline of protests after the May 9 demonstration. In the next week, as if to make their intentions clear, the forces of law and order murdered six people in Georgia and two in Alabama.[13]

It cannot be denied that a sizeable portion of the anti-war movement in 1970 did not condone militant confrontation. The actions of the thousands of students who converged in Washington, D.C. to lobby Congress are ample evidence, but at the same time, tens of thousands of people in the United States chose to battle the police rather than talk with Congresspeople. By their actions, millions of students showed a political understanding that making the system change its policies meant "raising the costs" of continuing the war by disrupting domestic tranquility, and the diffusion of militant tactics occurred despite the best efforts of the system (and many within the movement as well).

The burning of the Bank of America in Isla Vista, California on February 25, 1970, had set an important precedent. Like the Weatherpeople's Days of

Rage in October 1969, it was an action which defined a new level of struggle across the country. After Chicago's Loop was trashed by the Weatherpeople, window breaking and street fighting became commonplace; and after the bank was burned in Isla Vista, there were firebombings across the country. The diffusion of tactical innovations among students was not simply a national phenomenon. When students at Brandeis University took control of the campus telephone system, within ten days, students in England, Italy, France, and West Germany had attempted to do the same thing.[14]

In the course of the events of May 1970, students spontaneously generated new tactical approaches for confrontations designed to stop "business as usual." Across the country they blocked highways, expressways, railroad tracks, and city streets.[15] Blockading traffic might be seen as an extension of the sit-in, a tactic originally used by striking workers in the 1930s, but the students of 1970 contested the operation of the entire society, not only occupying their universities, but fighting for control of public space as well. On May 1, and again on May 3 and 14, thousands of students at the University of Maryland in College Park closed down Highway 1 and battled police and National Guardsmen who tried to open the road. On May 5, nearly 7,000 protesters from the University of Washington in Seattle blocked both the north and southbound lanes of Interstate 5 for over an hour, during which time they moved along the stopped cars to talk with motorists about the war and the strike. The next day the freeway was blocked again, but this time the police moved in and drove the protesters away.

At the University of California in Santa Barbara, a noon anti-war rally of 5,000 people took over the university center, where nearly 2,000 people formed affinity groups and moved onto Highway 101, which they blockaded for over an hour. One hundred feet of the main road leading into the campus was treated with lard, an action which also succeeded in stopping traffic. At Southern Illinois University in Carbondale, 2,000 demonstrators blocked downtown traffic and railroad tracks after the buses they had ordered to travel to the May 9 demonstration in the nation's capital were unexpectedly cancelled by the school's administration. A running battle with police and National Guard ensued, and scores of students were injured and over 200 arrested. One thousand people from the University of Cincinnati staged a ninety-minute sit-in in the midst of downtown traffic and were dispersed only after 145 were arrested. A contingent of 2,000 people marched from Columbia University onto the northbound lanes of the Henry Hudson Parkway, and at two campuses of the State University of New York (Stony Brook and Albany), at Mankato State College in Minnesota, and at St. John's in Philadelphia, hundreds of students marched off campus to block traffic. At John Carroll University in Ohio, more than 300 anti-war demonstrators succeeded in bringing traffic to a halt for more than an hour and one-half. In Austin, over 8,000 people battled hundreds of Texas Rangers who were called in to move the demonstrators out of the state capitol.

The tactic of blocking traffic first appeared spontaneously in May, but the *eros* effect carried it to other sectors of the population, and it has been widely used since 1970. A year later it was refined in the May Day attempt by 50,000 people to close down the nation's capital. In the 1970s, it was used by both farmers and truckers in protests at the Capitol. If blocking traffic quickly became a national tactic of the strikers, the black armbands worn after the murders at Kent State spread even further, finding their way to Indochina where GIs and Vietnamese fighters alike were reported to have worn them in solidarity with the striking students.

The explosion of the student movement in May 1970 created a situation without parallel in the history of the United States. As the editors of *Monthly Review* put it:

> All in all, it seems no exaggeration to say that the explosion touched off by the Cambodian invasion has been like nothing that has happened in this country in the more than hundred years since the Civil War. Nor is there much reason to doubt that it has created a situation qualitatively different from those which followed previous crises of the Vietnam war.[16]

What was new in May 1970 was the preponderant campus support for the strike demands. According to the report of the Scranton Commission, a blue-ribbon body appointed by Nixon to analyze the campus unrest, roughly 75 percent of all students favored the goals of the strike. The *New York Times* of June 15 reported that 42 percent of all students believed our Constitution needed major changes. As early as the fall of 1968, Daniel Yankelovich had reported that at least 368,000 people strongly agreed on the need for a "mass revolutionary party" in the United States, but after the strike of 1970, the same pollster announced that within the universities alone, more than a million people considered themselves "revolutionaries."[17] In early 1971, the *New York Times* discovered that four out of ten students (over three million people) thought that a revolution was needed in the United States,[18] and in 1976, sociologist Seymour Martin Lipset concluded that 75 percent of all students in May 1970 (about six million people) endorsed the need for "fundamental change" in the nation.[19]

The student strike was not confined to any geographical region (although it was strongest in the Northeast and weakest in the South), and it spread to technical, professional, and religious schools, to community colleges and non-elite universities, and to high schools across the country. Although the violence was widespread, it was not violent confrontations alone which marked the qualitatively new situation. Beginning in 1963, black uprisings had been brutally put down in the nation's inner cities, and there were many violently suppressed student demonstrations before Kent State. On May 15, 1969 ("Bloody Thursday" at People's Park in Berkeley), at least 128 people were hospitalized, most from gunshot wounds, and one person, James Rector, was killed by police gunfire. A day later in Burlington, North Carolina, the State Highway Patrol and National Guard broke up a student strike at a black college with bullets: One person was killed, several wounded, and over 200 were arrested. In April 1970, four students were wounded by birdshot in Santa Barbara, and another one, who was against the demonstrations and was guarding the Bank of America, was mistakenly shot and killed by police. In the same month, nearly 2,000 National Guardsmen, veterans of several tours of prison riot duty, were needed to arrest 600 people and restore order at Ohio State University after the unified demands of both black and white students were not met by the university's administration.

After the events of May 1970, however, a qualitatively new relationship existed between millions of Americans and their government: The violence of the Nixon administration became a threat to a broad cross-section of the population who had not previously perceived themselves to be targets of their own government. Nixon's "enemies list" (which eventually found its way into the pages of the mass media) included Hollywood celebrities, university faculty, hospitalized Vietnam veterans, business executives, GIs, and even university trustees and Congresspeople. In short, once the anti-war movement had won over the vast majority of students, the entire country became increasingly polarized and politicized, setting the stage for Watergate. At the same time as Nixon, Agnew, and Company were applauding the National Guard and making their "enemies list," a split developed in the nation's governing elite, a division which was originally revealed by the campus eruption of 1970. After the student strike, the split grew, extending beyond the university establishment to include the media (best exemplified by the *New York Times's* publication of the Pentagon Papers) and Congress in a power struggle against the executive and the military establishment.

Ever since the Atlantic City Democratic Convention of 1964 (when Walter Mondale, Hubert Humphrey, and the liberal leadership of the Democratic Party compromised the election of the Mississippi Freedom Democratic Party's delegation), the New Left had turned away from mainstream politics,[20] laying the groundwork for political confrontations such as the one that occurred in Chicago at the 1968 Democratic Convention. The strike of 1970, the high point of polarization, produced a concerted effort by liberals to "join" the movement, thereby bringing students into the established political arena.

One of the first indications of the academic elite's progressive swing was in May when nearly 200 college presidents publicly expressed their anti-war stand. Thirty-seven presidents of large universities sent letters to Nixon protesting the invasion of Cambodia. Once the strike began, a more moderate element linked to the campus administrations quickly assumed control of the rapidly spreading movement. Those at the top of academia joined the protests they had tried for years to stop, if only to better control them.

The administrators of many colleges ordered schools closed by executive mandate before students had the opportunity to strike. At Boston University, for example, students were given forty-eight hours to leave campus for the summer recess. Shutdowns from the top occurred at nearly one-third of the striking campuses. As the Scranton Commission put it:

> ...the massive number of moderates who joined the protests, partly because of the violent acts against students, then guaranteed by their involvement that the protests would be largely non-violent. In part, moderates were able to do this because they outnumbered extremists. But more important were their decisions: on campus after campus, students, faculty, and administrators set up

programs of action *designed to provide politically viable alternatives to violent action.*[21]

There was a host of such "politically viable" modes of action in May. The Princeton plan, which sought to alter the academic calendar by cutting down the Christmas holiday, thereby giving students two weeks off in the fall to work around elections, gained wide support until the Internal Revenue Service let it be known that they considered it a violation of university neutrality and therefore grounds for the withdrawal of tax-exempt status.

The president of Yale had greeted the demonstrators arriving for the May Day mobilization by joining them in support of Bobby Seale. By the end of the weekend, however, he declared the nascent national student strike to be an "irrationality which results from the inability to find any other way of shaking the regular political system into its senses: I hope we are smart enough to devise a better way to demonstrate our distress than to curtail education."[22] A week later, on May 11, he personally led a sizeable delegation from Yale to Washington, D.C. to discuss ways to immediately end the war. They met with more than 300 members of Congress and their assistants, particularly those who were Yale alumni. A 700-person delegation, comprising nearly the entire membership of Haverford College, also travelled to Washington to lobby for immediate de-escalation of the war, as did smaller groups from Stanford and other campuses on the West Coast. Altogether, delegates from one of every five colleges in the country went to lobby their Congresspeople in May 1970.[23]

In Washington, D.C., the National Student Association began to solicit support for the impeachment of Nixon during the strike. Letter-writing campaigns and petitions sprang up around the country. Protesters carried demonstrations to state capitals, and many local federal buildings became the site of lobbying, rallies, and in some cases, sit-ins as well. City Councils around the country found themselves voting on anti-war resolutions.

A year earlier, Joseph Califano, Jr., formerly of the White House and the Pentagon, had gone on a trip around the world sponsored by the Ford Foundation to evaluate the student movement. His findings included a call on the major political parties to include radical students:

> While the Communist Party to date has had little success in our country...it is clear that radical-anarchist groups, some armed with romantic views of Mao, Guevara, and Marcuse, are having an enormous impact on many of our brightest students...If the lessons of Western Europe and Japan are any indication, failure of the major political parties to attract vigorous and bright students will only enlarge the vacuum for radicals.[24]

By May 1970, it had been several decades since the United States had experienced a political strike, and the nature of the strike showed how far the gap between the established parties and the movement had become. Students on strike in 1970 were *not* simply motivated out of self-interest, but united around a set of demands oriented toward the needs of the most oppressed members of the world system. The universal nature of the strike's demands was one indication that students were not confined in their goals to the problems of one part of society—students and youth—but were consciously identifying in thought and deed with those at the bottom of the world's social and economic hierarchy. It was the international solidarity of Vietnamese and American, the active negation of the oppressor/oppressed duality, which was the essential meaning of the student strike. The nationwide strike demonstrated a motivation to nullify and move beyond the established system not only in the universal political *content* of the students' demands, but in the *form* of the strike as well. It was a new kind of strike in that the strikers not only attempted to stop ROTC and war research but also tried to make their institutions into what they should be: to create dual power based on a new set of ethics and values that would replace the old ones of partriotic chauvinism, international domination, hierarchy, and conformity.

The Form of the Strike

In 1970, students did not simply strike *against* their universities: They successfully mobilized both the members of the universities against national policy and, at the same time, they transformed the institutional structure of the academy. The eruption of the strike had a life of its own which could not be contained within the existing structures of power and authority. The energies generated were carried through into a redefinition of international relations, scientific research, and the goals of the whole society. Within the universities, the movement was not aimed at merely stopping "business as usual"; it sought to enact a new reality which broke with the assumptions of accepted rules and politics. At Northwestern University, as at many colleges, an alternative university and a new curriculum were established which raised questions about the role of the United States in international events. At Berkeley, experimental curriculum programs sprang up within many departments and were designed to create cooperative relationships based on mutual respect in place of the competitive and hierarchical atmosphere of the university's usual operations. The popularity of the new university was evidenced at a meeting in Berkeley's Greek Theater, when the assembled 17,000 people roared approval of a proposal to "reconstitute" the campus as a "center for organizing against the war in Southeast Asia." Before the meeting ended, Governor Ronald Reagan broke his sixteen-month-old vow to keep the schools open "at the point of a bayonet if necessary" and ordered all public universities and state colleges in California to close. Despite this executive order, more than 5,000 people gathered on May 8 for an illegal memorial to those killed at Kent State, and on Sunday, May 10, the school's newspaper appeared under a new title, *The Independent Californian.* As one astonished student at a school which the Governor had ordered closed summed up the situation, "My God, everywhere I go on campus, in every building, there are hundreds of people doing things. Organizing, meeting, writing leaflets—it's incredible."[25]

Challenging authority comprised only one of the many dimensions of the student strike. There was also a questioning of the everyday roles which are usually taken for granted. Berkeley's "reconstitution" led some staff members to write:

> [W]e are not an integral part of our typewriters; we are human beings with opinions on what is happening on this campus and in this country—and we have the right to express them as fully as the faculty and students are doing...[otherwise] it is hypocritical to say "I am opposed to the classification of people and peoples' rights in the campus community by fabricated differences such as race or sex or titles such as 'faculty, staff, students.'" We are all a part of a communal educational process; we should all share equally in all that goes on.[26]

Jocks and cheerleaders, fraternity and sorority members, engineers, campus workers, and doctors were all brought into the movement during the strike. Students naturally became a part of department meetings since that was where strike activities were being coordinated. Of course, after the strike, such participation diminished, but during the strike an entire generation of faculty, staff, and students developed new relationships to institutional (and national) authority. As one student put it, "I'll never feel comfortable in a lecture hall again."

The movement transcended a mere defiance of authority and formulated a vision of transformed institutions. One of the leaflets at Berkeley, for example, raised the notion of self-management (or "reconstitution" as it was called there):

> [R]econstitution is not a mechanical act, such as electing a senior prom chairman, but a political process—in the special sense, roughly, of a community of individuals publicly engaged in the enterprise of determining the management of the events and conditions that affect their lives on the basis of some approximation of a common good...There is no blueprint to be followed. There is no specific set of instructions that must be obeyed. The form and content of reconstitution will have to be worked out by the people who are themselves affected...decisions on how to implement the process are to be made not by professors, not by administrators, not by student leaders alone, but by the very people whose lives are involved, acting collectively in their communities.[27]

The participation of people in decisions formerly left to others helped to create a new situation: "Protest becomes an outmoded concept, for this reconstitution movement is not intent on petitioning any leaders to take action on our behalf. We are no longer protesting someone else's politics. Reconstitution is about making our own politics."[28]

Traditionally inactive engineering students joined the protests and began to consider their social responsibility. As one engineering action group's leaflet said:

In the past few days, a thousand Engineering students at Berkeley have redirected their usual daily activities to the cause of ending the war in Vietnam...Because of this concerted effort, Engineering students have been recognized for the first time as a socially responsible force. We can no longer afford to allow the stereotypes of us as socially irresponsible technicians to be sustained.[29]

The staff of the Engineering Library at Berkeley organized an ongoing Social Awareness Collection around the theme of "The Social Responsibility of Engineers in a Peace-Oriented Society," and at City College in New York 1,000 engineering students voted to join the strike there until U.S. troops left Cambodia.[30]

Law students commented that when they enter their profession they will "be more likely to change places and to raise political issues in the law firms." Some began to see their roles as "participant reformers" rather than "expert manipulators."

Music and drama students performed in the streets, while other art students built a mobile gallery which travelled around the state. One student wrote:

The University of California Berkeley has become a piece of art. Though its art museum has closed down, its concert halls are empty, its stages are dark, this campus for the first time realized the real function and meaning of art: to communicate, to change perception, to make us react.

All sorts of barriers are being broken down: art history students are silk screening alongside art practice students, journalism activists are working with design majors to make effective leaflets, sculptors are designing sets for drama students' street theatre. We've destroyed the artificial walls, and our energy and creativity are expanding at a rate unfathomable to us just one week ago.[31]

Among students, there was the feeling that the *process* of protest was a significant aspect of the movement and that the bureaucratic mode of work was to be prevented from setting in. At Berkeley, one action group's printed statement called on all strikers "to enjoy one's tasks and to learn from them. To prevent stagnation, various groups have begun to rotate positions to allow new ideas and faces to flow from one group to another and to prevent bureaucratic entrenchment of ideas and people in single positions."

Besides deepening and consolidating the movement within academia, campus activists also sought to spread the strike to consumers and workers. On May 8, the faculty at the University of Colorado in Boulder voted to accept a strike program which included a plan "to spark a national buyers' strike." Although the idea was popular from coast to coast and even included a call for a world economic boycott of the United States to begin June 1, 1970, the lack of ongoing national organization prevented it from becoming real.

A popular slogan in the Boston area during the strike was "Shut it Down! Open it Up!" As in many other parts of the country, the striking universities became a base from which working-class communities, high schools, and outlying areas were systematically canvassed by the strikers. Groups of students and faculty at 40 percent of the nation's universities went off campus to neighborhoods and workplaces during May, some groups travelling up to 200 miles to talk with people in isolated areas.[32] Around the country, there were a series of widely publicized haircuts which students hoped would make it easier for them to communicate with middle America.

On May 15, the Cambridge, Massachusetts underground newspaper, the *Old Mole*, called on the striking students to "deepen the strike inside the universities, and to spread it outside...Sure we're a long way from a general strike. But we were a long way from a student strike a few years ago." A wall poster in Cambridge called upon students to "spread the strike" into a general strike against the war, a strike modelled on May 1968:

> Students visited every factory in the Cambridge area Wednesday, May 6 with leaflets calling for a sick-out against the war. Liaison committees should be developed in every occupied university to communicate daily with the employees of each major enterprise in the university area. This is just what the French students did in the General Strike of May 1968. We should talk with workers individually, getting to know them, as well as leafletting.

The leaflets which students brought to factory gates were direct in their call for more than an end to war:

> We have acted not because we do not value education but because we refuse an education which trains officers and strategists; that equips us only to serve business interests as technicians making your work more profitable for them and unbearable for you; that produces "scholars" cut off from social realities...We are not so crazy as to believe that students by themselves have the power to end the evils that oppress us all. This can come about only when all of us act together to take power over our lives from those who wield it today.

As the above sources reveal, the aspirations of the campus strike went beyond even the transformation of the universities or opposition to the war. The attempts made to broaden the strike, however, detonated reactions among other sectors of the population, not only bringing new supporters into the movement, but also causing a reaction *against* the strikers.

The Crisis as a Whole

The present crisis is the most profound one in our entire national history: more profound than either World War I or II, more profound than even the Civil War, and more profound than the struggle for national independence in the 18th Century. In contrast to the previous crises, the present one finds the country not only divided, confused, and embittered, frustrated and enraged, but lacking the one vital element of self-confidence.

—Sheldon Wolin to the American Psychiatric Association,
May 1970

The chain reaction of events touched off by the invasion of Cambodia triggered widespread responses throughout the United States. No longer was it possible for middle Americans to concern themselves with their individual lives while they turned their backs on the international consequences of their tax dollars. With the shots fired at Kent State, the most important mental health problem in our society became the war in Indochina. While some chose to act out their aggressions on peaceniks, more focused their anger on the government that perpetuated a genocidal war.

The student movement created a context which affected tens of millions of Americans. Nearly everyone had relatives or friends studying at college, and when the entire university system appeared under attack, fired upon and occupied by the National Guard and police, and subjected to verbal barrages from the highest levels of government, everyday life became politicized. At the same time as some polls showed 79 percent of the American people wanted an end to the war, other polls said the major problem perceived in the country was campus unrest. Although these seem like contradictory findings, these polls indicate the polarization of the society into opposing viewpoints.

On the one side, the striking students found support for their movement outside universities. One hundred art galleries and several museums closed down to protest the war, and when the Metropolitan Museum of New York refused to close, 500 artists sat-in there. Forty-three Nobel Prize winners (75 percent of all U.S. winners) sent Nixon a joint letter urging an immediate end to the war. Significantly, the May strike also mobilized high school students, workers, soldiers, prisoners, activists from the women's movement, and professionals.

On the other side, many people went on an anti-student, anti-intellectual rampage. Skilled construction workers violently attacked anti-war marches in New York City, Buffalo, and St. Louis, and even a few students attacked campus demonstrations. At the University of New Mexico, three people were stabbed in a fight over whether or not to lower the flag after the Kent State murders. It seems as though the shots fired at Kent State signalled the start of a new Civil War. The *National Guardsman* warned in June 1970:

> And 'though there was shock, horror, and bitter denunciation in the wake of the Kent deaths, significant was the fact that the Guard as a whole and those involved in Kent as well—were supported verbally by thousands of Americans who have felt their lives and property endangered by the rising tide of violence and by the drift toward possible revolution.

The strike demand for an end to the incarceration of Bobby Seale and political prisoners in the United States reflected a consciousness of the connectedness of domestic racism and international genocide, and this connection was made frighteningly clear on May 11 when six black people

were killed—shot in the back—and twenty were wounded during a riot in
Augusta, Georgia, two days after a black teenager had been beaten to death in
the county jail. Three days later at Jackson State University, two people were
killed and twelve were wounded when the Mississippi Highway Patrol
opened fire on a women's dormitory.

Minorities and the Anti-War Movement

Prior to the murders in the South, black and third world students had not
participated in the strike or the anti-war movement to the same extent that they
had struggled against racism. In 1968 at Kent State University, for example,
400 of the university's 597 black students resigned to protest that institution's
racism, and a solidarity boycott by SDS helped build the impetus which led to
the demonstration of May 4, 1970. In February of 1970, over one-third of the
student body (894 out of 2,300) was arrested at all-black Mississippi Valley
State College at a demonstration in support of thirty demands related to
improvement of conditions on campus. As late as April 1970, racist university
conditions ranked first among the many reasons for campus disruptions. The
war in Indochina was close behind in second place,[33] followed by other issues
like student power, the quality of student life, and ecology.

When the student strike erupted, black students intensified their struggles
around domestic issues. At Southeast Junior College in Chicago, students
went on strike on May 13 (the day before Jackson State), not to protest the
war or the killings at Kent State (or in Augusta) but to rename the school after
slain Black Panthers Fred Hampton and Mark Clark, for the reinstatement of
the black studies director, and for a black college president.[34] Classes there
were suspended indefinitely on May 14 after police were called in to quell the
second day of demonstrations. On May 8 at Morehead State College in
Kentucky, black students interrupted a convocation concerning the war and
the deaths at Kent State to present twenty-one demands of their own.[35]

Prior to the strike, the student movement, like the progressive forces in
the country, was generally split along racial lines. On March 21, 1970, the day
after a shotgun blast had narrowly missed killing a black student, the chairman
of the Black League for Action at California State College in Pennsylvania said
he was tired of lip service and "hippies who cause trouble."[36] At San Jose State
College in California, a week-long ecology "Survival Fair" had culminated on
February 20 with the funeral and· burial of a new car to protest smog and
environmental pollution. About seventy-five black and Chicano students,
supporters of Huey Newton, protested the protest by passing out leaflets
saying: "It must be made clear that this is a plot by 'The Man' to mesmerize the
people into thinking their environment, meaning the air we breathe, is a basic
issue for change."[37]

Although anti-war sentiment was most widespread among minorities[38]
and it was disproportionately minorities who fought and died for the
Pentagon on the battlefields of Vietnam, there were only scattered demonstrations by minorities against the Cambodian invasion. In Tuscaloosa, Alabama,
thirty-seven students at an all black school were arrested, and in North

Carolina, hundreds of black students marched to the state capitol on May 8 to ask the Governor to withdraw his support for the Cambodian fiasco. It should be remembered that thousands of blacks had been killed or wounded during the urban riots of 1967 and 1968 and that blacks who demonstrated were taking far more risks than their white counterparts. Nonetheless, at Jackson State University, 500 students rallied on May 7 to protest the Cambodian invasion, and the next day, a boycott of classes began. As the movement was sustained, police began to hear reports that the students intended to march on the college ROTC building. When the police and the Mississippi Highway Patrol attempted to move onto the campus to secure the building, they unexpectedly opened fire on a women's dormitory, killing two students and wounding twelve others, thereby sending a message to the entire country.

Ten days earlier, the murders at Kent State had appeared to unite a racially divided movement, but the lack of response to the deaths in Augusta and at Jackson State served as proof to many people of the movement's racism. While the campus reaction to the murders at Augusta and Jackson State was small in comparison to the outrage after Kent State, it was not inconsiderable. It was, however, mainly black students who mobilized. The National Guard was called in once again to Ohio State University, this time to seal off the campus. Thousands of high school students in New York and Chicago closed their schools in solidarity with those murdered in the South. At Hunter College in New York, a third world coalition blockaded entrances on May 12 to protest the school's not having been shut down in response to the killings in Augusta.

Black students were joined by civil rights activists and college presidents in their protests. The president of Morehouse College issued a call to all 123 black colleges in the United States, requesting a meeting to protest the war in Southeast Asia and the murder of blacks at home. On May 20, a group of fifteen black college presidents went to the White House and met with Nixon for over two hours, even though the meeting was originally scheduled to last only forty-five minutes.[39] A march against repression through Georgia, during which more than 275 people were arrested, culminated in a rally of over 10,000 people in Atlanta, where anti-war and civil rights forces converged on May 22.

As the crisis intensified after the shootings at Jackson State, a coalition of thirty moderate civil rights and anti-poverty organizations formed the Mississippi United Front and called for self-defense. Gun shops reported a surge in black customers on the eve of a statewide boycott against white businesses. At Jackson State there was a vigil of students from May 15 to 23 in order to prevent evidence from being taken away by the same Highway Patrol which had just done the shooting. The FBI finally came to get the evidence.

In this same period of time, anti-war protests intensified among Puerto Ricans and Chicanos. The Puerto Rican Socialist Party, an organization formed in the 1960s, led massive anti-war demonstrations in Puerto Rico and New York. Anti-war sentiment among Chicanos brought a call for a Chicano Anti-War Moratorium in Los Angeles. On August 29, 1970, the police attacked the 30,000 marchers, killing three people (including journalist Reuben Salazar) and wounding sixty. More than 200 people were arrested, and after the night of fighting was over, property damage ran into the millions of dollars.[40] On January 31, 1971, another Chicano Moratorium was called to protest the war as well as police repression, and the police again attacked, killing one person and wounding at least nineteen.[41] The Chicanos responded by intensifying their struggle and building organizations like the Brown Berets.

Like never before, the *eros* effect of 1970 posed the possibility of unity among all the progressive forces in motion. When thousands of students in Washington, D.C. found themselves fighting with police, for example, they were frequently taken in by the black community there, which literally opened its doors to those in need of a safe haven. At the same time, the support for the Panthers provided by the four million striking students bore fruit when Huey Newton was released from jail on May 29 (in the midst of the student strike). With the coming together of blacks, Hispanics, and whites in 1970, the movement appeared to be moving toward a genuinely revolutionary position, one which went beyond existing social divisions.

In September, the Panthers' call for a Revolutionary Peoples' Constitutional Convention in Philadelphia was answered by over 10,000 people, including a sizeable contingent of students and young whites. As an indication of how much existing social antagonisms were transcended, one of the most spirited and well received groups was from the newly emergent gay liberation movement. The workshops drafted outlines to comprise an "Internationalist Constitution," not a national one. Its Preface began:

> We, the people of Babylon, declare an International Bill of Rights: that all people are guaranteed the right to life, liberty, and the pursuit of happiness, that all people of the world be free from dehumanization and intervention in their internal affairs by a foreign power...Reparations should be made to oppressed people throughout the world, and we pledge ourselves to take the wealth of this country and make it available as reparation.

The new Constitution contained similar statements from working groups of street people, women, gays, children, prisoners, students, health workers, and artists. (These documents are contained in the Appendix.)

Although the September convention roared its approval of the program as a whole, the gathering two months later in Washington, D.C. (on November 4) failed miserably, largely because of the Panthers' decision that the new Constitution was a mistake. The change in the Party's orientation "back to the black community" and the emergence of electoral politics as the defining tactic of the Panthers proved to be the beginning of a bitter and bloody internal feud which tore the organization—and the movement—apart.

Workers and the Strike

If the events of the past two weeks have done nothing else, they should have convinced the U.S. that the student protest movement has to be

taken seriously. . . . The invasion of Cambodia and the senseless shooting of four students at Kent State University in Ohio have consolidated the academic community against the war, against business, and against government. This is a dangerous situation. It threatens the whole economic and social structure of the nation.
                                        —Business Week, May 16, 1970

If there was one sector of American society besides the Pentagon that stood behind Nixon throughout the uprisings of May, it was the top leadership of the AFL-CIO. There were many workers, of course, and some labor leaders who opposed the war. Already in 1968, the United Auto Workers had quit the AFL-CIO because of George Meany's support for the war. During May 1970, however, Meany and the majority of top union bureaucrats stood by the President. They not only sided with Nixon against the striking students, but they also embraced the anti-labor policies used by the Nixon administration to amass the resources to fight the war.

Beginning in 1967, as real wages had begun to decline because of the inflation fueled by the Vietnam War,[42] there were more strikes, contract rejections, and wildcats by workers in the United States than at any time since the Great Depression. Many observers considered the thousands of construction workers thrown out of work because of high interest rates to be one of the costs of the war. On November 11, 1967, less than a month after 175,000 anti-war demonstrators had marched in Washington, D.C. and 50,000 had confronted the National Guard at the Pentagon, a two-day conference of unions was held. Keynote speakers Martin Luther King, Jr., UN General Secretary U Thant, John Kenneth Galbraith, and Victor Reuther addressed over 500 representatives of fifty international unions who gathered from thirty-eight states. The convention unanimously called for an immediate end to the bombings of northern Vietnam and a U.S. willingness to recognize the National Liberation Front in southern Vietnam.[43]

Two and a-half years later, at the same time as the students went on strike, many workers were involved in strikes as well. On May 13, the Federal Mediation and Conciliation Services reported it was mediating 391 strikes, including 166 walkouts involving the construction industry. In March, the first major walkout of postal workers had occurred over the heads of their union leaders. In defiance of public employee anti-strike laws, union orders, and federal injunctions, the wildcat strike had quickly spread to more than 200 cities and towns. It was only when Nixon brought out thousands of National Guard troops to handle the mail that the strike was broken. In the same month, special legislation from Congress had averted a national railroad strike. On April 29, despite a law prohibiting public employees from striking, teachers in Boston went on strike, joining their colleagues in Los Angeles, Newark, Atlanta, Muskogee (Oklahoma), and Baldwin (Pennsylvania) in demanding higher pay and smaller classrooms.[44] In Honolulu, a strike of blue-collar workers was joined by thousands of their white-collar associates and drastically curtailed all public services for almost three days.

In seven states during April and May, wildcat walkouts and other disruptions were set off by dissident Teamsters protesting a tentative national contract which their leaders had negotiated. At one point, the disruptions affected an estimated 500,000 workers who were on strike or idled by cutoffs of truck service.[45] Tensions ran highest in Ohio, where over 4,000 National Guardsmen were called up under a state of emergency after two-thirds of the state's eighty-eight counties had reported incidents of violence. In Cleveland alone, there was a month-long blockade of city streets and sixty-seven million dollars worth of damages.[46]

The original authorization to call up the National Guard in Ohio had not come because of the disturbances at Kent State but because of the Teamsters' strike. Two regiments, the 107th Armored Cavalry and the 145th Infantry, were on active duty in Akron as early as April 29. If was not until *the day after* the shooting at Kent State on May 4 that the April 29 authorization to call up the National Guard was amended to include the city of Kent.[47]

In St. Louis, trucks and police cars were bombarded with rocks and bricks on May 3 when 300 strikers tried to prevent a truck convoy from leaving a freight terminal. There were injuries and arrests followed by firebombings and shootings. Gunfire was reported in Illinois, Michigan, California, and Pennsylvania. The militancy of the Teamsters Union, however, was a double-edged sword, particularly since by late July, César Chavez and the United Farmworkers of California (UFWOC) were marching against attempts by the Teamsters to unionize in the Salinas Valley. The UFWOC had waged a five-year battle against the growers, and the Teamsters were obviously trying to undercut the UFWOC's base of support.

The epidemic proportion of rank and file contract rejections, dramatized best by the April Teamsters' revolt against their union leadership, had prompted a panel consisting of the construction industry, the top building trades unionists, and Secretary of Labor George Shultz (before his promotion to the White House staff) to propose that the right to vote on contracts be taken away from the rank and file in the construction industry.[48] In June 1970, in a decision which astonished many people, the U.S. Supreme Court ruled that employees could be forced back to work if their union agreements contained a no-strike pledge and an arbitration clause.

In the midst of this anti-labor campaign, Nixon and Company incited thousands of hardhats to attack student anti-war rallies. More than 60,000 construction workers rallied in support of Nixon, the country, and the war and beat up anti-war demonstrators on national television. They were skillfully manipulated by the "dirty tricks" of the White House "plumbers." Their union leadership was instructed to tell them that if they did not sign the daily roll at the mass rally, they would lose their pay for the day.[49] Smaller groups of several hundred hardhats had attacked anti-war rallies earlier in the week, and it was later revealed that their bosses had let these workers know they would be paid for time taken off to attack students.

It was a vicious circle: The hardhats were losing work because of the economic problems caused by the war; the students who opposed the war might have helped to remedy the situation of these workers but were attacked by them. Furthermore, more than 12,000 unskilled construction workers (mainly blacks) had shut down all construction in Philadelphia, laying off more than 3,000 skilled workers, in a strike for equal pay for skilled and unskilled labor alike. The racism of the construction industry and unions was under attack in Seattle, Pittsburgh, Buffalo, Washington, D.C., and Boston.[50]

The fragmentation of the population made it all the more easy for Nixon to maintain order through manipulation. From a pre-arranged meeting at the White House where he was presented with an honorary hardhat to the creation of an all-black police riot squad in Washington, D.C. for use against the mainly white anti-war demonstrators, Nixon proved that the age-old tactic of divide-and-conquer could work well even in the twentieth century.

Contrary to what was reported by the mass media, however, students and workers in the United States were not at war. As early as November 1969, workers at General Electric had gone on strike and had received demonstrations of support at many universities, including Boston University, MIT, the University of Wisconsin at Madison, and the University of Illinois (where the National Guard had to be called out to control the students). On May 21, 1970, the day after hardhats in New York City, Buffalo, and St. Louis had attacked peaceniks, some of their co-workers marched through New York City as part of a 40,000 strong labor-student anti-war rally. At this rally, representatives of twenty-eight unions and seventeen campuses came together in solidarity with those murdered at Kent State, Jackson State, and Augusta. They condemned George Meany and the thirty top labor leaders who, by a twenty-seven to three vote, had said that Nixon should not be influenced by the anti-war movement. At the end of the rally, nine people were injured when police unexpectedly rode their horses into the crowd.[51]

The relationship between striking students and workers on the West Coast was even better. After the invasion of Cambodia, every AFL-CIO county central labor council in the vicinity of San Francisco, representing some 400,000 workers, called upon Congress to censure Nixon "for his deception, dishonesty, and violation of our Constitution," to repeal the Gulf of Tonkin resolution, and to cut off funds for combat operations in Indochina by the end of the year.[52] A full page ad in San Francisco's two daily papers on May 18, signed by 463 trade union leaders (including fifty-three from the building and metal crafts), concluded: "We want a cease-fire NOW! We want out of Cambodia NOW! We want out of Vietnam NOW! We've had it!" A similar ad was signed by 100 union officers in Ohio.

In San Jose, California, a standing committee for cooperation between striking students and the Santa Clara County Central Labor Council already existed. A year earlier, there had been a significant alliance between striking workers at Standard Oil in Richmond, California, and striking students and teachers at San Francisco State College. Both strikes had been long and difficult, and the police were particularly brutal in their bloody suppression of the strikers at San Francisco State. At a joint press conference announcing the alliance, Jake Jacobs, secretary-treasurer of Local 1-561 of the Oil, Chemical and Atomic Workers said, "It is not just police brutality that united us. We are all exploited, black workers more than whites, but we all have the same enemy, the big corporations. And it is corporations like our enemy, Standard Oil, that control the Boards of Trustees of the state colleges the students are fighting."[53]

After the invasion of Cambodia, there were several union conferences which supported the anti-war movement. On May 8, representatives of 5,000 faculty from twenty-three California campuses met in San Diego and formed the United Professors of California. After three days of debate on how their union should relate to public stands on political issues, the delegates overwhelmingly voted to "condemn Nixon's escalation" and called for the remainder of the academic year to be devoted to bringing the war to an end.[54] A day earlier in Denver, a convention of the American Federation of State, County, and Municipal Employees (AFSCME) unanimously passed a resolution calling for immediate withdrawal from Indochina "consistent with the safety of U.S. troops." Union representatives of the Teamsters, United Auto Workers of California, and the AFL-CIO Amalgamated Clothing Workers signed resolutions calling for "Peace Now." On May 11, 800 of the 4,000 university employees at MIT voted to strike for the three demands of the students as did workers at Berkeley, Harvard, Columbia, and other universities.

Walter Reuther had personally addressed a message to Nixon on behalf of the UAW protesting the escalation of the war and the killing of students at Kent State, and the vice-chairman of the Union of Teamsters and Ware-housemen called on workers to speak out against the war and to take the lead in all actions against Nixon. In Detroit and Chicago, a planned three-minute work stoppage on May 15, called in memory of Reuther (who died in a plane crash on May 10), turned into a day-long anti-war wildcat: 2,000 workers walked off the job at one plant alone (Ford Assembly in Chicago's Southside), and in all, 30,000 workers struck at twenty plants.[55] As a gesture of solidarity, longshoremen in Oregon and Teamsters in Ohio refused to cross student informational picket lines. Ten Chicago union leaders supported the local student strikes, and in many counties across the country, central labor councils voiced opposition to the invasion of Cambodia.

At a conference in late June, over 1,000 trade unionists representing four and a-half million workers called for immediate U.S. withdrawal from Indochina and formed Labor for Peace, an organization dedicated to "inform, educate and arouse the membership to act to end the war now." Will Pary, a district secretary-treasurer of the Western Association of Pulp and Paper Workers said: "Unemployment, inflation, war, racism, repression and worth-less labor leaders leave the laboring man in desperate straits...Nixon is the worst anti-labor President we've had."[56]

In Washington, D.C., government workers began to question national policy. On June 1, 1970, *U.S. News* reported that: "Federal workers, supposedly non-political, are beginning to badger office holders, elected and appointed, on the course of national policy." At least one organization, the Federal Employees for a Democratic Society, modeled itself on SDS and grew out of anti-war protests by government workers. By the summer of 1969, they claimed a membership of hundreds within most bureaus of the federal government, and in 1970, Joseph Califano, Jr., credited them with the capability to "operate as a shadow government."[57]

In retrospect, the mass media stereotyped the working class as a solidly pro-Nixon, pro-war force, but the actions of American workers during May 1970 reveal that they were deeply divided on the issue of the war. Manipulated by reactionary leadership to attack students, the nation's hardhats provided a clear indication that the trade unions were no longer in the forefront of social progress. Even though many trade unionists supported the striking students and the idea of a general strike of workers and students repeatedly surfaced in May, the split in the working class and the racial polarization of American society made the actualization of a general strike a project for the distant future.

The Revolt Within the Military

In the Army, dissent is a major issue, on a scale unprecedented in the history of this nation. Radical newspapers are being published, anti-war coffeehouses are being opened, and military discipline is no longer accepted at its face value.

—Joseph A. Califano, Jr., 1970

After the deaths at Kent State, entire companies of U.S. troops in Vietnam refused to cross over into Cambodia. Their black armbands symbolized their solidarity with the striking students, and their actions were true to their convictions. Combat refusal became so commonplace that separate companies were set up for men who refused to engage the "enemy." It appears that the *eros* effect of the anti-war movement was more successful in reaching soldiers and sailors than anyone else. Across the country, groups of activists formed coffeehouses for GIs, helped start newspapers, leafletted incoming troop ships and planes, and set up counseling services for those who wished to leave the armed forces.[58] Although the nationwide participation of GIs in the anti-war movement reached its highest level in May 1970,[59] it began many years before that.

As early as 1967, the 198th Light Infantry Brigade had rioted at Fort Hood, Texas and went to the stockade rather than to Vietnam. In 1969, an entire company of the 196th Light Brigade had publicly joined the sit-in movement and sat down on the battlefield. That same year, another rifle company, from the notorious 1st Air Cavalry, had flatly refused (on CBS national news) to advance down a dangerous trail. The first GI-led march for peace was in February 1968 (during the Tet offensive), when 7,000 people demonstrated in San Francisco. By 1970, U.S. soldiers all over the world—England, Germany, and within this country—were marching for peace.

The anti-war movement and the counterculture were the forerunners of the GI movement, and when the campuses erupted, many soldiers were quick to join the spreading movement. For the first time, Vietnam veterans who were patients in VA hospitals got involved in the peace movement in large numbers during May 1970.[60] Members of the Vietnam Veterans Against the War helped to lead student strikes on many campuses. Membership in that organization jumped about 50 percent to 2,000 by the summer of 1970, and two years later there were 2,500 members on active duty in Vietnam alone.

Never before in the history of the United States had veterans so massively protested while the war in which they had fought was still going on. Not many active duty GIs in 1970 had spent time on the campuses, but the diffusion of the movement's thoughts and actions into the military, while organized by some, also took the course of music and cultural politics, an opposition to the "military madness" of authoritarianism, enforced short hair, and the overt repression of the base which contrasted so starkly with the comparatively "free" nature of society. *Scanlan's* reported in January 1971 that wigs were one of the biggest selling items at military post exchanges in the United States and abroad.[61]

Drug abuse became commonplace in Vietnam among American GIs. Dr. Joel H. Kaplan, who helped set up the Army's first formal drug abuse program in Vietnam, reported in June 1970 that:

> While I was there, the Pentagon announced that there were only 3500 marijuana users in the entire U.S. Army. My team alone saw that many in our own patient population. My KO (neuro-psychiatric specialist) estimated that 50 to 80 percent of the Army's enlisted men tried marijuana once . . . I would estimate that between 10 and 20 percent of the GIs in Vietnam were drug abusers. A drug abuser with a daily dependence would smoke a marijuana joint in the morning when he got up, like enjoying a cup of coffee. He would drop some barbituates during the morning, smoke a couple of more joints at lunch, and in the evening would wind up on opium.[62]

A Congressional study in 1971 found that there were at least 30,000 GIs addicted to heroin.

As morale broke down, officers became legitimate targets for the rifles and grenades of GIs. The Pentagon admitted to 209 "fragging" incidents in 1970, more than twice the toll for the previous year. The *Armed Forces Journal* reported that in one division, the Americal, fraggings were running at the rate of one a week and that news of fraggings "will bring cheers at troop movies or in bivouacs of certain units." In April 1970, an underground military paper interviewed a former platoon commander, Sergeant Richard Williams, who had served for seven years in Vietnam. "When I was a guard in the Long Binh stockade," he said, "there were 23 guys there for killing their C.O.'s [commanding officers] and 17 others were already on trial for killing C.O.'s."[63] Lieutenant-Colonel Weldon Honeycutt, a commander at Hamburger Hill, where his orders to attack had resulted in the deaths of most of his men, was proclaimed "G.I. Enemy Number One" by an underground publication which issued a wanted poster offering a $10,000 reward for his death. Subsequent reports of grenade and Claymore mine explosions near him indicated that attempts were being made to collect the bounty. According to Army records, beginning in 1969, there were at least 551 fraggings which resulted in 86 dead and over 700 wounded.[64]

Resistors Within the Army (RITA) units were established in Vietnam and the United States, a type of resistance which losing armies in World War I

(Russia and France in 1917, and Germany and Austria in 1918) and World War II (Italy in 1943) had experienced, but one which had never occurred in U.S. history.

The desertion rates were incredibly high during the period of the student strike. Officially, there were 65,643 deserters from the Army alone in 1970. The number of men who left the military in the six years (1967-1972) reached almost half a million. According to the *Wall Street Journal*, at least 500 GIs deserted every day of the week during May 1970. Many went over to the side of the "enemy." The *London Express* reported that U.S. intelligence estimates were that as many as sixty soldiers a week—the majority of them black—were crossing over to the NLF. The *Express* also reported a top-secret campaign to capture or kill these defectors, particularly since some were using their knowledge of U.S. operations to cut in on short wave transmissions to misdirect artillery fire and lead helicopters into ambush.[65]

Resistance occurred in the Navy as well. In March 1970, an ammunition ship was hijacked on the high seas by some of its crewmen and sailed to Cambodia, where the mutineers were granted political asylum. In late May, the destroyer *USS Robert Anderson* was set to leave San Diego for Vietnam when someone "threw something into the gears." The destroyer was drydocked for two months, and the incident was not reported until June 14, three weeks after it happened.

On Armed Forces Day, May 16, 1970, there were marches, rallies, and political rock festivals at twenty-two different bases in the country with the participation of at least forty-three different GI anti-war groups. The demonstrations at five of these military installations (Fort McClellan, Alabama; Charleston Naval Base, South Carolina; Fort Hood, Texas; Fort Benning, Georgia; and Fort Riley, Kansas) marked the first time that anti-war actions had taken place there. One thousand people, marching through the streets of Killeen near Fort Hood, shouted demands: "U.S. out of Southeast Asia now! Free Bobby Seale and all political prisoners! Avenge the dead of Kent State, Jackson State, and Augusta!"

The military high command was so threatened by the wave of uprisings rolling through the troops that regularly scheduled Armed Forces Day events were cancelled at twenty-eight other bases. At Fort Ord, south of San Francisco, most GIs were assigned to their barracks, riot control, or to digging a trench between the edge of the base and Route 1, a barrier against planned demonstrations later reinforced by miles of concertina wire. At Camp Pendleton in Oceanside, California, all Marines were restricted to the base, and, for the first time, platoons assigned to riot control received orders to shoot to kill in case of disturbances on the base. At Fort Dix, New Jersey, GIs were restricted to base, and the 3,000 demonstrators who attempted to march onto the base were gassed.

On July 4, 1970, 1,000 black and white GIs assembled in Heidelberg, West Germany, and were joined by Germans to call for "*Freiheit für Bobby Seale.*" As black soldiers stepped up their struggle against racism, 250 black GIs at Fort Hood burned down two reenlistment centers as well as one of the base dormitories. Also in July, 200 black soldiers seized a section of Fort

Carson and held it for a time by fighting off military police.[66]

The anti-war movement's political outreach to GIs was intensified after the student strike. By 1971, there were at least 25 anti-war coffeehouses and 144 underground GI newspapers. The massive rebellion in the military meant that it was only a matter of time before the United States had to withdraw from Vietnam since its GIs refused to fight. With the return of the veterans, the anti-war movement was provided with a nucleus of leadership in the period after the student strike. The students and soldiers of that time, although segregated into different worlds, came together in the struggle to end the war.

The Cultural Dimensions of the Crisis

> *Tin soldiers and Nixon coming*
> *We're finally on our own.*
> *This summer I hear the drumming*
> *Four dead in Ohio.*
> *Got to get down to it.*
> *Soldiers are gunning us down.*
> *Should have been done long ago!*
>
> —Crosby, Stills, Nash, and Young

The shots fired at Kent State and the attacks by hardhats in New York and St. Louis were forms of cultural as much as political conflict. Without the underlying current of resentment against long-haired peaceniks, no amount of manipulation could have made construction workers attack the children of the Be-Ins and the Summer of Love. Since 1967, a new territory had begun to emerge, one where careers and the compartmentalization of straight society had no validity, where money, prestige, and power had been rejected in favor of humanism and naturalism. This new dimension to the culture of industrialized societies may have since become absorbed and acceptable, but in 1970, it appeared as though it was under attack with no turning back.

As early as 1963, artists and crafts people had begun to gather in the East Village and Haight-Ashbury. In the summer of 1966, the Diggers began distributing free food in San Francisco, and after the 1967 Summer of Love, hippies and youth communities sprang up across the country (and around the world). The counterculture sought to create human community where it did not exist. Its political expression through the anti-war movement did not express its total rejection of technocratic culture. Young people broke away from deodorized bodies, shiny cars, and the plastic food of corporate America to live a different kind of life. Once the existence of Haight-Ashbury, the East Village, and other havens became widely known, people freely migrated to these meccas to live their lives according to their own values. At People's Park and elsewhere, they fought (and loved) police and National Guardsmen who were mobilized against them. The Berkeley Liberation Program, written at the height of the struggle for People's Park in 1969, expressed the militancy of a culture under siege:

The people of Berkeley must increase their combativeness; develop, tighten and toughen their organizations; and transcend their middle-class, ego-centered life styles...We shall create a genuine community and control it to serve our material and spiritual needs. We shall develop new forms of democratic participation and new, more humane styles of work and play. In solidarity with other revolutionary centers and movements, our Berkeley will permanently challenge the present system and act as one of the many training grounds for the liberation of the planet.

Communes and collectives sprang up in major cities, small towns, and rural regions. Experimentation in new ways of living and in raising new generations of children were begun, and free schools, food co-ops, and collective bookstores were created to preserve and spread the new culture.

The "underground" press quickly spread throughout the country. From five papers which reached an estimated 50,000 readers in 1966, the Underground Press Syndicate grew to include 200 papers with six million readers by the summer of 1970,[67] and in high schools, there were an additional 500 underground papers.[68] Liberation News Service began in 1967, and by 1970, it was supplying over 400 outlets with a weekly source of up-to-date information on progressive movements throughout the world. As early as March 1969, over 30,000 copies of the *Black Panther* were being distributed across the country.

The emergence of this new culture was a time of optimism, and the spirit of the New Age permeated all areas of society, making its way, for example, onto the stage in shows like "Hair" and performances of the Living Theater. Electronic music became a significant medium of communication for the new culture and for its proliferation to GIs and young workers. Free concerts in the parks helped create a space where political messages and musical energy flowed together. It appeared that the nihilism of the Beats and their withdrawal from political responsibility had given way to collective action.

After People's Park and Kent State, of course, the emergent culture increasingly became a culture of resistance. "We're finally on our own" was what the shots at Kent State meant to many people. The murders of students at Kent and Jackson State had an intimidating effect on many students and young people at the same time as they served to intensify the commitment of others and to spread the movement even further. As the Scranton Commission put it:

During the past decade, this youth culture has developed rapidly. It has become ever more distinct and has acquired an almost religious fervor through a process of advancing personal commitment. This process has been spurred by the emergence within the larger society of opposition, of political protest. As such opposition became manifest—and occasionally violently manifest—participants in the youth culture felt challenged, and their commitment to that culture and to the political protest it prompts grew stronger and bolder. Over time, more and more students have moved in the direction of an even deeper and more inclusive sense of opposition to the larger society. As their alienation became more profound, their willingness to use violence increased.[69]

A new wave of military attacks from the radical movement occurred during the summer of 1970, a wave which had been building steadily since 1965, as the map on the following page indicates. On June 9, 1970, the Weather Underground bombed police headquarters in New York City, and two months later, the Army Math Research Center in Madison was gutted (and a graduate student accidentally killed) by a massive explosion placed in retaliation for that institution's research and development of an infrared device which had been used by the CIA to locate and murder Che Guevara in Bolivia. On August 7, 1970, Jonathan Jackson stood up in a Marin County courtroom with an assault rifle in hand. He freed three prisoners, and they took a judge and a district attorney hostage, hoping to exchange their prisoners for George Jackson (a leading member of the Panthers who was imprisoned for life for his alleged role in a $70 robbery). A barrage of gunfire directed against their escape van left only Ruchell Magee alive. By September, half of the FBI's most wanted list were radicals, including Angela Davis (who was indicted for owning the gun used in the Marin Courthouse raid). These fugitives, some of whom have yet to be captured by the FBI, could depend on many loyal supporters who lived from coast to coast.

When the Black Liberation Army and Weatherpeople went underground to begin the armed struggle at the end of 1969, the mass movement lost many of its finest members, activists with experience accumulated over years of organizing. The type of leadership they exemplified in going underground was a self-destructive force in the New Left. By abandoning the mass movement, they negated the promise of a new fusion of politics and culture at the very time when an increasing number of people looked to them for direction.

The appearance of guerrilla warfare in the United States was one indication of the legitimation crisis of the state, a political dimension of the cultural crisis which spread to young workers like those at Lordstown, Ohio, who refused to produce forty hours a week, to soldiers in Vietnam who refused to fight, and to housewives who refused to remain politically marginalized. The rupture in the legitimacy of American power and authority, however, was nowhere clearer than among those confined to the country's prison cells. After the norms and values of the society had been publicly called into question by the student strike, a massive prisoners' movement erupted, reaching its high point at Attica State Prison in New York and San Quentin in California. By the end of September 1971, more than fifty persons had been killed in the bloody suppression of the wave of prison rebellions which rocked the nation. The majority of those killed were at Attica, where forty-two people died after Governor Nelson Rockefeller refused to negotiate with the inmate committee coordinating the revolt.

Attica symbolized the crisis of legitimacy which shook the United States in the early 1970s. Millions of people were no longer content to live by the previous rules governing social interaction. From blind patriotism to restitutive justice, previously accepted values lost their magical ability to mold

Map 2

Guerrilla Attacks in the U.S., 1965-1970

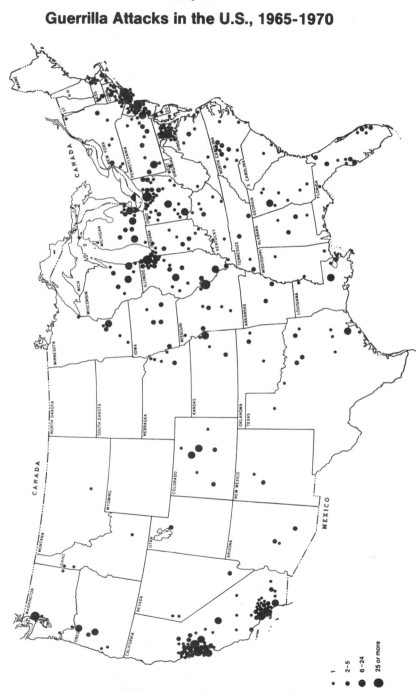

Source: **Scanlan's Monthly,** Vol. 1, Number 8 (January 1971), p. 48.

behavior. The work ethic, bureaucratic authority, and compulsive consumption were challenged by the generation born after World War II—a generation raised amidst unprecedented prosperity. As the baby-boomers began to develop a culture based on cooperation and communalism, it appeared to many Americans that their children had gone crazy, that the comfort they had struggled through the Depression to achieve for their families was being rejected as corrupt. What the Diggers had said in 1966 seemed to express the feelings of millions of people in the early 1970s:

> Don't drop half out. Drop all the way out. Anything that is part of the system is the whole system. It's all hung on the same string. Money is the system; reject it. Give all you have to the poor and do your thing. Wealth, success, security, luxury, comfort, certainty: they are all system-oriented goals. They're what the system uses to reward its subjects and keep them from noticing that they are not free. Throw it all away. The system has addicted you to an artificial need. Kick the habit. Be what you are. Do what you think is right. All the way out is free.

Previous generations of Americans had accepted material advancement as the goal of life, but with the advent of hippies, the baby-boom generation developed a new conceptualization of the good life, a vision not tied as much to material comfort as to ethical and moral concerns. Their aspirations to dignity and love, not wealth and expertise, and the belief that people—not things—are primary, were of paramount importance in defining their new culture. The genocidal war in Indochina became the primary focus of the culture which hippies opposed, and the synthesis of culture and politics in 1970 gave rise to political hippies (also known as "freaks"). Resistance and opposition to the war were heightened by the fact that although eighteen-year-olds were not allowed to vote, they were drafted to fight in the jungles of Vietnam.

From its beginnings, youth culture had contained a membership which was motivated by more than a desire to carve out easy lives for themselves. Material deprivation was not part of the experience of millions of younger people at the same time as technological innovations pointed to new possibilities for the reduction of scarcity and toil. It was common sense that the American Indians have been grievously wronged and that the Vietnamese posed no threat to the United States. The legitimacy of material rewards and the Protestant work ethic, so essential to the rise of capitalism in Europe, were being undermined by the material success of the system.

The hippies opted to live humanly in an age of specialization. A newspaper from California, *Incarnations*, put it this way:

> Scarcity is an historical condition that necessitates repression, not an unavoidable necessity . . . This generation is moving into revolutionary action through the discovery that television and new cars do not save. Salvation means wholeness. Wholeness is not found or made in the private consumption of commodities. The needs, limits, and potentials of organisms in their ecological relations must govern our science and our social being, not the needs of a market system or the fantasies of technicians.[70]

On the striking campuses of 1970, many students attempted to integrate questions of everyday life into their opposition to U.S. foreign policy. One action group at Berkeley wrote:

> Reconstituting the university means nothing without changing the relationships in our own lives. These relationships extend into our work and into our politics, as well as into our homes. The most typical form of relationship in American society is that of boss-worker (master-slave)...Our submission as subordinates makes us as responsible as the decision-makers for the policies which support the war ("I was just following orders") unless we, like those who refuse the draft, say "NO!"[71]

The Scranton Commission's report could make few recommendations for how to deal with the cultural revolt besides commenting on its underlying motivational force: "How long this emerging youth culture will last and what course its future development will take are open questions. But it does exist today, and it is the deeper cause of the emergence of race and war as objects of intense concern on the American campus."[72]

The protests themselves took on an imaginative character during the student strike. At Cornell University, students laid siege to the ROTC building using a homemade "peace tank" to fire flowers and candy at it. At the University of Connecticut, the ROTC building was occupied by over 1,000 students armed with paint and brushes. They covered the walls with flowers, cartoons, and peace symbols.[73] At Michigan Tech, about 200 ROTC cadets joined 1,000 other students to build a one acre park in a symbolic protest against the war and the deaths at Kent State.[74]

At the University of Denver, students erected a tent and board city near the student center which they dubbed "Woodstock West: Peace and Freedom Community." Over 1,000 students converged there during the weekend of May 9 to be part of the city which was constructed "as a protest against the war in Southeast Asia, against racism in America, and against the slaying of four students at Kent State University." Although the university chancellor ordered people to disperse, no one paid any attention to him, and he was forced to call in the police. Thirty people were arrested, and the city was destroyed, but almost immediately, 600 people returned to the site and rebuilt it, this time with heavier nails and bigger beams. While nearly 1,000 Colorado National Guard and Denver Police watched, workmen tore down Woodstock West for the second time. That night, students returned, but this time "to love to death" the thirty police guards. They moved from one guard to the next and "discussed, argued, agreed, and laughed together." According to the *Denver Post*:

> Several times during the afternoon and evening command officers reminded patrolmen, relaxed in conversation, that their helmets were supposed to be on their heads, not under their arms. The patrolmen responded quickly, but by nightfall the formality had been destroyed, and not one of the nightforce was wearing his helmet.[75]

The next day, 400 of the college's 430 faculty met and voted to support the "spirit of Woodstock West."

In Philadelphia, a National Guard M48 tank bumped a car when the tank's steering broke. A lunchtime throng of Temple University students surged around the tank. Flowers quickly appeared in the barrel and "Free Bobby Seale" was painted on the turret before police could clear a path and get another tank to tow the disabled hulk away.

At McComb County Community College in Michigan, students performed a guerrilla theater. An ear-muffed jury connected by strings to judges (who were themselves connected to a villain called "Wixon") condemned a black, a hippie, and a student as "un-American." The three were then crucified.[76]

The summer after May was a time of imaginative and symbolic actions. The flags of the United States, Canada, and the National Liberation Front of southern Vietnam flew above a summer rock concert attended by 250,000 people on the border between the United States and Canada. On August 6, hundreds of "long-haired undesirables" took over Tom Sawyer's Island at Disneyland and battled with police to stay there, causing a Disneyland ban on hippies for several years. As the politicization of everyday life progressed, repression of cultural events intensified: In Connecticut, 30,000 people were stranded at a cancelled rock festival; in Palo Alto, 260 street people were rounded up on July 12, a week after a July 4 street people's riot in Berkeley.

The cultural roots of the political movement were an important source of the energy of the popular movement, and the New Left's cultural subversion defined one of its most significant dimensions. The spontaneous integration of culture and politics provided a vitality to the movement, but it also accounted for the carrying-over of oppressive characteristics like sexism, racism, and authoritarianism into the life of the movement. The photograph of the advertisement on page 149, taken from the April 1970 edition of *Ramparts* (the forerunner of *Mother Jones*), is an indication of how sexism and de-politicization go hand in hand. Besides serving to prevent activists from giving and living to their full potential, sexism (like racism) undermines the avowed goals and aspirations of the movement. The consciousness that our personal lives have political implications may have been an insight of the counter-culture, but it was made self-conscious by feminists who rose to challenge previously unnoticed modes of oppression.

By 1970, the autonomous women's movement experienced phenomenal growth, as women's groups sprouted up on college campuses, in industry, in cities, and in suburbs. Like the black movement, the women's movement contained a diverse membership, and in 1970, radical feminists became the leading force within the feminist movement. That the "personal is political" had long been discussed by the New Left, but never before had the legitimacy of heterosexual relationships and patriarchal domination been challenged as it was in 1970. As radical feminists consolidated their hegemony within the women's movement, women occupied buildings and set up women's centers, and they fought the police for control of their newly won territory. In New York, the offices of the *Ladies Home Journal* were occupied by women whose

Photo 4
Ramparts, April 1970
Sexism and Depoliticization

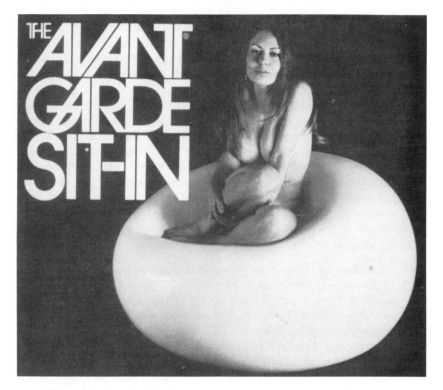

Protest against uncomfortable, heavy, square-looking furniture! Take a position in the revolutionary new Avant-Garde Inflatable Sculpture Seat. Use this seat anywhere—in your pad, the office of the university president, even the middle of the Atlantic Ocean. What's more, the Avant-Garde Inflatable Sculpture Seat is completely portable and it can be stored in a drawer. It's made of thick, triple-laminated vinyl and is available in six vibrating colors. Perhaps best of all, the Avant-Garde Inflatable Sculpture Seat easily supports the weight of two—and it bounces!

Chairs similar to the Avant-Garde Inflatable Sculpture Seat sell in department stores for $50. Our deflated price: **only $9.95!!**

To order your Avant-Garde Inflatable Sculpture Seat, simply fill out the adjacent coupon and mail it with $9.95 (plus 85¢ for shipping) to: The Avant-Garde Emporium, 110 West 40th Street, New York, New York 10018. Please be sure to hurry, since the Avant-Garde Inflatable Sculpture Seat is imported and stocks are limited.

You'll really be sitting pretty.

THE AVANT GARDE EMPORIUM
110 W. 40 ST., NEW YORK, N.Y. 10018

The Avant-Garde Emporium
110 West 40th Street
New York, New York 10018

I enclose $_____ for _____ Avant-Garde Inflatable Sculpture Seats at ONLY $9.95 EACH (plus 85¢ for shipping; total: $10.80). My color choice is: (Check)

☐ White   ☐ Red   ☐ Blue
☐ Orange   ☐ Yellow   ☐ Black

NAME

ADDRESS

CITY

STATE   ZIP

NEW YORK RESIDENTS PLEASE ADD 60¢ PER CHAIR FOR SALES TAX. ©AVANT-GARDE 1970. TRADEMARK "AVANT-GARDE" REGISTERED U.S. PATENT OFFICE. AGER1.

demands included an entire issue devoted to feminism and an end to the portrayal of women as mindless commodities.

Within this climate, the National Organization of Women (NOW) embarked on its most ambitious campaign: a general strike of women scheduled for August 26, 1970 (the fiftieth anniversary of women's right to vote). The preparations for the strike included a new symbol for feminism— the clenched fist inside the biological sign for women.[77] As the date for the strike approached, women staged "tot-ins" to dramatize the need for daycare centers, and Betty Friedan, president of NOW, promised "an instant revolution against sexual oppression." On August 26, over 10,000 women marched down Fifth Avenue in New York, and smaller demonstrations occurred in cities and towns across the country. The next day, a lobbying campaign for an Equal Rights Amendment began on Capitol Hill. Although the ERA never passed, the women's movement continued to gather momentum in the 1970s, changing the common sense of American society while providing women with new possibilities for their lives.

Not only did the crisis of 1970 produce cultural changes in the everyday lives of millions of people, there was a political readjustment in the United States as well, a readjustment necessitated by the impact of the student strike.

The Political Crisis

> *The American constitutional system makes no provision for mid-term changes in government, and we have no de Gaulle waiting in the wings to return to power in a crisis situation. The solution here would therefore have to take a form for which there is no obvious precedent, and the search for one would greatly complicate the war-related crisis. There is no assurance that the U.S. ruling class could find a way out of this tangle. Failure could lead to chaos, attempted military takeover, even civil war with various factions of the Armed Forces pitted against each other.*
> —Paul M. Sweezy and Harry Magdoff,
> *Monthly Review*, June 1970

With the intensity of action and emotion in May 1970, it was only a matter of time before a major change at the highest levels of government had to occur. The restoration of domestic tranquility demanded it. Nixon knew it when he could not sleep the night before the massive May 9 demonstration at the White House, when he went out at dawn to talk with some of the protesters. In May 1970, of course, few could guess whether the crisis would be resolved through elections or a military *coup d'état*, and practically no one would have believed that somehow the whole thing would come to be blamed on the one man who didn't want the United States to appear to be a "pitiful, helpless giant."

After the murders at Kent State, Nixon had said "they got what was coming to them," but by May 8, he personally invited students from that campus to visit with him, and he spent an hour listening to their comments. His frantic attempts to rally support for himself included summoning the states' governors for elaborate briefings on the Cambodian invasion, dropping in unexpectedly on a meeting of the AFL-CIO executive committee, granting a private interview to Roy Wilkins of the NAACP, and sending a condolence letter to the parents of Allison Kraus, one of the students killed at Kent State.

He had miscalculated the depth of the reaction to his invasion of Cambodia, and a master of Machiavellian politics, he frantically beat a hasty retreat. What he had called an "historic turning point" and "a challenge to the enemy everywhere" in his April 30 speech announcing the invasion was quickly turned into a two-month maximum penetration of not more than thirty-five kilometers into Cambodia. Not only was the Cambodian invasion a political fiasco, it had no hope of accomplishing its military objective: finding the headquarters of the Vietnamese Liberation Army. (When the war ended, it was revealed that this headquarters had been located underground just outside of Saigon.) Two weeks after the invasion began, Secretary of Defense Melvin Laird sent a top-secret cable to the U.S. Commander in Vietnam, General Abrams: "In light of the controversy over the United States move into Cambodia, the American public would be impressed by any of the following evidence of the success of the operation: (1) high-ranking enemy prisoners; (2) major enemy headquarters; (3) large enemy caches."[78]

The first official intelligence reports had stated that only a week's supply of ammunition had been captured. According to *Time* magazine: "A few days later, as if by magic...intelligence analysts overnight increased the value of the haul to an admirable four and a-half month supply." When the pictures of the captured caches were released to newspapers and magazines in the United States, however, they portrayed little ammunition amid many GIs waving the peace sign.

To make matters worse, the economy staggered from the huge expenditures demanded for the war. The Dow Jones Industrial Average was affected by the protests of May and closed at its lowest point in over seven years.[79] The market's eighteen-month slide reflected a 36 percent decrease in stock values, the greatest loss since 1929 and three times as large a loss on paper as the great crash.[80] The chairman of the New York Stock Exchange traveled to Washington to personally confer with Nixon. Corporate profits were down 10 percent from a year earlier, and the nation's factories were operating at only 80 percent of their capacity.[81] Not counting indirect appropriations, Vietnam War expenditures amounted to about $24 billion a year, fueling an inflation rate within the United States of 6 percent in 1970 (compared to 4.8 percent in 1968). Unemployment was measured at 5.8 percent in 1970 compared to 3.3 percent two years earlier, and many economists tied the growing federal deficit to the continuation of the war.

Despite the fact that the people of the United States were experiencing the beginnings of the economic crisis of the 1970s, many were a little better off than they had been in 1960. The median family income in 1970, relative to the purchasing power of the dollar in 1960, had risen 32 percent, and the number of persons living in poverty as defined by the government had dropped from nearly forty million in 1960 to twenty-five million. More families had incomes over $25,000 than ever before, and 80 percent of all families owned a car.[82]

As early as 1968, it was evident that continuing the war was a threat to the economic security of the nation, but after the Cambodian invasion and the student strike, Nixon's continuation of the war began to crystallize political problems at a level previously unimagined. On May 8, when the strike was at its height, over 250 officials from the Agency for International Development and the State Department signed a statement opposing expansion of the war. It was rumored that half of Nixon's cabinet was hostile to his decision to invade Cambodia, and in the days following Kent State, more than a dozen advisors and high officials in the White House, including Nixon's advisor for youth, resigned their positions in protest.

There was a crisis of legitimacy at the highest levels of power. The chairman of the board of Bank of America, the director of the Bank of Chicago, and the director of IBM all came out against the Cambodian invasion. As J. Watson Jr., director of IBM, said, "If we continue, I believe we will soon reach a point where much of the damage will be irreparable." On May 25, New York's Governor Nelson Rockefeller, never known for dovish views, called for a quick end to the war in order to avoid "greater disasters in the future."[83] The Wall Street Businessmen for Peace and the Corporate Executive Committee for Peace (representing 350 high level business executives) organized and immediately came out strongly for an end to the war. The Business Executive Move for Vietnam Peace, an organization with a membership of 3,000 owners and senior executives of private corporations, launched "Operation Housecleaning," a nationwide effort to help defeat pro-war members of the House of Representatives in the November elections.

Twelve hundred Wall Street lawyers converged on the Capitol on May 20 to lobby for an end to the war. Smaller groups of establishment lawyers from fifteen cities staggered their visits to maintain the pressure on Congress. The state legislatures of New York, California, Ohio, Kansas, Illinois, Rhode Island, Alaska, Michigan, Massachusetts, and New Jersey considered, and in some cases passed, legislation allowing draft age men to refuse to fight in the undeclared war. The Hawaiian State Senate passed a resolution on May 6 urging Nixon to stop the invasion of Cambodia.

Liberals did not begin opposing the war in 1970 because they had finally learned something new about it, developed a moral concern for massively bombarded civilians, or even become concerned about the well-being of American GIs—but because the rising economic and social costs of the war threatened their legitimacy and power at home. The "irreparable damage" and "greater disasters" they feared were precisely the growth of the movement, the deepening of its insights and commitment, and the broadening of its appeal. The split in the ruling class was tactical: In principle, they all agreed that U.S. world hegemony should be preserved. They disagreed on how best to accomplish it. As the editors of *Monthly Review* put it:

> If we seek analogies—often useful but always to be used with caution—Russia in 1903 and perhaps France in 1968 would seem to be more relevant to our present prospects than, say, Russia in 1917 or China in 1949...What about the other term in the present historical equation, the U.S. ruling class? There is no question

about its strength or experience. It certainly will not be shattered by even the most severe crisis arising out of the war. But there is no way now to predict how it might react to such a crisis... The U.S. ruling class is not even going to make an earnest effort to end the Vietnam War until it is convinced that its ability to govern can be assured in no other way.[84]

Apparently, the student strike and spreading social unrest convinced many corporate executives and Congresspeople of the need for a quick end to the war. On June 24, the Senate voted overwhelmingly (eighty-one to ten) to rescind the Gulf of Tonkin resolution (which had provided what scant legal grounds there were for U.S. military involvement in Indochina). In the next few months, the Senate's Foreign Relations Committee declared Nixon in violation of the Constitution for his conduct of the war without consent of the Senate. Finally, on December 8, the Senate reaffirmed its ban on committing U.S. troops to Cambodia, an act equivalent to a no-confidence vote, which, in Western Europe, would have forced the resignation of the head of the government.

From Watergate to the Iran-Contra Scandal _____

The people of this nation are eager to get on with the quest for new greatness... it is for us here to open the doors that will set free again the real greatness of this nation—the genius of the American people... a "New American Revolution"... a revolution as profound, as far reaching, as exciting as that first revolution almost 200 years ago.
                                                              —Richard Nixon
                              State of the Union Address, January 22, 1971

When the President of the United States echoed the New Left by calling for "Power to the People" and waving the peace sign, it appeared to be nothing more than another example of Orwellian double-talk from a government that claimed to be fighting for "freedom" and "democracy" in Indochina, that "urbanized" Vietnam through saturation bombings of the countryside, and that professed concern with "peace" at the same time as it waged war at home and abroad. Few people appreciated Nixon's rhetoric as a signal for the intensification of the war against Vietnam through massive air attacks which would target the major population centers. No one considered the possibility that the New Left had won a significant victory.

In the immediate aftermath of the student strike, it was unclear what the future held in store. Although most observers agreed that changes were needed, there was continuing debate whether or not the country would move further to the right. In the fall of 1970, a host of articles on the "death of the student movement" appeared, but even though the New Left had been officially declared dead, tens of thousands of people took to the streets of New York, Washington, and more than a dozen other cities in October to protest Nixon's new escalation of the war. A majority of the country was now opposed to the war, and with each new escalation—the invasion of Laos, the mining of Haiphong Harbor, and the Christmas bombing of Hanoi—the anti-war movement organized massive and militant responses. On May 1, 1971, nearly 50,000 regionally organized people attempted to bring morning traffic in Washington, D.C. to a halt. Their mobilizing call, "If the government doesn't stop the war, we'll stop the government," was direct enough, but the illegal arrests conducted by the Department of Justice—more that 15,000 in three days—prevented the movement from accomplishing its tactical objective.

Although historians have decided that the New Left died after the student strike, there is abundant evidence that it was only after the Watergate affair that the movement abated. The protests following the mining of Haiphong in the spring of 1972 were estimated to have had nearly as many participants as the more than four million people on strike in 1970. Students at Kent State were again in the forefront of protests, but this time off-campus at Wright Patterson Air Force Base, where 152 people were arrested for blocking traffic. There were large demonstrations on a few days' notice in New York (50,000 people), San Francisco (35,000), and Los Angeles (30,000). At the same time, street fighting broke out at ROTC centers and war-related targets in Berkeley, Madison, Ann Arbor, and Cambridge. Students from the University of Maryland spent three nights blockading Route 1 in running battles with the National Guard. When General William Westmoreland appeared on a base podium in El Paso, Texas, he was pelted with tomatoes by active-duty GIs.[85]

If the 1968 Tet offensive had demonstrated that the United States would never be able to achieve a military victory on the battlefields of Vietnam, the student strike of 1970 made it abundantly clear that the Pentagon and their President had bitter enemies at home, enemies who were able to muster considerable support. The Nixon administration became increasingly isolated, and in a desperate attempt to regain control of the situation, the man who entered office in 1968 promising "never to invade Vietnam or any country in the area" reversed himself yet again and contradicted his life-long promises to deal resolutely with the "Red Chinese." Given the new mood in the country, Nixon's trip to Peking was precipitated by the need to boost his image and carry him through the 1972 elections.

In 1960 it would have been ludicrous to suggest that the same politician whose reputation had been built upon the most crude anti-communism—the heir apparent to Joe McCarthy—would open relations with the People's Republic of China. It was in 1960, after all, that the need to better defend Quemoy and Matsu, the two Taiwanese islands being shelled by China, were made by Nixon into one of the chief points of contention in his televised debates with John Kennedy. Indeed, the attempt to blockade the revolution in China and to prevent its spreading throughout Asia was seen by some observers as the principle reason for both the Vietnam and Korean Wars.[86]

When Nixon announced his forthcoming journey to Peking, he was denounced by many of his former supporters, not only by conservative Senators and Congresspeople, but also by paramilitary right-wing groups, one of which went as far as issuing a "Wanted for Treason" poster of the

President, making a threat they intended to carry out in San Diego during the Republican Convention. After his trip to China, Nixon was cut off from his right-wing base of support, and when he came under increasing attack from anti-war forces, he blundered into the same mistake made by his forerunner Joe McCarthy and attacked an Establishment he thought he had grown too powerful for.

Despite revelations of secret bombings in Cambodia and Laos from the earliest days of the Nixon administration and the arrest of the Watergate burglars prior to the 1972 election, the President was re-elected by one of the most solid majorities ever obtained. After his re-election, of course, when Nixon himself was implicated in the attempted cover-up of the White House connections to the Watergate burglary, only then was he forced to abandon the ship of state. Although his administration had escalated the killing in Indochina with B-52 saturation bombings of Hanoi a month after his election, there had been no accusations of impropriety from Congress. By cynically scheduling these twelve days of carpet-bombing for the Christmas break, Nixon had avoided the possibility of student protests at campuses closed for the holidays. So long as his administration had quietly supervised the brutal repression of the black liberation movement and the illegal bugging and repression of the anti-war movement, Congress and the electorate had not considered his leadership of the imperial camp to be improper. Only when he directed the least violent of these same methods against members *of the Establishment* with the Watergate fiasco had he gone too far. In the skeptical view of Noam Chomsky, it was not until "the discovery that the directors of Murder, Inc. were also cheating on their income tax," that they crossed the line between propriety and impropriety.[87]

The chain of events which led to the Watergate hotel was obscured by the media's obsession with generating news stories relating to one particular bungled burglary (and an attempted cover-up). Among other revelations buried in the tons of newsprint was the fact that immediately following the student strike, Nixon had approved a "top secret" plan (the Huston plan) aimed at destabilizing the New Left. The government feared that the May 1970 revolt was spilling over to the whole society. As the first part of the plan, "Summary of Internal Security Threat," pointed out: "Increasingly the battlefield is the community with the campus serving primarily as a staging area." The Huston plan was implemented through a campaign of infiltration, mail tampering, burglaries, and wiretapping aimed at a selected list of domestic groups and individuals. Other government counter-intelligence operations were intensified: the FBI's COINTELPRO program, the CIA's Operation CHAOS, and similar programs by the Army, Navy, Secret Service, etc.[88] As activists refused to be intimidated, Nixon approved even more "dirty tricks"—the Liddy plan, the Segretti plans—aimed at the growing "enemies list" compiled by the White House, a list which came to include George McGovern's name.

As the Watergate scandal unfolded, the front men of the Oval Office (Haldeman and Ehrlichman) attempted to argue that the country was on the verge of insurrection and that the measures they had taken were necessary to insure "national security," but it was already too late. To be sure, such arguments persuaded many Americans that Nixon had only stretched his Constitutional limits as far as his Democratic and Republican predecessors had also done. Among members of the nation's ruling elite, however, Nixon's "attempted coup" was seen as itself a threat to national security. The established powers were no longer unified in supporting the war, and with the Watergate revelations, Nixon's colleagues were provided with a golden opportunity to resolve the national impasse.

It might have been expected that in the face of a potential insurrection, the system's rulers would close ranks, as the Oval Office insisted they should. Instead, the liberal wing of the Establishment—the heads of transnational corporations and Eastern bankers led by the Rockefeller brothers—redirected the focus of the popular resistance from the system as a whole to the man at the "highest" level of power. Richard Nixon became a scapegoat whose resignation prepared the way for the country to be "brought together again." The idea that a charismatic leader would come forth to take the country out of crisis was turned on its head: Nixon's "negative charisma" united the country, so much so that the ghost of Watergate haunted his party for years. The revolt of the students was co-opted and moved into the halls of Congress, but if Nixon's plumbers had not been caught inside the Watergate Hotel, it is difficult to see how the national impasse could have been resolved.

Although Watergate succeeded in changing the faces of some of the men holding the highest positions of power in the federal government, the legacy of Nixon and Company meant that the American political system would never be the same. Although implicated in the widespread network of illegal wiretapping and dirty tricks of the Nixon administration, Henry Kissinger, one of the great mass murderers of history, was promoted to Secretary of State, and he went on to carve out a new global constellation of power. Vietnam was bombed and defoliated, and after the U.S. got its prisoners of war back, not one cent of the promised billions of dollars in reparations was paid. An example had to be made for other countries to learn what the costs of fighting the United States would be. The tensions between China and the Soviet Union were heightened by the new U.S. friendship with China, thereby splitting the communist "enemy" and further destabilizing Indochina. In the Middle East, Kissinger's shuttle diplomacy breathed new life into Israel's decaying position: He pledged that the United States would not even talk with the Palestine Liberation Organization unless Palestinians gave up their struggle to regain their homeland. Although he was never an elected official, Kissinger's pledge has defined American policy for more than a decade.

Kissinger modeled his new world order on Metternich's leadership of the counterrevolutionary Holy Alliance which restored "order" to Europe after the French revolution. His college dissertation was a study of Metternich which portrayed him as the doctor who prescribed cures for revolution and whose diplomacy was founded on duplicity. Almost all of the "Nixon doctrine" can be found in Kissinger's dissertation: From slogans like the "generation of peace," "Peace with Honor," and the "silent majority" to the use of police lies to disrupt the popular opposition, Kissinger cold-bloodedly used his study of history to manipulate modern events. The modern-day equivalent of Metternich's twice quoted, "We should advance with the olive branch in one hand and with the sword in the other," can be found in the Christmas bombing of Hanoi at the same time that the Paris peace talks between the U.S. and Vietnam were underway. Based on what he considers the separations of ethics and politics in Anglo-American political theory, Kissinger argued that, "Domestically, the most difficult problem is agreement on the nature of 'justice.' "[89] Counterrevolutionary diplomats were lauded as fulfilling the "duty of diplomacy" whenever they disobeyed popular, governmental, and even "divine" commands.

Using his insights from the historical record, Kissinger helped turn the thrust of the world-historical events of 1968 to 1970 into a victory for the Rockefellers' Trilateral Commission, a strategic think-tank for transnational corporations based in Europe, Japan, and the United States. By 1976, these forces had not only helped to dislodge a President guilty of "ungentlemanly" conduct of office, but they could stage elections where the choice between Gerald Ford and Jimmy Carter was nothing more than a fraternal contest between Nelson and David Rockefeller.[90] The winner turned out to be the one with the least "negative charisma," as the ghost of Watergate lurked on the shoulder of Nixon's hand-picked successor. The loser was American democracy: The federal government had been "saved" by the Rockefellers only to survive as an instrument of their benign rule (as I discuss below).

With the 1976 election of Jimmy Carter (a protégé of the Rockefeller-financed Trilateral Commission), a "new era" was heralded in U.S. foreign policy, the era of "human rights." After the defeat suffered in Vietnam, massive and overt U.S. military intervention abroad was simply out of the question as the "Vietnam syndrome" refused to disappear. For nearly a decade, the Pentagon was unwilling to risk another major battlefield defeat or the possible regeneration of a domestic resistance movement, and they were unable to buy or conscript a fighting army. During that decade, the doors were opened to a flood of national liberation movements: Angola, Mozambique, Guinea-Bissau, Ethiopia, Nicaragua, and Iran were all able to free themselves from political systems tied to the United States.

No matter how much it may have masqueraded as Christian morality, the "human rights policy" of the Carter administration was formulated and conducted in the real world of a declining empire and the lack of popular confidence in the federal government at the beginning of the 1970s. It was tailored to fit the post-Vietnam international constellation of forces and the post-New Left climate of domestic opinion, and it was useful to the "powers that be" as a transition program to stabilize a new international order within which transnational corporations could continue to expand while the war wounds healed at home. Of course, it also served as a smokescreen hiding U.S. support for dictatorships in Indonesia, El Salvador, and other countries as well as covert U.S. intervention around the globe.[91] Cold warriors within the power structure also found much ammunition within the "human rights policy" to use against the governments of the Soviet bloc, thereby preparing the groundwork for the Reagan presidency.

One of the immediate effects of the Vietnam War was the breakdown of the U.S. Armed Forces among the rank and file. At the same time, however, there was a longer-term strengthening of its command structure. The Vietnam War provided the top command of the Pentagon with a training ground from which they have drawn lessons and made adjustments. In 1968, when General Westmoreland was removed as Chief of Combined Operations in Vietnam, he became the U.S. Armed Forces chief of staff and was entrusted with the command of all counter-insurgency operations in Latin America. In 1968, Philip Habib was the State Department coordinator for Vietnam, and immediately after Thieu fell, he visited Southeast Asia to assure U.S. allies in the region that the United States military presence and power in Asia would be maintained.[92] In 1983, during Israel's bloody invasion of Lebanon, the same man served as U.S. coordinator in the Middle East, a position he earned through his Vietnam experiences. Neither should it be forgotten that Ronald Reagan was Governor of California during the student strike. The man who advocated "paving over Vietnam" and who reacted to the New Left by declaring, "If they want a bloodbath, let's get it over with," went on to become the Commander-in-Chief.

After Carter's Iranian hostage debacle, the global prestige and interests of the United States were at stake, and there was an actor waiting in the wings, one who had been carefully prepared to play his greatest role. A last minute change of heart by David Rockefeller and the defection of the Trilateralists to the Reagan banner were the icing on the cake. His credentials were impressive. A decade before his election, Ronald Reagan had already performed in a dress rehearsal for his ascension to power. On February 10, 1969, he played the war-game role of the newly-installed Chief of State after a military takeover of the United States. (See the documents in the appendix.) After he had rehearsed "saving democracy," all that was left was for him to be "democratically" elected. The Pentagon could not have put anyone more to their liking in the White House.

Effects of the New Left

The Reagan Presidency's revitalization of American patriotism and military power serves as an indication to many people that the New Left in the United States was a movement of little or no consequence to the established system. As I discuss in the following pages, however, the domestic movement compelled the nation's governing elite to accept defeat in Vietnam and ushered in a vast program for modernizing the political, corporate, and university systems.

After the high point of the New Left had passed, cynicism became commonplace among a generation of activists whose sacrifices and courage remain historically noteworthy. As the psychic Thermidor (the internally-conditioned impetus to return to the *status quo ante*) intensified, the movement disintegrated from within. The Panthers turned on each other, and shoot-outs replaced discussions as their means of internal struggle. The Weather Underground embraced Charles Manson as a hero. "Radical" women began a series of attacks and physical assaults on individual activists they judged to be particularly sexist. As the movement splintered, various groups moved into its official bodies. The Revolutionary Union (a "new communist party" which was a split off of SDS and is today known as the Revolutionary Communist Party) took over the national offices of the Vietnam Veterans Against the War. In Boston, the Venceremos Brigade (the group coordinating the sending of activists to Cuba) was taken over in 1971 by a group which refused to endorse any white men who were not homosexuals, arguing that it was the duty of the American movement to struggle with "Cuban homophobia." While these dynamics may seem ludicrous to some, they serve to outline the nature of a social movement in decline.

In the remainder of this chapter, I attempt to clarify the powerful impact that the New Left had on the established system, an impact denied not only by the defeatism of many activists but also by official histories of what has come to be called "the Vietnam era." In the next chapter, I consider the post-1968 possibilities of renewing a movement like the New Left was in its ascendancy.

Political Reform

In his memoirs, Henry Kissinger argued that the war against Vietnam could have been won if public opinion in the United States had not blocked further escalations. Of course, it is highly unlikely that the outcome of the war could have been different given the moral and military superiority of the Vietnamese. In retrospect, however, it is clear that it was the tumultuous reaction to the Cambodian invasion which blocked U.S. plans to continue the war. On May 15, 1970—in the midst of the student strike—McGeorge Bundy, formerly a top military advisor to Lyndon Johnson and president of the Ford Foundation, warned that another escalation of the war "would tear the country and the administration to pieces."[93] In early August of 1970, another man near the center of corporate power, Clark Clifford, said that a reescalation of the war "would be traumatic for this country and cause a crisis far worse than the one following the invasion of Cambodia."[94]

The Carnegie Commission published a report on campus unrest in September 1971 (well over a year after the student strike). In what was generally a foreboding section, "It Can Happen Again," there was an acknowledgment that, although a psychic Thermidor had set in among activists, a new escalation of the war would have tragic consequences:

> To say that the campuses have been relatively quiet since May 1970 is not to say that they have been pacified. . . opposition to the war and current national policies run deeper than ever. The signal for any new large-scale confrontation is not likely to come from the campuses or the counter-culture. The student and intellectual communities are now too pessimistic about any movement they would launch having any impact. . . The spark for the conflagration, if there is to be one, will most likely be a deliberate governmental policy decision—to invade North Vietnam, or to use tactical nuclear weapons. . .[95]

There is abundant evidence that the necessity of defusing the domestic opposition demanded an end to the war. At the same moment, however, activists in the anti-war movement were less than impressed with their own efficacy. In Boston, for example, when there were approximately a quarter of a million students on strike in May 1970, a poster from the Left read:

> If students strike, there is no school.
> If workers strike, there is no war.

When this poster is contrasted with *Business Week's* evaluation of the student strike ("This is a dangerous situation. It threatens the whole economic and social structure of the nation.") or with Nixon and Company's appreciation of the insurrectionary potential, it verifies once again the insight that the class consciousness of the power elite is superior to that of any other class in the United States.[96]

Further evidence of the effect of the domestic movement on global policymakers can be found in documents of the Rockefeller-funded Trilateral Commission. In *The Crisis of Democracy*, a report on the situation in the industrialized countries after the New Left, Samuel Huntington—one of the authors of the report and also the chief architect of the "forced urbanization" of Vietnam—summed up what he called the consequences of the "democratic distemper":

> For a quarter-century the United States was the hegemonic power in a system of world order. The manifestations of the democratic distemper, however, have already stimulated uncertainties among allies and could well stimulate adventurism among enemies. If American citizens don't trust their government, why should friendly foreigners? If American citizens challenge the authority of American government, why shouldn't unfriendly governments? The turning inward of American attention and the decline of authority of American governing institutions are closely related, as both cause and effect, to the relative downturn in American power and influence in world affairs. A decline in the governability of democracy at home means a decline in the influence of democracy abroad.[97]

Outmaneuvered on the battlefields and undercut at home during the Vietnam War, U.S. policymakers were compelled to embark on an ambitious program aimed at pacifying the growing domestic opposition in order to rebuild the international power of the United States. From Watergate and Carter's "human rights policy" to the Civil Rights Acts, Constitutional Amendments, federal affirmative action programs, the suspension of the draft, and eligibility of eighteen-year olds to vote (which was signed into law *less than a month* after the student strike), the federal government appeared to conform to needs raised by the movement. The effects of all these reforms on the decline of the movement should not be underestimated. Even though fundamental problems like poverty, racism, and international starvation continue, the apparent swinging over of the state in this period made it an unlikely target for protests, thereby helping to depoliticize the burgeoning movement.

By themselves, reforms won by popular movements can be both beneficial and deleterious, bringing disillusionment from what might appear to be immediate failures as well as exhaustion from winning adjustments. Even when they appear to be beneficial, as was the case with the "human rights policy" of the Carter administration, such reforms do little to alleviate structural problems—as evidenced by the millions of dollars squandered on a government of "democratically" elected death squads in El Salvador. Reforms fundamentally depoliticize single-issue movements—precisely through their formal politicization. Not only is the movement deprived of a focus for opposition, but such reforms also serve to bolster the position of members of the corporate elite who, for reasons of their own, prefer co-optation to repression of popular movements. By bringing movement leaders and ideas into "acceptable" arenas of discussion and action, these very arenas are strengthened by the participation of former activists, rather than delegitimated by the opposition of popular movements. Andrew Young's service as U.S. ambassador to the United Nations, for example, although demonstrating the limits of Carter's "human rights policy" when he was fired for talking with representatives of the Palestine Liberation Organization, made it possible for the U.S. government to gain new prestige internationally and domestically at the same time as the legitimacy of American foreign policymakers had never been more precarious.

Since the defeat in Vietnam, the capacity for U.S. intervention in the internal affairs of other nations has become increasingly sophisticated. Policymakers now have several options which they may choose to implement. Their intervention can be open, without the benefit of rhetorical camouflage, as in Grenada or Libya; carried out through third parties as in the funding and training of right-wing Nicaraguans to attack the *Sandinista* government (in what appears to be a re-run of the ill-fated Bay of Pigs invasion of Cuba in 1963); or covert and economic, as in Allende's Chile. So far at least, it has not been as massive and brutally destructive as it was in Vietnam.

If anything is clear from the Reagan counterrevolution, it is the insight that reforms in the existing system are extremely tenuous: What may have been necessary to restore domestic tranquility in 1973 can easily be reversed a decade later, depending upon the balance of forces.[98] More often than not, reforms in the political system are designed to deflect the oppositional movement which provided the original impetus to make changes. The smooth functioning of the system is perfected, and once the oppositional movement has disappeared (or been channeled into more "appropriate" avenues of dissent), the system is even more capable of accomplishing its goals without future disruptions.[99] In order to appreciate the historical character of this observation, the nature of post-1970 reforms in the United States is examined below.

Reforms on the Campuses and in the Workplaces

Caught by surprise in May 1970, the administrators of the nation's 2,800 colleges and universities embarked on an ambitious program of modernization after the student strike—reforms designed to prevent future rebellions before they arose and to manage them more effectively when they do break out. From 1960 to 1970, the number of college students in the United States had more than doubled from under four million to eight and one-half million, [100] and the quantitative growth of the 1960s gave way to a fine-tuning of the academic assembly line in the 1970s. The nationwide student strike, the first real indication of the enormous energy of these millions of people brought together on campuses, was used to streamline authority structures and strengthen the centralized bureaucracy against which the movement had fought. Nearly all states today have "superboards," academic coordinating councils with new powers. Far more decision-making power is now concentrated at levels above the individual campus, a vast centralization of power which serves to insure the power of institutional elites.[101]

According to Nixon's Presidential Commission on Campus Unrest, the original impetus for campus reforms came from the need to "declare a national cease-fire." The leader of this group, William Scranton, prefaced the report by explaining:

> Our colleges and universities cannot survive as combat zones, but they cannot thrive unless they are receptive to new ideas. They must be prepared to institute needed reforms in their administrative procedures and instructional programs.

The report sponsored by the Carnegie Commission to study May 1970 was prefaced by a letter from its chairman, Clark Kerr, the industrial trouble-shooter who moved to the academic point of production during the 1960s. He found the report to contain ". . . not only an instructive view of what happened on the nation's campuses in the spring of 1970, but also some useful suggestions about ways in which the tragedies that marked that era can be avoided in the future. The Carnegie Commission on Higher Education agrees with his conclusion that May 1970 might occur again." According to the report, one of the major reasons why the campus uprising was not sustained was the quick reaction of administrators, specifically new and more partici-patory campus governance arrangements, better relationships between students and faculty, and greater freedom and flexibility in the curriculum. Quick reforms were needed because "the tinder of discontent on the campuses remains dry" and "any new mass reaction from the campuses could escalate into a conflict that could leave both university and society in extremely serious disarray."[102]

Following the strike, there was so much concern that the campuses would erupt again that the Scranton Commission called for immediate contingency planning to deal with new disorders, including the creation of what is today called SWAT, Special Weapons and Attack Team.[103] Everywhere empha-sizing the need for "professionalism" in law enforcement and better foresight in dealing with demonstrations, the Commission called for the creation of standing joint committees composed of university officials, the local chief of police, representatives of the state police and National Guard, and the district attorney. Following further recommendations of this Commission, the federal

Law Enforcement Assistance Administration began a vast program of financial assistance for policemen to take courses at nearby universities, and in the first six months of the new programs, 20,000 students and policemen received such funding.

Legislation was quickly enacted in many states to punish those who might participate in a new wave of demonstrations. Before the campuses reopened in the fall of 1970, state legislatures had considered bills aimed at repressing campus demonstrators, and over thirty states enacted a total of eighty laws dealing with campus unrest.[104] These new laws covered everything from firearms on campus to disrupting classes, from curtailment of financial aid to radical students to the discipline of faculty and university employees. Universities enacted new codes of conduct designed to lessen the willingness of those on campus to participate in protests and to take back concessions granted to the movement. On October 27, the president of Berkeley announced a new professional code for faculty which "attempts to outline a separation of personal political activity and professional and institutional activity." At the same time, he promised to continue improving the campus ROTC program, overriding a May 18 Academic Senate vote to phase out credit for ROTC.[105]

During the same period of time, new approaches in the workplaces were devised in attempts to increase worker job satisfaction and reduce confrontations. Techniques from Japan became increasingly experimented with in the United States, and co-management models were imported from West Germany. The "humanization" of work became an accepted goal of managers, and labor-management committees sprung up to deal with issues like working conditions and speed-ups, issues which had not been a part of the standard union bargaining package.

This new trend toward "industrial democracy," like university reforms, was won because of grassroots turmoil. Frustrated by the failure of their unions to win them control over their jobs, workers systematically substituted their own rotation of jobs and production plans for those of management.[106] After the student strike, unrest spread to thousands of factories in the United States, as workers developed "informal underground unions" to counter the deterioration in the quality of their daily job lives.[107] A 1973 report of a special task force to the Secretary of Health, Education, and Welfare entitled *Work in America* put it this way: ". . . absenteeism, wildcat strikes, turnover, and industrial sabotage (have) become an increasingly significant part of the costs of doing business." In the words of Peter J. Pestillo, Ford's vice-president for labor relations:

> We can't run our plants with guerrilla warfare and that's what we've had. We are moving from a law-driven to a personnel-driven situation. This is the Japanese distinction . . . We must motivate and lead, not direct.[108]

From the experiences of their European subsidiaries, American transnational corporations learned to live with and benefit from representatives of workers sitting on their board of directors—even General Motors agreed to such an arrangement. Since 1970, more than 3,500 U.S. companies have adopted Japanese management techniques which encourage management and workers to cooperate.[109] Although such arrangements have been used to break unions, there are sometimes other results: Worker safety in mines where miners are permitted to rotate jobs seems to be significantly higher than in mines where jobs are semi-permanent; worker satisfaction generally increases with an increase in their responsibilities in planning production; and, most importantly, corporations that give workers more such responsibilities have higher rates of profit and productivity.[110]

The End of *Pax Americana*

Despite the many reforms of the 1970s, not all observers regarded the popular insurgency of the 1960s as grounds for the system to expand the range of its liberties or to incorporate new constituencies within the prosperity of *pax Americana*. On one side, the system responded with reforms, but on the other side, there was also a sober appraisal of the possibility of *less*, not more, democracy. As Samuel Huntington put it in his report to the Trilateral Commission:

> Al Smith once remarked that "the only cure for the evils of democracy is more democracy." Our analysis suggests that applying that cure at the present time [1975] could well be adding fuel to the flames. Instead, some of the problems of governance in the United States today stem from an excess of democracy...[What's] Needed ... is a greater degree of moderation in democracy ... We have come to recognize that there are potentially desirable limits to economic growth. There are also potentially desirable limits to the indefinite extension of political democracy.[111]

It should not be forgotten that the wave of uprisings which rolled across the country terrified many people, and although the war was supposed to be in Vietnam, there was also one going on at home. In the three years leading up to the student strike, the National Guard was called to duty over 200 times to deal with major protests.[112] Between 1963 and 1968, there were nearly four times as many casualties from political violence in the United States as in Western Europe.[113] The four people murdered at Kent State alone are more than the number of fatalities during the entire near-revolution in France in 1968. Between 1964 and 1969, there were at least 239 major violent confrontations between black people living in the inner cities in the United States and the forces of law and order. At least 191 people died and over 8,000 were injured. In the same period, there were over 200 non-police attacks on members of the civil rights movement which caused at least 23 deaths and 112 injuries.[114] These federal statistics are quite low, and they do not include twenty-eight Black Panthers, many of whom were killed as a result of the FBI's COINTELPRO operations. In 1969, Fred Hampton, leader of the Black Panther Party in Chicago and founder of the original Rainbow

Coalition, was murdered while asleep in his bed after having been drugged the night before by an FBI informant.[115]

Although Nixon and Company were dispersed by the Watergate scandal, the structural imperatives of the system that created them remain unchanged. In the 1980s, the offices of groups opposed to U.S. intervention in Central America are regularly broken into, and the names and addresses of activists and supporters are stolen. Those seeking to publicly question American policy in the Middle East face even more severe official sanctions (as well as attacks from Zionist fanatics of the Left and the Right).

Even the most benign reforms in government have had their usefulness to the political heirs of Richard Nixon: The Civil Rights Acts, like the end of the segregated housing policies of the federal government, have been used to deconcentrate minorities, thereby lessening the potential for future urban insurrections. Federal Section 8 dollars have been channeled to minorities in order for them to leave the inner city, creating the preconditions for gentrification of neighborhoods adjoining urban financial centers. While affirmative action programs have had little impact on the black underclass,[116] racism and poverty remain significant issues for the national conscience.

The turmoil of 1968 and 1970 may have exposed American institutions as empty shells filled with little more than patriotic pride and ushered in a host of reforms aimed at reasserting institutional authority, but the dynamics of the economic system have been quietly at work transforming the role of the United States within the global structures of wealth and power. This new role of the United States has been summed up as resembling that of a "banana republic."[117] Because of the predominant global power of transnational corporations with worldwide interests of their own, the United States increasingly resembles countries whose energies and resources are controlled by outside interests. The distribution of wealth and income in the United States today is more in the tradition of the underdeveloped world than in that of an affluent society. Moreover, other characteristics of third world countries have appeared in the United States since 1968: the growing strata of homeless people (estimated at between 500,000 and three million people); the changing structure of the nation's inner cities into playgrounds for the rich and displays of corporate wealth; the importance of agricultural exports for the nation's economy; and, as I discuss below, the increasing irrelevance of domestic democracy.

The cynical dealings of the Nixon and Reagan administrations with Congress constitute a historical drama which highlights the new status accorded the United States within the world system. Behind the scenes of this political stage, however, its economic counterpart has been steadily in operation. As early as 1971, the end of American economic hegemony was evidenced in the collapse of the Bretton Woods monetary accords and President Nixon's decision to free the dollar from fixed foreign exchange rates. Within the post-1968 global system, the economic demise of the United States has been portrayed by the fall in the value of the dollar, the growing national trade deficit, the tremendous debt of the federal government, the declining power of unions, the redistribution of national income, and the de-industrialization of the country. During the same period of time, the people of the United States have experienced a decline in their standard of living. Between 1972 and 1982, non-agricultural real wages in the private sector fell more than 15 percent.[118] As always, it has been those least capable of defending themselves—unskilled and semi-skilled women and minorities as well as the elderly—who have been the hardest hit, but even unionized workers have been severely impacted. The pacification of the workplaces in the 1970s helped render unions impotent in the face of the Reagan administration's offensive on behalf of the wealthy. Membership in unions has fallen to about 15 percent of the workforce, the lowest fraction of any economically advanced society and more in line with a third world country.

As labor-intensive industries have migrated abroad, some specialized technical jobs have been created in the United States, but larger numbers of decently paying jobs have been lost as whole steel mills and auto plants have been closed.[119] New jobs in the service sector (which now account for more than 75 percent of all employees) are scandalously underpaid. The Council on International and Public Affairs estimates that roughly half of all private sector jobs pay average wages within 30 percent of the federally established poverty line. In 1986, a study commissioned by the Joint Economic Committee of Congress found that more than half of all the new jobs created in the 1980s pay wages too low to keep even small families above the poverty level.[120]

Rather than enacting legislation to protect the rights of workers, our public officials continue to court the new corporate aristocracy, perhaps in the naive belief that sentimental concern for the loyal American will bring future concessions. In a world where an international assembly line and an international money market exist, however, corporate loyalty has superceded patriotism as a motivating force of economic decision-makers. Even the Pentagon has suffered from this shift in loyalty. In 1973, for example, the Philippine subsidiary of Exxon refused to sell oil to American warships for fear of violating the Arab world's boycott of pro-Israeli governments. Three years later, Gulf Oil ignored the State Department's orders to refrain from paying royalties to the new socialist government of Angola, and the State Department had to act quickly in order to prevent Boeing 737 jets from being delivered there.

Of course, it has long been the case that the structural imperative of profit has outweighed any national loyalty or sense of morality that corporate executives may have. As Thomas Jefferson put it, "Merchants have no country of their own. Wherever they may be they have no ties to the soil. All they are interested in is the source of their profits." President Eisenhower recognized this same truth when he said, "capital is a curious thing with perhaps no nationality . . . It flows where it is served best." During World War II, monopolies like ITT, Pan Am, and other U.S. corporations operated factories for the Nazis.

Although it has long been the case that corporate interests have been those of profits alone, the power and resources of corporations have never been as great as they are today. Exxon has a fleet of ships larger than Great Britain's, and the total output of the overseas operations of American corporations is larger than the GNP of any country in the world except the Soviet Union and the United States. Moreover, the concentration of corporate wealth is proceeding at an alarming pace. Within the United States, the top 500 corporations increased their share of all manufacturing and mining assets from 40 percent to 70 percent between 1960 and 1974.[121] Between 1974 and 1984, as a merger mania swept corporate boardrooms, there were more than 23,000 mergers and acquisitions, and 82 of the Fortune 500 disappeared as they were swallowed up. By 1983, the 200 largest corporations held more than 60 percent of all manufacturing assets in the United States.[122]

On an international level, the same process of concentration is occurring. In 1968, transnational corporations accounted for 25 percent of all goods and services produced in the world. It has been estimated that by 1990, transnational corporations will account for 50 percent of the world's output.[123] These are global interlocking directorates which, in conjunction with huge commercial banks like David Rockefeller's Chase Manhattan, have clearly defined economic and political interests which go far beyond the national interests of any country (including the United States). They substantially control international production, investment, trade, media, technology, and exercise extensive control over national governments. In the epoch of the communications revolution spawned by the Third Industrial Revolution, it is possible for the central headquarters of transnational corporations to manage the daily activities of production lines anywhere in the world. Containerized shipping makes it extremely cheap to relocate whole factories, and manufactured goods can be partially assembled in two or three countries before the final product is completed.

Although economists have analyzed the reasons for the transformation of the U.S. economy (particularly the transfer of assembly line jobs to the third world), solely in economic terms (the lower wages and taxes paid abroad as well as the absence of pollution control laws), there has also been a dimension of political motivation. The policies of the federal government have served to provide windfall profits to American corporations which transfer capital abroad. The tax code was revised, allowing transnational corporations to subtract their foreign taxes from the *bottom* line of their tax returns. Taxes on profits abroad are allowed to remain uncollected unless they are brought into the United States, a provision which provides only further incentives for corporations to expand their foreign operations. Similarly the government's tariff regulations have been relaxed, encouraging transnationals to assemble domestically manufactured components abroad and re-import the final product for sale in the United States. The national Export-Import Bank has used hundreds of millions of dollars to subsidize the transfer of manufacturing equipment abroad for corporations like Ford, Kaiser, Alcoa, Goodyear, and Dow Chemical.[124] At the same time, revenues raised from corporate taxes fell to 6 percent of all federal income in 1983.[125]

In a phrase, the declining standard of living and the pillage of the national treasury can be understood as punishment for the eruptions of the 1960s. As long as unions guaranteed domestic tranquility, corporate policymakers predicated their decisions on the need for the material comfort of the vast majority of people in the United States. Once the "rebels in Eden" had stubbornly demonstrated their ingratitude, however, the ascribed role of the American people in the international balance of power and wealth was recalculated. Not only does the downward economic mobility of Americans provide an immediate cure to the problem of "rising expectations" (a problem considered by some to have caused the New Left), but it also offers some insurance that as the activist generation of 1968 moves into positions of power within the established institutions, these institutions themselves will be of reduced significance. It may be true, for example, that there are an increasing number of progressive American mayors (from Bernie Sanders to Harold Washington), but at the same time, the power of municipal governments has declined tremendously within the global system, leaving the cities all but powerless to deal with the hundreds of thousands of homeless within them. Even if Congress were to enact national legislation to control corporate flight, the economic power of the national government has been reduced. Keynesian economic planning is essentially obsolete in a global system where the scope and power of transnational corporations far exceed those of nation-states.

At least in part, the New Left was a reaction to the new global power of corporations, as were the political scandals of Watergate and Irangate. The national power elite is no longer capable of fulfilling its historic functions of developing the productive forces, expanding "democracy," and emancipating the individual. Rather, as the free enterprise system undermined itself by leading to the creation of monopolies, national monopolies have become international conglomerates serving no interest but that of continually increasing their own profits. In short, the American revolution of 1776 has seen its own gains undermined by an economic system which no longer serves the national interest.

One of the implications of these dynamics for the federal government of the United States is a weakened Congress, not only in its capability to effectively regulate the national economy but also in its ability to conduct foreign policy. In an age of electronic media and a world economic and political system, the power of the President is much greater than it ever has been (or was intended to be). The war against Vietnam was the first major example of the new powers of the executive branch of government. Congress never declared war against Vietnam, even though the Constitution stipulates that only Congress has the authority to declare war. Nonetheless, for more than a decade, the executive branch of government conducted a war which was never in the interests of the American people.

The invasion of the Democratic Party's inner sanctum at Watergate and the resulting ouster of Nixon and Company from the White House is widely regarded as proof that Congress was able to curb the new power wielded by the executive branch. The step from Nixon's fiasco to Reagan's Irangate (symbolically portrayed by the distance from the Watergate Hotel to the basement of the White House) serves to illustrate the everyday reality that unbridled executive actions continue to guide the formulation and imple- mentation of our country's policies. The similarities between Watergate and Irangate are striking. Both cases involve the conduct of illegal wars (ones specifically forbidden by Congress—Cambodia in 1973 and Nicaragua in 1986), the falsification of Presidential records in the face of Congressional investigations, and the spectacle of the nation's most powerful men being exposed as criminal operators. To be sure, the public existence of these scandals provides dramatic proof that Congress can temporarily succeed in restraining the machinations of appointed power brokers. The reappearance of the ghost of Watergate more than a decade after it had outlived its usefulness to the powers that be, however, serves to indicate that there are structural conditions causing such crises (and that there are similar solutions put forth to deal with them).

Common sense tells us that the Iran-Contra Affair, like the Watergate scandal before it, is the result of the strengths of American democracy, of the smooth functioning of a system of checks and balances. The mass media have presented the American public with abundant proof that Congress has again curbed the excessive powers appropriated by the executive branch of government. Beneath the surface of the apparent resiliency of American democracy, however, there are indications that our common sense comprehension of these events is insufficient to understand them. As I discuss below, the Iran-Contra spectacle, rather than verifying the pluralist view of American government, represents the reassertion of the corporate elite's will over that of the President (and people) of the United States.

Both Watergate and Irangate, although symbolized by scandals peripheral to the primary issues, have been used to create the preconditions for major policy adjustments demanded by the corporate elite. In Nixon's case, an end to the war against Indochina, restabilization of relations with China, and the restoration of domestic order were achieved via Watergate; in Reagan's case, renegotiation of arms control agreements with the Soviet Union and the rehabilitation of the less explosive system of global spheres of influence are the real stakes behind Irangate. It should not be forgotten that "improving ties with Iran," the strategic goal of the "arms for hostages" fiasco, necessarily meant channeling the Islamic revolution north against the Soviet Union, rather than letting it spread to regimes friendly to the United States like Kuwait and Saudi Arabia.

The difference of opinion which developed between the Reagan administration and trilateralist leadership was first made public in the pages of *Foreign Affairs* (a journal which serves as a trial balloon for the opinions of corporate leaders). Writing in *Foreign Affairs* in the spring of 1982, Robert McNamara, McGeorge Bundy, George Kennan, and Gerard Smith (spokesmen for the highest levels of corporate power) raised the need for the United States to change its nuclear policy—specifically to reverse its long-standing assertion that it would "use nuclear weapons if necessary to repel aggression from the East." In discussing the attitude of the Reagan administration, the authors noted that:

> The present American Administration has so far shown little interest in questions of this sort, and indeed a seeming callousness in some quarters in Washington toward nuclear dangers may be partly responsible for some of the recent unrest in Europe . . . The

day is long past when public awe and governmental secrecy made
nuclear policy a matter for only the most private executive
determination.[126]

Transnational leaders were well aware that Reagan's military build-up and the
burgeoning European movement threatened to disrupt the Atlantic Alliance
and alter the post-World War II division of Europe. In the short run, they
feared that as protests in Europe continued to mount and became increasingly
anti-American in content, there existed the potential for the radicalization of
the huge base of the domestic disarmament movement, a possibility which
could have led to a disruption of the smooth functioning of corporate
democracy. In their words:

> The principal immediate danger in the current military posture of
> the Alliance is not that it will lead to large-scale war, conventional
> or nuclear. The balance of terror, and the caution of both sides,
> appear strong enough today to prevent such a catastrophe, at least
> in the absence of some deeply *destabilizing political change* which
> might lead to panic or adventurism on either side. But the present
> unbalanced reliance on nuclear weapons, if long continued, might
> produce exactly such political change...Conversely, if consensus
> is re-established on a military policy that the peoples and govern-
> ments of the Alliance can believe in, both political will and
> deterrent credibility will be reinforced. [emphasis added][127]

In reading the above excerpts from *Foreign Affairs*, it should be kept in mind
that it was in the same journal after World War II that an article by one of the
same authors, George Kennan—using the pseudonym, "Mr. X," first
proposed the policy of containing the Soviet Union, a policy which was at the
root of the Cold War—and, as some insist—the wars against Korea and
Vietnam. Similarly, it was in the same journal that the need for what became
known as the Camp David peace accord was first raised.

Reagan's failure to produce an arms control agreement with the Soviet
Union during his first term in office led McNamara, Bundy, Kennan, and
Smith to issue yet another message (a much clearer one) to the President before
his summit meeting with Gorbachev in Iceland. This time, they put the matter
in no uncertain terms. President Reagan could enjoy his second term or
maintain his policies, but not both. Their second article concluded:

> This has not been a cheerful analysis, or one that we find pleasant to
> present. If the President makes no major change of course in his
> second term, *we see no alternative to a long, hard, damage-limiting
> effort by Congress* . . . He currently has some advisors who fear all
> forms of arms control, but advisors can be changed. We are not
> suggesting that the President will change his course lightly.
> [emphasis added][128]

Before the failure of the summit in Iceland, corporate opinion-leaders were
openly discussing some of the options they might have to implement to bring a
measure of nuclear sanity to the Reagan administration. Many establishment

figures were concerned about the intransigence of the Reagan administration in their dealings with the Soviet Union, particularly the insistence on spending untold billions of dollars on Star Wars, technically a dubious system and politically a violation of the Nixon administration's ABM treaty with the Soviet Union.

Apparently, their concern about the possibility of the present limited wars in Afghanistan, Lebanon, and Nicaragua escalating was so great that, after the failure to negotiate seriously in Iceland, they helped precipitate a domestic crisis (Irangate) aimed at disrupting the rightward drift of Reagan's staff. If the above analysis is correct, then it seems clear that the co-optive thrust of corporate policymakers remains a significant vehicle for the pacification of both insurgent movements and unbridled executive action. In an era of nuclear instability generated by Cruise missiles and a new generation of armaments, can anyone be sorry that corporate leaders precipitated Irangate to bring a measure of sobriety into the National Security Council?

The continuing crises of six American Presidencies (from John Kennedy to Ronald Reagan) appear to indicate the vulnerability of that office. In fact, the exact opposite is the case: Precisely because these men were the world's most powerful individuals did they became politically expendable. In short, the corporate elite created and then sacrificed Presidents in order to rejuvenate a system whose legitimacy rests upon the fact that no one person appears to run it. Is it a mere coincidence that the nation's political system has suffered crisis after crisis at the same time as American corporations have moved "their" wealth abroad?

It is not only the integrity of the national political system which has been undermined by the interests of transnational corporations. The fate of local communities is even more precarious. Whole towns have been poisoned by massive amounts of toxic wastes dumped by corporations. In one case alone, that of Woburn, Massachusetts, sixteen children died mysteriously from leukemia, and W.R. Grace Corporation (whose chief executive, Peter Grace, served as chairman of President Reagan's commission on inefficiency in government) systematically lied to local residents, priests, and the judicial system during the course of years of investigations. Although Congress passed a law requiring corporations to report to the Environmental Protection Agency (EPA) how they used and disposed of new synthetic chemicals like trichlorethylene (TCE), W.R. Grace filed no such report. Two years later, when the EPA demanded the information from Grace, the corporation reported that it had used only one five-gallon drum of TCE and then discontinued using it. A year later, Grace claimed that it had used only four drums of TCE over a twenty-two year period, not enough to have caused Woburn's leukemia problem. The testimony of plant employees, however, contradicted the statements of corporate executives. On the news program *Sixty Minutes*, Al Love, the Grace employee in charge of taking delivery of chemicals into the Woburn plant, estimated that at least four barrels of TCE had been used at that one location every year for more than ten years. Another employee testified that TCE was dumped in the backyard every day after it had been used to clean machinery. Grace, one of America's largest corporations, ultimately settled the civil suit against it for a multimillion dollar sum (spare change for a transnational giant), although the possibility of criminal charges against it remain open. W.R. Grace Corporation's actions in Woburn are part of a global pattern: The same corporation owns United Fruit Company, whose interests in Central America, according to Representative Henry Gonzales of Texas, exert a "tremendous influence" on the Reagan administration.

It goes without saying, of course, that Woburn is one example when hundreds—if not thousands—of other corporate dumps exist. Moreover, it would not be wise to rely upon federal agencies to control corporate crimes: At the same time as the EPA was investigating Grace, one of the top administrators of the EPA was forced to resign after perjuring herself during Congressional testimony. More recently, the Justice Department initiated a criminal investigation into unlawful collaboration between the nuclear power industry and the Nuclear Regulatory Commission (NRC) at the same time as the NRC filed regulations to strip states of their right to veto nuclear power plants.

Watergate and Irangate, although portrayed in the media as isolated examples, would appear to be indications of the daily method of operation at work in the economic as well as the political institutions of contemporary society. While, for some, the Congressional hearings into the whole Iran-Contra Affair serve to justify the view that democracy is alive and well in the United States, it should also be evident that the failure of Congress to even question the larger issues raised above reveals an unspoken acceptance of corporate power as both the means and ends of the policies of the federal government. Furthermore, there are serious questions which should be raised concerning the nature of the commissions which are appointed to investigate the "excesses" of federal agencies. Senator John Tower has become known for serving as chairing the "Tower Commission," the Congressional group entrusted with providing the government (and the public) with a comprehensive report on the Reagan administration's involvement in the Iran-Contra affair. It completely escaped the media's widely-publicized coverage of the Tower Commission, however, to even mention that Senator Tower had previously served on a Congressional investigating committee. In 1976, he was Vice Chair of the Senate Intelligence Committee which reported on the CIA's illegal domestic use of educators and the media to influence public opinion in the United States. While his service on that committee might seem to have enhanced his qualifications for chair of the Tower Commission, it should be pointed out that he was one of the committee's two members who refused to sign the final report because he felt its effect would be so damaging to the CIA. Much as corporate executives earn their spurs in profitable scams and move up the organizational ladder, so, it seems, do federal power-brokers operate in a similar mode.

The above dynamics demonstrate the fact that the federal government increasingly operates like a corporation and in the interests of corporations, and they illuminate an important reason why the public's confidence in the government continues to erode. Tendencies toward "corporate socialism" (as government's subservience to business has been called) significantly affect the quality of life in the United States, undermining as they do our democratic heritage as well as the standard of living taken for granted ever since the Great Depression. With the rise to global dominance of a few hundred transnational corporations and their subversion of the health and welfare of the people of the United States, there appear to exist the potential conditions for the popular rejection of the entire existing system, a rejection which, with the notable exception of the New Left, had not appeared since the 1930s.

In the next chapter, I discuss the political legacy of the New Left for future social movements. Before moving on to examine the prospects of qualitatively transforming the existing system, however, a final effect of the New Left should be considered: the strengthening of the existing system's capacity for domestic violence. Since 1970, local police departments have been beefed up with tanks, helicopters, and even submarines through federal funding. Specially trained "intelligence" officers and SWAT teams have been created and now routinely work within local police forces. The FBI has reconsolidated itself in the wake of Congressional investigations and public concern caused by its illegal operations, giving it greater capacity to function in infiltrating and disrupting domestic movements.

For the time being, at least, the control mechanisms of the established system are contained in an economic disciplining of the poor and working class, a disciplining reflected in the declining standard of living, the hundreds of thousands of homeless, and continual economic insecurity for millions of people. If these mechanisms of internal control prove to be insufficient in the years ahead, behind them stands a vast repressive apparatus. The strengthening of the structures of domination—not their weakening—remains an undeniable and unintended effect of the New Left.

Part III

INTERPRETING THE NEW LEFT

Chapter 5

THE POLITICAL LEGACY OF THE NEW LEFT

The fact that the time has come for a self-disciplined organization bears witness not to the defeat but to the prospects of the opposition. The first heroic period of the movement, the period of joyful and often spectacular action, has come to an end. The capitalist enterprise is rapidly approaching its inherent limits on a global scale and is resorting to intensified violence and intensified co-optation.

—Herbert Marcuse, 1972

Whether in the United States or Japan, Europe or Latin America, the New Left proved incapable of sustaining the momentum of the popular upsurge it helped set into motion. As the radical impetus of 1968 was blunted and dispersed, written out of history books and caricatured in the mass media and Hollywood, the New Left entered a period of crisis, a crisis brought on by the disintegration of a movement which had reached world-historical proportions. In May 1968 and May 1970, vast popular movements had unexpectedly erupted, creating crises of major proportions which challenged the global universe of cultural, political, and economic reality. After the uprisings had died down, however, the logic of the established system exerted a powerful influence in depoliticizing the counterculture and dispersing the New Left.

Despite the apparent failure of the New Left, the openings provided by its decisive breaks with the established system leave a significant legacy. The defeat of the United States in Vietnam ushered in an era of successful national liberation movements in the periphery of the world system at the same time as the U.S. military was restrained by the "Vietnam syndrome." The federal government remains unable to regain the kind of popular legitimacy it enjoyed before the 1960s. Moreover, there have been significant changes in domestic relationships as witnessed by the newly won rights and dignity for Americans of African descent and increasing opportunities for many minorities and women. The Jim Crow system of segregation has been largely dismantled on both the institutional and cultural levels; there exists a new set of norms, laws, and values regarding relationships between men and women (from legalized abortion and widespread birth control to open homosexuality—in some cases legally protected—and an increasing number of women who choose not to marry). As the political and cultural values of the New Left have become common sense, millions of people have experienced improvements in the daily conditions of their lives.

The expectation of many people in 1968 was that there would be a linear progression from the New Left to a new society. Despite the many legal reforms and cultural shifts since the 1960s, however, it appears that there has been as much regression as progression in world affairs since 1968. The aspirations of the New Left to rationally reorganize international relations, to transform authoritarian structures of power into their opposite, and to build a qualitatively new way of life appear as utopian speculation in the real world of increasing starvation, growing militarism, and fresh outbreaks of bloody wars. Although the New Left in the United States challenged the racism and patriarchy of the society, these dynamics continue to shape cultural and social reality. Civil rights reforms and formal equality notwithstanding, the overall economic situation of minorities and women in the United States has improved very little since 1968. More than one-fourth of all black families have incomes below the federally established poverty line, and the number of impoverished female-headed families continues to rise.

Despite continuing injustice, the New Left leaves its imprint in the ongoing attempts to create a new world culture—a culture posing the possibility of qualitatively new relationships between core and periphery of the world system, between men and women, and between human beings and Nature. The cultural and political redefinition of freedom remains a vital question in the wake of the New Left. At the beginning of the twentieth century, when the struggle for socialism shifted away from the industrialized societies to the underdeveloped countries of the third world, the idea of a free society was redefined as one which had eliminated hunger, poverty, disease, and illiteracy. Socialism as the "leap into freedom" was defamed as "utopian" at the same time as the atrophy of the utopian imagination proceeded at an alarming rate. With the rising tide of socialisms in the third world and the reintroduction of its possibility in the industrialized countries by the New Left, the vision of a free society again needs to be redefined, going beyond the far-sightedness of even the most "utopian" ideas of the nineteenth century. The vision of a world without hunger or an arms race, without alienation, boredom, domineering nation-states, and arbitrary authorities—a vision prefigured in the praxis of the New Left—is an unabashedly optimistic prognosis for the future of the world system and possibly an unattainable one. There exists no guarantee of its realization; the alternatives remain, as they were vocalized in 1968, "socialism or barbarism."

A genuine revolution in the advanced capitalist societies, particularly the United States, would be either "world-historical" or nothing at all. Without such a qualitative leap, there will only be further degeneration of a world society administered by and for centralized elites and transnational corporations, a world in which production and distribution of the vast social wealth will not serve self-determined human needs, but as levers of environmental destruction, starvation, and militarism. These are the only realistic alternatives given the fact that the United States is the strongest nation-state in the world. Self-determination for oppressed people and self-management of institutional power in the United States would break up the world economy as it exists and render meaningless the existing geo-political power blocs. It would mean the goals of the disarmament movement would be realized—the world would *dis*-arm. As Marcuse realized in 1972:

> The fall of the capitalist superpower is likely to precipitate the collapse of the military dictatorships in the Third World which depend entirely on the superpower... The Chinese and Cuban revolutions would be able to go their own ways—freed from the suffocating blockade and the equally suffocating necessity of maintaining an ever more costly defensive machine. Could the Soviet world long remain immune, or for any length of time capable of "containing" this revolution?[1]

A genuine revolution in the United States, while national in form, would be international in content: It would be based upon the universal interests of the human species and all life, not just the self-interest of a particular nation or sector of the population. It would be a working-class feminist revolution against racial domination or nothing at all.

In this chapter, I discuss the political legacy of the New Left for future social movements in the core of the world system. Although the immediate prospects of revolution in the economically advanced societies are none too bright, a theoretical exploration of such a possibility is one dimension of the legacy of the New Left. Some of the analysis in this chapter compares social movements in Europe with those in the United States, but my primary concern is the center of the modern world system: the United States of America.

Rebellion and Revolution

The men in power had their universities,
The students took them.
The men in power had their factories,
The workers took them.
The men in power had their radios,
The journalists took them.
The men in power only have their power now.
We shall take it.

—Poster, Beaux-Arts, May 1968

Even though the first seven lines of this poster were true, the grand finale failed to materialize. Of course, a one- or two-month long revolution is not possible. But revolution should not be viewed simply as a mechanistic problem of seizing state power or as some other technical transformation of the structures of society. Rather, revolution is a process through which large numbers of people qualitatively transform the values, norms, and institutions of society—not simply overthrowing the old rulers and replacing them, but creating new kinds of social realities and human beings.

A revolutionary situation is one which opens the possibilities for the transformation of the totality of social reality. A revolt, on the other hand, merely demonstrates discontent with the present state of affairs. When people revolt, they rise up against those perceived to cause a common problem, not to take control of their own destinies. A revolt culminates in the negation of the previous rulers, values, or institutions, not in the affirmation of new modes of life. As Sartre put it:

> The revolutionary wants to change the world; he transcends it and moves toward the future, toward an order of values which he himself invents. The rebel is careful to preserve the abuses from which he suffers so that he can go on rebelling against them...He does not want to destroy or transcend the existing order; he simply wants to rise against it.[2]

As discussed in the previous two chapters, the New Left in France, West Germany, and the United States reached its culmination in massive strikes and revolts touched off by attacks on the movement. These high points of resistance were touched off in Germany by the near-assassination of Rudi Dutschke in April 1968 and by the passage of the *Notstandsgesetze* (emergency legislation enabling the government to curtail individual rights in times of declared emergencies) in May 1968; in France, by the arrests at the Sorbonne in May 1968; and in the United States by police attacks on black people in 1967, the assassination of Martin Luther King in April 1968, attacks on the Black Panther Party, the invasion of Cambodia, and the murders at Kent State and Jackson State Universities in May 1970, and the mining of Haiphong Harbor in 1972. The *reactive* origins of these explosions indicate that the time and space of the movement's eruptions were determined by the pace of externally-defined events, testimony to the power of the system to define reality and not to the power of the people to *redefine* it.

There is general agreement that major historical outbreaks of social conflict have been precipitated by some event or series of events (wars, rising expectations concomitant with deprivation, repressive measures). In the case of New Left general strikes, however, the eruptions were particularly diffuse and spontaneous. In May 1968, for example, when ten million French workers went one strike, no one in the government (or the opposition) seemed to know what the strikers really wanted. The workers themselves were unable to formulate a general consensus for demands and action. As time went on, there quickly set in a psychic Thermidor, an impetus to return to the pre-crisis situation, a reaction demonstrated by the many workers who continued to punch their time-cards when they arrived for strike duty. When all was said and done, the crisis inevitably led to the restoration of order and to a streamlining of the existing system. Despite the momentary establishment of dual power in the factories, universities, and neighborhoods, the forces of order not only remained intact, but they were actually strengthened by the crisis.

The diverse qualities of the global New Left as manifested in each particular country where it appeared can be traced, in part at least, to a rebellion against (rather than a revolution of) national cultural characteristics. The content of the revolt in Germany was (and is) specifically anti-authoritarian in contrast to traditional German authoritarianism. In the United States, New Left activists all but took vows of poverty in opposition to the opulence of their society, and in France the cultural hegemony of the nation and the extreme centralization of the state were challenged by the twin aspirations of internationalism and self-management. At the same time, however, national characteristics were also spontaneously reproduced within the movement: the theoretical strengths of the German New Left, the romantic and imaginative actions of the French, and the militant pragmatism of Americans. These characteristics stand out historically, although they were also evident in 1968 to Stephen Spender:

> If one were asked to sum up in a word the expression on the faces of
> the students in different countries, one would say of the Americans
> "hysterical" (driven to it), of the French "romantic," of the West
> Germans "theoretic"—but of the Czechs one would say "modest!"[3]

The influence of specific cultural traits and national conditions on the New Left can be further observed in the form of action taken by the movement vis-a-vis the mass media. German activists launched all-out attacks on the trucks and offices of the Springer newspaper chain (the largest in Germany); in France, journalists, broadcasters, and media technicians stayed out on strike as long as any others, and they raised imaginative slogans like, "The police on the television mean the police in your home"; and the incredible proliferation of the underground press in the United States was an indication of the "Do it!" mentality.

National conditions help explain why, in Germany and Italy, the insurrectionary impetus has not evaporated, as seems to be the case in France and the United States. In the formerly fascist states, there remains an historically-conditioned legitimation crisis of the "democratic" corporate state—a comparative inability to fulfill its integrative and co-optive functions—conditions which provide a background to the continuing armed struggle. It should not be forgotten that, in 1968, the German Social Democrats decided to form a Grand Coalition with the Christian Democrats and that the Chancellor of Germany was Kurt Georg Kiesinger, a former member of the Nazi party. Neither should the incapacity of more than forty governments since World War II to rule Italy be overlooked.

Of course, the legitimation crises engendered by the New Left were not confined to Italy and Germany. In the aftermath of the rebellions and strikes from 1967 to 1970, guerrilla groups and "new communist parties" formed throughout the industrialized countries in the belief that they could accomplish what the actions of millions of people had failed to do: destroy the existing system so that a new society could be born. Table 2 indicates the extent to which the armed struggle by small groups replaced the popular movement of 1968. The armed struggle testified to the inability of the movement to realize its spontaneously generated forms of a new society at the same time as it contributed to the decline of the popular impetus.

Table 2

International Incidents of Political Violence Classified as "Terrorism," 1971-1985

Year	Incidents
1971	278
1972	206
1973	311
1974	388
1975	572
1976	727
1977	1257
1978	1511
1979	2585
1980	2773
1981	2701
1982	2492
1983	2838
1984	3525
1985	3012

Source: Risks International Inc., as reported in the **Christian Science Monitor,** May 13, 1986, p. 20.

In contrast to traditional views of revolution as a change in elites or the destruction of the existing economic and political structures, however, the New Left had raised the idea of the transformation of power into a decentralized and self-managed form. Such a revolution, unlike a revolt, would be more than a struggle against inherited injustices and irrational structures and would not culminate in the mere seizure of national power, but in the transformation of centralized power through the building up of dignified processes of life and alternative structures for the expansion of the democratic rights of the individual. Such a transformation would depend upon the continual liberation of the sensibilities and needs of the vast majority of people, not simply the seizure of power by an armed vanguard. The leap which would be the real "leap into history" would be prepared by the aesthetic and cultural transformation of individuals and groups, whose new needs would prefigure the political and economic transformation of society.

With the consolidation of the global counterrevolution in 1968, the New Left proved itself incapable of reconsolidating a popular base and moving to the second phase of struggle: going from the contestation of power to the building of a hegemonic bloc capable of leading the entire society in a new direction. In the vacuum created by the dispersal of the New Left, there has been a resurgence of parties from the traditional Left, and at least in the short run, this renewal of socialism has not been an entirely unsuccessful one, as rejuvenated Socialist Parties in France, Greece, and Spain have won electoral victories. In Latin America, there has also been a reconsolidation of traditional organizations of the Left. After the defeat of guerrilla movements in Bolivia, Brazil, and Uruguay and the brutal repression of popular movements in Chile and Argentina, a new stage was reached. As one observer analyzed the dynamics of the early 1970s:

> The "new left" in Latin America consisted primarily of Gue-vara/foco and Marxist tendencies, neither of which proved capable of guiding the revolution. As these currents fell into disarray, most conventional Communist Parties remained consolidated around a conception of peaceful, reformist, and electoral transition to the revolutionary process. By the early 1970s the Cuban party also became reunited somewhat with this perspective. Cuba endorsed the 1975 Havana declaration of Latin American CP's which, in the wake of the tragic defeat in Chile, held up the military-led reform process in Peru as typifying the strategic path of the Latin American revolution.[4]

Not all currents in the Latin American Left flowed toward conceptions of revolution from above. The armed struggle of the Sandinistas culminated in the ouster of Somoza, and in El Salvador, revolutionary forces consolidated under the banner of the Farabundo Marti National Liberation Front, whose unified forces would have already driven the "democratically" elected government of death squads out of the country if not for the mammoth amount of U.S. aid pumped in. It would be a mistake to view the radicalization of the Left in El Salvador as an isolated occurrence, since a similar process seems to be underway in other Latin American countries. In those countries where traditional organizations of the Left remain pacified, radical organizations like *Sendero Luminoso* in Peru have emerged. In the Middle East, the New Arab Left has maintained its commitment to popular revolution and armed struggle despite tremendous repression at the hands of the Israeli and Arab regimes.

New Left cultural politics continue to define the form of *radical* oppositional movements in the economically advanced countries. Since the high point of 1968, the contours of this movement have been found in the Metropolitan Indians of Italy and the Punk Left in England, Germany, Switzerland, and Holland.[5] The New Left's impetus toward decentralization and cultural autonomy finds expression today in the increasing regionalism in Europe (partially indicated by the map below), in movements for community control of neighborhoods, and in the plethora of groups opposed to nuclear

Map 3

Devolving Europe: Nations Emerging from States

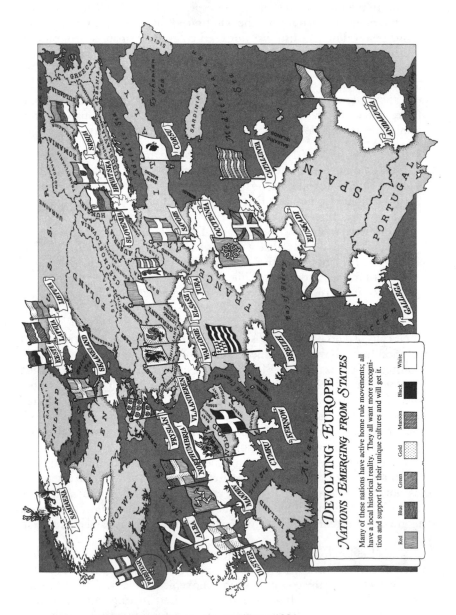

Source: **CoEvolution Quarterly,** No. 32, Winter 1981.

power and weapons, patriarchy, and international domination of small nations by superpowers. In West Germany, an extraparliamentary movement emerged in 1979, and the Green Party has consolidated itself along the lines of self-managed and decentralized theory and practice. Beginning in the fall of 1986, a new generation of student activism appeared in France, Spain, Mexico, Palestine, South Korea, and China, further indications that the New Left-style student-led revolts continue to define the constituency of modern social movements.

Throughout the world in the 1980s, political movements have emerged which draw energy from the impetus of 1968, but in the United States, a period of reaction has set in, and the movement is depoliticized, fragmented, and seemingly unable to reconsolidate its energies. To be sure, new social movements in the United States are much more widespread than is commonly realized. The impulse of the 1960s continues in the civil rights program of the Rainbow Coalition, the emergence of widespread movements against apartheid (including the appearance of more than seventy-five shantytowns on college campuses in the spring of 1986), the disarmament initiatives, the tremendous growth of feminism, the gay liberation movement, the resurgence of radical thinking in academia, and the new political involvement of senior citizens, farmers, rock n' roll bands, and Hollywood celebrities. In the 1980s, there have emerged thousands of locally-based neighborhood movements; a diverse array of single-issue pressure groups; hundreds of ballot propositions—more than at any time since the 1930s;[6] rising interest in radical theory off the campuses; a series of protracted strikes and intense labor struggles; massive movements against nuclear power and U.S. intervention in Central America; and hundreds of ongoing worker-controlled collectives and alternative institutions. The women's movement was nationally prominent in the campaign for abortion and the Equal Rights Amendment, and the anti-nuclear weapons initiatives have found widespread support.

Despite these and other activities, however, the oppositional movement in the United States remains atomized and depoliticized when compared with its counterparts in Europe. In the short run, it appears that the kind of focused—and increasingly "socialist"—social movements which exist in Europe will not appear in the United States. Why have the movements in Europe had such clear impact on national politics (whether in the electoral victories of Mitterrand in France, Papandreou in Greece, Gonzales in Spain, or the Greens in West Germany), while in the United States the trend of national politics is toward increasing military power, cutbacks of aid to poor people and the most needy, and a resurgence of global intervention? This question has long been a subject of analysis and debate in many different contexts. As long ago as 1906, Werner Sombart asked, "Why is There No Socialism in the United States?" The legacy of the New Left leaves more than sufficient reason to ask it again.

The answer to this question cannot be found by comparing the relative numbers of New Left activists in organizations of the 1960s in the United States with those in Europe. In 1968, the Socialist Party in France was practically non-existent, and prior to May 1968, there were no more than

2,000 members in all the French New Left groups combined.[7] The movement among students alone in the United States was far bigger than the entire German New Left. Membership in Students for a Democratic Society (SDS) in the United States (that is, not counting SNCC, the Black Panther Party, or other movement organizations) was far greater both absolutely and proportionally than in its counterpart in West Germany. Even at its high point, the *Sozialistischer Deutscher Studentenbund* (SDS) in Germany never had more than 2,000 members, and although the New Left created quite a stir there, it never attracted the widespread participation so essential to the larger movements in France or the United States.[8] The ratio of SDS members to total population was 1 to 7,000 in the United States compared with 1 to 30,000 in West Germany.[9] In 1984, Jesse Jackson and the Rainbow Coalition gathered a percentage of votes that was two to three times higher than those received by *die Grünen* in *any* German election. The victory of Harold Washington in Chicago—to say nothing of similar campaigns in Berkeley, Santa Cruz, Madison, Boston, and Burlington, Vermont—indicates a far greater level of popular support for post-1968 "new" politics in the United States than in Germany.

How then can the decline in radical movements in the United States be explained? A number of factors should be mentioned: first and foremost, the end of the war against Vietnam. With the end of overt U.S. intervention, the urgency of mobilizations against ongoing genocide was gone, and the movement was left without a unifying focus for action. Since the war was also a focal point for the New Left in Europe, however, its end alone does not explain the relatively greater dispersion of the New Left here. Similarly, if the reason for the relative absence of a focused social movement in the United States is sought in economic factors like the onset of the Great Recession of 1979, it again becomes difficult to distinguish between Europe and the United States, since the post-Vietnam economic downturn was a global one with similar effects throughout the economically advanced societies.

In my view, there are three factors which account for the fragmentation of the movement in the United States: co-optation by the two-party system; the professionalization of the movement; and its displacement to the realm of culture.

Co-optation by the Two-Party System

Compared with many other countries, citizens of the United States enjoy extensive democratic rights like free speech and assembly. At the same moment, the apparent flexibility of the political system helps to account for the incorporation of the New Left by the established system of politics. In the name of political "effectiveness," the pragmatism of the American way of life demands that those who seek to institute social change join the Democratic or Republican Parties. In contrast to European forms of representative democracy where governing coalitions are formed *after* elections, in the United States divergent interest-groups come together *before* elections to select one candidate. Such a system of elections provides for the institutional incorporation of emergent political tendencies, de-emphasizes the value of ideological questions, and focuses energy on specific candidates or issues, not ideas or long-term concerns.[10] These dynamics were clearly illustrated in 1984, when the new opportunities for minorities and women created by the struggles of the 1960s became symbolized by Jesse Jackson and Geraldine Ferraro. Their participation in the Democratic Party strengthened the existing two-party system at the same time as it helped to explain why no black, feminist, or post-New Left parties exist. Despite the increase in the number of black elected officials (from a meager 103 in 1964 to 6,424 in 1985)[11] and a 300 percent increase in the number of female elected officials between 1970 and 1985,[12] it is the two-party system which has gained, not political parties of blacks and women (or a post-New Left party like the German Greens).

It is not only the New Left which has been dissipated by the two-party system. To a large extent, the decline of social movements in the United States has accompanied the rejuvenation of a dominant party: The Workingmen's Parties of the 1830s were absorbed by the Jacksonian Democrats; the National Labor Union (the U.S. affiliate of the First International) was outmaneuvered in 1872 when the Democrats nominated the socialist Horace Greeley; in 1896, the People's Party was absorbed by the Democratic Party's nomination of William Jennings Bryan; in 1908, the same candidate was again used to blunt the thrust of the Socialist Party;[13] and the New Deal of the 1930s brought enthusiastic support from many socialists, both for the Roosevelt presidency and for the Democratic Party. In the 1940s, the Communist Party of the United States went as far as making it their official policy to carry the flag and uncritically support Roosevelt during World War II, a policy which compromised their autonomy and led to their demise long before their repression in the 1950s.[14]

The co-optive thrust of corporate democracy is nowhere greater than in the United States because those brought into established politics are brought into the two-party system. In Europe, third parties can win a share of the seats in the government according to their proportion of the votes. At a minimum, such a situation encourages a plurality of dissenting public voices, and it can also give smaller parties a position to bargain for reforms when neither of the major parties can form a clear majority without them. If the United States had a parliamentary form of government like France or Germany, there would probably be at least ten black Senators today—as opposed to none. Furthermore, it is the experience of the German Greens that if the political integrity of their elected representatives remains uncompromised—that is, *if* the membership refuses to allow bureaucratic tendencies to develop, *if* representatives remain tied to their local base, and *if* the party continues to enunciate its radical vision *after elections*—such parliamentary representatives can help popularize an extraparliamentary movement. Within the existing political system in the United States, however, voting for a party other than the Democrats or Republicans is seen as "throwing your vote away," since candidates are not elected by a proportion of votes. American pragmatism militates against breaking out of the system of established politics.

Short of changing the structure of the U.S. political system to allow representatives of smaller parties a proportional number of seats in the House of Representatives and the Senate, state and local elections offer the possibility of educating and mobilizing a popular base of support as a means of building a broad consensus for change. At the same time, however, as long as national elections offer nothing more than the political equivalent of Coke vs. Pepsi, public apathy will continue to define the primary characteristic of national elections, and the absence of meaningful public debate within legislative bodies will continue to foster unbridled executive action.

Important as the co-optive impetus of the two-party system may be in keeping the population passive and the opposition loyal, this factor alone does not adequately explain the political incorporation of the radical movement in the United States. From its beginning, the New Left was an *extraparliamentary* movement, and even if some of its members operated within Establishment politics, there remained hundreds of thousands of activists and millions of supporters who did not. To account for the dispersion of their political energy, it becomes necessary to consider additional factors: the professionalization of the movement and its displacement to the realm of culture.

Professionalization of the Movement

The tremendous impact of the New Left coupled with the historical discontinuity of social movements in the United States combined to germinate a motley assortment of reformist groups in the aftermath of the 1960s. Increasingly, activists' energies were directed into specialized and professionalized outlets. Some worked with political action committees as "professional" activists; others devoted their energy to electoral campaigns, not only around special interests or personalities, but toward some form of Rainbow politics or "economic democracy"; and still more focused their energies on particular instances of injustice (the nuclear arms race, atomic power, apartheid, the oppression of women, or U.S. intervention in Central America).

What unites these seemingly different tendencies is their *professionalization*[15] and *specialization*, tendencies which have contributed to the fragmentation of the movement. Where these various concerns were once fused together in a dynamic movement, today they have become specialized groupings with professional leaderships. Where there was once a focus of opposition to the system as a whole, today there are well-organized avenues of specialized protest orchestrated by professional activists and experts who reproduce the middle-class values of the system within the movement.

Although the New Left was a global movement able, for years, to focus on the needs of the most oppressed, the fragmented logic of the system reasserted itself in the formation of specialized interest-groups (the *social* equivalent of individualism). As professional bureaucrats came to redirect the trade-union movement into a mechanism of stability, so too were paid political activists able to bring the New Left into the system it opposed. Besides serving as an integrative mechanism, the transformation of activism into a spectator sport is the ultimate effect of the professionalization of the movement. Where political education and activities were once a *means* of mobilization, their professionalization gradually changed these means into an *end* in itself: the maintenance of professionals whose jobs are "educational."

Intentional or not, the effects of paid functionaries who bring grievances into the arena of established politics are often to undermine the vitality of grassroots movements which raised the issues in the first place. The specialization of focus engendered by paid professionals helps narrow the questioning process and directs it into "appropriate channels." In the case of the New Left, the tendency to question how society determines its goals and to challenge the system's irrationality was transformed into technical problem-solving and reforming the established system.

If grassroots activism involves a questioning of the system's structures, the praxis of professional activists implies the system's validity. Even when social reformers are convinced that more is needed than small adjustments or better people (or more women and minorities) making the decisions, their professional status preempts the vitality of popular movements.[16] In order to appreciate the insidious effects of professional activists on popular movements, two examples are discussed below: the disarmament movement and the campaign to enact the Equal Rights Amendment (ERA).

The Disarmament Movement and the Campaign for the Equal Rights Amendment

The Reagan administration's plan to install new medium-range nuclear missiles in Europe aroused a wide spectrum of international opposition which continued to intensify as the missiles' arrival date grew closer. On October 10, 1981, a quarter of a million people in Bonn marched against the missiles. Similar large-scale protest marches with distinctly anti-American overtones were held two weeks later in Paris, London, Brussels, and Rome. Earlier, on September 13, amid a flurry of guerrilla attacks on U.S. personnel and bases in West Germany, over 7,000 riot police were needed to guard Secretary of State Haig from at least 50,000 demonstrators in West Berlin, and in the ensuing turmoil, hundreds were arrested and over 150 police injured.[17]

The disarmament movement in the United States quickly mobilized as the repercussions of the global anti-nuclear impetus were felt on this side of the Atlantic. On June 12, 1982, the high point of the movement was reached when 800,000 people (some estimates were as high as one million) converged on New York City to express their support for a nuclear-free world. In the months prior to that march, organizers of Ground Zero Week had conducted anti-nuclear educational events in 150 cities and 500 towns, and the Union of Concerned Scientists had sponsored teach-ins at 360 campuses, events which drew an estimated 350,000 observers.[18] The success of nuclear freeze initiatives on the ballot in the fall of 1982 was even more stupendous: It won in eight of nine states and in thirty-six of thirty-nine cities and counties where it was on the ballot. Besides the more than 11 million votes (out of a total of 19 million) which the nuclear freeze received in these initiatives, it was approved in 321 city councils, 446 New England town meetings, 63 county councils, and 11 state legislatures.

Professional politicians and corporate leaders quickly jumped on the disarmament bandwagon. Before the massive June rally in New York, Ronald Reagan declared: "I am with the people marching against nuclear weapons."[19] A month earlier, 19 Senators and 122 Representatives had voiced their support for the nuclear freeze. The speed with which the disarmament movement garnered supporters demonstrates the international connections between European and American social movements at the same time as it shows that the American political establishment is ready to co-opt a European movement even before it appears in the United States.

Of course, it is difficult to fault the disarmament movement for being useful to the more benign members of the corporate elite, particularly if a measure of nuclear security is negotiated in Geneva. At the same time, however, there were longer-term questions dealing with the causes of the arms race and the militarization of the planet which were not part of the discourse created by the professional leadership of the movement. One could begin by asking whether the long-term effects of the teach-ins, rallies, and electoral initiatives have been to enhance the legitimacy of scientific specialists and professional politicians or to enhance the vitality of a popular movement. The parade of experts who spoke at the movement's events was one indication of the technocratic ideology of its leadership. Another indication was the channeling of the movement into the Democratic Party. At their annual conference in February 1983, for example, delegates representing the more than 20,000 Nuclear Weapons Freeze Campaign activists in the United States reached a consensus that their most immediate goal should be the passage of a freeze resolution by both houses of Congress. A further agreement was reached that the campaign should work to "elect in 1984 a President and Congress who will actively support the freeze."[20]

Missing from the theory and practice of the disarmament movement is an understanding that it is the economic and political structures of the existing world system which are responsible for the systematic militarization of our planet. To put forth the belief that lasting world peace and genuine disarmament can be achieved within the framework of the present world system is to fail to understand the causes of war, its roots in the irrational structures of the existing system. No matter how goodhearted they may be, liberal advocates of disarmament foster the illusion that the present system has the capability of achieving the goals of lasting world peace and genuine disarmament. The urgency of their appeals often serves to stifle the possibility that it might be the very nature of the economic and political structures of the present system—of capital as a self-expanding value—which *necessitate* militarism.[21] Why are wars and increasing military expenditures the system's solutions to its economic crises? Didn't World War II and the vast expansion of the Pentagon pose the system's solution to the Great Depression? Are there structural reasons for Reagan's vast increase in military expenditures? Why are we spending over one million dollars per minute on armaments when there already exist over three tons for every man, woman, and child?[22]

The professional climate of the disarmament movement not only stifled such questions, but its leadership actually reproduced society's racism within the movement. The huge rally of June 12, 1982 is a case in point. At the same time that hundreds of thousands of people converged to express their aspirations for peace, a U.S.-sanctioned genocidal (but "conventional") war was occurring in Lebanon. The organizers of the rally took great pains to ensure that *nothing* critical of Israel was allowed to be said from the speakers' platform. Even though Menachim Begin, as Prime Minister of Israel the man responsible for the ongoing bombing of population centers (to say nothing of his role in the 1948 massacre at Deir Yassin), was to arrive in New York that week, the rally organizers would not permit the planned demonstrations against his visit even to be announced.

There are, of course, legitimate political differences between single- and multi-issue approaches to organizing, but at the same time, single-issue campaigns can be a guise for allowing only the viewpoints of a rally's leadership to be publicized. Although the rally's leadership used the argument that the single issue uniting the participants was the threat of nuclear war, they refused to consider that it is in the third world, specifically in Israel and South Africa, that the main danger of nuclear escalation exists. In fact, in the last twenty years, it has been at Khe Sanh in Vietnam in 1968 and in the Middle East in 1973 that the use of nuclear weapons was closest to occurring.[23] In 1973, a decision was actually made to load Israeli bombers with nuclear weapons when it appeared that Israel was losing the war. It may be that the exclusionary ideology of Zionism and the history of the Nazi holocaust will lead Israel to be the world's second detonator of an atomic bomb in the name of "defense."

Despite the danger of a nuclear war being started by Israel, the leadership of the June 12 rally prevented "side issues" from being discussed. Using such excuses as "time pressures," and "technical considerations," the rally's leadership was "freed" from any political responsibility for excluding speakers critical of Israel. The organizers' support for Israel was neatly hidden by the pragmatic application of their professional ethos and specialized focus.

As the "technologically and economically most advanced, but politically and culturally most backward" country in the world,[24] there exists a general climate of reaction in the United States, one which pervades even the most "radical" movements. The climate of Zionism is the most shameless form of racism among "radicals" in the United States, but it serves as a mirror image to the more general racism which makes the unity and vitality of the movement highly problematic. Evidence of these connections prior to the June 12 march is, unfortunately, abundant. Six months before the rally at an organizers' convention, a black delegate had proposed that the slogan, "No U.S. Intervention in the Third World," be adopted by the coalition, but parliamentary maneuvers and a long tirade by Bella Abzug were enough to defeat the proposal on the grounds that the "disarmament movement would be ineffective if 'side' issues were allowed."[25] To be sure, it was not only Abzug who temporarily succeeded in compromising the integrity of the disarmament movement. A whole range of groups (among them Greenpeace, the Quakers, and Physicians for Social Responsibility) refused to accept speakers and slogans focused on U.S. intervention in the third world because they preferred to try reaching conservative American groups on the disarmament issue.[26] At one point, the National Black United Front was actually excluded from the

June 12 leadership because they insisted on the need to address racism from the speakers' platform.

Finally, after continuing debates, the issues of racism and U.S. intervention in the third world (but not anything related to Israel) were scheduled to be included in the speeches planned for the rally. At the last minute, however, several speakers were changed to the end of the list, and their turn to speak did not come until after the rally was supposed to end. The Reverend Ben Chavis of the National Black Independent Political Party was cut off after a few minutes. Johnston Makatini of the African National Congress was only allowed to deliver brief greetings, and Carlos Zenón, an activist in the struggle against the Navy's use of Vieques (a Puerto Rican island) for bombing practice, was cut off in mid-sentence by "time-conscious" members of the rally committee.

To some observers, the issues in question were ones of timing and effectiveness, a pragmatic interpretation of these dynamics which serves to downplay the larger issues at stake. The continuing strength of American pragmatism and instrumentalism, when coupled with the cult of individualism, defines "effective" in ways which neatly match the short-term power and needs of media stars and "professional" activists. Rather than helping to build a movement which calls the irrational nature of the structures of the present global system into question, short-term effectiveness serves to reform that system, to patch it up so that it functions more smoothly. Moreover, single-issue movements with professional leadership, as discussed in the previous chapter, are useful to the more benign members of the corporate elite, particularly those whose interests are tied to transnational corporations.

The disarmament movement contains the potential of questioning the entire global system at the same time that it is a reflection of the continuing legitimation crisis of the nation-state. Challenging the secret formulation of foreign policy by a handful of generals and politicians represents a rekindling of the democratic spirit. In potential, the disarmament movement could enunciate a new relationship among human beings and between humans and Nature. The rights of living beings to exist without the threat of destruction may well become the basis for the eruption of this movement.[27] Contained as it is by a leadership which channels it into the system of middle-class values and established politics, however, the radical *potential* of the disarmament movement remains latent, and in actuality, the movement becomes useful to those who would futher streamline the present global system to ensure its survival for profit-making.

Similar questions could be asked about the campaign for the ERA—a campaign which provides another example of far-reaching political and social questions being made into technical matters for professional politicians. When the women's movement was brought into national prominence during the campaign for the ERA, the questions being raised concerned neither the entire system of capitalist patriarchy nor even the formal rights of women. Rather it was technical questions which concerned the organizers and the public. How many votes could be mobilized? What would it cost an elected official to lean a certain way? How much money could be raised for each side? How many more states were needed? When would time run out? Despite support from over 450 national organizations and opinion polls showing that more than two-thirds of the country favored it, the ERA was defeated. Whether or not it had passed, however, the professionalism of the campaign and its narrow focus blunted the questioning of the entire system of capitalist patriarchy, a system whose structurally-caused militarism conditions male domination and *vice versa*. In its potential, the women's liberation movement represents the most radical break possible with the established system of domination; it calls into question both political structures of power and domination in everyday life. In the campaign for the ERA, however, a feminist questioning of the entire system of capitalist patriarchy was transformed into a question of formal equality within the *status quo*.

Although professionalism and specialization define the nature of post-1970 activism in the United States, the potential for creating new social structures and values still exists within these movements, a potential which is a dormant legacy of the New Left. Both in its internal organization and its vision of a new society, the New Left contained the promise of popular participation in the decisions affecting life, in questions like war and peace and the structure of power in factories, offices, and schools, as well as in questions of everyday patterns of interaction. The New Left raised the issue of the goal-determination of the whole organization of society, a questioning which—then as now—lies outside established politics and social theory (as I discuss in the next chapter). The promise of the New Left was not only to negate the passivity and routinization of a society built upon a world system of exploitation, but to create a new participatory quality of experience for human beings, a legacy which remains confined to the margins of U.S. politics.

Culture and Politics

In the long run, the dispersion of the New Left may prove to have been a blessing. Particularly in the United States, the youthfulness and immaturity of the activists, the weakness of a continuous radical tradition, and the genocidal war against Indochina combined to produce a desperate and unreliable movement. Despite its fundamental righteousness, the New Left included many of the worst characteristics of the society it opposed: Middle-class authoritarianism and elitism, racism and male domination, competition, gangsterism, and the anti-intellectualism of the society were also contained within the movement. Because the ideas and substance of the movement did not culminate in a revolution, its promise of a new and qualitatively better society continues to exist in the *imagination* of it.

As much as it might appear that the New Left simply evaporated, to a large extent, the global political revolt of 1968 to 1970 was displaced to the cultural arena. The New Left's radical impetus continues in the "new cinema" in Germany, Senegal, and Brazil; in reggae, new wave music, and punk rock; in the new women's culture and in black and Chicano cultures in the United States; in the feminist and science fiction literature of Marge Piercy, Alice Walker, and Ursula LeGuin; in the rise of peoples' theatre in France and

England;[28] in the alternative institutions (collective bookstores, printing presses, food networks, childcare centers, etc.); in the many struggles for neighborhood democracy; and in Hollywood as well as in many churches. In the aftermath of the New Left, new strata of radical professionals appeared, and there has been growing interest in radical theory both within academia and in the society at large: English translations of Gramsci, Lukács, Adorno and even Karl Marx have been published for the first time; previously out-of-print books dealing with general strikes in 1877 and 1905 have been reprinted, and radical professional associations and "New Left schools of thought" have appeared in economics, sociology, literature, political science, history, and psychology—associations with a combined membership of over 12,000.[29] There has been an unending stream of journals and books concerning various aspects of radical change—one bibliography alone listed over 500 references on socialist alternatives for America.[30]

For the most part, these diffuse intellectual and cultural energies do not exist in the headlines and spectacles of the media but carve out their own space, however fragmented and isolated it may be. The political intuition of the New Left was to live differently—according to new values—and even after the radical impetus of the movement has been dispersed, individual and collective attempts to live and think differently have not. Many people live and work within self-managed institutions, communal alternatives which stand in opposition to the institutions of established society.

The numbers of these new communards are much larger than is commonly realized. In 1980, there existed somewhere between 1,000 and 1,800 alternative communities and land cooperatives in the United States, some involving as many as 1,000 people.[31] According to other estimates, there were between 30,000 and 100,000 group living experiments in the cities and the countryside of the United States in 1979.[32] In addition, there exist hundreds, if not thousands, of cooperative and collective work groups (over 50 in the Boston area and at least 150 in the Bay area),[33] about 1,000 alternative food stores and two dozen food warehouses doing a half-billion dollar annual volume, at least 150 employee-owned firms in larger industry,[34] and scores of alternative communities and land cooperatives in the United States, some numbers seem, they account for a decline since the first stage in the proliferation of these alternative institutions in the late 1960s and early 1970s. In 1972, there were over 340 free clinics and more than 8,000 documented free schools in the United States.[35] A list of nearly 1,000 co-ops which was published in 1974 noted that only 5 percent of these existed prior to 1970.[36]

Although there may now be fewer of these energy centers being formed, there continues to be a large network of anti-profit collectives who have tried to build up non-hierarchical institutions. Food co-ops and food stores, bakeries and bookstores, newspapers and magazines,[37] women's centers, free schools, peoples' health centers, and childcare centers have been created in accordance with the logic of building a new way of life from the grassroots. These counter-institutions continually suffer from a lack of funds and cannot hope to drive agribusiness or large circulation daily papers out of business. Nonetheless, they provide a space for the self-development of the individuals who work within them, and they provide a living example that the imperatives of profit-making and top-down structures of power are not the only possibilities for institutional organization. The communities and individuals who have created and work within these counter-institutions may serve as base areas and become a source for new leadership which could be decisive factors in the formation of future social movements. As "red-diaper" babies, children of Communist parents, were an important sector of New Left activists, the children and activists of the New Left and those who live and work within the counter-institutions may become a significant nucleus for future political energy.

More often than not, however, the isolation of the counter-institutions from each other and from a larger movement has the effect of depoliticizing them, leaving them open to the criticism that, at best, they provide an escape for a few from the problems of society and that, at worst, they have degenerated and become a part of the very system they oppose—a fate suffered by the "old waves" of co-ops in the United States, seven of which proudly proclaim their membership in the Fortune 500.

Although their history is largely unknown, co-ops have existed in the United States since 1768 and have long since become big business. According to statistics from the Cooperative League, one of every four Americans belonged to a co-op in 1979, and their total dollar volume in that year was over $230 billion. Cooperatives are some of the biggest producers of pesticides (sales worth nearly two billion dollars in 1975), and their political involvement in the Establishment was only hinted at when the dairy co-ops were exposed for giving huge bribes to the Nixon administration in the early 1970s.

By themselves, co-ops are merely a way in which producers and consumers can share in the material wealth of their society. Depending on their relationship to larger cultural and political questions, co-ops can be either enslaving or liberating. Some Israelis, for example, practice settler-colonialism by setting up co-ops and land communes on Palestinian lands. According to the testimony of Dr. Steinar Berge, a Norwegian doctor, as Palestinian prisoners from Lebanon were transported to jails in occupied Palestine in 1982, the buses "stopped at kibbutzim to let people beat them."[38] This extreme example of the ways in which co-ops can be a means for brutal participation in society should not obscure the fact that every institution of society has tremendous pressures exerted on it (both from within and without) to conform to the imperatives of the system: to hierarchy, domination, and war.

Within West Germany, it has been argued by some that the alternative institutions and the West Berlin movement of the 1980s are nothing more than political Disneylands where young people can go through their adolescent rebellion, after which they will "come to their senses" and fill the niches of the bureaucracy and the offices of big corporations. Others respond that the building of a new society is not an abstraction or to be reserved for the far-off future and that it is precisely in the abandoned inner cities where the space to begin building a new society can be found.

Because many radicals bitterly condemn the alternative institutions as "the middle class within the movement," there is seldom the space to recognize that the alternative institutions (like parties which participate in elections) can have either liberatory or integrative functions, *depending on their relationship to a larger social movement.* The alternative movement is progressive insofar as it: provides some activists with non-alienating jobs; creates non-hierarchical institutions; and provides a sense of community rooted in friendship as opposed to the depersonalized mode of life in the corporate world. On the other hand, the alternative institutions serve as mechanisms of integration because they can lead to the commercialization of previously uncommercialized needs; fulfill unmet needs within an oppressive system and thereby help to fine-tune and mitigate the worst excesses of the system; and provide the system with a pool of highly skilled but low-paid social workers within "alternative" institutions. If there are connections to a larger political consciousness, however, they may serve as structures of dual power within which some individuals are freed from the tyranny of bosses, from the schizophrenia of the employer/employee mentality, and from the alienation of heteronomously-determined work. If they exist within a context of international solidarity and participatory democracy, co-ops and collectives could be concrete embodiments of a liberated political culture. They might be seeds of a new society, serving as base areas within which personal power trips and the isolation of the individual are transformed, as crucibles for the creation of new values, ethics, and a revolutionary global culture.

Stated differently, part of a strategy for the creation of a new society demands a protracted struggle at the level of everyday life—the building up of human beings with new needs and the construction of institutions and communities whose values, goals, and methods run counter to the need for domination and the hierarchy and specialization of the system. As the ascendant bourgeoisie first established itself economically before being able or ready to conquer political power from the monarchies, so the subjects of a new global society might create for themselves a culturally-rooted existence before being capable of decentralizing international political power and institutional decision-making into the built-up forms of a free society.

To break the overall structure of the system requires the prior construction of an *alternative* to it, an alternative which will not automatically develop from the inner dynamics of the capitalist system. New needs and critical strata may be spontaneously created by the dynamics of capitalism, but the system has continually proven itself capable of finding ways to partially satisfy these new needs by absorbing them into the market system.

Like the degeneration of the old wave of co-ops, the depoliticization and commercialization of the counterculture is an indication of the capacity of the system to absorb (and profit) from pragmatic attempts to construct a better life, especially those attempts which are made without the consciousness that the system's structures must be broken. Where San Francisco music once expressed the energy of the free space created in Haight-Ashbury, today there are professional entertainers whose music is an important part of consumer markets, not of a counterculture. In place of the "underground" newspapers in the 1960s which sprang up in nearly every major city, today there are commercially funded entertainment guides with press runs in the hundreds of thousands. Although in Boston, Rockefeller money bought out the largest of the underground papers, the *Boston Phoenix*, the cash incentives of the market were themselves strong enough to lure other hip-capitalist editors into creating newspapers which by their depoliticized nature were able to assemble an advertising base that drove many underground papers out of existence. What appeared to be the very flexibility of the system in allowing the space and resources for the formulation of cultural and political avenues of protest also turned out to be means of blunting the global movement's political thrust: By building up reformist and pacifying forces within the radical strata (forces which are loyal to the comfortability of the system and not to the mass base of a radical global movement), co-ops and depoliticized newspapers harnessed popular insurgency for the increased stability of the system.

Many efforts to build alternative institutions have been half-hearted and have suffered a "psychic Thermidor," that is, the reintroduction of deeply ingrained patterns like greed and power-trips. Here as elsewhere, the values of the dominant culture provide obstacles which could be overcome with time. The construction of free individuals, like that of a free society, cannot occur overnight, neither in the breaking of the structures of domination nor in the creation of new forms of freedom. Without a protracted struggle to transform individual personality structures, patterns of racism, sexism, ageism, authoritarianism, and homophobia reassert themselves and render the movement incapable of breaking with the established way of life. If the movement is a dehumanized one, then a free society remains utopian: If we ourselves are not free, how can we obtain freedom? Day-to-day progress in the building of new institutions and communities from below is not only a possibility; it is a necessity if the vision of a free society is to be realized.

Perhaps art is a dimension of the cultural revolution on which human imagination is most freed from the intrusion of the system's values. Art is a domain within which the reworking of human aspirations and dreams is possible even when the nightmarish qualities of the *status quo* appear to be most vivid.[39]

Those who argue that the existing economic and political structures must first be broken before any meaningful cultural change can occur assert an *a priori* belief in the automatic theory of cultural revolution—that once the economy is transformed, the rest of the society is quick to follow—a theory which has been thoroughly discredited in the practice of the last sixty years. In relation to the alternative institutions and communities, many Leftists have adopted a narrow point of view and play a regressive and depoliticizing role at a time when political direction could be an important counterforce to the depoliticization of cultural politics. Much of the politics of the Left is correctly seen as irrelevant and repressive by those activists whose theory may not be contained within traditional socialist theory but whose practice in alternatives is radical and far-sighted.

At the same time, however, it should not be forgotten that a thorough political revolution is necessary for the complete transformation of society. The fate of previous generations of co-ops—their integration into the smooth functioning of the existing system—should be proof enough that the apparent flexibility of the world system constitutes a mechanism by which the radical potential of alternatives can be blunted and turned into their opposite.

The "new narcissism" of the 1970s can be seen as a consequence of the New Left's depoliticization—a dynamic in which the "we" defined by the movement was reduced to an "I." As the popular base of the New Left became increasingly dissolved in avenues of purely personal advancement and in the openings provided for the expression of professional dissent, tendencies within the movement developed which, if anything, only served to deepen the popular disillusionment with politics: sectarian "Marxist-Leninists" who destroyed alternative institutions because they were not explicitly socialist; dictatorial individuals who forced their own self-interests on others; and real (or aspiring) millionaires who made alternative institutions into their own vehicles for enrichment. These problems, like those of dogmatism and sectarianism, are not simply conscious political phenomena: They should be understood as having psychological roots as well. In such dynamics as the masochism of "anti-intellectual intellectuals"[40] and the self-hatred of white radicals can be found obstacles to the vitality of popular movements. Such activists reproduce the values of the system within the movement: the Protestant work ethic, authoritarianism, and the quest for power.

The United States is one of the most materially wealthy and morally amorphous societies ever to appear in history, the society *par excellence* of the cash nexus—and not coincidentally, one of the world's most violent societies. It would be a mistake to underestimate the "debilitating comforts" of "one-dimensional" society, the toll which industrialization and imperialism have taken on the psyche of the American people, and the authoritarianism, racism, and sexism which have been built into the consciousness and the unconscious of the participants in a system that has evolved within the struggle for the "survival of the fittest." The prevalence of such values is a cultural corollary to the existing economic and political structures, and their existence defines the necessity of a cultural revolution accompanying a political one.

The Question of Revolutionary Subject _____

By themselves, the accumulation of specialized political education, single-issue struggles, and alternative lifestyles for marginal sectors of the population will not lead to a qualitative break with the irrational structures of the world system. The qualitative transformation of the existing society—the break from what has been called "pre-history" and the "survival of the fittest"—demands not only the breaking of the structures of the existing system but also the formulation of a new self-consciousness of the human species, one where the national and social fragmentation of humanity engendered by the global system of capitalist patriarchy would no longer be of any consequence. In 1968, Harold Cruse pointed out that:

> The Negro rebellion in America is destined to usher in a new era of human relations and to add a thoroughly new conception of the meaning and form and content of social revolution. In order to make social progress the world as a whole must move toward unification within the democratic framework of a human, national, ethnic or racial variety.[41]

Similarly, a genuinely feminist revolution would need to free our species from the entire system of capitalist patriarchy: Nothing less could redefine the existence of the individual and transform the instinctual needs of men and women in everyday life.[42] The current systematic stratification by gender would have little to do with the lives of free women and men.

Not only does the goal of genuine human liberation call into question today's fragmentation of humanity, the practicality of history, evidenced in the practice of the New Left, demands the forging of a revolutionary subject capable of forming a hegemonic bloc—that is, a political formation capable of providing the entire society with a socially legitimate alternative to the present system. Such a revolutionary subject is not *automatically* or *spontaneously* formed by the dynamics of the system. Capitalism may "create its own gravediggers," but it creates them in its own image, according to its own peculiar logic of atomization, competition, and fragmentation—dynamics which antagonistically pit one individual against another, class against class, white against black, man against woman, nation against nation, etc. The logic of capitalism is the systematic struggle for material gain and self-interest, a logic which reduces all relations to the "equality" of the cash nexus.

If it is possible to create a new society, it will be the result of the formulation and consolidation of a different logic, one where mutual respect based on autonomy and unity amid diversity are encouraged. Such dynamics run counter to the logic of the system, a logic which exerted a powerful influence on the New Left. Today hindsight allows us the privilege of asserting that the New Left in the United States played out a role in a script dictated by *reactions* to the injustices perpetrated by the Pentagon, the police, and the system. In the midst of an escalating spiral of repression and resistance, both the black movement and the anti-war movement reached violent and spectacular culminations. From 1964 to 1968, the ghettos in hundreds of cities spontaneously rose up, demonstrating the key location and power of blacks in the inner cities at the same time as their isolation from allies made it possible for the rebellions to be ruthlessly suppressed. In 1970, the universities were momentarily taken over by millions of striking students, faculty, and staff, but the revolt was managed and dispersed by those at the highest levels of power. If nothing else, the practice of the New Left makes clear that neither students nor blacks alone have the capacity to break the structures of the present system. Although millions of blacks and students spontaneously rose up, doing everything in their immediate power to transform their conditions of existence, the system remained in control.

In contrast to the patience and vision characteristic of a revolutionary movement, neither the student nor the black movement were able to break with a cataclysmic, now-or-never, instant coffee mentality. Although ghetto riots may have provided a temporary sense of community, the rioters burned their own turf to the ground rather than organizing to take it over, actions which reveal their meaning as reactions to injustices, not the consolidation of a revolutionary force. If the student movement was dispersed into the already atomized middle class, it was, in large part, because of its middle-class nature to begin with. The student movement was not capable of carrying through a protracted struggle which included the universities as a focal point, and the students' instant coffee consciousness and the movement's proletarian dogmatism and third world idolatry (the political tendencies within SDS when it dissolved) brought the New Left out of the one institution where it had been able to win majority support. Of course, after the national student strike, the practical limits of a campus-based movement were clear enough, but to realize that students alone cannot carry through a program of fundamental change does not mean abandoning the student movement. In the 1990s, enrollment in the nation's colleges will climb from over eleven million people to between thirteen and fourteen million.[43] However, it is not just numbers that enhance the importance of political work on the campuses. As one sociologist cautioned:

> No society should find it remarkable that a segment of its student population should be involved in activist student politics that is directed militantly against the *status quo*. It can be strongly argued, as C. Wright Mills did, that students are the one group who will continue to supply recruits for such causes, even when no other stratum is available ... Any efforts to analyze the future of politics, whether on the domestic or international scene, will ignore the students at the peril of being in error.[44]

There can, of course, be no revolution without the participation and leadership of the vast majority of workers but that insight should not obscure a key political lesson and legacy of the New Left: the enlarged base of the subject of social change. The mobilization of blacks, young people, the middle strata, women, and students has yet to be comprehended within traditional frameworks of analysis.[45] It is not only an analysis of the subjective forces of change—the composition of the New Left—which challenges traditional proletarian dogmatism (although even at that level of analysis, dogmatic theory ignores such dynamics as the Pullman Union's leadership of the civil rights movement in the 1950s and the surveys of the 1960s which showed that a majority of participants in the ghetto riots were working people, particularly unskilled laborers).[46] Even in terms of objectively defined occupational categories, any analysis of revolutionary subject in the United States should consider that Hispanics, blacks, and women have come to make up a greater portion of the traditionally defined working class; that the proletarianization of the middle strata, the Taylorism of the university, and the historical decline of self-employed small business owners have been carried to the point where more than 80 percent of employees today labor in non-managerial jobs.[47]

In the modern world, the economic imperatives of the existing system have brought the vast majority of American people into the labor market while the logic of capital has simultaneously demanded an ever-increasing fragmentation in the production process. As a "class-in-itself," the working class reflects the existing global inequalities and the specialization and compartmentalization of modern production. It reflects the militaristic mis-use and scandalous under-use of vast new global powers, powers made possible by one dizzying breakthrough after another in science and technology and the accompanying concentration of capital under the control of transnational corporations. The increasing mechanization of production through robots (and the effects of the Third Industrial Revolution), the export of industrial production to the third world, and the vast growth of the education, health, and service sectors are ascendant dynamics, ones which have further contributed to the fragmentation of the population (and to the need for rethinking categories of past eras).

In addition to this transformation of the objectively defined working class, another dimension of the way in which revolutionary subjects constitute themselves should be considered. One of the New Left's legacies is the historical insight that the formation of a revolutionary subject is *not* simply determined by objectively defined categories of production. The formation of a "class-for-itself" takes place both on a material and symbolic level, within dimensions of economic exploitation in the factories *as well as* within patriarchal oppression and political domination of individuals, communities, and nations. The transformation of atomized individuals into a revolutionary subject in the modern world includes national liberation movements in the third world as well as movements among students, women, communities, and most significantly, national minorities.

The central role of black people in constituting the leadership and base of the New Left in the United States was conditioned by their concentration in the inner cities, the factories, and the military as well as their status as the "most oppressed." Writing in 1968, Leo Huberman and Paul Sweezy noted that the idea of blacks as leaders of an American Revolution was not widely accepted:

> Today, we venture to believe, it will be taken very seriously indeed; and we do not hesitate to predict that a year from now it will be widely accepted by the Left, and even beyond, as the key to our national future. That this view is not already widely accepted is owing, we think, to a certain myopia which afflicts most Americans, including most radicals. They can see the Negro question only as a race question, not as a social question. They do not understand that the Negro struggle has its deepest roots in the most fundamental contradictions of the American social order and that it can achieve its aims only by eliminating these contradictions which means by transforming the social order itself.[48]

More than any other part of the population in the United States, blacks have the most pressing need to fundamentally transform the economic and political structures of the established system. By themselves, however, black people in the United States do not have the power to qualitatively transform the whole society. Moreover, the fate of the New Left provides new evidence that isolated struggles by sectors of the population ultimately become useful to the existing system, organized as it is to serve the needs of special interests at the same time as it maintains its control by antagonistically pitting the interests of the various sectors against each other. As James Boggs succinctly summarized the history of both the black and the labor movements:

> [T]he labor movement is unable to lead the American people today
> in the struggle for a new society because it is concerned chiefly with
> the interests of labor and not with those of the whole society or of
> the whole human being, which is what any movement must center
> around if it is to advance Humankind... today the black movement
> has degenerated just as the labor movement of the 30s degenerated
> into a special interest group concerned only with what will benefit
> blacks.[49]

In reconsidering the constituency of a hegemonic bloc, one capable of
leading the whole society through a protracted series of fundamental changes,
it should be remembered that the meaning of a free society is very different
today than in the nineteenth or early twentieth century. A genuine revolution
in an economically advanced country like the United States would include the
quantitative reduction and qualitative transformation of work, not its glorification.[50] A free society would be one where the vast majority of people, not
merely a handful or even a fraction, would themselves control production and
consumption. In such a society, the individual's freedom to determine *all*
aspects of his or her social life, not simply the economic dimensions, would be
of paramount importance, and social freedom would liberate the individual
from being defined simply according to gender, race, or sexual preference.

Because the New Left reflected the existing fragmentation of the population and was comprised of many diverse constituencies organized around
specific issues (the civil rights movement, the anti-war movement, the feminist
movement), it has often been the case that each part of the New Left has been
analyzed while the movement's political positions in relation to the entire
established system have been neglected. Moreover, because the New Left was
not comprised of the traditionally defined working class, it is often assumed
that the movement was simply a reformist one. A review of the New Left's
understanding of national political power helps to reveal its impetus to replace
the existing system.

As early as the huge civil rights march on Washington in 1963, SNCC
leader John Lewis raised the possibility of creating a power source outside the
established system. In the summer of 1965, only a few months after SDS had
helped pull together the first national anti-war march on April 17, the issue of
building an alternative national political structure was raised by Staughton
Lynd:

> Ultimately this movement might lead to a Continental Congress
> called by all the people who feel excluded from the higher circles of
> decision-making in this country. This Congress might even
> become a kind of second government, receiving taxes from its
> supporters, establishing contact with other nations, holding de-
> bates on American foreign and domestic policy, dramatizing the
> plight of all groups that suffer from the American system.[51]

In January 1966, Bob Parris, a member of SNCC, asked California activists,
"...why can't we set up our own government and declare the other one no
good and say the federal government should recognize us?"[52] The rupture in

the legitimacy of the U.S. government continued to gather momentum in 1966 with the enunciation of Black Power by SNCC and the draft resistance of the anti-war movement. As the system exposed its own viciousness in the violence it exported to Indochina, the brutality it brought to the nation's inner cities, and the force it used in Chicago in 1968 at the Democratic National Convention, millions of people came to see the U.S. government as an enemy of freedom and democracy. With the widening of the system's crisis of legitimation, there were increasing attempts to put forth alternatives to it, attempts which culminated in the Revolutionary Peoples' Constitutional Convention of 1970.

When the Panthers convened the Revolutionary Peoples' Constitutional Convention, they had developed the outline of a new conception for the organization of society: "revolutionary intercommunalism." Huey Newton's enunciation of "revolutionary intercommunalism" summed up the popular aspirations of the entire movement, and then as now, there is a great deal of promise in the conception of a decentralized society of self-governing institutions and communities. At least in the attempt to build a revolutionary alliance of oppressed people, the Panthers looked beyond the fragmentation engendered by the present system. At the same time as the constituency of the Revolutionary Peoples' Constitutional Convention negated the social divisions of capitalism, the more than 10,000 participants sought to preserve their unique cultural diversity, a diversity reflected in the calls for self-determination for blacks, women, students, and gay people. (See the documents in the appendix.)

In theory, the New Left may have begun to enunciate the outline of a new society, but in practice it was never able to win over a majority of Americans. Although many who joined the movement or became sympathetic to it had been well integrated into the system, the movement's base was among those marginalized from positions of power and privilege: blacks, women, young people. A majority of the country was won over to the cause of civil rights and later to demanding an end to U.S. military involvement in Indochina, but a majority mandate for fundamental change in the economic and political structures of the established system was never achieved. Even if there had been a popular mandate, however, the movement itself was unable to sustain its organizations.

For its part, the Black Panther Party proved unable to maintain unity even among its own membership—let alone to continue to provide leadership to the New Left (or the entire society). As the popular impetus faded away, shoot-outs within the Party evidenced its internal disintegration. The gangsterism which ensued testified to the regression of the Panthers to the streetways of their past. The thousands of black street people who had surged into the Panthers and momentarily crystallized a decisive break with the system failed to break with their own previous *patterns* of behavior. Although they were the most militant revolutionary social force within the United States, the example set when their leadership split apart caught on, and their militance became directed once again against each other, not the state.

One of the reasons for the lack of continuity among those who would transform this society was their inability to draw appropriate lessons from recent historical praxis. As I discuss below, previously developed revolutionary theories were spontaneously adopted by the New Left, and the movement's failure to consciously determine its own internal structure helped lead to its demise. If it is true that each revolution takes place according to unique conditions of time and space, there needs to be a re-evaluation of the frozen metaphysical theories which continue to define social movements' self-perception.

Political Organization of the Avant Garde

What theory can today bring into focus—the legacy of the struggles of the past and the possibilities for the future—remains speculation unless revolutionary leadership emerges to crystallize and consolidate the historical process. Theory may help to prepare the groundwork for a better society, but without a "collective intellectual" prepared to translate the insights provided by theoretical analysis into historical reality, theory remains cut off from practice; reason is divorced from sensuality; and the unity of *Eros* and *Logos* is shattered. In the dialectical tension between theory and practice, the question of organization is a vital one.

If the New Left showed anything, it demonstrated that without revolutionary leadership providing for the fusion of interest groups into a hegemonic bloc, spontaneously generated movements remain defined according to the logic of the system. Direct actions may have the effect of restraining the machinations of politicians and generals with their fingers on the nuclear trigger or of weakening the impetus toward conventional military intervention. They may help to dramatize the legitimation crisis of the system and usher in reforms which deal with some of its obvious injustices. Massive and militant demonstrations may be crucibles for the formation of a revolutionary consciousness, but they are not sufficient for the realization of revolutionary goals. Like parliamentary and trade-union struggles, direct actions may create a deeper understanding of the nature of the system—its limits and flexibility, violence and rewards—and they may even create major crises as they mount in intensity. But the complete redefinition of the "rules of the game" depends on the prior reorganization of power relationships and the emergence of a socially legitimate alternative to the existing system.

Revolutionary organization would prefigure the political and cultural forms of a new society: decentralized power, autonomy for minorities and women, and a pluralism of cultures, religions, and ethnic groups. The need for organized leadership to break the structures of the present system and the goal of a decentralized society call into question the idea that a strictly hierarchical and centralized party should lead the revolution. The organization of a movement which prefigures a new society would be based on *self*-management and *self*-discipline, not on orders dispatched from above by a central committee. Could such a leadership lend coherence to popular movements, help to formulate universal interests, and at the same time provide for the disintegration of central power and centralized decision-making?

An affirmative answer to this question rests on the redefinition of traditional notions of "mass" and "cadre." Rather than seeing "the revolution" as an abstraction to which they sacrifice their lives, rather than "serving the people," it would be incumbent upon activists to question accepted conceptions of politics, to serve as examples of initiative and free thought—not to hold back opinions or spout a party line. Philosophical, aesthetic, and political concerns would not simply be "internal" questions, but would have a popular vitality in an open democratic forum. Counter-bureaucratic activists would be rooted within the building of counter-institutions and forms of dual power in factories, offices, universities, and neighborhoods. Revolutionary organization would enhance their ties to a popular base, develop their individual intelligence, deepen their capacity for critical reflection, and transform their individualism into a new individuality.[53] Here a dogmatic application of the Bolshevik form of organization veers precisely in the wrong direction. In the standardization of thought, not its multiplication, in the subservience of the class to the Party, the individual to the organization, and the "mass" to the cadre, such parties can often restrict the historical possibilities of change (as they did in France in 1968).

The failure of Leninist parties in the economically advanced societies to contribute to the vitality of popular movements since World War II has led many people to believe that all parties are superfluous to the revolutionary process. The "iron law of oligarchy" is accepted as a fixed truth. While a decentralization of power is necessary, a hegemonic bloc is needed to prevent spontaneous struggles (immediate contestations of established powers and policies) from doing little more in the long run than "perfecting the machine, instead of smashing it."

Furthermore, the guidance of a visionary leadership is needed to integrate the spatial and social fragmentation of popular movements. In 1968 and 1970, few people outside the inner circles of government were aware of the national (and international) proportions of the crises. The insurgents themselves were not even aware of the threat they would have posed if they had been able to integrate the intensity of their various struggles, to bring in new strata of supporters, and to continue growing. Similarly, the continued lack of movement leadership in the seventies and eighties has resulted in radical movements' inability to draw appropriate lessons from single-issue struggles and isolated strikes or to develop some consensus on how to most effectively work for change.

Like a baby first learning to speak, the initial phase of a revolutionary movement involves mimicking elders and learning about the past. In the United States, the rapid growth of the New Left and the transformation of its goals from reform to revolution helped precipitate the transition from what had been the pragmatism of the civil rights movement and the early New Left to the ideological post-1968 period. The importation of theory from revolutionary movements in Russia, China, and the third world was a spontaneous and mechanistic one: Che's *foco* theory was adopted by the Black Liberation Army and the Weather Underground; some of Huey Newton's speeches were nothing but restatements of Lenin; and the "new communists" within the

New Left metaphysically transported the Bolshevik form of organization across time and space.

The organizations of the New Left (SNCC, SDS in Germany and the United States, the March 22 Movement in France, and the Black Panther Party) initially arose from the concrete needs of emergent movements which were expressions of the restricted activities of students, intelligentsia, and racial minorities in the 1960s. These organizations developed in a specific time and space; they were vehicles used in the struggle for civil rights and against the war in Indochina, struggles which culminated in the eruptions of 1967 to 1970 and collapsed after the first phase of the movement.[54] Although these organizations may have started out building from the bottom up with a great deal of internal flexibility and democracy, by 1970 New Left politics, particularly in the United States, was caught up in withstanding the assaults from national political power, and movement organizations became increasingly centralized and hierarchical. As the movement's aims developed from reform to resistance to revolution, it became increasingly feared by the federal establishment which executed concerted attacks on the New Left through the FBI and local "red squads." After the assassinations of Malcolm X, Martin Luther King, and Fred Hampton, the FBI assaults on the Black Panther Party spread throughout the country, and the black liberation movement closed their organizations to new members, helping cut themselves off from their base of support and making internal democracy practically impossible. By 1970, the "powers that be" had murdered or locked up the entire central committee of the Black Panther Party. Would a decentralized revolutionary party have been better able to withstand the assaults of the centralized state? In the words of Herbert Marcuse:

> The sweeping concentration of power and control in the nation-wide political and military Establishment necessitates the shift to decentralized forms of organization, less susceptible to destruction by the engines of repression... The technical and economic integration of the system is so dense that its disruption at one key place can easily lead to a serious dysfunctioning of the whole. This holds true for the local centers not only of production and distribution, but also of education, information, and transportation...However, such points of local dysfunctioning and disruption can become nuclei of social change only if they are given political direction and organization.[55]

Moreover, the Bolshevik form of organization does not bode well for the new society it seeks to bring into existence. Were the militarization of the Russian economy and the failure of the revolution to realize its initial aims, in part at least, contained within the Bolshevik organizational form? According to André Gorz:

> Co-ordination and political-ideological vision and leadership must not be superimposed from above or imported from outside: if they are to lead to the building of popular power and a new state, they must be internal to the mass struggles themselves, so as to not create

from the outset a new social division between those who lead and those who are led, between the workers and their "spokesmen," between the masses and the vanguard, between state power and the people. The history, structure and ideology of the Bolshevik Party—conceived as a vanguard separated from the masses, as an elite who had to bring to the mass of ignorant people the truth whose sole depository it conceived itself to be—can be held to contain the matrix of later deviations and degenerations.[56]

The Leninist party, refined and suited to the needs of social movements in China and Vietnam, has been an important element in the successful consolidation of centralized nation-states freed from foreign domination. Of course, new forms of organization have also emerged in the third world: The *Sandinistas* and the Palestine Liberation Organization are both fusions of several organizations and ideological positions. Because the extreme economic, political, and social problems of the third world demand radical solutions, it is in the underdeveloped countries that revolutionary movements today are most viable. As in 1968, social movements in the industrialized societies will continue to be motivated by international dynamics, but the differing material conditions of existence which define the core and periphery of the world system make the organizational models of third world movements highly problematic for social movements in the capitalist metropoles. Specifically there are:

1. different economic realities: mass production of luxuries and a predominant tertiary sector in a consumer society vs. minimal production of necessities;

2. different immediate aims: decentralization of increasingly powerful centers vs. national consolidation of power in the face of international imperialism;

3. different primary contradictions: technological and economic overdevelopment and political/cultural underdevelopment vs. economic underdevelopment and intense class struggles/cultural awakening;

4. different political conditions: mass "democracy" vs. dictatorship.

The question of organization faced by revolutionary movements in the industrialized societies involves negating the spontaneous vitality of popular insurgency *while preserving it at a higher level*. This dilemma is a vital one in the aftermath of the New Left, particularly since traditional Left organizations in the industrialized West played regressive roles in the 1960s, acting as a brake on the French movement of May 1968 and hastening the dissolution of the New Left in both Germany and the United States.[57] To be sure, there are alternative models for the organization of a political avant-garde in economically advanced societies, and a brief discussion of two of them (the German

Greens and the Rainbow Coalition) will help make clear their differences with a traditional vanguard party.

The movement in Germany today (including the extraparliamentary opposition and not only the Greens) has posed an alternative theory and practice, one capable of crystallizing the gains and lessons of isolated struggles and of reformulating the relationship of reform and revolution, of legal and extraparliamentary struggles. Much to the chagrin of some, leadership is rotated as much as possible to ensure internal democracy as well as the personal development of thousands of activists.

The German Greens are the product of a diverse but unified constituency whose needs and aspirations stand in opposition to the anti-ecological and militaristic functioning of the present system. In comparison with their counterpart in the United States (the Rainbow Coalition), the membership of the Greens is theoretically well-developed, and they do not use charisma, huge amounts of money, or celebrities to win votes. Rather they attempt to involve thousands of people in creating a political force within the government as part of a larger movement aimed at qualitatively transforming the entire society. It is not uncommon for the organization to have all-night meetings where global questions like East-West relations and the divided status of Berlin are debated. Hundreds of position papers on a whole range of issues are written and discussed in the course of their preparations for any given set of elections.

In its present form, their program includes a strong position against German participation in NATO and advocates a model of self-management which they believe is "incompatible with the existing system."[58] Their official program calls for a "fundamental alternative" in the areas of "economy, politics, and society," and it is quite explicit that:

> We oppose an economic system in which the economically powerful control the work process, the end products, and the living conditions of the vast majority of the population. A fundamental change in the short-sighted, goal-oriented economic way of thinking must take place, along with decisive changes in the economic, political, and cultural arenas if a truly ecological and social economy is to be achieved.[59]

With regard to workers, the program of the Greens includes "equal pay for equal work, for both men and women, German and foreigner" as well as the point that "workers themselves must be able to determine the work process, the planning, performance, and end result of their work." Their program also calls for a fixed percentage of Germany's Gross National Product to be transferred to the underdeveloped countries.

In one of their more controversial statements, some Greens came out in favor of the reunification of Germany as a way of developing a nuclear-free Central Europe, and other Greens strongly opposed the idea of a reunified German nation. Such divisions are often presented by the media as a sign of weakness and disorganization, and even among movement activists in the

United States, they are commonly understood in a similar fashion. In fact, the Greens are far from being a monolithic organization. Among their diverse membership, two main points of view have emerged: *realos* (who favor short-term governing alliances with the liberal Social Democrats) and *fundis* (who favor publicizing the group's position for fundamental change by refusing to help govern an irrational system). As much as the divisions in the Greens reflect the decentralized nature of the party and its ability to conduct regional campaigns in accordance with local needs, the diversity of political viewpoints strengthens the organization, makes participation possible by a wide variety of people, and provides for daily political discussions among a broad public. Apparently, the open diversity of viewpoints within the organization has not damaged the Greens' appeal to voters: They have won more than 3,000 positions in local elections, and in the national 1987 elections, their portion of the vote rose (from 5.6 percent in 1983) to 8.3 percent.

In the United States, Jesse Jackson's continuing campaigns for the Presidency have galvanized thousands of grassroots activists and hundreds of groups into a new Rainbow Coalition,[60] an umbrella organization providing for the articulation of an alternative national politics at the same time as it has revitalized the political participation of millions of black Americans. The Rainbow has been created by and for non-integrated minorities seeking their entrance into the system, a system they believe must be reformed in order for the now disenfranchised to receive a fair share of its power and resources. The Rainbow Coalition has inherited the legacy of the New Left—not only the civil rights movement but also the multi-racial impetus led by the Black Panther Party—but to the extent to which the Rainbow is dependent upon the Democratic Party, its radical potential remains latent, and its ability to openly enunciate a genuine alternative to the existing system remains compromised.

The Rainbow Coalition epitomizes U.S. pragmatism at the same moment that it seeks to negate the efficiency-orientation of society. By carefully operating within the existing system of primary elections in 1984, the Jackson campaign mobilized three and one-half million votes in support of his candidacy. He won a majority of votes in the primaries in three states, the District of Columbia, sixty-one congressional districts, and most big cities of the Northeast, Midwest, and South, and he decisively won the eighteen to twenty-nine year-old vote in the Northeast.[61] Moreover, he registered over two million new voters and stimulated a plethora of local campaigns. In contrast to both Reagan and Mondale, Jackson raised a number of issues which otherwise would not have been placed before the electorate. His "New Directions Platform" included a non-interventionist foreign policy; a pledge of no first use of nuclear weapons; a two-state solution in the Middle East; re-opening of diplomatic and trade relations with Cuba; passage of the ERA; plant-closing legislation to deal with runaway shops; an end to corporate tax breaks; cessation of "chemical warfare" by corporate polluters; and full employment.

Of course, the professional politicians of the Democratic Party were far from convinced of the need to embrace—or even to discuss—Jackson's proposals, and at the party's platform hearings, "Jackson delegates were shocked at the 'undemocratic' nature of the proceedings."[62] Despite the Democratic

Party's consistent refusal to even deal with Jackson's platform proposals, the Rainbow Coalition remains firmly within that structure. Apparently, there exists the hope that the current leadership of the Democratic Party will be replaced by the progressive trend of the Rainbow. A leader who was less patient, less self-assured, or less pragmatic than Jesse Jackson would have long since brought his forces out of the Democratic Party, but, if the Rainbow's analysis is correct, it may become the case that Jackson's moderating influence will significantly transform the structure and platform of the Democratic Party.

At the same time, however, Jesse Jackson's predominant leadership role accounts for the failure of the Rainbow Coalition to spark democratic debate and discussion among the many forces of the Rainbow. As long as the Rainbow's unity is based on Jackson's charisma and talent rather than on an ongoing process of struggle and change, the Rainbow Coalition stands closer to reformist groups like Mitterrand's Socialist Party (at best) than to groups like the German Greens. Even from a pragmatic point of view, Jesse Jackson's role as sole spokesperson for the Rainbow Coalition has made it possible for his attempts to offer even a moderate alternative to the existing universe of discourse to be thwarted through personal attacks rather than political debates. The best example, of course, is the label of anti-Semitism hung on Jackson by the media, a treatment suffered by nearly every progressive American who has attempted to bring the homelessness of millions of Palestinians and their persecution by Israel to the consciousness of the American people. If the Rainbow Coalition were to publicly debate its own internal differences about U.S. policy in the Middle East, not only would many people gain insight into an area currently misunderstood by most Americans, but it would also be far more difficult for the media to replace substantive discussion of the issue with personalized attacks on the Rainbow's leader.

If, in reality, there remains hope that the economic, political, and military structures of the present world system can be qualitatively transformed, such a leap forward depends upon the fusion of a common vision-in-action among ecologists, feminists, blacks, Mexican-Americans, workers, i.e. among the diverse and now fragmented majority of the population. In potential, both the Green Party and the Rainbow Coalition share the spiritual dimension and utopian vision which could pose the idea of such a qualitative change, a type of change which traditional political parties have long abandoned because of its "impossibility" or "undesirability." The fragmentation of the potential constituency of the Rainbow, however, especially along the lines of race, mirrors the structure of the society and only serves to weaken the possibility of a genuine alternative to it.

Although the Rainbow Coalition remains predominantly focused on Jesse Jackson's continuing campaigns for the Presidency, local Rainbow Coalitions, notably the one in Vermont, have built up programs and campaigns which appear to be independent of the Democratic Party. If independent local campaigns were enhanced in many parts of the country, they could serve as vehicles for uniting the fragmented base of the Rainbow around a program that breaks with politics-as-usual. Apparently, that is one of the goals of the national Rainbow Coalition, an organization which was formally constituted on April 17, 1986 at a convention attended by 750 delegates. The resolutions adopted at the convention were far from aiming at the qualitative transformation of the existing world system. They included organizing to "repeal Gramm-Rudman-Hollings legislation" and a "fair tax structure," although the importance of a "toxic-free environment and a nuclear-free world" as well as a "non-interventionist foreign policy" were also stressed.

Although the delegates were firmly convinced of the need to work within the Democratic Party, the participation of local activists provides a basis for optimism about the future of Rainbow politics in the United States, since, as one observer put it, they "will insist on a process of organizing and intellectual development that reflects the new, alternative society they are working to build."[63] Moreover the convention approved a resolution critical of the pragmatism which has weighed so heavily on past social movements:

> We will seek to revive ethical and moral values in American democracy and foreign policy by building an ethically and culturally diverse coalition that is itself founded on the ethical and moral common ground of what is politically *right* rather than merely expedient.[64]

The U.S. movement's emphasis on concrete accomplishments as opposed to theoretical critiques may not only be a handicap for the emergence of a radical movement, since it also implies that the movement here need not carry the ideological baggage which weighs down European movements. The relative freedom of popular movements in the Americas from the conventions of European dogma can be seen in the names taken on by the Left organizations: In Europe, besides the Greens, there are Socialist Parties, Communist Parties, Social Democrats, and Unified Socialists; while in the Americas, there have emerged *Sandinistas*, *Tupamaros*, Black Panthers, *Fidelistas*, and a Rainbow.

As discussed, the New left posed the international decentralization of resources and power as an alternative to the structure of the existing world system, a goal which might imply the need for several coalitions, groups, and parties rather than one centralized vanguard party as a model for movement organization. If a radical Green party (or some other formation) were to emerge in the United States, would it be allowed to become part of the Rainbow, help solidify a new American majority, and, at the same time, *move that majority from trying to integrate into the existing national system of power to the creation of a new and better system?*

The Green Party of West Germany, unlike the Rainbow, is an explicitly internationalist organization. Indeed, the international cross-fertilization of theory and practice is one of the most dynamic elements of Green politics, particularly since the German Greens continue to challenge modern society's existing structures at the same time as they question the nationalistic solutions offered by traditional parties. The need for an international dimension in the organization of a political avant garde is called forth by the existence of problems that have no simple national solutions: acid rain, the Greenhouse effect, the nuclear arms race, world hunger, and military interventions by the superpowers in the affairs of the third world. The phenomenal achievements of the nation-state as a form within which the economy, science, and industry have been developed are themselves the strongest arguments for the obsolescence of the nation-state. If given a choice, who would agree to grant any national political elite the ability to push the nuclear button? Are there those who would consider it proper that the national organization of the global economy relegates hundreds of millions of people to starve? As social problems have become increasingly internationalized, so too must solutions to these problems be conceived and implemented on a global scale.

As happened before in history, it could very well be ideas crystallized from the experiences of the German movement which provide the context for a new International. What occurred in the aftermath of the world-historical movements of 1848 (i.e. the formation of the First International), might recur in the post-1968 epoch (the formation of a new International). Such a historical recurrence might not, as has often been stated, follow the pattern of "the first time as tragedy, the second as farce." The fate of such a new International might depend as much on its own internal capabilities and boldness of vision as upon any "iron law" of history.

Socialism or Barbarism? An International Question ___

As the twentieth century draws to an end, not only is the scope and power of corporations increasingly internationalized, so too is the class struggle: South Africa, Palestine, and El Salvador are the scenes of struggles within a global society, struggles which pit international reaction against international revolution, bringing into play all the problems of political alliances and coordination on a global level. This international struggle is intensifying, both in the movements for national liberation and the reaction against them. What was raised by Che as a slogan of the international movement—"Create 2, 3, Many Vietnams"—today exists in the bloody realities of Beirut and San Salvador, of Namibia, Eritrea, and South Africa.

Socialist and national liberation movements in the third world, however, involve breaking "weak links" in the chain of international domination. This commonly used metaphor, as much as it explains how a prisoner is freed when one link in the chain of captivity is broken, fails to explain the transformation of the world system. Many "weak links" in the chain of imperialism have been broken, but the world system has used all means at its disposal to condemn these liberated nations to economic isolation and technological backwardness. From attacks on the Russian Revolution beginning in 1917 to the blockade of Cuba, the denial of agreed-upon reparations to Vietnam, and attempts to isolate and militarize Nicaragua, the capitalist metropoles have exerted an over-determining influence on the possibilities and characteristics of modern revolutions. To be sure, the possibility of revolution in the economically advanced nations rests upon the step-by-step progress made by movements in the periphery of the world system and the subsequent weakening of the entire structure. At the same moment, however, the blockades and attacks against the successful movements in the periphery—from Vietnam and Cuba to Angola,

Mozambique, and Nicaragua—helps make clear that the possibility of a world-historical revolution rests upon the transformation of the strongest links in the imperialist chain.[65]

As more and more of the world break the "weak links" in the chain of international domination, the result will be an intensification of crisis tendencies and unrest within the industrialized societies, and the question on the historical agenda will be: socialism or barbarism? As revolution in the third world remains a necessary and growing force, racism in the United States will be further compounded by a growing *national* chauvinism. Recently evidenced in hatred of Iranians and Arabs and in resentment toward the Japanese, this systematic tendency is institutionalized for Mexican workers, tens of thousands of whom are thrown into detention camps each month (about one million every year). The mass media and even liberal politicians have only exacerbated the situation. In Nazi Germany, Jews were stereotyped as the big bankers and communists, but in the United States today, it is Arabs who are portrayed in what are structurally analogous terms: as sheiks and terrorists. The crematoria are portable F-16s, and the United States supplies them freely to Israel, which uses them without the slightest hesitation. Israeli scientists have been hard at work designing bombs disguised as toys, weapons which have been dropped on Palestinian camps; special bombs were developed to explode only after penetrating underground shelters where civilians have taken refuge; new "vacuum bombs" were used to destroy major structures containing hundreds of people with one hit.[66]

Within the United States, there is but scant opposition to providing billions of our tax dollars for military purposes to Israel every year. Indeed, a new McCarthyism has been on the rise in the 1980s, an anti-terrorism which has supplanted the anti-Communism of the 1950s. Anyone daring to publicly challenge Israel is immediately outcast. Even Democratic Congressmen like Representative Paul McCloskey and Republican Senators like Charles Percy have been unseated for timid remarks critical of Israel. The media, institutional elites, and much of the "Left" converge in their support of Israel, a convergence which indicates the distance of Americans from a revolutionary consciousness and the existence of a new barbarism vis-a-vis the Arab world.

In the long run, the extreme Right—the forces behind the Iran-Contra operations—may supplant the rule of the more liberal corporate elite in the United States. Despite the apparent strength of corporate policymakers (as revealed in their successful "uncovering" of the Watergate burglary and the Iran-Contra Affair), it would be a mistake to rely on them to protect the remnants of democracy which exist in the United States. Try as they may, the forces of the international economic order are unable to stabilize the economies of nations which have remained loyal to U.S. corporations. We see this most clearly in Mexico, where the refinancing of the foreign debt has resulted in windfall profits for United States banks—in what amounts to the theft of the entire oil reserves, a larger gain in reality than the French and Maximilian could ever have imagined.

Within the post-Vietnam world constellation of power, the scope and possibilities for the expansion of capital are increasingly limited, and banks and corporations are forced to squeeze ever greater profits from a shrinking "Free World." The structural imperatives of capital (its nature as a self-expanding value) demand the intensification of exploitation in those areas of the globe where capital is given free reign. The irrationality of this structural imperative can most obviously be found in the increasing poverty and indebtedness of the third world at the same time as these countries transfer billions of dollars to transnational banks. The violence necessary for maintaining this structural relationship is increasingly used against those who have no choice but to fight to change the impoverished conditions of their existence. The more the system labels these growing numbers of increasingly marginalized people as "terrorists," the longer it refuses to offer them even the semblance of a dignified life. The more openly the established order displays its own irrationality, the faster it undermines its long-term chances for survival.

Examples of the system's irrational nature abound. At the same time as there has been an exponential growth in the debt of the "developing" countries (from $87 billion in 1971 to $456 billion in 1980)[67] and massive interest payments have been made, as many as 20 million Latin American children died before the age of one—more children than were born in all of Europe during the same time.[68] In 1980 alone, thirty million of the world's children under the age of five died of starvation. Modern agriculture now produces enough food to provide every person on earth with a decent diet, yet more people suffer from malnutrition today than ever before in history.[69]

As the system's goals of power and profit reach new dimensions of technical implementation on a global scale, the daily incorporation of lands and lives into the world system intensifies, and the structure and goals of the system become increasingly destructive. I have already indicated that systematic starvation in the periphery of the world system accompanies the expansion of the world system. The dimensions of this problem are much larger than is commonly realized. In 1981, a study by Harvard University began with the fact that:

> Half of the people in the developing world are malnourished—over 1 billion individuals do not consume enough food to meet their daily caloric requirements. Of these, 895 million have daily caloric deficits in excess of 250 calories... Malnutrition is fundamentally a poverty problem. It is not, at least presently, a result of inadequate global supplies of food, for the world produces enough food to meet everybody's nutrient requirements. Rather, it is the unequal access of countries and people to that food that causes malnutrition.[70]

In other words, the economic structure of the world system accounts for the one billion starving human beings on our planet.

Let me cite another example of the irrational impact of the system's "successful" operation: Nearly half of the earth's tropical rain forests have already been destroyed, and each year, an area roughly the size of England and Wales combined are leveled for commercial purposes.[71] The result is that one or more species of life is made extinct every day, and the Greenhouse effect is intensified. Has this expansion of the industrial system been approved by the species as in our best interests? What of the three million homeless children who roam the streets of Brazil's cities? Are they the conscious result of the system's urbanization of people, or is their fate a reflection of the unconscious operation of a social machine which is out of control? According to the United Nations, an additional 28 million children in Brazil (the "economic miracle" of the 1970s, a country with a total population of 120 million) have a lower standard of living than that stipulated in the UN Declaration of Children's Rights. Is this outcome of the present industrial system capable of being considered rational?

Although the system's ability to deliver the goods to the majority of the people in the economically advanced societies may remain intact, the comforts of the system can be debilitating; its food contains harmful chemical preservatives; its electricity is generated in atomic power plants; and its whole structure is built upon the poverty of the vast majority of the world. The structures of the existing world system not only dictate increasing starvation and cultural poverty: Their potential effect is to destroy the entire planet, a possibility calmly discussed by generals in the Pentagon and in the Kremlin and politicians in Washington, D.C. and Moscow at the same time as they oversee "small-scale" wars in El Salvador and Afghanistan, to name only two instances.

Whether or not the uncontrollability of the world system results in nuclear war, economic incapacitation, or ecological devastation, in the final analysis, the decisive factor in the creation *of a better society* will be the consciousness in action of a majority of people in the United States, the strongest link in the world system. Will the people of the United States assume their historical responsibilities? Perhaps in the unwillingness of so many to support their government's war against Indochina can be found some basis for optimism.

In 1776 the people of the United States provided the world with a model of human progress and freedom, but in the last 200 years, our government has changed from the inspiration of national independence and freedom into its enemy, and the dollar interests of U.S. transnational corporations have come to dominate more and more of the world. Is it possible to break the international chain of economic exploitation and political and cultural domination? Can the human species emerge from its present state of high-tech barbarism? Will the people of the United States be capable of enacting our right of revolution? If the possibility of an affirmative answer is blocked, is there also the possibility that the United States, like Nazi Germany, could be defeated from the outside?

Such speculation is possibly the most accurate means of assessing the future, since the crisis tendencies of the existing system are profound. Who knows what the cumulative effects of the intensifying poverty in the third world will be? What would happen in the United States if transnationals were expelled from the Middle East or if there were an international financial crisis? What if the current political unrest in Central America made its way north to Mexico? Already the influx of economic refugees from Mexico to the United States is in the millions, and in all probability the continuing economic crisis in

Mexico will bring political repercussions, posing the radicalization of the entire Southwest where over 70 percent of Mexican-Americans live. Such a radicalization of the Southwest may coincide with the next baby boom—the "echo baby boom," whose members are expected to begin entering the universities in the 1990s. This new baby boom may very well carry on some of the radical ideas of its parents, the generation of the New Left, who themselves might not have been fully integrated into the system. As noted by conservative sociologist Seymour Martin Lipset in 1970:

> [I]n the United States, a more radicalized student generation is gradually moving into the lower and sometimes even the upper rungs of important parts of society...Despite the coercive pressures on them to conform which come from participation in the bureaucracy, many aspects of their environment will continue to support their youthful opinion. It is likely, therefore, that the current generation of radical university students will continue to affect the larger body politic in many countries ten, twenty, or even thirty years from now...generations sometimes may even appear twice, first in their own right and then through their influence over their children who are given a set of ideals that they try to activate, ideals that stem back to the conditions of their parents' formative political years.[72]

The confluence of all these dynamics may produce another period of upheaval in the core of the world system, and the United States may experience an explosion of the depth and magnitude which France experienced in 1968. *If* the working class in the United States has developed beyond the racial and political polarization which defined its limitations in 1970 during the student strike; *if* a black revolt and/or Hispanic civil rights movement and a new student movement were synchronized; and *if* the powers-that-be are again divided and provide another set of precipitating events, it might well be the case that the coming crisis could even surpass the one that France experienced in 1968. It should be remembered that the May events in France occurred in the epoch after two colonial defeats had been suffered (Vietnam and Algeria). The United States has already been devastated once (by Vietnam). With the current adventurism in Washington manifested in its Central American and Middle East interventionism, another major setback might loom in the not-too-distant future.

That a major new upheaval might occur is not unlikely given the crisis tendencies of the system, but even if it did, unless there are prior changes in popular consciousness and an emergent hegemonic bloc capable of leading the society in a new direction, such an explosion could very well precipitate a massive right-wing response, one which undoubtedly would constitute a giant step backwards in history. On the other hand, if the established institutions were able to remain intact, an explosion on the scale of May 1968 might become little more than an opportunity to debate whether it was another "missed opportunity" or a further demonstration of the flexibility of the current system—of its ability to incorporate and benefit from spontaneously generated protests. In either event (and even if a new explosion fails to materialize in the near future), the possibility of yet another period of crisis would remain open, posing the question once again for the emergence of a genuine alternative to the existing system.

To be sure, if there is any chance of the aesthetic transformation of the established world system, such a possibility does not rest entirely on any organization. The self-activity of popular movements, the spontaneous emergence of an escalating spiral of strikes, sit-ins, and insurrectionary councils (what I have referred to as the *eros* effect), cannot be brought into existence by any conspiracy or act of will. Neither can these forms of struggle be predicted in advance of their appearance, resting as they do upon the accumulation of political experiences and the needs of millions of people as shaped by the changing constellation of historical conditions. The unpredictable power of the *eros* effect as a weapon in the class struggle should not be underestimated, *particularly* in the aftermath of the world-historical events in 1968. If nothing else, such examples as the fall of the Shah, Marcos, and Duvalier demonstrate the uselessness of weapons in the face of the mobilized power of the people.

At the same moment, however, without an organized political avant-garde, one capable of expressing the popular will and consolidating the resistance *through enlightenment*, such crises might be resolved in regressive directions. Without a visionary leadership posing the many-sided dimensions of oppression—and the means to transcend them—the direction of change can be defined by charismatic absolutism or reaction rather than enlightenment and social revolution. Above all else, historical transformations have proven that when the moment arrives for the emergence of the *eros* effect, there is no time left to prepare for the defeat of the forces of *thanatos*.

Chapter 6

THE
RATIONALITY
OF THE
NEW LEFT

The inability to grasp in thought the unity of theory and practice and the limitation of the concept of necessity to inevitable events are both due, from the viewpoint of theory of knowledge, to the Cartesian dualism of thought and being. That dualism is congenial both to nature and to bourgeois society in so far as the latter resembles a natural mechanism. The idea of a theory which becomes a genuine force, consisting in the self-awareness of the subjects of a great historical revolution, is beyond the grasp of a mentality typified by such a dualism.

—Max Horkheimer

Some analyses of the New Left have been chiefly concerned with its theory, others with its practice. Such a dualism has been detrimental to the integrity of both theoretical endeavor and practical action. Two errors are commonly made in conceptualizing theory and practice. On one side, militant activists often conceive of theory other than cookbook-style recipes as meaningless (or worse), while, on the other side, pure and "neutral" technicians of academic thought maintain the "scientific" separation of their facts from human values, of theory from practice. To attempt to resolve the contradictory nature of praxis by conceiving of it as practice being guided by theory (as most activists do) or as theory being verified by practice (as most academicians maintain) is to completely miss the point: Every action simultaneously contains *within it* theoretical considerations, and every theory has a moment of practical repercussion embedded *within* its enunciation.[1] Viewing theory and practice as external to each other already presupposes their separation. Genuine praxis negates both "pure theory" and "pure action" by preserving each at a higher level. When millions of people self-consciously articulate and act upon their vital needs, as they did in May 1968 and May 1970, they move beyond isolated contemplation and knee-jerk responses to the established conditions of their existence.

To conceive of either theory or practice as constituting an autonomous realm of social reality is one particular manifestation of the subject-object duality. This dualism is expressed in the split between thinking and being, mind and body, idealism and materialism, and it has its roots in the dualistic relationships of human beings and Nature, man and woman, organization and individual, capital and labor, and Party and class. It is a dualism which has made possible vast technical progress at the same time as it has helped blind the human species by reducing our vision of perfectibility "to the way things are." The blindness inherent in splitting reality in two can be observed in many theoreticians' disregard of the practical effects of their theories and in their inability to comprehend moments of the unity of subject and object (the *eros* effect) in social revolutions.

As the practice of the New Left went beyond the existing categories of political experience, so its theory transcended the established forms of social thought. The New Left rejuvenated the critical philosophy of European social thought, a philosophy which had been conceptualized after the French revolution, recast in the wake of the "failed" revolutions of 1848, and reformulated as "critical theory" after the demise of a European-wide revolution from 1917 to 1919. Critical theory differs from traditional theory in two ways. Traditional theory confines itself to contemplation of its constructed facts and with its methodologies of verifying facticity. In contrast, critical theory traces the construction of truth in relation to history and embraces the origins of thought in the evolution of the human species.[2] Through reflection on itself, thought becomes more than observation and description: It becomes thought to the second power.

More importantly, critical theory questions the social goals served by the ways in which facts are asserted as truthful. It not only seeks to uncover the origins of thought in evolution but also attempts to understand the effects of thinking on the process of the self-formation of the human species. In this sense, critical theory seeks to sublate the isolation of theory from practice. By questioning both the origins and purpose (*telos*) of thought, critical theory orients itself to the process of human enlightenment and emancipation. In a period where the possibility of a genuine praxis seems remote, critical theory concerns itself with the anticipation of its realization and, in so doing, critical theory becomes a catalyst in the process of social transformation. Critical theory aims at achieving an explanation of society which is so comprehensive that it embraces the general interrelationship of theory's own enunciation with its practical effects. In this sense, critical theory views itself as an agent of enlightenment.[3]

In this book, I now move from theoretically reconstructing historical events to analyzing social thought in relation to its practical repercussions. In the first chapters, I emphasized the form and content of emergent forces during periods of the *eros* effect. By studying the actions and aspirations of millions of people during social crises, I revealed characteristics of social movements generally overlooked by traditional social theory (including Soviet Marxism). As I show in this chapter, Soviet Marxism, sociology, and systems analysis are each based on similar philosophical presuppositions that blind them to such newly emergent social facts, a theoretical problem which underlies their practical disregard of previously non-existent aspects of reality which unexpectedly appear.

My focus on the emergence of new forms of life in the midst of crises has both advantages and disadvantages. By uncovering the content and form of the conscious aspirations of participants in social movements during moments of the *eros* effect, the concrete historical meaning of "class-for-itself" was investigated in a way that did not bury it beneath a conception of social life as merely conditioned by sacred or secular external forces. In contrast to either an idealistic or deterministic analysis, I developed an analysis of the qualities of *social* actors, one which avoided both the error of qualitative reduction to statistics as well as that of narrowly focusing on the "Great Men" of history. By focusing on the emergence of previously nonexistent qualities of human aspirations as they were articulated and realized in the spontaneous creation of new forms of social life, I hope to have made clear that social movements are concrete proof of the *changing* nature of social reality and the *non-reducibility* of human actions to fixed laws.

A danger with such a study is that it could become infatuated with the *act of creation* of new social values and aspirations and thereby lose sight of the creation of the creators. At the same time as humans emerge from their biological and social existence and create new dimensions to themselves, they are themselves products of that which already has been created. They act within the framework of historical possibilities posed by the objective and subjective constellation of reality and are themselves the product of these forces.

Another possible problem with my focus is that an uncritical presentation of the content of the participants' vision in general strikes could lead to the false assumption that these events provide a true picture of the interests and existence of the participants. There were many reasons for people's participation in the events of May 1968 and May 1970, and I do not claim to have comprehensively explained their motivations. All I hope to have accomplished is to have uncovered the meaning of their actions in history. Once a book is written, for example, it has a life of its own independent of the author: In the same way, the New Left strikes have a meaning in history which can not be reduced to purely personal motivations.

The choice to study the self-constitution of "class-for-itself" in social crises rests upon specific epistemological assumptions. Specifically, my work departs from the notion that the *self-activity* of life defines its life-ness, that the "facticity" of social life depends upon the human beings whose consciousness presupposes the possibility of determining the existence and nature of a fact. "Facts," if they are to have the status of facticity, need to be viewed in relation to the whole society. Such a perspective is grounded in dialectical thought from Plato to Hegel and Marx, a kind of negative thought embodied in the modern world in the work of Herbert Marcuse and German critical theory.[4]

Rather than dealing with this tradition descriptively, I seek to develop it in this chapter through a critical analysis of established social theory. I have two goals: to show how and why established theory was (and is) incapable of comprehending the New Left, thereby indicating what its reaction to social movements in the future will be; and to illustrate the theoretical inability of sociology, systems analysis, and Soviet Marxism to deal with the question of the goal-determination of society. The case studies of May 1968 and May

1970 revealed that the New Left contested the goals and organization of the existing world system. As I discuss below, the theoretical stagnation of sociology, systems analysis, and Soviet Marxism helps to explain their hostility to the New Left, and more importantly, it also reveals their role in the maintenance of irrational forms of social organization.

The practice of Soviet Marxists and social scientists during the crises induced by the New Left provides a practical glimpse of the more general implications of their philosophies. Some social scientists consciously worked against the student movement since they saw it as a threat to the *status quo*. An extreme example is Samuel Huntington, who helped design the forced "urbanization" of Vietman—the bombing of the countryside at such a brutal pace that peasants were forced into the cities. With regard to students, he had this to say:

> Students are typically the most active and important civilian middle-class political force. In non-praetorian societies (western "democracies"), their opportunities to political action are restricted by the strength of the political institutions and the prevailing concepts of legitimacy. Their attitudes and values, however, fall into the same oppositional syndrome which exists in the praetorian societies. In traditional political systems, the university in the capital city is typically the center of hostile attitudes and plotting against the regime . . . This opposition does not stem, in most cases, from any material insufficiency. It is an opposition which stems instead from psychological insecurity, personal alienation and guilt, and an overriding need for a secure sense of identity.[5]

Huntington went on to discuss how to best control student movements, noting that reforms often make the situation worse. He analyzed various State Department tactics employed in the third world and concluded that it is often best to close down the universities in a crisis situation.

Sociological analysis has also been oriented around fragmentary aspects of the problems of the youth. Louis Feuer's *Conflict of Generations* portrayed the student movement as merely the result of the Oedipal complex—as sons fighting their fathers—and never attempted to deal with the more substantive issues raised by the movement. Many sociologists only considered the post-World War II baby boom and the massive influx of college-age students into the universities twenty years after the war in their analysis of the New Left. One of the best collections of articles and documents on the New Left, *The University Crisis Reader*,[6] was concerned with analyzing the New Left almost solely in terms of its campus activities and critics.

There has been little sociological analysis of the New Left which understands the movement in terms of society as a whole—the economic and political realities as well as culture and lifestyles—as pointed out in 1970 by Seymour Martin Lipset.[7] Instead, the idealism and universality of the concerns of young people have been recognized by many sociologists. As the same analyst commented in trying to analyze the Berkeley student revolt in 1964:

University students, though well educated, have generally not established a sense of close involvement with adult institutions; experience has not hardened them to imperfection. Their libidos are unanchored; their capacity for identification with categories of universal scope, with mankind, the oppressed, the poor and miserable, is greater than it was earlier or than it will be later in life . . . Youthful idealism, even when it leads to sharp rejection of adult practices and the use of extreme methods is often expected and respected by older people.[8]

The degradation of the New Left by the Soviet Left follows a similar pattern. The attitude of the French Communist Party toward the 1968 student movement, as I discussed in Chapter 3, is similar to that of the Soviet Left in general. In their view, the New Left was "petit-bourgeois," a movement that was an historical accident (at best) or composed of the children of the "big bourgeoisie."

There was, of course, much affinity between some social theorists and the student movement. Herbert Marcuse dedicated his *Essay on Liberation* to the militants of the French student movement, noting that:

The young militants know or sense that what is at stake is simply their life, the life of human beings which has become a plaything in the hands of politicians and managers and generals. The rebels want to take it out of these hands and make it worth living; they realize that this is still possible today, and that the attainment of this goal necessitates a struggle which can no longer be contained by the rules and regulations of a pseudo-democracy in a Free Orwellian World.[9]

Another consistent friend of the student movement was Ernest Mandel. On the "Night of the Barricades," one of the initial confrontations between students and police in France, he emerged from addressing the student militants to find his own car burning in the streets of Paris. Climbing onto a barricade, he joyfully shouted: *"Ah! Comme c'est beau! C'est la revolution!"*[10] Writing in the midst of the student movement of 1968, he said:

It would be hard to understand the dimensions and importance of the universal student revolt in the imperialist countries without taking into account the tendencies which we have sketched here: the growing integration of intellectual labor into the productive process; the growing standardization, uniformity, and mechaniza-tion of intellectual labor; the growing transformation of university graduates from independent professional and capitalist entrepre-neurs into salary earners appearing in a specialized labor market...[11]

It is one thing to discuss the actions of intellectuals and another to analyze their theories in order to understand their actions. Having briefly enumerated the practical orientation of some theorists, I deal in more detail with theoretical questions below.

Nature and History _____

To the extent that the world economic system is an inherited structure, one which has never had a mandate from a majority of its members, it is non-rational. At the same time, however, to the extent that the existing system is a reflection of the "survival of the fittest" and embodies the historical need to dominate Nature as conditioned by the necessity to overcome problems of material scarcity, the world system is *irrational*: unconsciously reflecting goals and forms of social organization developed in the epoch of our instinctual struggle for survival. Long ago, humans began to scientifically produce more than enough to satisfy their survival needs, but that accomplishment alone does not mean that we have created rational forms of social organization. The material conditions that determine the what and how of production and the whole organization of society evolve in "pre-historical" time according to the logic of natural evolution and the struggle for survival. So long as the whole organization of society continues to develop in an unplanned, Nature-like way (*Naturwuchs*), so long as it is not the consciousness of the species but spontaneous, unplanned developments which create the whole organization of society, the human species is not yet rational.[12]

From this perspective, it becomes possible to grasp a fundamental insight into revolution by contrasting it with evolution. The process of evolution is defined by Nature, but through revolution, *Nature becomes history:* Human beings, the product of natural evolution, leap from unplanned evolution ("pre-history") into the realm of genuine "history" through revolution. It follows that the essential nature of revolutionary social movements is to prepare the leap from unreflexive survival and adaptation ("pre-history") to consciously determined history.

This theoretical realization informed my choice to focus this book on New Left general strikes as an indication of possible future leaps from the realm of "pre-history" to "history." It matters little, at least from this theoretical viewpoint, that these situations began spontaneously: Pre-history is essentially spontaneous, and it is this spontaneity that genuine revolutions both negate *and preserve* at a higher level of development. Nor is it theoretically significant that these small leaps did not culminate in a big jump—that the New Left did not complete a "successful" revolution. The unleashed energies of these leaps were transitory moments in history, but they were concrete embodiments of what could become genuine "history."

The self-formative praxis of social actors throws light upon the concrete meaning of the leap from "pre-history" to "history," and an understanding of that process grasps the essential meaning of revolution in general and the New Left in particular. May 1968 and May 1970 were moments of the actualization of the species as a species-being, moments when new goals for the whole organization of society were conceived (and temporarily actualized) in the lives of millions of people. The visionary aspect of New Left general strikes— the development of new values like internationalism, new forms of social organization like self-management, and new goals opposed to profit-making— makes clear that the movement was more than spontaneous opposition to perceived injustices derived from the unplanned goals of the system as it has evolved.

To be sure, natural evolution alone did not produce the world system: It did not create the consumer societies, on the one side, and the poverty of the third world, on the other. *But neither is the existing world system a conscious, self-determined creation of the human species.* There has been no vote, no conscious or democratic determination of the structure and goals of society by its members. The world system has developed through economic and political revolutions, through the extinction of a whole series of prior forms of economic and social organization, but it is not the creation of a democratic community of freely associated human beings. To the extent that it simply represents the power of the past over the present, the existing system is an *irrational* organization, and its irrationality might prove to be the cause of its downfall more than its inability to "deliver the goods" to the majority of people in the economically advanced countries.

The scientific and technological breakthroughs of the past two centuries, while guaranteeing material comfort for the majority of people in the economically advanced societies, provide no guarantee of an improving quality of life. The assumed goals of the social system—continuous economic expansion, "national" security, and the accumulation of individual wealth—militate against qualitative progress in the human condition. The accomplishment of these goals demands the domination and destruction of the natural environment, an environment which includes Nature as it is commonly thought of (i.e. external Nature) as well as dimensions of Nature within human beings. The channeling of basic drives into acquisitiveness and aggression *(thanatos)* negates the potential for harmonious and mutually satisfying relations *(eros)*.

The objectification of the natural world (of which the human body is but one example) logically proceeds from a social system organized on the basis of achieving the assumed goals of the present society—as do nationalistically organized militaries and the existing poles of wealth and poverty. In historical terms, the domination of external Nature necessarily preceded the domination of human by human for the simple reason that power and the state, social status, prestige, wealth, and money are humanly created (and therefore artificial) concerns, concerns which necessarily had as their precondition the satisfaction of survival needs. In another sense, these two aspects of domination go hand-in-hand: The domination of external Nature has a price; the desensitization of inner Nature, that is, the banishing of awe at the complex contradictory harmony of the universe through its replacement by awe with techniques aimed at certainty and control.[13] As the precondition for "society" to emerge was the overcoming of fragmentary pre-capitalist formations, so the precondition for modern economic and technological progress was the overcoming of "awe" by "fact," the separation of *Eros* and *Logos*.

At the dawn of social thought, *physis* and *nomos* expressed roughly the same fundamental opposition which today is found between *scientistic* and *humanistic* social science. Aristotle's development of formal logic stands as a key step in the divorce of *Logos* and *Eros*, in the break between the useful, on the one side, and the beautiful, on the other.[14] Plato's logic was ironic, natural subversive, and self-contradictory in contrast to Aristotle's linear and progressive dialectic.[15] Once the link between *Logos* and *Eros* was broken, the door was open for scientific rationality to emerge as essentially neutral, for theory to be divorced from practice.[16] To be sure, the conscious aim of both Plato and Aristotle was "the good life," but Aristotle's reduction of logic from Plato's internal subversion of the human mind to the logical classification of external Nature has served as a basis for the reduction of human progress (the "good") to scientific progress (the "useful").

Modern scientific progress seems to have taken us (at least the majority of people in the economically advanced countries) to the threshold of freedom from material scarcity. That condition does not mean that we have achieved a free society, unless of course, human progress is equated with scientific-technical progress.[17] Within the classical tradition of Western philosophy, differing views of the question of freedom have been reflected in the ideas of the "two cultures," the scientific and the humanistic. Although humanists have long been critical of the limits of scientific progress, these two paradigms share a common conception of the relationship of Nature and humans, a common ground which makes them both incapable of transcending the established goals of modern society.

The Unity of Scientism and Humanism

Within established forms of social theory, there have evolved two seemingly incompatible paradigms: the scientistic and the humanistic.[18] By scientistic, I refer to the acceptance of the established routings of science. Much of modern sociology, systems analysis, and Soviet Marxism uses a model taken from natural science: History is seen as reproducible (not unique); the creation of instruments of study which are not themselves affected by the study are assumed to be possible (computerized mathematical correlations, for example); and social interaction is assumed to be predictable by the development of laws (the same conditions here producing the same results there). The goals of scientistic research are the creation of theories, laws, generalizations, and principles which can be used to deduce and predict future events.

Humanistic theory, on the other hand, is premised on the qualitative difference between human beings and natural reality. The reflexive nature of humans make us an object to ourselves; humans interact symbolically as well as instrumentally; human behavior contains a moment of unique and unpredictable spontaneity; and finally, humanistic theory recognizes the reactive nature of humans on the instruments of investigation as well as the human creation of these instruments (implying that the instruments of social analysis cannot be separated from their object). The seeming incompatibility of humanistic and scientistic sociology can be made apparent by contrasting Kenneth Burke with Ralf Dahrendorf. Dahrendorf asserts that:

> If in this study I speak of "theory," "hypothesis," "empirical test," "refutation," and "science," I use these terms in the strict sense of

the methodological characteristics of an empirical discipline. At least logically, physics, physiology, and sociology are subject to the same laws—whatever may render one or the other of these disciplines empirically preferable in terms of exactness.[19]

Kenneth Burke, on the other hand, points out that:

> [A] physical scientist's relation to the material involved in the study of motion differs in quality from his relation to his colleagues. He would never think of "petitioning" the objects of his experiments or "arguing with them," as he would with persons whom he asks to collaborate with him or to judge the results of his experiment. Implicit in these two relations is the distinction between the sheer motion of things and the actions of persons.[20]

Unlike the natural sciences, social science has proven itself unable to develop a unified theoretical paradigm, to agree on the method and content of investigation that research must use to arrive at some form of truth. Although one or another conceptual scheme may claim such a validity, it has been the case—and seems likely to continue to be for quite some time—that social science will be composed of a number of disparate strategies for conceptualizing society. Both the scientistic and humanistic paradigms contain premises which seem incompatible with the other. The scientistic view reduces human life by ignoring a key insight into the difference between natural and human history: Human actors (consciously or unconsciously) have helped to create history but not Nature, and that which humans have made, humans can change. On the other hand, humanists sever humans from their natural origins: Human thought and imagination distinguish us from the animal and mineral world. If the scientist tends toward the creation of laws and systems which contain human behavior, the humanist tends to deny the existence of any law or reproducible pattern of human behavior.[21]

At first glance, these differences seem insurmountable, but from a wider perspective, these two paradigms complement each other in their very contradiction: They unite in their denial of concrete history. The scientist poses eternal laws; the humanist argues their impossibility. They agree, however, to the terms of the contest—that is, on the evaluation of human behavior outside history. The scientistic view collapses history into eternal laws—the humanist denies the possibility of history as a process. For the scientist, natural history *is* history and for the humanist, history has no *nature*, only uniqueness. For the scientist, humans are conceptualized according to science; for the humanist, human thought is separated from *Nature*; it is not seen as Nature reflecting upon itself.

The above analysis helps to explain why both scientistic and humanistic sociology have been unable to comprehend revolutions. Scientistic theories pose categories of social reality modeled on Nature as eternal: There is no room for humans in "pre-history" to transform themselves and the whole organization of society—to make a leap into "history." Humanistic views, on the other hand, contain a model of humans as already distinct from Nature:

They have no eyes to see the leap from "pre-history" to "history," since to their eyes, human history already exists.

The unity of the contradiction between scientistic and humanistic social theory lies not only in their rejection of history, but also in their undialectical separation of humans and Nature. The scientistic conception of Nature not only reduces humans to the same categories as animals and minerals, it goes on to fragment and objectify Nature, an objectification which accompanies the abolition of the knowing subject. The humanistic conception denaturalizes humans, thereby depriving Nature of any reflexivity. *These two paradigms unite in their celebration of the domination of Nature*—not only the domination of "external" Nature but "inner" human Nature as well.[22] The "humanistic" denial of Nature in humans was viewed by Adorno and Horkheimer as *the* regressive thrust of the Enlightenment, as a cause for the irrationality of modern society:

> In class history, the enmity of the self to sacrifice implied a sacrifice of the self in as much as it was paid for by a denial of Nature in humans for the sake of domination over non-human Nature and over other humans. This very denial, the nucleus of all civilizing rationality, is the germ cell of a proliferating mythic irrationality: With the denial of Nature in humans, not merely the *telos* of the outward control of Nature, but the *telos* of one's own life is distorted and befogged. As soon as humans discard the awareness that they themselves are Nature, all the claims for which we keep ourselves alive—social progress, the intensification of our material and spiritual powers, even consciousness itself—are nullified, and the enthronement of the means as an end, which under capitalism is tantamount to open insanity, is already perceptible in the prehistory of subjectivity.[23]

The way in which the dialectical relationship of humans and Nature is conceptualized is a key to understanding the nuances and orientation of theory, to grasping the cultural universe of the theorist, and to appreciating the ultimate effects of the theory. Humans and Nature, conceived in the form of scientific fact, described by abstract symbols and impersonal adjectives, function in a system of *co-determination*; but humans and Nature, conceived as a living, changing, inseparable, and contradictory unity, described in their process of interpenetration and concrete particularity, make the construction of a system problematic (if not impossible) and assert the essential feature of life as *self-determination*.

The differences between these two conceptions are immense. Only the latter allows for the possibility of a qualitatively new species-existence (the leap from "pre-history" to "history," and the actualization of genuine "species-being"). In this sense, it becomes a perspective that allows us to see the ways theorists reify the given reality, and it reveals the ways existing categories of life are posited as eternal. According to Jürgen Habermas:

> The resurrection of Nature cannot be *logically* conceived within materialism... The unity of the social subject and Nature that comes

> into being "in industry" cannot eradicate the autonomy of Nature
> and the *complete otherness* that is lodged in its facticity.[24]

Certainly it has not always been the case that Nature has been "completely other," since at the beginning of the human species, we emerged from Nature. Nonetheless, Habermas asserts this position in the name of logic, even though the logic of Hegel considered the enunciation of an "other" as the first step toward its domination. Habermas's position is based on a model of the human actor which considers the unconscious, following Freud, as "inner foreign territory;"[25] and he maintains what seems to be an overly rational (that is, ego-oriented) ideal for human perfection.[26] He criticized Marcuse's notion of a "New Technology," one not based on the domination of Nature but one which conceives of Nature as a partner in life, as one "which will not stand to *logical* scrutiny."[27] In each case, Habermas argues on the basis of *logic* that Nature must be an "eternal" other. Isn't it possible that, as in a love relationship, the "other" can simultaneously become "self"?

Nature is an eternal other from the point of view of *rationalistic* understanding, specifically from a conception of rationality which excludes intuition as one of its forms. German speculative philosophy, the tradition from which Habermas derives his thinking, could never pose the subject without the object. (Nor could it be one with the natural world; indeed it was its incessant criticism of empiricism which informed its development.) A *holistic* conception of rationality, on the other hand, would include the forms of rationality (instrumental, hermeneutic, critical) of the left side of the brain as well as intuitive and aesthetic moments of the right side.[28]

Much of Habermas's work is concerned with the explanation of the distinction between instrumental reason (reason oriented to technical ends), hermeneutic reason (reason oriented to explanation), and critical reason (reason oriented to emancipation). His treatment of these three categories of reason, however, seems to deny the possibility of their simultaneity (and in this sense is derived from Kant rather than Heidegger). In contrast to Habermas, Marcuse opens the possibility of a liberated human relationship with Nature. The present technical domination of Nature could conceivably be replaced by a "New Technology," one which would preserve, foster, and release Nature's potentialities.[29] There is a deeper level at which Marcuse imagines this possibility; namely, that it may be precisely the natural essence of humans, the instinct for freedom, which drives humans toward liberation and perfection.[30] In *Eros and Civilization*, Marcuse notes the anthropological description of Arapesh culture as a "fundamentally different experience of the world: nature is taken, not as an object of domination and exploitation, but as a 'garden' which can grow while making human beings grow."[31] He goes on to discuss this question not in terms of the past, but in terms of the future of mature civilization.[32] He imagines a future where work can become play, where *Logos* and *Eros* are reunited, where Nature and humans lovingly embrace each other.

Marcuse's theory was developed after World War II, a time when the material wealth of the economically advanced nations provided the majority of their members with sufficient wealth to enjoy the newly emergent consumer society. The "end of ideology" was but one of the many descriptions of the popular acceptance of a one-dimensional social order which "delivered the goods." At the same moment that Marcuse's theory analyzed most people's integration into one-dimensional society, he anticipated the possibility of new oppositional forces emerging from within these affluent societies. In 1968, the social movements which appeared concretely embodied his theoretical formulation of work becoming play, the useful becoming the good, and life becoming art. As discussed in the case studies of May 1968 and May 1970, the practice of the New Left transcended the one-dimensionality of the societies from which it arose. The spontaneity of the movement, although widely criticized by orthodox Marxists, represented the reintegration of work and play, of politics and art. The aesthetic dimension of the movements, symbolized by the takeover of the Odeón theater, the appearance of costumed demonstrators, and love at the barricades empirically demonstrated the fusion of the Good, the True, and the Beautiful in an epoch when their separation has never been more necessary to the established order. The political values of the New Left (self-management and internationalism) were derived from this *Weltanschauung,* a world-view which was present as much in intuitive as rationalistic form. The new unity of aesthetic and technical rationality, portrayed in the actions of millions of people in May 1968 and May 1970, has come to define the innermost meaning of a free society. Whether or not such a society is achieved, its outline is now visible, and our technological advances make it feasible.

Of course, the movement of history—what Hegel referred to as the *Weltgeist*—is not mandated from above or organized by conspiracies. Rather, as the dynamic process of historical change unfolds, the actions of millions of people actualized in moments of the *eros* effect confirms the new stage reached in the realization of freedom. The insight that it is the deeds of millions of people which determine the direction of society may be obvious today, but it is a recent insight in historical terms, one derived from the French and American revolutions.

It is widely recognized that the American Revolution of 1776 and the French Revolution of 1789 profoundly changed our understanding of history, ending the epoch of divine right and beginning that of national democracies. With the New Left, our thinking has again been changed, and our understanding of the nature and goals of history has been transformed. It has become widely accepted that there exists today—in contrast to the *whole of history*—an entirely new balance in the relationship of human beings and Nature: The human species is now the domineering factor, not the dominated one. Not only are we domineering, we are increasingly ecocidal. The accumulation of technical power over Nature which capitalism (and the French, American, and Russian revolutions) have made possible means today that the "striving" of the species, technologically and politically, might even result in the annihilation of all life on earth. Under these conditions, traditional world views have become outdated: It is no longer assumed, for example, that "more is better"; rather, there is now the insight that "small is beautiful" and that the "human scale" defines an optimum size for communities, enterprises, and politics.

These recent theoretical insights oppose the trend in the twentieth century to redefine the Good, the True, and the Beautiful according to technical expertise, instrumental fact, and the "elegance" of mathematics. As *homo technicus* has come to define modern human beings (in contrast to Aristotle's *homo politicus* and Adam Smith's *homo economicus*), the accomplishments of the industrial revolutions and the scientific breakthroughs of the twentieth century, taken together, have resulted in the change from quantity to quality: From a situation of human powerlessness and awe in the face of Nature, we stand today as conquerors of Nature and hold our technology in awe. The realistic alternatives posed by the species' technical progress are fundamentally those of life versus death: On the one side, nuclear war, ecological catastrophe, blatant barbarism and its "refined" counterpart in the economically advanced countries; or, on the other side, disarmament, a New Technology working in harmony with Nature, and fundamental changes in the structure of the world system. How do we as a species decide between these alternatives? How does our social theory account for the goal determination of society? How does it comprehend social movements which question the system's goals?

Such questions as these are not discussed within the predominant discourses of sociology, systems analysis, and Soviet Marxism. Although the intellectual basis of the Soviet Union and the United States appear to be as incongruous as their geopolitical domains, the practical repercussions of the two systems are as similar as Chernobyl and Three Mile Island. Their seeming incongruity, however, functions to stifle the questioning of the structures of either system by its members. In the United States, proponents of the restructuring of the world economy are immediately identified as "Communist," and in the Soviet Union, those who aspire to reform the absolutist political structures have been similarly outcast as pro-Western. Each superpower respects the rights of the other to intervene in the affairs of the small nations, and Nicaragua and Afghanistan figure neatly into the equations of generals in both the Kremlin and the Pentagon.

From the perspective of the New Left, the *intellectual* frameworks of the Soviet Union and the United States are quite similar to each other. They each contain assumptions which unquestioningly maintain the structures of world order, assumptions which make both systems of thought incapable of dealing with the question of the goal determination of society. In order to appreciate this New Left perspective, the ways in which sociology, systems analysis, and Soviet Marxism understand the goal determination of society are now examined.

The Sociology of Social Movements

It has long been recognized that our social goals are not given to us by divine right, but the insight of the French Revolution (that they can be determined through Reason), was precisely the insight that Comte's formulation of the science of sociology sought to negate. By subordinating imagination to observation, Comte hoped to concern himself with "facts," not speculation, with scientific laws not fanciful contemplation, and "with organization and order instead of negation and destruction."[33] By sticking to the facts, Comte hoped to attain objectivity on the model of the natural sciences: formal and mathematical, on the one hand, substantive and empirical, on the other. Comte originally designated this new science as "social physics," and it was not until 1838 that he used the word "sociology."[34]

For Comte, sociology was not merely aimed at description: "To see in order to foresee: that is the permanent distinguishing feature of true science."[35] In other words, sociology was originally conceived as a science capable of prediction. The goal which was to be served by such a science was the "continuous improvement of our individual and collective conditions of life—in opposition to the vain gratification of a sterile curiosity."[36] For Comte, the progress of science and technology was a basis for a better life for all members of society. This was reflected even in his definition of technology as "no longer exclusively geometrical, mechanical, or chemical, etc., but also and primarily political *and moral*."[37]

From this statement on technology, it should not be inferred that Comte conceived of sociology as an activist science. On the contrary, theory and practice were sharply divorced, since, in his view:

> All intermixture or any links of theory and practice tend to endanger both equally, because it inhibits the full scope of the former—theory—and lets the latter vacillate back and forth without guidance . . . The new social philosophy must thus carefully protect itself from that tendency, only too general today, which would induce it to intervene actively in actual political movements; these must above all remain a permanent object of thorough observation for it.[38]

If as a discipline, sociology did not exist until after the French revolution, it was for the same reason that the conception of "society"—understood as comprising the whole of social reality—did not appear until around the same time.[39] For the ancient Greeks, the *polis* was the focus for social and political thought; for Machiavelli, it was the feudal state. But with the rise of capitalism, the whole world was subjected to a unified economic process for the first time in history. Previously independent monarchies, city-states, and remote self-sufficient communities became integrated into a world system which broke down the parochialism of manorial life and freed serfs and lords alike from the bondage of feudal obligation. In short, as a world system came into being, the fate of individuals and groups was seen as determined by unified laws and existing in a unified reality: "society."

Social theory of all ideological viewpoints around the time of the French revolution attempted to discover scientific explanations for the nature and development of "society." We see this same search in the work of such different theorists as Comte and Hegel, Condorcet and Saint-Simon. The intellectual climate in post-revolutionary France demanded that knowledge be sequential, that it move from the less rational to more rational, from multiple explanations to a unified explanation. Within this post-religious context, the question was posed: What kind of agent could find the order, clarity, and rationality within itself which was embodied in the emergent "society." For Hegel, Comte, and Condorcet, the answer lay in the human mind. The search for the "motor force" to history, conceived by Aristotle as the "immovable mover" and deified by Christians, Moslems, and Jews as "God," was for Hegel, Comte, and Condorcet the mental organization of the human mind and its "eternal" laws. For Hegel, history was embodied in the "spirit of the people" or in the "Great Men" of history, and history "had a feature entirely different from that of Nature—the desire toward perfectibility."[40]

It was not until the outbreak of class conflict in the revolutions of 1848 that Karl Marx posited human beings involved in class struggles as the agents of history. Marx negated the abstract universals of philosophy and preserved them in his portrait of a *concrete* universal with two manifestations: establishment of a "world market" and the self-formation of humans as *Gattungswesen* or "species-being." History, for Marx, was nothing but the concrete actions of human beings in their society:

> *History* does *nothing*, it "possesses *no* immense wealth," it "wages *no* battles." It is *humans*, real, living humans who do all that, who possess and fight; "history" is not, as it were, a person apart, using humans as a means to achieve *its own* aims; history is *nothing but* the activity of humans pursuing their aims.[41]

The belief in "eternal" laws of history was criticized as "the reflection of man's plight in bourgeois society and of his helpless enslavement by the forces of production."[42] In other words, even though modern history might appear to be determined by immutable, eternal laws of Nature, these laws are not eternal but the *historically-bounded* laws of the capitalist world system. The "discovery" made by Marx was that history consists of concrete relationships between human beings, social relationships that "are just as much the product of humans as linen, flax, etc.,"[43] and that these relationships in "pre-history" were (and are) primarily conditioned by the economic organization of society. Social relationships were seen as simultaneously inherited from the past and reproduced in the present. That is the meaning of his famous passage:

> Humans make their own history, but they do not make it just as they please; they do not make it under circumstances chosen by themselves, but under circumstances directly encountered, given and transmitted from the past. The tradition of all the dead generations weighs like a nightmare on the brain of the living.[44]

Human relationships were seen as "not those between one individual and another, but between worker and capitalist, tenant and landlord . . .," that is, relationships between concrete human beings *in history*.[45] Theories which pose abstract laws of society as eternally valid take the existent reality and project it as true for all time. To his credit, Marx realized that the laws which govern capitalism (laws which he *incompletely* discovered and critiqued in *Capital*[46]) are valid only within the particular epoch of the "separation of the producers from the means of production." In the *German Ideology*, Marx analyzed both the *rise* and *fall* of the world system:

The further the separate spheres, which act on one another, extend in the course of this development and the more the original isolation of the separate nationalities is destroyed by the advanced mode of production, by intercourse and by the natural division of labor between various nations arising as a result, the more history becomes world history . . . In history up to the present it is certainly likewise an empirical fact that separate individuals have, with the broadening of their activity, become more and more enslaved under a power alien to them (a pressure which they have conceived of as a dirty trick on the part of the so-called world spirit etc.)—a power which has become more and more enormous and, in the last instance, turns out to be the *world market*.[47]

Whether or not we are Marxists, we now recognize the world as a system, but if it is a system whose goals have not been democratically (or scientifically) determined, how does modern sociology explain attempts to redefine these goals?

At the beginning of the twentieth century, sociological theories sought to explain revolutions and social movements through analogies to Nature. Lyford Edwards did this quite clearly in *The Natural History of Revolution*: "A revolution, in certain respects, resembles an elephant. The elephant is the slowest breeding of all living creatures, and revolution is the slowest forming of all social movements."[48] Crane Brinton's *The Anatomy of Revolution*, first published in 1938, drew a similar parallel: "The best conceptual scheme for our purposes would seem to be one borrowed from pathology. We shall regard revolutions as a kind of fever."[49]

These analogies to biology were the defining characteristic of the natural history conception of revolutions. A cyclical pattern was gleaned from the dynamic of past revolutions, and a temporal sequence not dissimilar to the four seasons in New England was posited as their inevitable cycle: from the appearance of symptoms (the defection of the intellectuals, the onset of economic crisis etc.); to a "crisis frequently accompanied by delirium" (the Reign of Terror); to a period of convalescence (Thermidor); and finally and inevitably, to a return to "normality" (the Restoration of a ruling elite). Such was the natural history view of revolutions. Although the assumption of an analogy to biology was made with some reservations, it was carried out. This assumption overlooks the fact that human values must be interpreted, and unlike animals, whose goals of survival are simply given to them by Nature, human beings construct goals and values other than those given to us by Nature.

Ten years after the publication of *The Natural History of Revolution*, Talcott Parson's *The Structure of Social Action* appeared, a work destined to be of monumental importance to sociology. Parsons synthesized a systematic model of social action by combining social theory from England (a utilitarian individualized means-end framework), France (normative order and a structural-functional system), and Germany (phenomenological analysis of the subjective state of the actor).[50] His work had the effect of producing a shift from understanding social reality through temporal biological analogies to a static system of analytic determinants whose existence was posited as universally valid. The building block of the Parsonian system was the unit act:

> Just as the units of a mechanical system in the classical sense, particles, can be defined only in terms of their properties, mass, velocity, location in space, direction of motion, etc., so the units of action systems also have certain basic properties without which it is not possible to conceive of the unit as "existing."[51]

In other words, for Talcott Parsons, an understanding of the goal-determination of society was built from the fact that each "unit act" has its goal, and the goals of the whole system flowed from the integration of the various parts. This position neatly paralleled the economic theory of Adam Smith, but it became increasingly problematic in an era of huge industrial corporations and massive economic intervention by the state (features of both the modern Soviet Union and the United States).

Although it is widely recognized today that revolutionary social movements are an important force in the redefinition of social goals, Parsons's theory could not even begin to analyze social movements since it was based on a spontaneously given normative order, an order challenged by revolutionary movements. For Parsonian structural-functionalism, the notion that the normative order "naturally" tended to insure the cohesion and equilibrium of the social system was a presupposition carrying within it the notion that non-normative action could not be a part of the social system—that is, that the vehicle of social change lay outside the boundaries of the system. Within the scope of the Parsonian system, the emergence of new social forces could only be comprehended as *externally* induced; disturbances must, as Parsons tells us, be "introduced into the system" from the outside.[52] In discussing this topic, C. Wright Mills commented:

> The idea of the normative order set forth leads us to assume a sort of harmony of interests as the natural feature of any society . . . The magical elimination of conflict, and the wondrous achievement of harmony, remove from this "systematic" and "general" theory the possibilities of dealing with social change, with history . . .[A]ny systematic ideas of how history itself occurs, of its mechanics and processes, are unavailable to grand theory and accordingly, Parsons believes, unavailable to social change . . .[53]

It is not my intention here to develop a comprehensive critique of Parsons's system but only to indicate his views of how social goals are determined and the role social movements play in transforming existing social goals.

Parsons derived his theory of action in the first place from what he called "individualistic positivism" beginning with Hobbes. He criticized Hobbes for being "almost entirely devoid of normative thinking," and at the same time, applauded him for "defining with extraordinary precision the basic units of a utilitarian system of action." For Hobbes, the totality of social reality was the sum of the individual parts, but within that formulation, the problem of social cohesion arose: why and how these separate parts came together to form a whole. If, as for Hobbes, the whole is equal to the sum of the parts and the parts are in a natural state of "war of all men against all men," then the whole's existence is possible only through a "visible power to keep men in awe," a "mortal God," a "Leviathan." The power of the strong in the state of Nature becomes the legal power of the state.

For Emile Durkheim, the whole was not merely equal to the sum of the parts—it was a reality "existing in its own right independent of its individual manifestations."[54] The whole was the integration of the parts—that is Durkheim made the leap from arithmetic to calculus in his social thought, a leap which can also be understood as corresponding to the leap from the circular, simple reproduction of capital to its expanded, spiral reproduction. For Durkheim and Parsons, "normative order" played the role of Hobbes's "Leviathan" in maintaining social cohesion. It follows that within this conceptual scheme, theories relapse into an uncritical acceptance of common sense notions of fact and value, the most obvious (and most criticized) example being the perception of the "normal" as opposed to the "deviant." For Parsons, the social system naturally tended toward equilibrium, and any disturbance of this equilibrium was not normal. Parsons shared a world-view with the natural history school in their similar treatment of social movements (and unconventional behavior generally) as pathological or deviant, and because of that assumption, the Parsonian system exiled collective behavior from the realm of normative behavior.

This banishment of collective behavior from the Parsonian system should not be viewed in isolation from the nearly simultaneous emergence of "symbolic interactionism," a term coined in 1937 by Herbert Blumer. In opposition to Parsons's reification of human action into structurally induced categories, Blumer developed a model of society stressing the cognitive interaction of human actors. He went as far as denying the existence of social structures, modeling human behavior instead as a striving for symbolic meaning in the flux of social interaction. For Blumer, collective behavior was meant to include any behavior "not based on the adherence to common understanding or rules."[55] His perspective shared with Parsons a sharp distinction between normal functioning and non-conventional behavior, even though for Blumer, that which was disrupted was a cognitive system of norms, values, beliefs, and attitudes, not a system of interdependent social structures. From this viewpoint, collective behavior was seen as a social-psychological attempt to reconstruct the symbolic meaning and order of the social world. The breakdown of established norms gave rise to behavior that Blumer identified as no longer being cognitively mediated, as irrational:

> The loss of customary critical interpretation and arousing of impulses and excited feelings explain the queer, vehement, and surprising behavior so frequent among members of a genuine crowd. Impulses which ordinarily would be subject to a severe check by the individual's judgment and control of himself now have a free passage to expression. That many of these impulses should have an atavistic character is not strange nor, consequently,

is it surprising that much of the actual behavior should be violent, cruel, and destructive.[56]

In short, the symbolic-interactionism of Blumer and the structural-functionalism of Parsons shared a valued orientation toward the *status quo*; their belief in the normality of order and the abnormality of conflict made both theories highly problematic as time went on.

Parsons had succeeded in building a steady-state system of social equilibrium in theory, but the practical movement of history soon gave him reason to try and adjust his model to the changing political environment. His system more or less accurately reflected the situation in the United States immediately after World War II. It was American in another sense as well: Parsons's system was oriented to action, not to thought. It was an action-oriented version of Kant's philosophical system. Although thought was a form of action for Parsons, he posited "doing" as eternal and focused his system on a theory of action, not of thinking. Where German philosophy generally concerned itself with the *goals* of human endeavor *as a whole*, Parsons took the goals (and cultural values) of the social system as "given" in much the same way as the goals of a biological or mechanical system are "given."

The early Parsonian system had attributed relatively little importance to the role of the state in defining social goals and maintaining social equilibrium. To Parsons, the social system was held together by its normative order, and he did not—at least in his early theories—concern himself with the role of the state in maintaining social stability. As Alvin Gouldner pointed out:

> The focus of early Positivistic Sociology was largely on "spontaneous" social arrangements that grew "naturally". . . . There was no doubt that Durkheim believed the state incompetent to manage what he regarded as the decisive problem of modern Europe, its "poverty of morality," *anomie*. . . In a similar vein, early Parsonian theory, warning of the unpredictabilities of "purposive social action," expressed suspicion of the Welfare State then crystallizing in New Deal reforms.[57]

Only after World War II was it the case that functionalism "began to give explicit support to the Welfare State as a way to satisfy the need for action to regulate the economy and to protect society against the 'international Communist conspiracy.'"[58] The consequences of this charge in the Parsonian system should not be underestimated. Once it is admitted that the goals of society are no longer "spontaneously" determined, the problem of how these goals are determined becomes a key issue, one which drove Parsons, the master system builder, to reorient himself to the problems of power in society and the relationship of the economy to politics. He republished new versions of his system both in *The Social System* (1951) and *Economy and Society* (1956). In the latter work (written together with Neil Smelser), the political system was "analytically defined as a functional subsystem of the larger system."[59] Writing in 1969, Parsons criticized his three earlier works on social systems for their "asymmetry between the economic and political." His earlier treatment of politics was one which he recognized "to have been quite unsatisfactory."[60]

After Parsons admitted the defects in his earlier formulations of the social system, he attempted to account for the role of the state in determining society's goals. His newly found emphasis on the polity led him to redefine the state as "the goal attainment subsystem of any social system."[61] This change meant abandoning his emphasis on the primary role of individualized moral values in holding society together. By jettisoning the belief that the social order was naturally normative (that society maintains equilibrium without the need for purposive-rational action *aimed at control*), Parsons helped pave the road for the rise of modern systems analysis and for the eclipse of grand sociological theory.

Current Research on Social Movements

Prior to 1957, there was not a single textbook on the subjects of collective behavior or social movements in the United States.[62] In that year, Turner and Killian published their *Collective Behavior*[63] and compared emergent norms in collective behavior to conventional, institutional behavior. In 1962, Talcott Parsons's student and colleague, Neil Smelser, reformulated his teacher's system in such a way that purposive social action, including unconventional behavior and social movements, could be analyzed from within the same conceptual framework as conventional behavior.[64] In so doing, Smelser helped sociology make the same leap that economics had made through the theories of Keynes.[65] In 1968, Smelser went on to single out the "government-and-control apparatus" as the one variable which could be seen as "determining the long-term direction of change" in the social system.[66] If the government is capable of rational action, then the same could potentially be true of social movements.

For Smelser, however, collective behavior and social movements are the "action of the impatient"; they display "crudeness, excess, and eccentricity"; they are "clumsy and primitive."[67] There may be short-term instances "when institutionalized means of overcoming the strain are inadequate," but even then, non-conformist collective behavior should be contained by *social control which "channels the energy of collective outbursts into more modest kinds of behavior."*[68] Smelser perceived collective behavior as irrational, as based on generalized beliefs that are "short-circuited." Although he attempted to analyze conventional and collective behavior from the same perspective, he distinguished between the beliefs underlying each type of action. The notions which guide collective behavior "involve a belief in the existence of extraordinary forces—threats, conspiracies, etc.—which are at work in the universe." They are "akin to magical beliefs"[69] insofar as the participants do not believe in the ability of the system to resolve social strains.

Following Parsons, Smelser assumed a spontaneously defined normative order, and he excluded the possibility that it might be the goals and organization of society which are irrational. In short, Smelser assumed that a consensus exists which approves of the whole organization of society, and any behavior which departs from such a belief was conceived as irrational. The view that the whole organization of society has evolved in an unplanned, Nature-like way (*Naturwuchs*)—that the whole system in its present form could be irrational—lies outside the domain of Smelser's theory. He accepted the system as it has evolved and as it exists. The very language of his theory indicated his values since he did not discuss human beings but components of action. He neglected to mention that these components exist within humans and that humans may rationally choose to transform themselves. The term "collective behavior," used as it is in contrast to conventional behavior, contains within it a distinction between "normal" and "abnormal" which rests upon a cognitive acceptance of the equilibrium of the *status quo*.

Despite these conservative biases, Smelser's theory (along with that of Ralph Turner)[70] played an important role in legitimizing social movements as a proper focus for sociological inquiry. In the last two decades, social movements have emerged as a reality for sociological analysis more or less distinct from those social phenomena covered by the collective behavior field. In 1966, Zald and Ash used organizational analysis to analyze the dynamics of social movement organizations.[71] In 1968, at the same time as worldwide movements were a key feature of social reality, Joseph Gusfield sketched a view of social movements as "socially shared demands for change in some aspect of the social order. This definition emphasizes the part played by social movements in the development of social change . . . it has the character of an explicit and conscious indictment of whole or part of the social order, together with the conscious demand for change."[72] With Gusfield's article, sociology had finally arrived at an understanding of social movements as rational attempts to determine society's goals and structures.

Unfortunately, sociological studies since 1968 have more often than not attempted to fit social movements into preconceived theoretical frameworks rather than constructing investigations of them as attempts to transform an irrational system. The goal of such studies is either to build upon the accumulated knowledge of past studies or to validate a specific theory by empirically demonstrating the correspondence of the generated facts to the accepted theory. Smelser's *Theory of Collective Behavior*, for example, has been used to analyze anti-pornography campaigns,[73] "race" riots,[74] student riots,[75] alienation,[76] and the student New Left.[77]

Generally speaking, the study of social movements since 1968 consists, on the one side, of middle-range theoretical systems and, on the other side, of fragmentary social research which attempts to validate one of the variants of middle-range theory. The principal approaches to studying social movements include: structural-functional consensus theories generally derived from Smelser's model;[78] social-psychological theories from Blumer to Gurr;[79] conflict theories exemplified in the work of Anthony Oberschall and Charles Tilly;[80] organizational theories like those of Mayer Zald and John McCarthy;[81] symbolic-status theories as in the work of Joseph Gusfield;[82] world system and mass society models derived in large part from the work of William Kornhauser and recently refined by Theda Skocpol;[83] and finally various types of Marxism found in the work of Roberta Ash Garner, Eric Hobsbawm, and George Rudé.[84]

Each of these theories seeks to explain social movements in relation to *partial* aspects of social reality, aspects which the theory defines as significant. Consensus theorists focus on the maintenance of social equilibrium and have little to offer about conflict; social-psychological theorists focus on the changing norms of human actors and have little to say about power and economics; conflict theorists focus on the structures of power but fail to explain the formation of collectivity; organizational theorists offer insight into the mobilization of resources by activists but neglect their "hearts and minds"; status theorists focus on the ways in which social problems are cognitively defined and the interests such definitions actually serve but give little insight into objective structures; mass society theorists deal with the relationship of elites to masses but have little to say about the subjectivity of human actors and the cultural sources of cohesion and conflict.

What all of these theories have in common is the fragmentation of the object of inquiry. By presupposing an empirically fragmented social reality, that is, by failing to deal with totality of society and with the question of how social goals are determined, these theorists narrow the possibility of discussion without grounding this reduction historically or theoretically. Fragmented theory restricts the questions under discussion without advancing a single argument for the appropriateness of such a reduction. Methodology stream-lines the question of epistemology as schools of thought compete for hegemony within the universities and professional associations while scholars vie for tenure and grant money.

For these (and other) reasons, sociological analysis of social movements is replete with attempts to generate objective laws of the rise and decline of revolutionary movements in order to determine specific cause-effect rela-tionships which might be useful in other times and places. Such an empirical use of generalized theory may have the effect of overlooking significant facts as much as making them apparent. It may be possible to mathematically and "scientifically" prove theories which in actuality could be utterly false. Although there may be a certain utility, for example, in understanding the relationship of family background and activism, such a study cannot account for periods of inactivity when child-rearing practices remain fairly constant. The inability of empirical research to comprehend rapidly changing situations and outbreaks of the *eros* effect makes its usefulness in the study of social movements highly dubious. As Gramsci cogently observed:

> The fact has not been properly emphasized that statistical laws can be employed in the science and art of politics only so long as the great masses of the population remain (or at least are reputed to remain) essentially passive...It should be observed that political action tends precisely to rouse the masses from passivity, in other words to destroy the law of large numbers. So how can that law be considered a law of sociology?[85]

There is, of course, a perspective from which finely focused empirical social research can be accorded a moment of truth. Insofar as the standardization of modern society has been conditioned by the extreme concentration of economic power, methods which are standardized are not only a reflection of the situation but also a suitable means for describing it.[86] Description, however, is not the same as scientific understanding, particularly when that which is described is but a fragment of the whole. Significantly, the fact that individual "problems" are studied in isolation leads empirical inquiry to seek solutions that don't take into account the organization of society as a whole— *which itself may be a cause of the particular problem.* In this sense, fragmented empirical research not only reflects and describes society, but it may also have the effect of contributing to the problems of society, even if the researcher is oriented to values of "change" rather than "order."

Conceived as a scientific discipline capable of passively understanding and predicting social behavior, sociology serves as an instrument for the existing control center of society. At best, a partnership between sociologists and social managers can be built to co-manage social relations. Conceived as an active moment of the popular reconceptualization of society (as is the "interventionist sociology" which has recently appeared in France), sociology might become a means of reconstituting the social order on an enlightened and democratic basis. Given the present ideological separation of fact and value, however, sociology remains tied to a system of beliefs which perpetuates the existing system.

Fact and Value

Both scientistic and humanistic sociology are in agreement about the need for a "value-free" social science. In the case of scientistic sociology, the "facts" are "given" in the external world, and the facts generated correspond to that world. So, for example, Durkheim's proposition that "social facts are things" is nothing but the carrying over of the commodity form to the analysis of social reality.[87] Knowledge thereby becomes a "thing" which can be bought and sold on the marketplace. Such a sociology not only reflects the economic structure of society, but more often than not, it also serves to reproduce it. Modern humanistic sociology, derived from the theory of Max Weber, assumes that human values can be made external to the process of inquiry. It assumes that it is possible (and desirable) to separate research from values, knowledge from action, and theory from practice.

The bifurcation of fact and value has its roots in Aristotle's formal logic, but it was *explicitly* systematized by Machiavelli. He wrote *The Prince* in the hope that weak Italy could become strong, and in the interests of princely domination, Machiavelli wrote:

> But my intention being to write something of use to those who understand, it appears to be more proper to go to the real truth of the matter than to its imagination; and many have imagined republics and principalities which have never been seen or known to exist in reality; for how we live is so far removed from how we ought to live, that he who abandons what is done for what ought to be done, will rather learn to bring about his own ruin than his

preservation...Therefore it is necessary for a new prince, who wishes to maintain himself, *to learn how not to be good*...[88]

In modern times, the idea of a "value-free" sociology was enunciated by Max Weber, who also lived in a weak nation that desired strength. Weber maintained that although values were relevant in choosing a *topic* for scientific inquiry, the process of inquiry itself demanded a suspension of value judgments. Weber's views have been the subject of intense debate, and it seems that the modern reading of Weber takes him far afield from his own statements.[89]

Historically, "value-free" social scientists have not been so free of values. Pitrim Sorokin, for example, took great pains to assert his neutrality in *The Sociology of Revolution*:

> The phenomena of revolution are very exotic and romantic— therefore the investigator must be especially prosaic; he has to study with the methods and purposes of a naturalist. The purpose of this book is neither to blame, praise, apotheosize nor to condemn revolution. It is only to study revolution in all its reality.[90]

This passage stands in Chapter 1, entitled "The Perversion of Human Behavior in Revolution."

Gustav Le Bon similarly spent considerable space asserting his scientific posture in his book, *The Crowd:*

> I have endeavored to examine the difficult problem presented by crowds in a purely scientific manner—that is by making an effort to proceed with method, and without being influenced by opinions, theories, and doctrines, This, I believe, is the only mode of arriving at the discovery of some few particles of truth, especially when dealing, as is the case here, with a question that is the subject of impassioned controversy. A man of science bent on verifying a phenomenon is not called upon to concern himself with the interests his verification may hurt.[91]

The reader need only continue a few pages to find Le Bon comparing crowds to worms: "In consequence of the purely destructive nature of their power, crowds act like those microbes which hasten the dissolution of enfeebled or dead bodies." Max Weber, the most "value-free" of all sociologists, called for members of the radical Left to be sent to the madhouse, the zoo, or the firing squad.[92]

In theory, value-free sociology asserts a superiority to "value-laden" research, but in practice, the effect of value-free sociology in a highly specialized industrial society is to provide the "control center" with information that can be used to maintain the social order as it exists. That "value-free" sociology succumbs to the control center was demonstrated in horrifying ways during the Vietnam War. Using "value-free" methods, Ithiel de Sola Pool analyzed questionnaire results from interrogations of prisoners in order to determine the motivational sources of "enemy" actions.[93] Samuel Huntington helped design the "forced urbanization" of Vietnam: the saturation bombing of the countryside which forced hundreds of thousands of peasants into the U.S.-controlled urban areas and "strategic hamlets"—a "value-free" version of concentration camps.

How is it possible that "value-free" social science could come to these overtly value-laden deeds? To some, this question should be answered according to the nature of the particular personalities involved, but what is really at stake here is much more. If, in the name of "value-free science," such actions have been committed, it is also because "value-free" science has taken on a larger than life meaning, that is, it has become a belief system which obscures its values and impact. In their call for "value-free" sociology, scientists are making commands similar to those of church in medieval society:

> The positivist command to conform to facts and common sense instead of to utopian ideas is not so different from the call to obey reality as interpreted by religious institutions, which after all are facts too. Each camp undoubtedly expresses a truth, under the distortion of making it exclusive... Both schools are heteronomous in character. One tends to replace autonomous reason by the automatism of streamlined methodology, the other by the authority of a dogma.[94]

Already in the theory of positivism—its abolition of the conscious human subject and its reification of objective fact—is contained its practical effect: the elimination of morality and the reduction of human reality. Writing after World War II, Horkheimer put it this way:

> The death factories in Europe cast as much significant light on the relations between science and cultural progress as does the manufacturing of stockings out of air... It must be observed here that the division of all human truth into science and humanities is itself a social product that was hypostatized by the organization of the universities and ultimately by some philosophical schools, particularly those of Rickert and Max Weber. The so-called practical world has no place for truth, and therefore splits it to conform it to its own image: the physical sciences are endowed with so-called objectivity, but emptied of human content; the humanities preserve the human content, but only as ideology, at the expense of truth.[95]

Herbert Marcuse and Jürgen Habermas have similarly interpreted modern science and technology as forces of social domination and as ideology.[96] In Marcuse's view, it is the "value-free" character of science which makes it ideology:

> It is precisely its neutral character which relates objectivity to a specific historical subject—namely, to the consciousness that prevails in the society by which and for which neutrality is established.[97]

"Value-free" empirical social research reaches its logical focus by slicing social reality into pieces small enough to be analyzed in much the same way that modern physics focuses on atomic particles, or modern biology is defined by the investigation of chromosomes and DNA. These methods owe a great deal to technical advances like the electron microscope and computers. In the case of social science (and possibly natural science as well), the instruments of analysis cannot be exempted from the process of inquiry as if they were neutral methods of viewing reality. They focus attention on only certain aspects of the whole, and by studying partial aspects of society, empirical research (implicitly or not) idealistically posits a fragmented social reality without first proving the validity of such a method. Systems theory attempts to remedy the fragmented comprehension of empiricism by focusing attention on the whole system, but in so doing, posits the existence of the system without proof.

I now turn to a discussion of systems analysis, a modern body of theory which claims to be capable of overcoming the fragmentation of empiricist knowledge. Moreover, because systems analysis has become widely used in both the Soviet Union and the United States since 1968, its adherents claim that it is a value-free method of analysis, a neutral means of controlling complex systems which, in contrast to Soviet Marxism, does not place political ideology above "objectivity."

The Limits to Systems Analysis

Modern systems analysis is based on the attempt to control increasingly complex social systems without necessarily understanding the subjectivity of the members of the system. Systems analysis is thus nothing but social engineering, as Jay Forrester, one of its key exponents, proudly admitted in 1961:

> Before World War II, basic scientific developments in the world's universities lacked close ties to the practice of engineering...Over the last two decades engineering has developed an articulate recognition of the importance of systems engineering.[98]

In Forrester's view, previous methods of social control have been unsuccessful:

> Labor turmoil, bankruptcy, inflation, economic collapse, political unrest, revolution and war testify that we are not yet expert enough in the design and management of social systems.[99]

Systems analysis grew out of the technological developments made during World War II when new weapons systems capable of mass destruction on a scale never before possible were invented. Since ballistic missiles and nuclear weapons require machines to direct their use, humans are no longer capable of making the quick decisions typical of the automated battlefield. "Friend and foe identification," "weapon selection," and "fire-control" became machine functions. In Forrester's words:

> The battle commander can no longer plot the course of his enemy on a chart and personally calculate the aiming point. In fact, with a ballistic missile he would have no time even to select his defensive weapon.[100]

The influence of modern systems theory has been quite widespread. Under Lyndon Johnson, systems analysis became a tool used in the quest for the "Great Society." After Pompidou proclaimed *"le grand société,"* systems analysis has been used in the renovation of the French central planning system. Since 1967, there has been a West German law concerning economic stabilization (*Stabilitätsgesetz*) which explicitly requires features of cybernetic control policies, and in the Soviet Union, systems analysis is an important tool for state planning.[101]

In the period of rapid technological change after World War II, systems analysis perceived a tendency for "all sectors of a highly industrialized society to amalgamate into one big organization." Two consequences became apparent: "Social problems became more complex," and "there are rapid and often unexpected reactions on socio-economic or political activities."[102] Systems theory is concerned with "problems" which disrupt the normal functioning of the system, but the tendency of the modern system to become involved in crisis remains incompletely explained by systems theory. In Forrester's system, the word "noise" is used to denote such phenomena, and he is quite explicit in his belief that computers can understand social problems better than human beings:

> Our intuitive judgment is unreliable about how these systems will change with time, even when we have good knowledge of the individual parts of the system. Model experimentation is now possible to fill the gap where our judgement and knowledge is weakest—by showing the way in which the known separate system parts can interact to produce unexpected and troublesome over-all system results.[103]

Systems analysis is a logical outcome of and justification for modern scientific progress. Decision-making was first automated in warfare, and then used to replace decision-making in the society which waged war in the name of preserving its human values. Systems theory assumes that the human mind cannot, by itself, understand the problems of modern systems, but its calculations do not include a thoughtful consideration of social goals and values.[104] The goals and values of the society controlled and managed by systems theory are those which are given to us by the past. Maintenance of the social system as it exists becomes an end in itself, an unquestioned goal helped along by "neutral" technicians and programmers.

Perhaps the most influential study produced by modern systems theory, *The Limits to Growth,* does make an attempt to deal with the goals and values of society. This concern does not *originate* in any way from a rationalistic critique of the whole organization of society but from a realization that unlimited growth is impossible in a finite environment.[105] The study asserts that the modern world system's collapse is inevitable because of the impending exhaustion of earth's non-renewable resources, the accumulation of pollution, the limits of arable land fit for food production, the expanding world population, and the exponential growth tendency of industrial capital.[106] The authors simulate various interplays of these factors in order to develop a possible model for the steady-state stability of the industrial world system.

Their suggested policy changes (needed if the world system is to avoid collapse) include:

1. popular access to 100 percent effective birth control.
2. an average desired family size of two children.
3. a steady average industrial output per capita (excess industrial capability being employed for consumer goods rather than expended in capital investment).[107]

Within the dynamic, steady-state society which the authors propose as the only alternative to impending collapse, "corporations could expand or fail, local populations could increase or decrease, income could become more or less evenly distributed." The authors seek:

> to create freedom for society, not impose a straitjacket... The state of global equilibrium could be designed so that the basic material needs of each person on earth are satisfied and each person has an equal opportunity to realize his individual human potential.[108]

The authors straightforwardly present the real possibility of what appears to be the leap from "pre-history" to "history," from the realm of material scarcity to abundance. They carefully note that such a change would require more than technical solutions. It demands a "change in human values"; it would "certainly involve profound changes in the social and economic structures," particularly since, in their view, the structure of the system "is often just as important in determining its behavior as the individual components themselves."[109]

As they are quick to admit, their analysis is nothing new:

> For the past several decades, people who have looked at the world with a global, long-term perspective have reached similar conclusions. *Nevertheless, the vast majority of the policy-makers seems to be actively pursuing goals that are inconsistent with these results.*[110]

At this point, they reach the limits of their own analysis. They have arrived at the conclusion that the current system is headed for collapse and that the world's policymakers are doing nothing to avoid it—indeed, these policymakers may be contributing to the very possibility of collapse. But how do they explain this? *Can* they explain it using their tools of analysis? What are the dynamics of the structures of society which account for this headlong dash for collapse?

In one phrase, *they cannot explain why this condition exists.* As they themselves are careful to point out, social factors cannot be included in their model:

> Neither this book nor our world model at this stage in its development can deal explicitly with these social factors, except insofar as our information about the quality and distribution of physical supplies can indicate possible future social problems.[111]

The authors note with concern that the gap between the core and periphery—between rich nations and poor nations—is widening and that between ten and twenty million people die each year from malnutrition.[112] Their analysis makes clear that the present system, one based on continual economic growth, cannot relieve this situation but actually is making it worse.[113] Within the confines of their system of analysis, however, this problem becomes an "imponderable political question."[114] They can neither explain why the world's policymakers are rushing headlong towards collapse nor why the gap between rich and poor nations is widening.

The blindness of even the best-intentioned systems analysis is shared by all forms of analysis which pose the categories of the present system as eternal ones. In *The Limits of Growth,* "capital" is considered an eternal "fact" and large-scale industrial production an eternal need. From these premises flow such assumptions as the cause of pollution lying in the *individual* desire for a higher standard of living[115] (a crucial assumption in terms of their specific model since a direct correlation between population growth and pollution is one of the key reasons they support birth control). Decentralization and self-sufficiency cannot be comprehended by their analysis as possible solutions to the crisis of the centralized world system; on the contrary, their view is that: "many nations and people, by taking hasty remedial action or retreating into isolationism and attempting self-sufficiency, would but aggravate the conditions operating in the system as a whole."[116]

It is here that the limits of the systems analysis become quite clear: By posing the system as the unit of analysis in the first place, there is no capacity to comprehend a reality which contradicts the existence of the system. The presuppositions of systems analysis as well as its goals of systematic control render it incapable of any point of view other than that of the control center. The logic of systems analysis, reflecting as it does the historical reality of the growth of the world system, eternally binds it to the continuation of that system.

Other possibilities such as a decentralized, self-determined, self-sufficient network of bio-regional communities[117] cannot be imagined from within the scope of systems analysis. By defining its goal as control of the social system, systems analysis joins hands with whomever sits at the control center. Whether or not it attempts to influence policymakers to adopt new policies, systems analysis conceives of problems and solutions from the point of view of the centralized system, and its values and morality reflect the needs of the control center. It has helped automate "judgment" so that weapons of mass destruction can be used in warfare between competing states, without asking whether or not these weapons *should* be used. Similarly, it has helped design methods of coordinating the modern social system without questioning the rationality of the system itself. Systems theory's promise for "constructing a rational and decent society"[118] seems to be falsified in its acceptance of the meaning of the "rational" as merely instrumental rationality (*Zweckrationalität* or rationality for technical results). Its roots in nuclear war should be cause for concern with its present application in social control. Systems theory knows no human subjectivity, no morality: Its rationality knows no genuine values

(*Wertrationalität*). So long as it works to help the system deliver the goods and maintain its stability, it can at best guarantee "prosperity without freedom."[119] Systems analysis is a useful tool in maintaining what C. Wright Mills called "the Cheerful Robot,"[120] but its utility in helping design a genuinely rational society is dubious.

Systems theory appears to be only a method, but insofar as it is a method which does not explicitly take up the question of the goals of the whole organization of society, it is a method for perpetuating the social goals which already exist.[121] The possibility that the members of society could democratically enunciate more rational goals than those inherited from the past is excluded in advance. According to Niklas Luhmann, a leading German theoretician of systems theory, the expansion of democracy is incompatible with the "rationality" of systems theory:

> Decision processes are...processes of eliminating other possibilities. They produce more "nays" than "yeas," and the more rationally they proceed, the more extensively they test other possibilities, the greater becomes their rate of negation. To demand an intensive, engaged participation of all [members of society] in them would be to make a principle of frustration. Anyone who understands democracy in this way has, in fact, to come to the conclusion that it is incompatible with rationality.[122]

Non-participatory central planning may (or may not) be the most efficient way for the modern system to function, but it is indeed the most rational only if "rationality" is understood as *purely* instrumental, devoid of moral and ethical questions.[123] Such a view does not allow the questions to be raised: What if the centralized structures of the system as they exist prove unable to solve the control problems? Indeed, what if these existing structures are themselves the cause of these problems?

In short, systems theory reduces *human* problems to *technical* ones. By viewing problems of *social* integration as problems of *system* integration, systems theory translates potential problem solutions to the one dimension of improving the system. Progress is thereby transformed into the process of increasing the power of the system over environmental complexity. The perceived tendency of "society to amalgamate into one big organization" is thereby reproduced by the theory which perceives this tendency *and attempts to control it.* Systems analysis is useful only insofar as a solution to problems of centralized control is involved. By positing itself as a means for control of the system, systems theory obstructs genuine understanding and serves to maintain the *status quo.* Real understanding, that is, *Social Science,* as opposed to *social technology,* must begin elsewhere, as Habermas argues:

> Among other things, social systems are distinguished from machines (with learning capacity) and from organisms by the fact that subjective learning processes take place and are organized within the framework of ordinary language communication. A systems concept which is more appropriate to the social sciences... can therefore not be taken over from general systems theory; it

must be developed in relation with a theory of ordinary language communication, which also takes into consideration the relationship of intersubjectivity and the relation between ego and group identity.[124]

Inasmuch as the system is a model of mathematical constructions which are taken as reality, systems theory is ideology. As Adorno analyzed it:

> The system, the form of presenting a totality to which nothing remains extraneous, absolutizes the thought against each of its components and evaporates the content in thoughts. It proceeds idealistically before advancing any arguments for idealism.[125]

Systems theory knows no life, no flesh and blood humans. Its *alpha* and *omega* are contained in its models and "mathematical elegance" which cannot be empirically verified nor epistemologically justified.[126] When this "elegance" of mathematics is held up for closer scrutiny, its human content is found to be non-existent. Indeed, in Marcuse's view, formal and mathematical logic is fundamentally untrue:

> Thought is true only insofar as it remains adapted to the concrete movement of things and closely follows its various turns. As soon as it detaches itself from the objective process and, for the sake of some spurious precision and stability, tries to simulate mathematical rigor, thought becomes untrue.[127]

In its "mathematical elegance," systems theory imagines itself to be free from biases and values which might obstruct its "pure understanding." Society is perceived as eternally existing as it is: There is no room for the creation of new dimensions to it. Within their models, systems theorists cannot conceive of new technological means of production which do not consume and dominate Nature. Their "mathematical elegance" cannot accurately predict technological developments whereby limited supplies of raw materials could be renewed or replaced. Neither can they predict with certainty the concrete mechanisms of population growth and the earth's capacity to absorb industrial pollution.[128] In short, their "mathematical elegance" is in their model: The real living world is not.

Critique of Soviet Marxism

Since the October Revolution, Marxism in the Soviet Union has been transformed from a means for liberation and subversion of the established reality into an instrument of domination and justification for the new social order. After 1917, the quantitative proliferation of Communist Parties throughout the world under the leadership of the Comintern resulted in the qualitative reduction and standardization of what had been the diverse theory and practice of the European socialist movement. By developing a critique of Soviet Marxism as it exists, I hope to locate theoretical presuppositions which led to the hostility of Soviet Marxists to the New Left and to explain why Soviet Marxism is incapable of questioning the existing structures of society.

Philosophical Foundations

What unites the various categories of Soviet Marxism in the modern world is a reduction of Marxism from a synthesis of rationalistic philosophy and empirical science to a scientific naturalism independent of human will and imagination. Following in the footsteps of Engels, modern Soviet Marxism considers natural reality to be the ultimate touchstone upon which the facticity of the dialectical method can be evaluated. Given only this empirical foundation, the humanistic critique of the established reality, an essential element of revolutionary Marxism, is lost. A dialectical Marxism worthy of its name is rooted both in the internal development of philosophy as well as in the empirical foundations of natural science.[129] By posing the "existence of Nature as it is," Soviet Marxism fails to comprehend the mental activity required to construct a fact—the epistemological problematic—and instead asserts the rules of natural science as the only methodology useful for the study of social reality.

The rules of natural science, such as those used by Marx in *Capital* to exhibit some of the necessary laws which operate within the capitalist system, have a validity rooted in the structures of the world system. But the moment of truth in such a methodology reaches its limit when the focus of investigation becomes the human transformation of the existing system. Soviet Marxism insists that the science of history can be as precise a science as biology and can be applied to practical decisions. This variety of "scientific" Marxism fails to differentiate between the naturally given realities of biology and the humanly constructed nature of the social world. However, a better reading of Marx is found here:

> The distinction should always be made between the material transformation of the economic conditions of production which can be determined with the precision of natural science and the legal, political, religious, aesthetic or philosophic—in short ideological forms in which men become conscious of this conflict and fight it out.[130]

It should be said here that Marx never tired of criticizing what he called "crude Communism" for not centering on the human essence, the human subject of social reality, but operating in a world of things. The discovery of the *Economic and Philosophic Manuscripts* in 1930 gave impetus to a revolutionary transformation of the conceptual framework within which Soviet Marxism continues to operate today. In the early work of Marx, and in his last work, *Capital*, political economy was derived from philosophical concepts. Indeed, the crucial breakthrough made by Marx was the transformation of economic facts into human factors.

Capital was never defined as a thing by Marx. On the contrary, at every point in the development of his scientific theory, he unmasked what had been regarded as the property of the capitalist as stored-up dead labor, as "objectified labor, i.e., labor which is present in space."[131] Even the exchange value of Nature was seen by Marx (rightly or wrongly) as contingent upon the embodied human labor required to extract raw materials from their natural locations. Soviet Marxism does just the opposite, making economic facts out of human relationships.

But even in the writings of Marx, there are elements which may be said to have been preconditions for the hegemony of positivism within contemporary Soviet Marxism. Marx approved of the comparison made by some between the phenomena of economic life he analyzed in *Capital* and the history of biological evolution analyzed by Darwin, and Marx's disciples, particularly Engels, admiringly referred to *Capital* as following in the scientific tradition of Copernicus and Galileo. More recently, Althusser has referred to this analysis by Engels as "pages of extraordinary theoretical profundity."

Within the writings of Marx, the roots of the scientistic reduction can be traced to his conception of the self-constitution of the human species as taking place only within the sphere of material production. That presupposition excludes important aspects of human existence from consideration. Furthermore, the fetishization of work, not its quantitative reduction or qualitative transformation, has become the position of dogmatic theory. The theoretical reasons why Soviet Marxism romanticizes the working class and the process of production can be found in the belief that the self-formation of the human species occurs solely through labor. Within the empirical parameters of Soviet Marxism, labor means work, not the broader process of the human transformation of Nature ("inner" as well as external Nature).

Although Marx's emphasis on the role of labor in the self-formation of the species has been interpreted to exclude other dimensions of human action (like political praxis, art, and communication), these comprise significant domains within which the human species transforms itself into a "species-being." In other words, revolutionary praxis is a second dimension of self-formation, and events like May 1968 and May 1970 constitute a vital means through which the human species becomes rational.

From this perspective, Soviet Marxism's hostility to the New Left can be traced to its labor metaphysic and its belief in the Party's absolute righteousness. The "absolute truths" of Soviet Marxists are predicated on theoretical presuppositions like the formal logic of natural science and the Party's claim to be the exclusive embodiment of the scientific application of the logic of historical development. By making Marxism into an abstract scheme universally applicable through the Communist Parties of the world, the living subjects of the concrete history of human society—the "little people" (as well as the dialectical logic of Marx which conceived human beings as the creators of their social reality)—are destroyed, buried beneath the rule of bureaucratically organized science. Such a Marxism regards the workings of things—particularly the "economic base"—as determining the consciousness and praxis of human beings.

By transforming the dialectical method into a universally applicable system of "base-superstructure," Soviet Marxism elevates its truth to a new metaphysic. Reality is poured into a bottle of static "scientific" propositions, reducing knowledge from a living human praxis to a dead formalistic model. As Marcuse pointed out:

> While not a single of the basic dialectical concepts has been revised or rejected in Soviet Marxism, the function of the dialectic itself has undergone a significant change: it has been transformed from a mode of critical thought into a universal "world outlook" and universal method with rigidly fixed rules and regulations, and this transformation destroys the dialectic more thoroughly than any revision...The first step in this was made by Engels in his *Dialectics of Nature*.[132]

It is not only the formalistic methodology of orthodoxy but the content of its imposed forms which are called into question by a critical social science. The language itself—that is, the words "base" and "superstructure"—belie a simplicity of analysis which, within the methodology of universally valid scientific knowledge, destroys the possibility of the transformation of the qualities of human beings and of our collectively constructed reality. Especially in the modern world where the state plays a greater role in the economy, it is increasingly difficult to accept the vulgar dichotomy of base and superstructure.

It is within this framework that Soviet Marxism can be seen as predicated on a metaphysical, trans-historical idealism. As Lukács observed in *History and Class Consciousness,* what is common to all bourgeois systems of analysis is the inability to formulate the categories of the present as other than eternal ones. Modern orthodoxy is predicated on a negation of the power of human reason and imagination as being ideological and unscientific. Parallel to the effect of sociological positivism, reality is thereby reduced to what exists as it is, and the definition of the totality of human existence excludes the possibility—indeed the necessity—of the qualitative transformation of the categories of social reality. As Marcuse put it:

> In a society whose totality was determined by its economic relations to the extent that the uncontrolled economy controlled all human relations, even the non-economic was contained in the economy. It appears that, if and when this control is removed, the rational organization of society toward which critical theory is oriented is more than a new form of economic regulation. The difference lies in the decisive factor, precisely the one that makes society rational—the subordination of the economy to the individuals' needs. The transformation of society eliminates the original relation of substructure and superstructure.[133]

By negating philosophy, Soviet Marxism fails to strengthen liberatory mass movements, and in practice, as we have seen in 1968, seeks to crush them. Philosophy provided the basis for Marx's theory and practice, but Soviet Marxism misses the dynamics of society and revolution in their human essence by rejecting the rationalistic foundations of Marxism. The class struggle, proletarian revolution, and freedom are retained, but as metaphysical truths. The "scientific" method of Soviet Marxism has become a static shell of empty logic universally applicable yet increasingly irrelevant to the liberation of human beings.

In the modern world where the technocratic ideology permits the rule of experts and elites, is it surprising that a justification for the reduction of Marxism from the philosophy of the revolutionary proletariat to the science of the Party is done in the name of Science? The dominant ideology of our time, in contrast to the era in which Marx articulated his revolutionary philosophy, is technocratic materialism, not religious idealism. The elites of today, whose hegemony depends on the docility of their followers, rely on people remaining convinced of their own inability to think and act properly without the presence of experts.

Within the Communist Parties, a strata of high priests of Marxism has been created to interpret the needs of "the revolution" for the members of the Party as well as for the working class. In the United States, under the conditions of monopoly production, the reduction of Marxian theory to a set of rigid categories has resulted in the standardization of thought common to the sectarian Left. Under similar conditions in France, but with a more conscious base among the working class, the reification of Marxism is an important reason for the Communist Party's antipathy toward the popular movement of May 1968, whose constituency and visions were not and are not comprehensible from within the myopic world view of "scientific" Marxism.

The "scientific" treatment of Marxism may be seen as a reinterpretation of Marx from within the dominant scientistic ideology of the modern world system. A failure to break with the mentality of mass society has resulted in a fetishized treatment of Marx and Lenin. These "great men" of history have been turned into commodities by the savants of orthodoxy. Each sect resembles a collective capitalist struggling to reap as much profit (cadre) from the popular movement as possible, each selling their version of the "real thing." The house dogmas which party members freely recite are more in the tradition of a catechism than a questioning and critique of the established reality. In few groups do activists learn to think about issues as a process of open scientific investigation. Instead the answers (and the questions) are provided by "higher ups." Such standardization of thought parallels, not negates, the dominant ideology of our society.

The reduction of Marxism from the philosophy of the proletariat to the science of the Party has necessitated its rejection of humanism. In the aftermath of the New Left, Louis Althusser consistently reinterpreted Marxism from a "scientific" perspective, attacking intellectuals like Sartre and Marcuse as "petit-bourgeois" and systematically revising Marxism in an attempt to exorcise the "evil spirit" of humanistic philosophy. The events of May 1968 may have brought the French Communist Party thousands of new members, but as I discuss below, the theory of the Party after 1968, at least as Althusser developed it, helped contribute to the continuing irrelevance of that group.

The Ideology of Althusser's Marxism

The scientific interpretation of the works of Marx as enunciated by Louis Althusser posit an "epistemological rupture" between the early "philosophical" Marx and the older "scientific" Marx: "This 'epistemological break' divides Marx's thought into two long essential periods: the 'ideological' period before, and the scientific period after, the break in 1845."[134] Althusser went on to classify the writings of Marx into four more precise periods culminating in the "mature Marx" after 1857.

The impositions of these constructed periods, and most importantly, the "essential" duality between the young, philosophical and old, scientific Marx, are themselves ideological. Despite the beliefs of the Althusserians that they are "non-ideological" scientists, it is possible to indicate the self-serving nature of their interpretation of Marxism by discussing epistemological aspects within the Althusserian paradigm: the abolition of the subject of history and the differentiation between ideology and science.

In contrast to the humanism of the young Marx, Althusser insisted that Marxism is a science devoid of humanistic considerations. Humanistic Marxism was viewed as ideology, which if accepted by scientific Marxists, would "cut ourselves off from all knowledge."[135] Unlike scientific theory, philosophy was seen by Althusser as a reflection of ideology from which a science might develop, but only as a result of an "epistemological rupture." According to Althusser:

> Without sciences, no philosophy, only world outlooks... The ultimate stake of philosophical struggle is the struggle for hegemony between the two great tendencies in world outlook (materialist and idealist). The main battlefield in this struggle is scientific knowledge: for it or against it. The number one philosophical battle therefore takes place on the frontier between the scientific and the ideological.[136]

To draw the line between science and ideology as Althusser does in the above quotation is to fail to recognize the ideological nature of science. Fortunately, in the course of dehumanizing Marxism, Althusser dealt squarely with our objection while criticizing Gramsci:

> Gramsci constantly declares that a scientific theory, or such and such a category of science, is a "superstructure" or a "historical category" which he assimilates to a "human relation"... Science can no more be ranged within the category "superstructure" than can language, which as Stalin showed escapes it.[137]

By elevating science to the status of pure knowledge, Althusser served the cause of the ideology of science which today is the primary system of belief within the economically advanced societies. This scientific ideology manifests itself in a variety of myths, particularly in the belief that all problems can be solved through the application of technology and the authority of experts.

After asserting that science is not part of the "superstructure," that it is an eternal truth, Althusser's next step was to make philosophy the "study of theoretical practices," providing a framework for the activity of philosophers as the "high priests" of the Communist Party, while divorcing philosophy from the rank and file. For Althusser, "historical materialism" was the science of history or the science of social formations, while "dialectical materialism" was Marxist philosophy. This dualistic conception of reality is, of course, ideological. The specialization and compartmentalization of knowledge, reflecting the fragmentation of the productive process, is itself false consciousness which overlooks the philosophical basis of all science, and, in particular, overlooks the development of the Marxian critique of political economy from its philosophical roots and method. Furthermore, Althusser's contrived "epistemological rupture" in Marx, meant to purge the philosophical aspects of the "young" Marx, demonstrates how different his notion of rupture was from Marx's notion of "*Aufhebung,*" the development of the new from within the old, negating the old while retaining key properties at a higher level, and decidedly not jettisoning the past altogether.

In the name of science, Althusser insisted upon the need not to stray into the "individualist-humanist error" of conceiving that "the subjects of history are 'real, concrete men.'" Who, then, if anyone, are the subjects of history? The reply from Althusser:

> The "subjects" of history are given human societies. They present themselves as totalities whose unity is constituted by a certain specific type of complexity, which introduces instances, that, following Engels, we can, very schematically, reduce to three: the economy, politics, and ideology. So in *every* society we can posit... the existence of an economic activity as the base, a political organization and "ideological" forms.[138]

In a later work, Althusser went on to comment on the rejection of the views of the young Lukács by the Comintern:

> The Marxist tradition was quite correct to return to the thesis of the *Dialectics of Nature,* which has a polemical meaning that history is a process without a subject, that the dialectic at work in history is not the work of any Subject whatsoever, whether Absolute (God) or merely human, but that the origin of history is always already thrust back before history, and therefore that there is neither a philosophical origin nor a philosophical subject to History.[139]

In the context of the ossification of the Communist Parties of Europe as bureaucratic structures above the people, Althusser developed a scientific defense. History has no subject, or if it does, it is given as society. "The people make history," a truism of Marxism, is rejected, and the role of revolutionary philosophy as a part of the autonomous actions of the people is eliminated in favor of a science which guides the Party. Thus, the implications of Althusser's dissection of the works of Marx are a reduction of the substance of Marxism to a technocratic ideology, that is, the degeneration of scientific Marxism into a justification for the facticity of the given.

In a period when the working class became contained within the consumer society of the "Free World" and the ideology of the Party became a means of justifying the bureaucratic reality in "socialist" societies, the New Left transcended each development from the perspective of the un-freedom of the modern world, and in its imagination was the potential of a qualitative step forward for human beings. In contrast to the view put forth by academic sociology and by Soviet Marxism that philosophy is nothing more than the expression of a specific social situation—ideology—the New Left returned to a conception of human beings as creative, rational beings who are not simply determined by the given reality. In this context, philosophy becomes socially realizable through the human transformation of the *status quo*. The New Left's philosophical project was the pursuit of "Reason" and "Truth" as part of the popular reconstruction of the social world, not simply an ideological activity reserved for the upper echelons of the Party or the inner sanctum of the corporate university. In so doing, it helped preserve the possibility of a real "leap into freedom" at a time when even the notion of human liberation was in danger of scientific reduction.

APPENDIX: DOCUMENTS

Document 1

*Governor Ronald Reagan's Speech
during "Operation Cablesplicer"
Governor's Orientation—10 February 1969[1]*

Thank you, General Ames, General Larson, members of the Military, members of the Legislature, and Administration and you gentlemen who are present.

You know there are some people in the state, who, if they could see this gathering right now, and my presence here would decide their worst fears and convictions had been realized—I was planning a military takeover.

If I hesitate, and incidentally, I think you should know, as Mark Anthony said when he entered the tent of Cleopatra, "I did not come here to make a speech." I am supposed to say a few words of welcome and perhaps mention the subject that has brought you together. If I hesitate to do that, to use the term emergency in discussing law and order and crime, I hope you will understand I am a little fed up with emergencies lately. I have thought it would be nice if we could lump some of our emergencies together. Like certain people in certain academic circles who have been of trouble lately; if we could mix them with the oil and then have the flood. I'm even denied the usual thing that any speaker in California can start with—he can always have a few words about the weather and I'm a little sensitive about that lately. It has been raining so much here that it's hard to tell land and sea apart. But then, we figured that out—the ocean is the part with the oil on top.

But you are here to discuss plans and the furtherance of your occupation and your professions, you are concerned with lawbreaking, with preserving the peace and the rights, preserving at the same time the rights of the citizen— this is your business—your daily work. Whether you are of the military and

---

[1] This document was provided by the Center for National Security Studies. Stamped "For Official Use Only," it provides us with the speech given by Ronald Reagan at the conclusion of "Operation Cablesplicer," a command-level exercise which simulated a military takeover of the United States (as explained in Document 2).

N.B.: These documents are reproduced here exactly as they appeared in the original, including all spelling mistakes and grammatical errors.

the national level or whether you are here from local law enforcement, the rights of the people, the peace and the freedom that must be preserved must be preserved not only in the local community from the lawbreaker but also on the international scene. So you have this in common. As a matter of fact, at any level of government I have always subscribed to a belief that protecting the rights of even the least individual among us is basically the only excuse the government has for even existing. In the context, some days ago I used a term and answered a question from a member of the press using the word bayonets and it caused a certain reaction among a number of people. I will admit that the manner in which it was reported was somewhat distorted—probably because the question was asked and answered at a noisy airport without the ability to exchange views and the wind of this in depth. It was done in the contact of keeping our campuses open at the point of bayonets, if necessary, and I will admit that this does bring a somewhat harsh picture to mind. Actually, the context in which I used it, I would re-affirm; because I used it in the context of government's responsibility to protect the people. And in answer to the question "was there any limit to the force that government should use in the protection of the individual?" I used the illustration of saying, "no, that government was obliged, at the point of bayonet, if necessary, to preserve these rights." Now, I want you to know your gathering here that not only do I mean that, but whatever more, or additional, that the State Government can do, and this Administration can to provide cooperation in what I believe is the most pressing task confronting us on the domestic scene today, the most immediate task, the preservation of the rights of the individual to feel free and safe in his own neighborhood, on his city streets and in his home—this is the problem that must be solved and must be met.

Now I know that you here are going to hear later today something about our 24-hour around-the-clock State operation; so I won't go into detail about that in my few remarks. But you will find out of course—some of you already know—that not only in this procedure we have this kind of cooperation but that we have a single number that can be called in the event of an emergency that will automatically alert every agency of the State Government that could possibly be concerned or involved. In the meantime you are all familiar with the program of Mutual Aid and the State is grateful for this. It has provided that the sacrifice of local State, local enforcement agencies, local resources are very often extended to their very limit and then Mutual Aid extends to the State and bringing in of the Guard, if required. But as I say this will be discussed later this afternoon. But let me just say in that context in making this Mutual Aid work—I believe that local law enforcement in California is without an equal any place in the world. I think we have the finest local law enforcement in the State of California by enlarge [sic] and with few exceptions that can be found in any part of the world today. And for the most part, in our cities, local law enforcement is doing the job magnificently and in the face of fearful odds. Now we need more and here too, I believe, there is more that the State can do. I think that there is a moral persuasive power to government, to my office and to the State Administration and I think that we should use that power to bring about the other addition that is needed to help you and that is a kind of moral resurgence on the part of the people. A return to the kind of philosophy in this February season that caused an Abraham Lincoln to be known in the copy books for walking several miles at the end of his days [sic] work to return a few pennys that he had mistakenly overcharged a customer. The kind of moral resurgence that will even go into the home and the things that are taken as commonplace today. In the event of the motor accident, the getting additional repairs because it only comes off the insurance company and they can afford it. The little bit of cheating that goes on with regard to the expense account, on the playing field, the idea the youngster that finds himself encouraged to do something as long as the referee can't see it. We need the mind of memorial resurgence that was responsible a few years ago for, I think, one of the most unusual incidents in a college football game that I have ever heard of—and yet it should be commonplace. I don't know how many of you know of this but TCU was playing Oklahoma when Bud Wilkinson's teams were the surge of the nation and held the National Championship and in the closing minutes of the fourth quarter a TCU end made a diving catch of a pass in the end zone for what looked to be the winning touchdown over the National Champions. The stadium was going wild, the TCU pass receiver stood up, walked over to the officials and said, "no, the ball touched the ground before I caught it." Now most coaches [sic] today first instinct would be—turn in your suit. It just happens that at TCU they are taught that way and I think it should be more widespread—it's an indication to me of the things we need. It begins with those who are so obsessed today, perhaps rightly so, with the need for social reform that they have gone beyond to the point of encouraging civil disobedience—suggesting amnesty for those who have broken the law and created disorders. That they must recognize that the ending of the social ills, the treating of the problems of human misery and poverty and want are noble in themselves are in a long range category and all of us are involved and have a sacred obligation to carry them out. But they can not, at the same time, result in this postponing the immediate enforcement of the law. The immediate problem that confronts us now that you can not have even civil disobedience without infringing on the rights of others. Now, let me turn for a second to the campus idea and where it figures in and here again is some of what I believe is "fuzzy" thinking. A group of students presents some demands—now some of those demands have merit. Indeed some of them in many cases in our own State have been a part of the existing college plans [that] have been going forward in the academic circles. Some of their demands are presumptuous, unwise and impossible to fullfill [sic]. But once they have presented the demands and then taken to the streets as we have seen them do, as for example, at San Francisco State or Berkeley. Those demands, regardless of how just some of them may be, cease to be the issue when those students threatened to use force unless their demands are met. When they turn to the rock and club and the firebomb and the physical beating of fellow students and faculty members, destruction and vandalism of property as a means to their end—then that becomes the only issue—the only issue that must be resolved and yet we have drifted so far in our basic values, from our basic values and the fundamental issue there is that the orderly processes of education cannot go forward under a threat of coherence. To do so, is to commit the fatal mistake one makes when he makes the first payment to the blackmailer. Their demands if presented as proposals can be discussed, dissected and debated—but not so long as they are ultimatums on a fight or surrender basis. And so it is with crime, we do our utmost to solve the problems of human misery that perhaps underlay and bring about and cause some of the crime. But at the same time we cannot tolerate for one minute those who, because of their frustrations, take the law into their own hands. A few days ago, a not to [sic] pleasant task and a thing I would hope to be avoided, I reached a point with regard to one of our campuses at Berkeley. For a long time I have hoped that academic forces, administration of our educational institutions coupled with law enforcement would take emergency measures to cope with the problem of the dissident outside and on the campus. Somehow this never quite came about. You were saddled the task—those of you who come from college towns and university communities. Saddled with the task of being called in after the disorder started, trying to arrest those that you could find that were responsible, try to get the evidence that would make a charge of battery and assault and vandalism stand up and the next day called back again until you have exhausted your resources. You have used up all the overtime that you could possibly have with your local law enforcement. And so we took the action of calling a State of Emergency on the campus at Berkeley. By calling State of Emergency we were able, with the use of the Highway Patrol, to put the forces on the campus in advance of the trouble to prevent the trouble from starting. And just on the way here I was handed a bulletin that was torn off the Associated Press Wire and it reads; For the first time since last month, early classes at the University of California at Berkeley got underway today without any pickets outside. About 50 Highway Patrol are stationed in a garage on the campus and one squad of Sheriff's Deputies are near by. The presence of law enforcement there in advance of the problem has evidently brought the order that we have been seeking for a long time. Therefore, as harsh as it may sound, I will tell you—that whatever, from now on a situation arises similar to the one at Berkeley that prompted this action, there will be no delay in declaring a State of Emergency on that campus wherever it may be to bring about the same results.

    As I say you are gathered here—I know the purpose of your meeting—to further the kinds of plans that we have started to make sure that the process is the six thousand year history of man of pushing the jungle back creating a clearing where men can live in peace and go about their business with some measure of safety for themselves and their family; you are on the firing line for that as the local level and at the international level. I commend you for it and again pledge you the all out support that we can give you in achieving your purpose because of late the jungle has been creeping in again a little closer to our boundaries. The boundaries of those clearings that man has created over these centuries and these thousands of years and so I wish you God speed and great success in the meetings that will take place and have taken place so far—the orientation for the program you are putting together. Again, thank you very much.

Document 2

Gram Metric Cable Splicer[2]

The exercise will simulate simultaneous multiple civil disturbances involving widespread rioting, arson, and looting in approximately 15 selected cities within the CONUS [Continental United States]. The Revolutionary Liberty Front (RLF), a radical organization advocating and practicing violence, acts as a catalyst in expanding the civil disturbances. These simulated disturbances will develop to the degree that the National Guard is either alerted or called to State or Federal duty in all 15 cities, and Federal military assistance will be requested in up to 12 cities. The requests for Federal assistance will include requests for loans of DOD equipment in most of these 12 cities, and requests for Federal military forces in up to six cities. In response to these requests, there will be simulated deployment of Federal military forces in up to six cities and simulated employment in up to three cities.

PURPOSE OF THE EXERCISE. To exercise key personnel, relationships and plans and procedures applicable in civil disturbance operations involving DOJ, DA, DN, DAF, USMC, MTMTS, USASTRATCOM, USAMC, USAINTC...USCONARC, CONUS Armies, MDW,[3] District of Colombia, designated task forces and support installations under simulated deteriorating domestic conditions which culminate in deployment of multiple Federal military task forces. Specific objectives are to exercise key personnel, plans, and procedures in the following areas:

(a) Deployment of employment of GARDEN PLOT forces (to include Quick Reaction Forces) within CONUS...loans to civil, National Guard, and Federal agencies by exercising support installation capabilities and loans of prepositioned civil disturbance supplies...designation and simulated deployment of the personal liason officer of the Chief of Staff, U.S. Army (PLOCSA), and the Department of the Army Liason Team (DALT)... (and) liason with civil authorities...

5(B) Information

(1) No voluntary releases, national or local, will be made on the CPX.

(2) Responses should be made at the lowest practical level to direct inquiries only. Responses will be limited to a statement of purpose of the CPX—"This routine civil disturbance Command Post Exercise is being conducted to exercise the existing contingency plans and procedures. Command, staff, and communications personnel will be the primary participants. No troop unit movements from home stations will be involved."

* * *

---

[2] Source: *Counterspy*, Vol. 2, Issue 4 (Winter 1976), p. 57
[3] Initials represent in order the Department of Justice, Department of Army, Department of Navy, Department of Air Force, U.S. Marine Corps, Military Traffic Management and Terminal Service, U.S. Army Strategic Communications Command, U.S. Army Material Command, U.S. Army Intelligence Command...U.S. Continental Army Command, Continental U.S. Armies, Military District of Washington.

Commentary by *Counterspy:*

The tone for GRAM METRIC can be judged from the game plan scenario. In all, "coordinated violence" occurs in 25 cities and stems form such diverse situations as a strike in Tacoma, a boxing match in New York City, a rock concert in Orlando, a sit-in in Sacramento, and the shooting of a civil rights leader in Washington, D.C. In the 24 hours prior to the official beginning of the CPX, the scenario called for 696 fires, 50 shootings, and 134 incidents of looting in Baltimore, Washington, D.C., Chicago, Cleveland and Detroit alone.

CPXes were not limited to the federal level, however. In order to coordinate federal and local response and resources, CPXes have been held on the state and regional level since OPLAN GARDEN PLOT was established. Interviews with Pentagon officials show that such CPXes are considered routine and have been conducted in every state of the Union.

Investigative reporter Ron Ridenhour of *New Times* obtained copies of the regional war games held in the 6th U.S. Army area, the states of California, Washington, Oregon, Nevada and Arizona. These war games, called CABLE SPLICER, borrowed the GRAM METRIC concept of management preparation and carried it to the local level. CABLE SPLICER even involved officials of major corporations.

Present at the CABLE SPLICER III (1970) after-action conference were: representatives from 13 state National Guard Commands; active duty military officials from the 6th U.S. Army; officials from the Department of Justice, the FBI, the Secret Service; the Selective Service, U.S. Army Intelligence command, Naval Intelligence, Air Force Intelligence, the Law Enforcement Assistance Administration, the Bank of America, Lockheed, Boeing, Sylvania, Pacific Gas and Electric, Pacific Telephone and Telegraph, Standard Oil of California, Jet Propulsion Laboratories, SCM, Dictaphone, John Hancock Mutual Life Insurance Co., and several University of California officials.

This excerpt, from the CABLE SPLICER documents obtained by Ridenhour, gives an indication of the matters discussed at the after-action conference:

> (1) General. The problem was designed to exercise two task force headquarters with four task forces conducting operations in four major cities or Oregon. Each player unit received background information initially as an intelligence summary covering the period preceding the exercise. A deteriorating situation was then progressively developed for each locale through a series of prepared messages. Each task force operated on the basis of actual assigned strength and equipment on hand during the actual exercise period. The exercise general situation developed a simulated gradual increase in lawlessness and disorder on the Pacific Coast during the spring months of 1970. Three new simulated radical leftist organizations (the Scholars Democratic League [SDL], on the campuses; the International Brotherhood of Labor Reform

[IBLF] among the blue collar workers; and the International Fraternity of Progress of Non-Caucasian [IFPC] among the minority groups), created confrontations at the universities and high schools as well as within the major cities. The situation continued to deteriorate until 0700 hours, 24 April 70. Then the Governor of the State of Oregon issued a proclamation of a state of emergency and directed the Adjutant General, Oregon, to assist civil authorities in the restoration of law and order. At the start of the exercise play at 0730 hours, 25 April, player units had been called to state active duty and had assembled and moved to assembly areas in problem cities (simulated)...play was advanced 48 hours and players were informed that the National Guard was called to federal service and assistance of federal troops had been requested (simulated). For duration of the CPX players planned actions required on being mobilized...

> Sixth U.S. Army Final Report
> CPX Cable Splicer III
> Section III, Field Operations
> pages 11-12
> "For Official Use Only"

Document 3

Revolutionary Peoples' Constitutional Convention
September 1970, Philadelphia

WORKSHOP ON INTERNATIONALISM AND RELATIONS WITH LIBERATION STRUGGLES AROUND THE WORLD

The Revolutionary Peoples' Constitutional Convention supports the demand of the Chinese people for the liberation of Taiwan. We demand the liberation of Okinawa and the Pacific Territories occupied by U.S. and European imperialist countries. The Revolutionary Peoples' Constitutional Convention supports the struggles and endorses the government of the provisional revolutionary government of South Vietnam, the royal government of National Union of Cambodia, and the Pathet Lao.

> Huey P. Newton
> Minister of Defense
> Black Panther Party

In order to insure our international constitution, we, the people of Babylon, declare an international bill of rights: that all people are guarnteed the right to life, liberty and the pursuit of happiness, that all people of the world be free from dehumanization and intervention in their internal affairs by a foreign power. Therefore, if fascist actions in the world attempt to achieve imperialist goals, they will be in violation of the law and dealt with as criminals.

We are in full support with the struggle of the Palestinian people for liberation of Palestine from Zionist colonialism, and their goals of creating a democratic state where all Palestinians, Jews, Christians and Moslems are equal.

We propose solidarity with the liberation struggle of the Puerto Rican people, who now exist as a colony of the United States and have many groups who are fighting for liberation, such as C.A.L. (Armed Commandos for Liberation), M.I.R.A. and the Young Lords Party.

We propose that, whereas the universities in the United States are used by the imperialist system to provide the knowledge that that system uses to perpetrate the exploitation of the Third World and repression against national liberation struggles, we propose that the universities and their resources be turned over to use for, by, and of the peoples of the world so that they may implement their vision of a new socialist world.

1.   The United States is an international federation of bandits and we denounce its rights to nationhood.

2.   We should provoke the destruction of all racists and fascists in capitalistic countries and the world over. We should not rest until all of them are wiped off the face of the earth.

3.   We support all liberation struggles throughout the world and we oppose all reactionary struggles throughout the world.

4.   Our constitution will guarantee the right of all people to travel and communicate with all peoples throughout the world.

5.   We stand resolute in our unrelenting convictions to destroy Pig Amerikka.

6.   Wherever the word "men" appears it should be replaced with the word "people" to express solidarity with the self-determination of women and to do away with all remnants of male supremacy, once and for all.

7.   We propose that we declare a just peoples' war against capitalism and remain in that state until capitalism is abolished from the face of the Earth.

8.   We should have an organization or army to defend the kidnapping and terror of pigs as a means of freeing political prisoners of war.

9.   We oppose such organizations as NATO and SEATO and all lackeys of U.S. imperialism.

10.   We damand immediate withdrawal of all American forces around the world.

11.   Reparations should be made to oppressed people throughout the world, and we pledge ourself to take the wealth of this country and make it available as reparations.

12.   We will not allow or accept this country going into other countries and utilizing their wealth.

13.   We will administer all foreign aid given by the U.S. by an international body composed of representatives from revolutionary peoples.

14.   We will use our more advanced revolutionary brothers and sisters to better the struggle.

15.   We demand an end to the genocide caused by sterilization programs in different forms—nationally and international.

All Power to the People

SELF-DETERMINATION OF STREET PEOPLE

What we want:

We want an immediate end to the crimes of pimping, prostitution, number rackets, gambling, dope pushing, fencing, loan sharking, sexism, rape, theft, pick pockets, bribery, extortion, union corruption, etc., committed on the people by organized crime syndicates which work hand in hand with the pig power structure and those lackeys within our communities who refuse to deal with these problems.

1.   Creation of investigative councils run by the people.

2.   Encourage informers to turn over information to these councils.

3.   Remove by force those elements which have been exposed.

4.   Confiscation or destruction of property controlled by organized crime syndicates.

5.   The encouragement of all progressive forces and elements to change corruption in government and enforce revolutionary justice.

Education—

All people will be provided with the kind of schooling they desire and need. All levels of schooling will be provided free by the government. Schooling must be non-compulsory. The community will control the schools, education, curriculum, and educators. Education must be part and parcel of the political realities of the time. Education must always serve the people by teaching the true nature of this decadent society.

Dope—

We recognize that hard drugs (smack, speed, etc.) are counterrevolutionary, sapping the strength of the people in their struggle. This problem must be dealt with on two levels. The seller of hard drugs must be eradicated from the community by any means necessary. The user must be helped to rid himself of addiction by the people. We urge setting up of a People's Rehabilitation Center by the people.

We recognize that psychedelic drugs (acid, mescaline, grass) are important in developing the revolutionary consciousness of the people. However, after the revolutionary consciousness has been achieved, these drugs may become a burden. No revolutionary action should be attempted while under the influence of any drug. We urge that these drugs be made legal. Or rather than they should not be illegal, that is, there should be no law made against them.

Land—

We hold that private property is theft.

We demand that the use of parks, streets, rural areas, and unused land to carry on our revolutionary struggle for survival. We will seize the land we need by any means necessary. Streets and urban parks must be liberated to be used for people's needs such as: 1) mass meetings, 2) concerts and recreation, 3) sleeping area, and other everyday activities.

Rural land and large state parks must be liberated to be used for: military training in the techniques of self defense and urban guerilla warfare in order to fight a war of liberation, and land to be used for farming and other productive needs.

Grievance—

All private rural land has been stolen from the people. It originally belonged to the people. It is being used for capitalistic goals and is being destroyed ecologically.

Food, Housing, Clothing, Health—

We demand the right for all people to have free food, housing, free clothing, free medical care and all other rights established by the Revolutionary People's Constitutional Convention.

Recognizing our responsibility as revolutionary street people in this period of transition—

1. We call for free de-centralized medical care and the availability of medical information (curative and preventive) for all the people in the neighborhood to meet the daily situations in a revolutionary manner.

2. We call for the establishment of free inter-relative community food cooperatives to collect, exchange, store, distribute and provide food and cooking facilities for the community needs.

3. We demand community control of the means of production of clothing and adequate sharing and distributing of clothing to meet the needs of the people.

4. We demand the replacement of deteriorated housing with the construction of adequate low-income housing which is available for those people whose housing is replaced and the control of community removal programs by the people in those communities.

Finally, we call for the formation of Revolutionary People's Community Councils to be responsible for the implementation of all collective needs of the community.

WORKSHOP ON THE SELF DETERMINATION OF WOMEN

—We recognize the right of all women to be free.

—As women, we recognize that our struggle is against a racist, capitalist, sexist system that oppresses all minority peoples.

—This capitalistic country is run by a small ruling class who use the ideas and practices of chauvinism and racism to devide, control and oppress the masses of people for their own greedy gains and profit.

—We want equal status in a society that does not exploit or murder other people.

- We will fight for a socialist system that guarantees full, creative, non-exploitive life for all human beings.

—We will not be free until all oppressed people are free.

Family—

Whereas in a capitalist culture, the institution of the family has been used as an economic tool or instrument, not serving the needs of the people. We declare that we will not relate to the private ownership of people. We encourage and support the continued growth of communal households and communal relationships and other alternatives to the patriarchal family.

We call for socialization of housework and child care with the sharing of work by men and women.

Women must have the right to decide when and if we want to have children. There should be free and safe birth control, including abortion, available upon demand. There should be no forced sterilization or mandatory birth control programs which are now used as genocide against third world sisters and against poor people.

Every women has the right to decide whether she will be homosexual, hetrosexual or bisexual.

Employment—

Whereas women in a class society have been continuously exploited, through their work, both in their home and outside their home, we call for:

1. guaranteed full, equal and non-exploitive employment, controlled collectively by the working people.

2. Guaranteed adequate income for all. This would entail the sharing of necessary, non-creative tasks and the maximum utilization of revolutionary technology to eliminate these tasks.

3.   An end to the sexism which forces women into the lowest paying service jobs and the racism that insures that third world women will be the lowest payed of all.

4.   Guaranteed payed maternity leave.

Education—

Whereas women historically have been deprived of education, or only partially educated and mis-educated in those areas deemed appropriate for us by those ruling powers who would benefit by our ignorance; we call for:

1.   the right to determine our own goals.

2.   The end of sex roles regarding training or skills.

3.   Self-knowledge: the history of women, our relation to society and the knowledge of our bodies.

4.   Guaranteed technological and professional training and in the interim, special programs should be set up in every feild in which women have been denied equality, such as child care.

5.   Men to be trained in those areas in which they have been denied equality, such as child care.

6.   Control of non-authoritarian education by the people it serves in the language and culteral style of the people.

Services—

Whereas the services provided for the people have been inadequate, unavailable or too expensive, administered in a racist and sexist manner, we declare that:

1.   All services—health care, housing, food, clothing, transportation and education—should be controlled by the people: and should be free.

2.   Services for women should be controlled by the women of the community which they serve.

Media—

The mass media is not permitted to exploit women's bodies in order to sell or promote products. Women must be treated with respect and dignity at all times by the peoples' media. The peoples' media will work to eliminate sexist terminology: he, man, mankind; when we mean person, people, humanity.

Self Defense—

Whereas the struggle of the people must be borne equally by all the people fighting for their liberation, we declare that women have the right to bear arms. Women should be fully trained and educated in the art of self-defense and the defense of the peoples' nation. We recognize that it is our duty to defend all oppressed people.

Women in Our Own Right—

Whereas we do not beleive that any person is the property of any other person, we declare that women have the right to bear their own surnames, not names determined by their husbands or fathers. We demand that all organizations, ranging from health insurance to social security to banks, deal with women in our own right as people, rather than as the property of men.

Equal Participation in Government—

Whereas all revolutionary people must share equally in the decisions which effect them, we are dedicated to the national salvation of all humanity.

All Power to the People!!

STATEMENT OF DEMANDS FROM THE MALE REPRESENTATIVES OF NATIONAL GAY LIBERATION

We Demand:

1. The right to be gay anytime, anyplace.

2. The right to free physiological change and modification of sex upon demand.

3. The right of free dress and adornment.

4. That all modes of human sexual self-expression deserve protection of the law and social sanction.

5. Every child's right to develop in a non-sexist, non-possessive atmosphere, which is the responsibility of all people to create.

6. That a free educational system present the entire range of human sexuality, without advocating any form or style. . . that sex roles and sex determined skills not be fostered by the schools.

7. That language be modified so that no gender takes priority.

8. That the judicial system be run by the people through people's courts and that all people be tried by members of their peer group.

9. That gays be represented in all governmental and community institutions.

10. That organized religions be condemmed for aiding in the genocide of gay people, and enjoined from teaching hatred and superstition.

11. That psychiatry and psychology be enjoined from advocating a preference for any form of sexuality, and the enforcement of that preference by shock treatment, brainwashing, imprisonment, etc.

12. The abolition of the necular family because it perpetuates the false categories of homosexuality and hetrosexuality.

13. The immediate release of and reparations for gay political prisoners from prisons and mental institutions; the support of gay political prisoners by all other political prisoners.

14. That gays determine the destiny of their own communities.

15. That all people share equally the labor and products of society, regardless of sex or sexual orientation.

16. That technology be used to liberate all peoples of the world from drudgery.

17. The full participation of gays in the Peoples' Revolutionary Army.

18. Finally, the end of domination of one person by another.

Gay Power to Gay People

All Power to the People

Seize the Time

WORKSHOP: THE FAMILY AND THE RIGHTS OF CHILDREN

1. The discussion was not truly representative of all oppressed groups, since, for example, there were no children present.

2. Some people felt that the traditional family was so oppressive that it must be abolished and replaced by a different family grouping. Others felt that there were positive things in the traditional family that should be perpetuated in the new world. It was also pointed out that we can't predict what the traditional family might be like under socialism.

3. It was agreed that children are not possessions and are not to be treated as possessions by parents, collectives or the state.

4. General agreement was that children are entitled to the broadest possible education.

5. Children are entitled to be brought up to have the greatest trust, confidence and sense of sharing with the other people in their society.

6. The responsibility for creating those conditions that would enable a child to be a whole human being rests with all of us.

7. We agreed that children's feelings and viewpoints should be respected.

8. It was agreed that children have the right to be breast fed.

9. A child must be reared to be sexually free and have his choices respected.

10. Children are essential to adults as teachers because children naturally resist oppression.

11. Children must be loved in a truly revolutionary manner. Children are people. ALL POWER TO THE PEOPLE!!!!

CONTROL AND USE OF THE LEGAL SYSTEM AND
POLITICAL PRISONERS OF WAR

The present judicial system in the United States is nothing more than an instrument and tool of class rule, representing the will of the racist ruling class, made into a law for everyone. The laws themselves and the procedural aspects such as bail, cater to the customs and mores of the ruling class.

At this time, in the transitional stage prior to the post revolutionary society, the call for peoples' revolutionary tribunes will be made. The function of these tribunals will be as the peoples' tribunals for revolutionaries who might be at the same time, on trial in the existing legal system of the ruling class. These tribunals will be decentralized and arise out of the area where the incidents or alleged crimes themselves took place.

While the struggle is still being waged, the people must learn to manipulate and utilize the existing court system, through political trials, in order to develope a revolutionary political consciousness and illustrate the true nature of this corrupt legal system before the people.

The courts should serve the people and in this racist society that can only be done by a jury of one's peers. Understanding of the laws is a matter of interpretation which directly reflects one's social, economic and racial background. So if one is to be judged, he must be judged by a jury of his peers instead of by those with the standards and ideas of the racist ruling class.

If we are to talk of creating a legal system that has its foundation in man's human nature, we must talk of transforming the entire society. Therefor it becomes necessary to define for ourselves what is criminal.

Therefor:

Principles are the foundation by which the will of the people is insured. And if we are to talk of legality, criminals and crime, we must first talk of the ultimate crime. That is the crime of exploitation of man by man and the legal system that endorses and upholds it.

Since exploitation deprives people of the necessities of life and the fruits of their labor, it is the supreme crime and the exploiters are the supreme criminals.

We feel that all of the natural recourses of the earth belongs to, an and any exploitation, usurpation of man's labors and of the natural resources of the earth is an attack on man's survival and a crime. Any lack of action that denies human beings their right to exist are crimes against the people. Therefore, if the people are to control their destiny and thereby assure their own survival, then we must have a legal system that insures the abolishment of all forms of exploitation.

We recognize the armed body of the state, the fascist police force, is the protector and perpetrator of criminal acts and crimes. Not because the police per se are criminal by nature or criminal men, but because the function of the police and the armed forces in a capitalist society is criminal by nature. So we feel that the police should come from the community in which they live and that there should be no distinction between the people and the police because of their function.

Every man was born and therefore he has a right to live, a right to share in the wealth. If he is denied the right to work then he is denied the right to live. If he can't work, he deserves a high standard of living, regardless of his education or skill. It should be up to the administrators of the economic system to design a program for providing work or a livlihood for the people. To deny him this is to deny him life.

Because the present constitution in words guarantees us the right to live, in practice we are denied this most basic human right, we list the following guidelines as essential to our continued survival and prosperity:

1. All juries must consist of one's peers.

2. All courts should be peoples' courts.

3. All decisions of the people should be implemented in a collective manner by the people.

4. No judge, no policeman, no advocate should serve more than one year in any position of administrative trust without being reviewed by the people.

These guidelines, we, the people feel, are the best pre-requisites needed to insure a just and humane system.

Rights of Oppressed People and Political Prisoners—

1. Because of the genocidal acts of the government of the United States, against the people of this country and the world:
    Oppressed people (any class, ethnic group or social group that has its rights restricted by any means by any other group) have an absolute right and responsibility to defend themselves by any means necessary and effective against all forms of aggression, whether this aggression be by a direct act of violence or by the violation of their human rights, among which are the rights to food, clothing, shelter, adequate medical care, education and the inalienable right to self determination.

2. The people have not only the right to self-defense by any means necessary, but also the right to organize against all oppression and exploitation, to alter or abolish all existing legal structures, and to reorganize the society for the benefit of all the people.

3. Because the legal system of the U.S. exists to serve the ruling class and facilitate oppression and exploitation of the people, those people that are held in jails and prisons have not necessarily been incarcerated for crimes against the people; that therefore all prisoners be returned to their communities for trial by the peoples' court under a revolutionary process.

4. That all charges be dropped against the peoples' leaders that they can return to leadership of their communities from jail and from exile because they have not committed any crimes against the people... Bobby Seale, the Conn. 9, N.Y. 21, L.A. 18, Angela Davis, Soledad Brothers, Ahmed Evans, Martin Sostre. We say that while held, all political prisoners of war must be treated under international agreements regarding humane treatment.

CONTROL AND USE OF THE EDUCATIONAL SYSTEM

1. Liberation schools set up for pre-school age children.

2. Entering school with a political consciousness.

3. Community control of schools:
   a. Parents controlling curriculum
   b. Community elected board officers
   c. Power to hire and fire teachers belongs to community elected board.

4. Intellectual and cultural education shall be available to all persons:
   a. Education will deal with the means of survival of the various portions of society
   b. Education for students will deal with the student as an individual
   c. The workings of the system or political education should be taught for constant political consciousness
   d. Schools and institutions will be free and make advanced study available to any person
   e. The schools will encourage all persons to expand and realize their creative aspirations. it will especially encourage study in socialist society, human survival, and the truth and workings of the present society.

Student's Rights—

1. Students in any school will have the right of freedom of speech, dress and assembly

2. Student government should be controlled by the students
   a. No rules set up for who runs for office, ex., grades, conduct, politics, participation in other actives
   b. Student controlled press (paper), student board to decide what goes in paper and what does not go into it
   c. Freedom to assembly whenever problems arise that the students feel should be solved collectively on a face to face basis

   d. Student activities not mandatory

   e. Assemblies left to student decision in accordance with what they feel should be solved relevant to those things that directly relate to them
   f. No guards in schools for any reason. Community and students will deal with all problems, major and minor

   g. Students decide their courses according to what they want and think they need. No set curriculum. Courses will be fit to students, not students to the courses.
   h. New grading system established.

We the people believe that education should serve the people. It should expose the true nature of this society. Education should assist in teaching us our socialist ideas, and stand as a basis for our socialist practice.

The power of education should and will belong in the hands of the people. We believe that education plays a major role in this system of programming. So we the people must penetrate and seize this tool of the power structure and turn it into a weapon to be used against it.

All Power to the People

WORKSHOP: CONTROL & USE OF MILITARY AND POLICE

Proposals on the Military—

1. National defense shall be provided by a system of peoples' militia, trained in guerilla warfare, on a voluntary basis and consisting of both men and women.

2. The U.S. shall not maintain a standing army, since historically a standing army has been used for offensive actions against the people of the United States and around the world.

3. No genocidal weapons shall be manufactured or used.

4. All presently existing offensive equipment and installations shall be made inoperable and unservicable for its original purpose.

5. The people shall be educated and informed on the action of the militia, and all records shall be open to the public.

6. The government shall be prohibited from sending any personnel, funds, or equipment to any nation for military or police purposes. It should also be prohibited from spending more than 10% of the national budget for any military or police purposes. This can be overriden by a majority vote in a national referendum.

7. No person shall serve full-time in the militia; those serving in the militia shall be paid a fair wage.

8. Militia members shall be governed by the laws of the community in which they serve (or governed by the laws of the nation??)

9. National defense shall be provided by a system of peoples' militias.

10. There shall be no conscription for any armed forces.

11. No peoples' militia shall be stationed outside national boundaries.

12. Government people and military personnel should be defined as one and the same, and not as separate entities in or of the power structure.

13. The people shall have the right to bear arms.
     a. No citizen shall be prohibited the possession, control or purchase of small arms without the due process of law.
     b. Free programs shall be set up in the training and use of small arms.

Organization, Use of, and Control of the Police—

1. The police force shall be a rotating volunteer non-professional body coordinated by the Police Control Board from a (weekly) list of volunteers from each community section. The Police Control Board, its policies, as well as the police leadership, shall be chosen by direct popular majority vote of the community.

2. There shall not be set up, or permitted to exist, a national body of police, or secret body of police, nor shall un-uniformed police be permitted to exist.

3. Any citizen can bring charges against any member or officer of the police force before the Control Board, and the Control Board shall have the power to relieve that member or officer of the police force of his or her duty.

4. Community Police Councils may set up working relations and exchange information with police forces in other communities.

5. The purpose of the people's police force shall be to serve and protect the community.

6. No person can serve on both the police force and the Control Board at the same time.

7. Any member of the Control Board can be removed by direct, popular vote of the people.

8. Funds for community police and for the community's Control Board shall be provided for by national government under direction of the local Control Board.

HEALTH

Health care is a right, not a priviledge. We say that comprehensive medical care should not be sold as a commodity by a class of exploiters, interested in profit only. We recognize this profit motive is the outgrowth of a capitalist system which thrives on the exploitation of people and divides them on racist, sexist and class lines. Our solution is to make all aspects of health care meet the demands of all people through prevention, education and community control of health services.

1. Prevention (health checkups)
    a. nutrition (educating people with regard to eating the right diets)
    b. Maternal and child care to put an end to:
       1. genocide
       2. experimentation in the hospitals of oppressed people
       3. experimentation in the public school system as a so-called mental health program
       4. exploitation of children's behavior; children are given tranquilizers and put in a category as threats to the capitalist system.

    c. Senior citizens services (the right to be able to work as long as they can function)
    d. Regular examinations for all people
    e. Better detection facilities (more emphasis should be placed on diseases that are more prevalent in minority group areas, e.g. sickle cell anemia)
    f. Medical teams should be sent out into the communities to seek out diseases and illnesses.

2.   Education
    a. health education of the masses (symptoms of diseases in the home, first aid in the home)
    b. training and retraining of present health workers
    c. ending professionalism (titles, etc.)
    d. open admissions to all who want medical training

3.   Community Control
    a. right of self determination to have children (not to be told by the capitalist system how many to have)
    b. right to adequate economic means
    c. community boards should run all medical institutions

4.   Mental Health
We consider mental health to include both physical and mental well being. We recognize that much of the mental illness in our society is caused by the oppression of the capitalist system where psychiatry is used as a tool of fascism. It has also been used against homosexuals.

We are opposed to the medical industrial complex of medicine. We believe in socialized medicine. Inherent in this concept is prevention and free comprehensive, community controlled medicine. The only way to socialize medicine is through revolution.

REVOLUTIONARY ART

The workshop on the Revolutionary Arts and Artists hereby submits the following declaration to the Plenary Session of the Revolutionary People's Constitutional Convention:

We Recognize:
1.   That all people are born with a creative potential and that the society must guarantee that every person has the opportunity to develop and express that potential.

2.   That art is a creative expression of a people's culture or way of life.

3.   We recognize the right of every people's culture to its form of expression and that those forms of expressions should be preserved, encouraged and developed.

4.   We recognize that art should be related to the interest, needs and
      aspirations of the people.

NOTES

Chapter One:
The New Left as a World-Historical Movement _____

1. Eric Hobsbawm, "1968—A Retrospect," in *Marxism Today* (May 1978), p. 130.
2. As quoted in John Hersey, "1968: The Year of the Triphammer," *San Diego Union*, October 22, 1978, p. C-8.
3. Theda Skocpol, *States and Social Revolutions* (Cambridge University Press, 1979), pp. 23, 286-8.
4. Aristide R. Zolberg, "Moments of Madness" in *Politics and Society* (Winter 1972), pp. 183-207.
5. Karl Marx, *The 18th Brumaire of Louis Napoleon* (International Publishers, 1972), p. 15.
6. Zolberg, *op. cit.*, p. 184.
7. What the student movement expressed in the slogan, *"L'imagination au pouvoir,"* originally came to France from Vietnam. See Jean-Paul Sartre, *Between Existentialism and Marxism* (Morrow Quill Paperbacks, 1979), p. 125.
8. See Karl Marx, *The German Ideology* (International Publishers, 1973), p. 56.
9. Antonio Gramsci, *The Modern Prince* (International Publishers, 1972), pp. 165-6.
10. Herbert Marcuse, *Reason and Revolution* (Beacon Press, 1960), p. 141.
11. G. W. F. Hegel, *Philosophy of History* (Colonial Press, 1899), p. 56.
12. Marcuse, *op. cit.*
13. Hegel, *op. cit.*, pp. 108, 343.
14. Rosa Luxemburg, *The Mass Strike* (Harper and Row, 1971), pp. 44-5. (Emphasis in the original.)
15. G. Sorel, *Reflections on Violence* (Collier Books, 1950), pp. 127-8.

16. Priscilla Robertson, *Revolutions of 1848: A Social History* (Princeton University Press, 1952), pp. 221, 269, 274, 289, 291, 300, 304, 391; Karl Marx, *The Revolutions of 1848-9* (International Publishers, 1972), pp. 108-9, 262; Sidney Harcave, *The Russian Revolution of 1905* (Macmillan, 1964), p. 203.

17. Alfred Willener, *The Action-Image of Society: On Cultural Politicization* (Pantheon Books, 1970), p. 93.

18. *The Commune of 1871* (New York Labor News, 1978), p. 7.

19. See Chapter 6 for further discussion of this concept.

20. Rosa Luxemburg, *op. cit.*, p. 36.

21. Thomas Jefferson, Letter to John Adams, September 4, 1823.

22. André Gunder Frank, *Crisis: In the Third World* (Holmes and Meier, 1981).

23. Alexis de Tocqueville, *Souvenirs d'Alexis de Tocqueville* (Gallimard, 1942), p. 30.

24. Priscilla Robertson, *op. cit.*, p. 81.

25. L. S. Stavrianos, *Global Rift: The Third World Comes of Age* (William Morrow and Company, 1981), p. 389.

26. See Rosa Luxemburg, *Theory and Practice* (News and Letters, 1980), p. 45; Richard Boyer and Herbert Morais, *Labor's Untold Story* (UE Press, 1974), pp. 142-164.

27. Azar Tabari and Nabid Yaganeh, *In the Shadow of Islam* (Zed Press, 1982), p. 30.

28. Harcave, *op. cit.*, p. 133.

29. Max Gordon, "The Communist Party and The New Left," *Socialist Revolution* (January 1976), p. 19.

30. Klaus Mehnert, *Moscow and the New Left* (University of California Press, 1975), pp. 41-2.

31. Valdo Spini, "The New Left in Italy," *Journal of Contemporary History* (January-April 1972), pp. 51-71.

32. Mihailo Marković, "The New Left and the Cultural Revolution," in *The Contemporary Marx* (Spokesman Books, 1974), p. 175.

33. D. Rousopoulos, *Canada and Radical Social Change* (Black Rose Books, 1973), pp. 51, 183.

34. Herbert Marcuse, *Counterrevolution and Revolt* (Beacon Press, 1972). Also see Chapter 5 of this book for further discussion.

35. Herbert Marcuse, "Reexamination of the Concept of Revolution," *Diogenes*, No. 64 (Winter 1968), pp. 17-27.

36. Earl Hutchinson, "Misunderstood Legacy of King," *Guardian*, January 17, 1987, pp. 1, 19.

37. See Willener, *op. cit.*, for a book-length study of this insight.

38. Wilfred Burchett, *Vietnam Will Win!* (International Publishers, 1968).

39. Frantz Fanon, *The Wretched of the Earth* (Grove Press, 1968), p. 136.

40. Harry Braverman, *Labor and Monopoly Capital* (Monthly Review Press, 1974).

41. United States Office of Education, *Projections of Educational Statistics to 1977-1978* (Government Printing Office, 1968).

42. James and Grace Lee Boggs, *Revolution and Evolution in the Twentieth Century* (Monthly Review Press, 1976).

Chapter Two:
Social Movements of 1968 _____

1. Liz Hodgkin, "People's War Comes to the Towns: Tet 1968," *Marxism Today* (May 1978), pp. 147-152.
2. Don Oberdorfer, *Tet* (Avon Books, 1972).
3. Hodgkin, *op. cit.*, p. 147.
4. See "Historic Victory in Indochina," *Monthly Review* (May 1975), pp. 1-13; Noam Chomsky and Edward Herman, *The Washington Connection and Third World Fascism* (South End Press, 1979), pp. 345-54.
5. See John Hersey, "1968: The Year of the Triphammer," *San Diego Union*, October 22, 1978.
6. See Daniel Ellsberg's Introduction to *Protest and Survive* (Monthly Review Press, 1981); Michio Kaku and Daniel Axelrod, *To Win a Nuclear War* (South End Press, 1987).
7. Interview with Noam Chomsky, *Indochina Newsletter* (November-December, 1982), p. 4.
8. Oberdorfer, *op. cit.*, pp. 289-90.
9. François Houtart and André Rosseau, *The Church and Revolution* (Orbis Books, 1971), p. 148.
10. *Ibid.*, p. 154.
11. *Indochina Newsletter* (November-December, 1982), p. 12.
12. Oberdorfer, *op. cit.*
13. Houtart and Rousseau, *op. cit.*, p. 167.
14. See Troung Chinh, *To Mobilize and Unite All Anti-U.S. Forces in the Country and the World*, edited and published by Asia Information Group (Berkeley, 1971). Also see *Vietnamese Studies* (Hanoi), particularly numbers 26 and 31, *Glimpses of U.S. Neo-Colonialism* (Parts I and II). For a specific analysis of Tet, see *South Vietnam: A Month of Unprecedented Offensive and Uprising* (Giai Phong Publishing House, March 1968).
15. David Triesman, "Cultural Conflict and Political Advance in Britain," *Marxism Today* (London, May 1978), p. 166.
16. This speech is fully reprinted in *Venceremos: The Speeches and Writings of Che Guevara*, John Gerassi (ed.), (Simon and Schuster, 1969), pp. 413-424. For an explanation of Che's "*foco* theory," see Régis Debray, *Revolution in the Revolution* (Penguin Books, 1968).
17. Tareq Ismael, *The Arab Left* (Syracuse University Press, 1976), pp. 92-125, 183.
18. Unsuccessful is a mild word for the bloody repression suffered by these movements. The repeated calls for armed insurrection from the Tri-Continental Conference in Havana (January 1966) and the OLAS

conference in 1967 brought swift reactions from Latin American
governments and the United States. In 1967, the Organization of
American States condemned Cuba and recommended economic sanctions against it. The United States, as sole coordinator and source of
military supplies (at that time), had established a Southern Command in
Panama. By 1968, special forces who had received anti-guerrilla
training in Panama carried out fifty-two operations. In 1966-67, they
intervened in Guatemala, Venezuela, Nicaragua, and, of course, in
Bolivia. See Houtart and Rousseau, *op. cit.*, pp. 206-7.

19.   Martin Kenner, Introduction to *Fidel Castro Speaks* (Grove Press, 1969),
      p. xvi.
20.   Daniel Ellsberg, *op. cit.*; *Los Angeles Times*, June 2, 1983, p. 12.
21.   Jaime Suchlicki, *University Students and Revolution in Cuba, 1920-1968*
      (University of Miami Press, 1966). Fidel Castro's first political
      involvement was at the University of Havana in the late 1940s, when he
      was active in the *Union Insurreccional Revolucionaria.*
22.   *Vietnam Courier* (October 1982), p. 24.
23.   Franz Schurmann, P.D. Scott, and R. Zelnik, *The Politics of Escalation in
      Vietnam* (Fawcett Publications, 1966), p. 45.
24.   C. Wright Mills, "The New Left," in *Power, Politics and People*, edited
      by Irving Louis Horowitz (Oxford University Press, 1963), pp.
      257-58.
25.   Clayborn Carson, *In Struggle* (Harvard University Press, 1981), p. 16.
26.   Edward Shils, "Dreams of Plenitude, Nightmare of Scarcity," in
      Students in Revolt, Lipset and Altbach (eds.), (Beacon Press, 1970), p. 5.
27.   Lipset, "The Possible Effects of Student Activism on International
      Politics," *ibid.*, p. 495.
28.   R. F. Tomasson and E. Allardt, "Scandanavian Students and the Politics
      of Organized Radicalism," in Lipset and Altbach, *op. cit.*, pp. 96-126.
29.   Claude Durand (ed.), *Combats étudiants dans le Monde* (Editions du Seuil,
      1968).
30.   Otto Klineberg, *et. al.* (eds.), *Students, Values and Politics* (Free Press,
      1979), p. 293.
31.   William J. Hanna, "Student Protest in Independent Black Africa," *The
      Annals of the American Academy of Political and Social Science* (May 1971),
      p. 172.
32.   Anthony Eisler, *Bombs, Beards and Barricades: 150 Years of Youth in
      Revolt* (Stein and Day, 1971); Edith H. Altbach, "Vanguard of Revolt:
      Students and Politics in Central Europe, 1815-1848" in Lipset and
      Altbach, *op. cit.*; J. Habermas, *Toward a Rational Society* (Beacon Press,
      1972), p. 40.
33.   Ernest Mandel as quoted in Tariq Ali, *1968 and After* (Blond and
      Briggs, 1978), pp. 47-49.
34.   Alexander Cockburn and Robin Blackburn (eds.), *Student Power:
      Problems, Diagnosis, Action* (Penguin Books, 1969), pp. 141-62.
35.   *Kursbuch* (Berlin), No. 18, p. 155.
36.   Arthur Liebman, "Student Activism in Mexico," *The Annals of the*

American Academy of Political and Social Science (May 1971), p. 165; Elena Poniatowska, *Fuerte es el Silencio* (Ediciones Era, 1980).

37. Heinz Rudolf Sonntag, "Versuch über die lateinamerikanischen Universitäten," *Kursbuch 13* (Berlin, June 1968); Jean Meyer, "Le mouvement étudiant en Amérique latine," *Esprit* (Paris, May 1969), pp. 740-53.

38. Robert Scott, "Student Political Activism in Latin America," in Lipset and Altbach, *op. cit.*, p. 404.

39. M. Phéline, "Crise universitaire et mouvement étudiant au Brésil," *Partisans,* No. 44 (Oct.-Nov. 1968), pp. 93-113.

40. Luisa A. Brignardello, *El Movimiento Estudiantil Argentino: Corrientes ideológicos y opiniones de sus dirigentes* (Buenos Aires: Ediciones Macchi, 1972).

41. Tilman Fichter and Siegward Lonnendonker, *Kleine Geschichte des SDS* (Rotbuch Verlag, 1977).

42. SDS, *Der Kampf des vietnamesischen Volkes und die Globalstrategie des Imperialism* (Berlin, February 17-18, 1968).

43. F.C. Hunnius, *Student Revolts: The New Left in West Germany* (War Resisters' International, 1968).

44. Heinz Grossman and Oskar Negt (eds.), *Die Auferstehung der Gewalt* (Europäische Verlagsanstalt, 1968).

45. H.J. Giessler, *APO-Rebellion Mai 1968* (Pamphlet-Verlag G. Rosenberger, 1968).

46. The emergence of post-New Left cultural politics in Central Europe at the beginning of the 1980s is empirical evidence of the world-historical nature of the New Left, and an entire chapter of this book was originally written to document the emergence of the Punk Left in Central Europe. That chapter was deleted in order to focus this book on the events of 1968-1970. It appeared in an abbreviated form as "The Extraparliamentary Left in Europe," *Monthly Review* (September 1982).

47. *Kursbuch 13* (Berlin, 1968), p. 55.

48. *Facts on File* (1968), pp. 205-6.

49. Barbara and John Ehrenreich, *Long March, Short Spring* (Monthly Review Press, 1969), p. 60

50. Valdo Spini, "The New Left in Italy," *Journal of Contemporary History* (January-April 1972), pp. 65-66.

51. Arrigo Levi, "Italy: The Crisis of Governing" in *Foreign Affairs* (October 1970), pp. 147-60.

52. Donald Katz, "Tribes: Italy's Metropolitan Indians," *Rolling Stone* (November 17, 1977), pp. 60-65; "Indios Metropolitanos," *El Viejo Topo* (Madrid, July 1977).

53. Bernhard Schutze, "Wiederstand an Spaniens Universitäten," *Kursbuch 13* (June 1968).

54. Manuel Tuñón de Lara, "Le problème universitaire espagnol," *Esprit* (Paris, May 1969), p. 848.

55. *Democracia Popular* (Madrid), January 1968.

56. *London Times*, April 2, 1969.

57. David Widgery, *The Left in Britain, 1956-1968* (Penguin Publishers, 1972).
58. Nobua Aruga as quoted in *Youth Up In Arms* by George Paloczi-Horvath (David McKay Co., 1971), p. 197.
59. Michiya Shimbori, "Student Radicals in Japan," *The Annals of the American Academy of Political and Social Science* (May 1971), p. 153.
60. Yoshihiko Hanawa, "Le radicalisme de la violence chez les étudiants japonais," *Esprit* (Paris, May 1969), pp. 754-63.
61. Jeanne Habel, "Les luttes étudiants et ouvrières au Japon," *Partisans*, No. 44 (October-November 1968), pp. 79-92.
62. Quoted in Robert N. Kearney, "Youth Protest in the Politics of Sri Lanka," *Sociological Focus* (August 1980), p. 304.
63. Samar Sen (ed.), *Naxalbari and After* (Calcutta, 1978)
64. Sumanta Banerjee, *India's Simmering Revolution: The Naxalite Uprising* (Zed Press, 1984).
65. Luis Aguilar (ed.), *Marxism in Latin America* (Temple University Press, 1978), pp. 152-7.
66. See *The Kapetanios: Partisans and Civil War in Greece, 1943-1949* by Dominique Eudes (Monthly Review Press, 1972). Further analysis of the Comintern's sabotage of popular social movements in the 1930s and 1940s can be found in Fernando Claudin, *The Communist Movement* (Monthly Review Press, 1974).
67. *Telos*, Number 25.
68. K. Mehnert, *Moscow and the New Left* (University of California Press, 1975), pp. 117-8.
69. Vladimir Kusin, *The Intellectual Origins of the Prague Spring* (Cambridge University Press, 1971), p. 63.
70. *Ibid.*, p. 139.
71. *Ibid.*, p. 60.
72. Robin A. Remington (ed.), *Winter in Prague: Documents on Czechoslovak Communism in Crisis* (MIT Press, 1969), p. 17.
73. "Studenten in Prag," *Kursbuch 13* (Berlin, June 1968), pp. 69-70.
74. Remington, *op. cit.*, p. 162.
75. Kusin, *op. cit.*, p. 128.
76. *Ibid.*, pp. 114-15.
77. Serge Mallet, *Bureaucracy and Technocracy in the Socialist Countries* (Spokesman Books, 1974).
78. Remington, *op. cit.*, pp. 5-7, 195-212.
79. M. Randle and A. Carter, *Support Czechoslovakia* (Houseman's Press, 1968), p. 10.
80. Remington, *op. cit.*, p. 455; *Voices of Czechoslovak Socialists* (Merlin Press, 1977), pp. 6-7.
81. Remington, *op. cit.*, p. 455.
82. Jiří Pelikan, *Sozialistische Opposition in der ČSSR* (Europäische Verlagsanstalt, 1973).
83. Hans-Peter Riese (ed.), *Since the Prague Spring* (Vintage Books, 1979).
84. Randle and Carter, *op. cit.*, pp. 14-17; *Facts on File* (1968), pp. 387, 489.
85. Kusin, *op. cit.*, p. 127.

86. *Ibid.*, pp. 127, 147-48.
87. M. Markovíc, *Student* (May 21, 1968).
88. "The Topic is Action," *Student* (May 14, 1968), p. 4 as quoted in *Revolt in Socialist Yugoslavia: June 1968* (Black and Red, 1973), p. 7.
89. *Susret* (May 15, 1968), pp. 7-8.
90. *Politika*, December 29, 1968.
91. "Warschauer Bilanz," *Kursbuch 13* (June 1968), pp. 91-107.
92. *Revolutionary Marxist Students from Poland Speak Out, 1964-1968* (Merit Publishers, 1970).
93. Zugmunt Bauman, "Le combat des étudiants polonais," *Espirit* (May 1969), p. 865.
94. *Boston Globe*, May 9, 1981; *Le Monde*, January 28, 1971.
95. Informations Correspondence Ouvrières, *Poland, 1970-71: Capitalism and Class Struggle* (Black and Red, 1977), pp. 11-12.
96. *Ibid.*, p. 23.
97. Michael Dobbs, K. S. Karol, and Dessa Trevisan, *Poland, Solidarity, Walesa* (McGraw Hill, 1981).
98. Informations Correspondence Ouvrières, *op. cit.*, p. 43.
99. Risto Bajalski in *Le Monde*, January 2, 1971.
100. *Der Spiegel*, January 23, 1971.
101. *Contemporary Poland* (March 1971), p. 48.
102. William Hinton, *Hundred Day War: The Cultural Revolution at Tsinghua University* (Monthly Review Press, 1972), p. 187.
103. Houtart and Rousseau, *op. cit.*, p. 214.
104. *Between Misery and Hope: Documents from and about the Church in Latin America* (Maryknoll Documentation Service, 1970), p. 144.
105. Speech to the Peasants, August 23, 1968 in *La Documentation Catholique*, No. 1524 (Bonne Press, 1968), col. 1545, as quoted in Houtart and Rousseau, *op. cit.*, p. 215.
106. Houtart and Rousseau, *op. cit.*, p. 214.
107. *Between Misery and Hope, op. cit.*, p. 211.
108. Houtart and Rousseau, *op. cit.*, p. 228.
109. *Informations Catholiques Internationales* (Paris: October 15, 1968), p. 17.
110. Houtart and Rousseau, *op. cit.*, p. 243.
111. *Ibid.*, p. 253.
112. Arthur Gish, *The New Left and Christian Radicalism* (Erdman's Publishing Co., 1970). For a discussion of Black Power and the church, see James Cone, *Black Theology and Black Power* (Seabury Press, 1969).
113. Houtart and Rouseau, *op. cit.*, p. 214.
114. Stephen Rousseas, *Death of a Democracy: Greece and the American Conscience* (Grove Press, 1967).
115. *Report of the National Advisory Commission on Civil Disorders* (United States Government Printing Office, March 1, 1968).
116. *Ibid.*
117. *Ibid.*, pp. 89, 95-112.
118. Amy Uyematsu, "The Emergence of Yellow Power in America" in *Roots: An Asian-American Reader* (UCLA, 1971), pp. 9-14.

119. Richard Gartner, *Grito! Reies Tijerina and The New Mexico Land Grant War* (Harper-Colophon, 1970); Patricia Blarvis, *Tijerina and the Land Grants* (International Publishers, 1971).
120. See Carlos Muñoz, *Quest for Identity and Power: The Chicano Student Struggle* (forthcoming from Verso Books, 1988).
121. Garth Buchanan and Joan Brackett, *Survey of Campus Incidents* (The Urban Institute, 1970), p. 15.
122. Robin Morgan (ed.), *Sisterhood is Powerful* (Random House, 1970), p. xxv.
123. Redstockings, *Feminist Revolution*, 1975, p. 21.
124. John Hersey, *op. cit.*, p. C-5; Joe Fagin and Harlan Hahn, *Ghetto Riots* (Macmillan, 1973), p. 105.
125. *Facts on File*, 1968, p. 212.
126. *Ibid.*, p. 200.
127. Daniel Bell, then professor of sociology at Columbia, as quoted by *U.S. News and World Report*.
128. See Immanuel Wallerstein and Paul Starr, *The University Crisis Reader*, Vol. II (Random House, 1971), pp. 160-62.
129. *Ibid.* pp. 162-65.
130. Sara Evans, *Personal Politics* (Vintage Books, 1980), pp. 200-1.
131. *Rights in Conflict* (Signet Books, 1968).
132. Hersey, *op. cit.*, p. C-5.
133. Morgan, *op. cit.*, p. 521.
134. Herbert Lottman, *The Left Bank* (McGraw Hill, 1982).
135. Hersey, *op. cit.*
136. The international nature of the counterculture is graphically displayed in Joseph Berke, (ed.), *Counter-Culture* (Peter Owen Press, 1969).

Chapter 3:
The New Left in France

1.   Ernest Mandel, "Lessons of May," *New Left Review*, Number 52, pp. 9-32.
2.   Patrick Seale and Maureen McConville, *Red Flag, Black Flag* (Ballantine Books, 1968), p. 79.
3.   An anthology of documents from the participants in the May events is contained in *The French Student Uprising*, edited by Alain Schnapp and Pierre Vidal-Naquet (Beacon Press, 1971).
4.   Seale and McConville, *op. cit.*, p. 92.
5.   *Ibid.*, pp. 177-78.
6.   *Ibid.*, pp. 48, 183-8, 231.

7. Chris Harman, "The Crisis of the European Revolutionary Left," *International Socialism* (Spring 1979), pp. 49-54.

8. André Glucksmann, "Strategy and Revolution in France 1968," *New Left Review*, No. 52, p. 70.

9. Daniel and Gabriel Cohn-Bendit, *Obsolete Communism: The Left Wing Alternative* (McGraw-Hill, 1968), p. 131.

10. Daniel Singer, *Prelude to Revolution*, (Hill and Wang, 1971), p. 70.

11. See Daniel Bell, *The Coming of Post-Industrialized Society: A Venture in Social Forecasting* (Basic Books, 1973), pp. 165-266.

12. Seale and McConville, *op. cit.*, p. 79.

13. Schnapp and Vidal-Naquet, *op. cit.*, p. 12.

14. Herve Bourges (ed.), *The French Student Revolt* (Hill and Wang, 1968), p. 29.

15. *Ibid.*, p. 11. Also see Raymond Boudon, "Sources of Student Protest in France," in the *Annals of the American Academy of Political and Social Science*, Volume 395 (May 1971), pp. 141-2. He notes that in the wake of May, the findings of a French sociologist bore out Sauvageot's belief: "When the students were asked what were, in their opinion, the causes of the May-June revolt, they quoted much more often the anxiety which they themselves felt in the face of unemployment."

16. Walter Kreipe, "Studenten in Frankreich: Hintergrund und Potential einer politischen Bewegung," *Kursbuch 13* (1968), pp. 156-58.

17. Schnapp and Vidal-Naquet, *op. cit.*, pp. 500-9.

18. See J. Habermas, *Toward a Rational Society* (Beacon Press, 1972), pp. 50-81.

19. Schnapp and Vidal-Naquet, *op. cit.*, pp. 437-45.

20. Singer, *op. cit.*, p. 85.

21. *Ibid.*, p. 38.

22. See R. Dahrendorf, *Class and Class Conflict in Industrial Society* (Stanford University Press, 1959), and A. Gouldner, *The Future of Intellectuals and the Rise of a New Class* (Oxford University Press, 1979).

23. See André Gorz, *Socialism and Revolution* (Allen Lane, 1975); Michel Crozier, *The World of the Office Worker* (University of Chicago, 1971), pp. 11-12; "White Collar Unions: The Case of France," in Adolf Sturmthal, *White-Collar Trade Unions* (Urbana, 1966); and Anthony Giddens, *The Class Structure of Advanced Societies* (Harper & Row, 1975), pp. 179-89.

24. Singer, *op. cit.*, p. 80.

25. Alain Touraine, *The May Movement* (Random House, 1971), pp. 39-40.

26. Singer, *op. cit.*, p. 211.

27. See Gorz, *op. cit.*, pp. 9-29.

28. This quote and much of the analysis in this section is from R. Gregoire and F. Perlman, *Worker-Student Action Committees* (Black and Red, 1969), p. 49.

29. See H. Lefebvre, *The Explosion* (Monthly Review Press, 1969); and C. Wright Mills, *The Power Elite* (Oxford University Press, 1956), especially Chapter 13.

30. H. Lefebvre, *op. cit*, p. 93.
31. Schnapp and Vidal-Naquet, *op. cit*, p. 172.
32. A. Willener, *The Action-Image of Society: On Cultural Politicization* (Pantheon Books, 1970), p. 311.
33. Sylvia Harvey, *May '68 and Film Culture* (British Film Institute, 1978), p. 14.
34. Willener, *op. cit.*, p. 194.
35. Rene Lourau in Willener, *op. cit.*, pp. 82-3.
36. Norman Birnbaum, *The Crisis of Industrial Society* (Oxford University Press, 1969), p. 140.
37. H. Marcuse, *Counterrevolution and Revolt* (Beacon Press, 1972).
38. Andrew Feenberg, "Remembering the May Events," *Theory and Society*, No. 6 (1978), pp. 37-38.
39. Schnapp and Vidal-Naquet, *op. cit.*, p. 438.
40. *Ibid.*, p. 439.
41. See Chapter 2.
42. Cohn-Bendit, *op. cit.*, p. 166.
43. André Hoyles, "General Strike: France 1968" (*Trade Union Register*, 1969), p. 29. (Reprinted by STO, Box 8493, Chicago, IL 60680.)
44. *Ibid.*, p. 27.
45. "Universities in Europe Draw Elite," *San Diego Union* (December 25, 1978), p. A-46.
46. Ernest Mandel, "Lessons of May," *op. cit.*
47. Schnapp and Vidal-Naquet, *op. cit.*, p. 427.
48. V.I. Lenin, *Left-Wing Communism* (International Publishers, 1940), p. 18.
49. Herbert Marcuse, *An Essay on Liberation* (Beacon Press, 1969), p. 56.
50. Hoyles, *op. cit.*, p. 3.
51. A. Belden Fields, "The French Student Revolt of May-June 1968," *Students in Revolt*, Lipset and Albach (eds.), (Beacon Press, 1970), pp. 163-64.
52. Charles C. Lemert, *French Sociology: Rupture and Renewal Since 1968* (Columbia University Press, 1981); Sherry Turkle, *Psychoanalytic Politics: Freud's French Revolution* (MIT Press, 1978).
53. Richard Barnet and Ronald Müller, *Global Reach* (Simon and Schuster, 1974), p. 18.
54. "French Polynesia: Trouble in Paradise," *San Diego Union*, December 25, 1981, pp. A22-23; *Liberation* (Paris), November 9, 1981.
55. *In These Times* (January 26, 1977), p. 10.
56. Régis Debray, "A Modest Contribution to the Rites and Ceremonies of the Tenth Anniversary," *New Left Review*, No. 115, pp. 45-65.
57. Marx, *op. cit.*, p. 122.
58. M. Crozier, *Le phénomene bureaucratique* (Editions du Seuil, 1963), pp. 359-61.
59. *Los Angeles Times* (March 23, 1979), Part VII, p. 11.
60. Elaine Marks and Isabelle de Courtivron (eds.), *New French Feminisms* (Schocken Books, 1981).

61.   Judith Miller, *Theater and Revolution in France Since 1968* (French
      Forum Publishers, 1977).
62.   Leo Huberman and Paul M. Sweezy, "Reflections on the French
      Upheaval," in *Monthly Review* (September 1968), pp. 6-7. For
      discussion of Mitterrand's administration, see Daniel Singer, "Imagina-
      tion Has Not Yet Taken Power," *The Nation*, January 29, 1983, and
      "Mitterrand's Achievement," *Monthly Review* (June 1986).

Chapter 4:
The New Left in the United States _____

1.   Reports gathered for the President's Commission on Campus Unrest
      indicated that there were many more "disruptive" demonstrations in
      1969-70 *before* the invasion of Cambodia than in the two previous
      school years. The proportion more than doubled again for protests after
      the invasion. Garth Buchanan and Joan Brackett, *Summary Results of the
      Survey for the President's Commission on Campus Unrest* (Urban Institute,
      September 1970), pp. 9-10.
2.   John Taft, *Mayday at Yale: A Case Study in Student Radicalism* (Westview
      Press, 1976), p. 87.
3.   *The Report of the President's Commission on Campus Unrest*, William
      Scranton, Chairman, September 26, 1970, p. 17.
4.   *Ibid*, p. 19 and Urban Research Corporation, *On Strike... Shut It Down:
      A Report of the First National Student Strike in U.S. History* (Chicago,
      1970), p. 1.
5.   Kirkpatrick Sale, *SDS* (Vintage Books, 1974), p. 637.
6.   *U.S. News and World Report*, May 25, 1970, p. 20.
7.   "The Guard vs. Disorder," *The National Guardsman*, Volume 24 (June
      1970), p. 2.
8.   Richard E. Petersen and John A. Bilorusky, *May 1970: The Campus
      Aftermath of Cambodia and Kent State* (Carnegie Commission on Higher
      Education, 1971), p. 127.
9.   *Washington Star*, June 24, 1970.
10.   Dave Dellinger, *More Power Than We Know: The People's Movement
      Toward Democracy* (Anchor Press, 1975), p. 136, and Sale, *op. cit.*,
      p. 637.
11.   Dellinger, *op. cit.*, p. 137.
12.   It was the fourteenth time the District of Columbia's National Guard
      had been called to riot duty since the 1967 Pentagon march. "The
      Guard vs. Disorder," *op. cit.*, p. 9.
13.   A year later, during the first week in May 1971, the frustrated needs for
      a militant confrontation in Washington were fulfilled in the attempt by
      thousands of people to close the city of Washington by sitting down in
      the streets during the early morning rush hour. Nearly 15,000 of the
      50,000 demonstrators were arrested in three days of civil disobedience.
14.   Joseph A. Califano, Jr., *The Student Revolution: A Global Confrontation*
      (W.W. Norton and Company, 1970), p. 53.

15. Urban Research Corporation, *op. cit.*, p. 12.
16. Paul M. Sweezy and Harry Magdoff, "War and Crisis," *Monthly Review* (June 1970), p. 5.
17. Daniel Yankelovich, *The Changing Values on Campus* (Simon and Schuster, 1972). Also see Joseph Califano, Jr., *op. cit., p. 64.*
18. *New York Times*, January 2, 1971.
19. S. M. Lipset, *Rebellion in the University* (University of Chicago Press, 1976), p. 58.
20. Local movements in San Francisco and Cambridge, Massachusetts, had put the war on the ballot in November 1967, but less than 40 percent of those voting favored immediate withdrawal.
21. Scranton Commission, *op. cit.*, p. 45. (My emphasis.)
22. Taft, *op. cit.*, p. 161.
23. Petersen and Bilorusky, *op. cit.*, p. 17.
24. Califano, *op. cit.*, pp. 79-80.
25. *The Daily Californian*, May 8, 1970.
26. Petersen and Bilorusky, *op. cit.*, p. 140.
27. *Ibid.*, pp. 141-42.
28. *Ibid.*
29. *Ibid.*, p. 160.
30. Urban Research Corporation, *op. cit.*, p. 91.
31. *The Daily Californian*, May 13, 1970.
32. Petersen and Bilorusky, *op. cit.*, pp. 14-16.
33. *Urban Crisis Monitor*, Vol. 3, No. 23 (June 5, 1970), pp. 3-4.
34. Urban Research Corporation, *op. cit.*, p. 50.
35. *Ibid.*, pp. 58-59.
36. *Urban Crisis Monitor*, March 27, 1970, p. 44.
37. *Ibid.*, p. 18.
38. In Puerto Rico, failure to report and refusals to be inducted into the military reached 75 percent of those called in June 1970. *Repeal the Draft*, Vol. 2, No. 7 (July 7, 1970), p. 3 as compared with 50 percent failing to report in Los Angeles and Oakland and a California average of almost 40 percent.
39. *Newsweek*, June 1, 1970, p. 25, and Petersen and Bilorusky, *op. cit.*, p. 3.
40. Carlos Muñoz, "Toward a Chicano Perspective of Political Analysis," *Aztlan* (Fall 1970), p. 15.
41. *San Diego Street Journal*, February 17, 1971.
42. Stanley Aronowitz, "Trade Unionism and Workers' Control" in *Workers' Control*, Gerry Hunnius, G. David Garson, and John Case (eds.), (Vintage Books, 1973).
43. *Veterans Stars and Stripes for Peace*, Vol. 1, No. 3, p. 1.
44. *Urban Crisis Monitor*, March 27, 1970, p. 18.
45. *U.S. News and World Report*, May 25, 1970, p. 20.
46. *Cleveland Plain-Dealer*, May 11, 1970.
47. Scranton Commission, *op. cit.*, p. 286.
48. Al Richmond, "Workers against the War," *Ramparts*, September 1970, p. 32.

49. *New York Post*, May 19, 1970.
50. *Urban Crisis Monitor*, Vol. 5, No. 11 (March 13, 1970), p. 3.
51. *Guardian*, May 30, 1970.
52. Richmond, *op. cit.*, pp. 28-29.
53. *Ibid.*, p. 31.
54. *Los Angeles Times*, May 11, 1970, Part II, p. 2.
55. *Guardian*, May 30, 1970.
56. *Vietnam Courier*, No. 305 (January 25, 1971), p. 6.
57. Califano, *op. cit.*, p. 88.
58. R. Heinel, *The Collapse of the Armed Forces*, in House of Representatives Committee on Internal Security, *Investigation of Attempts to Subvert the Armed Forces* (U.S. Government Printing Office, 1972).
59. James R. Hayes, "The Dialectics of Resistance: An Analysis of the GI Movement," *Journal of Social Issues* (November 4, 1975), p. 132.
60. Vietnam Veterans Against the War, *History*, published by the VVAW national office, 1972.
61. *Scanlan's*, January 1971, p. 55.
62. *Look*, June 16, 1970, p. 72.
63. *Scanlan's*, January 1971, p. 58.
64. David Cortwright, *Soldiers in Revolt* (Doubleday, 1975), pp. 44-5.
65. *Scanlan's*, *op. cit.*, p. 57.
66. J. Hayes, *op. cit.*, p. 132.
67. *Washington Post*, July 6, 1970.
68. Howard Zinn, *A People's History of the United States* (Harper & Row, 1980).
69. Scranton Commission, *op. cit.*, p. 61.
70. Steve Shapiro, "Political Ecology: An Introduction" in *Incarnations* (Irvine, California), January 15, 1970. This document and the Diggers' papers are contained in the archive of the Hoover Institution at Stanford University.
71. Petersen and Bilorusky, *op. cit.*, pp. 162-63.
72. Scranton Commission, *op. cit.*, p. 69.
73. Urban Research Corporation, *op. cit.*, p. 37.
74. *Ibid.*, p. 75.
75. *Ibid.*, pp. 34-35.
76. *Ibid.*, pp. 37.
77. Sharon Howell, *Metaphorical Analysis of the Evolution of the Female Identity, 1961-1982*, doctoral dissertation, Wayne State University, 1983.
78. *Newsweek*, May 25, 1970, p. 43.
79. *Newsweek*, June 1, 1970, p. 24.
80. *Life*, June 5, 1970, p. 28.
81. *Ibid.*, p. 32.
82. Basic data from U.S. Departments of Labor, Commerce, Transportation and Health, Education, and Welfare.
83. *Newsweek*, May 25, 1970, p. 30.
84. *Monthly Review*, May 18, 1970.

85. *Liberated Guardian* (May 1972), pp. 8-9.
86. Carl Oglesby and Richard Shaull, *Containment and Change* (Macmillan, 1967).
87. Noam Chomsky, "Watergate: A Skeptical View," *New York Review of Books* (September 20, 1973), pp. 3-8.
88. *Counterspy*, Winter 1976; Geoffrey Rips, *Unamerican Activities* (City Lights, 1981).
89. Henry Kissinger, *A World Restored* (Houghton-Mifflin), p. 328.
90. For further analysis of high levels of power in the United States, see Carl Oglesby, *The Yankee and Cowboy Wars* (Sheed, Andrews and McMeel, Inc., 1976); and see Holly Sklar, *Trilateralism* (South End Press, 1978) for background on the Trilateral Commission.
91. Noam Chomsky and Edward S. Herman, *The Washington Connection and Third World Fascism* and *After the Cataclysm* (South End Press, 1979).
92. *Vietnam Courier*, No. 5 (1982), p. 22.
93. *New York Times*, May 17, 1970.
94. *New York Times Magazine*, August 8, 1970.
95. Petersen and Bilorusky, *op. cit.*, p. 85.
96. C. Wright Mills, *The Power Elite* (Oxford University Press, 1956), pp. 30-31, 283.
97. Michael Crozier, Samuel Huntington, Joji Watanuke, *The Crisis of Democracy: Report on the Governability of Democracies to the Trilateral Commission* (New York University Press, 1975), p. 106.
98. Ralph Miliband and Leo Panitch, "Socialists and the 'New Conservatism,' " *Monthly Review* (January 1987).
99. See J. Craig Jenkins and Craig Eckert, "Channeling Black Insurgency: Elite Patronage and Professional Social Movements in the Development of the Black Movement," *American Sociological Review* (December 1986), pp. 812-29.
100. Carnegie Commission on Higher Education, *Priorities for Action: Final Report* (1973), p. 63.
101. *Ibid.*, p. 53.
102. Petersen and Bilorusky, *op. cit.*, p. 85.
103. Scranton Commission, *op. cit.*, pp. 169-70.
104. *Ibid.*, p. 39; Carnegie Commission, *Dissent and Disruption: Proposals for Consideration by the Campuses* (June 1971), pp. 165-66; and John and Susan Erlich, *Student Power, Participation and Revolt* (Association Press, 1970), pp. 247-54.
105. Petersen and Bilorusky, *op. cit.*, p. 115.
106. Bill Watson, "Counter-Planning on the Shop Floor," *Radical America* (May-June 1971).
107. Stanley Weir, *USA—The Labor Revolt* (New England Free Press, 1969), p. 2 as quoted in John Zerzan, *Creation and Its Enemies: The Revolt Against Work* (Mutualist Books, 1977), p. 30.
108. As quoted in the *San Diego Union*, February 17, 1982, p. A-21.
109. *San Diego Union*, February 5, 1982, p. D-2.
110. Daniel Zwerdling, *Workplace Democracy* (Harper & Row, 1978); Bruce

Stokes, "Productivity and Production Go Hand in Hand," *Los Angeles Times*, April 22, 1979, Part IV, p. 1.

111. *The Crisis of Democracy, op. cit.*, pp. 113-15.

112. Scranton Commission, *op. cit.*, p. 12.

113. Hugh D. Graham and Ted R. Gurr, *The History of Violence in America* (Bantam Books, 1969), p. 578.

114. National Commission on the Causes and Prevention of Violence, *Progress Report* (U.S. Government Printing Office, 1969), p. A-11.

115. National Lawyer's Guild, *Counter-Intelligence: A Documentary Look at America's Secret Police* (1978).

116. See Peter Bohmer, *The Impact of Public Employment on Racial Inequality: 1950-1984*, doctoral dissertation, Economics Department, University of Massachusetts, Amherst, Massachusetts, 1985.

117. Richard Barnet and Ronald Müller, *Global Reach* (Simon and Schuster, 1974).

118. United States Bureau of Labor Statistics quoted in Gilda Haas, *Plant Closures: Myths, Realities and Responses* (South End Press, 1985), p. 13.

119. Barry Bluestone and Bennett Harrison, *The Deindustrialization of America* (Basic Books, 1982).

120. Mieke Meurs, "Political Implications of Changing Class Structure," *Guardian* (February 4, 1987), p. 7; *Boston Globe*, December 10, 1986, p. 1.

121. Barnet and Müller, *op. cit.*, p. 230.

122. Statistical Abstract of the United States, Table #886; Robert Heilbroner and James Galbraith, *The Economic Problem* (Prentice-Hall, 1987), p. 550.

123. Robert Heilbroner, "None of Your Business," *New York Review of Books* (March 20, 1975), p. 6.

124. Bluestone and Harrison, *op. cit.*, pp. 129-133.

125. See Corporate Taxes and the Federal Deficit," by Craig Melden, and "The Need for Tax Reform," by Paul Sweezy and Harry Magdoff, *Monthly Review* (November 1984).

126. McGeorge Bundy, George Kennan, Robert McNamara, and Gerard Smith, "Nuclear Weapons and the Atlantic Alliance," *Foreign Affairs* (Spring 1982), pp. 762-63.

127. *Ibid.*, pp. 765-66.

128. McGeorge Bundy, George Kennan, Robert McNamara, and Gerard Smith, "The President's Choice: Star Wars or Arms Control," *Foreign Affairs* (Winter 1984-85), p. 277.

Chapter 5:
The Political Legacy of The New Left _____

1. Herbert Marcuse, *Counterrevolution and Revolt* (Beacon Press, 1972), p. 2.

2. Jean-Paul Sartre, *Baudelaire* (New Directions, 1967), pp. 51-52.

3. Stephen Spender, *The Year of the Young Rebels* (Vintage Books, 1968), p. 77.
4. William Bollinger, "Revolutionary Strategy in Latin America," *Monthly Review* (February 1983), p. 28.
5. For further discussion, see my article, "The Extraparliamentary Left in Europe," *Monthly Review* (September 1982).
6. "Legislators' Inattention Spawns Burgeoning of 'Direct Democracy,'" *San Diego Union*, December 12, 1982, p. C-1.
7. Chris Harman, "The Crisis of the European Revolutionary Left," *International Socialism* (Spring 1979), pp. 49-54.
8. Tilman Fichter and Siegward Lonnendonker, *Kleine Geschichte des SDS* (Rotbuch Verlag, 1977).
9. My calculations are based on data in Fichter's book and in *SDS* by Kirkpatrick Sale (Vintage Books, 1974).
10. See Seymour Martin Lipset, "Why No Socialism in the United States?" in *Sources of Contemporary Radicalism*, edited by Seweryn Bailer and Sophia Sluger (Westview Press, 1977).
11. *Guardian*, July 2, 1980, p. 16; *New York Times*, January 9, 1984, p. B8; *Boston Globe*, July 28, 1986.
12. *Time*, July 12, 1982, p. 20; *Working Women*, October 1986.
13. In 1912, the Socialist Party received 6 percent of the vote and won a number of local elections, and in 1916, Eugene Debs received even more votes while in jail for opposing World War I, but the Socialist Party soon sank into political oblivion.
14. Xavier Nicholas, "Questions of the American Revolution: Conversations with James Boggs" (The Institute of the Black World, 1976), p. 7.
15. I do not use the word "professional" in contrast to "amateur" but in its similarity to specialized, paid functionary. One of the real faults of the New Left was its amateurism: There were reports of years of unanswered correspondence turning up behind old file cabinets in the SDS national office in Chicago. The current professionalism seems to be the other extreme of what previously was amateurism. See John McCarthy and Mayer Zald, "The Trend of Social Movements in America: Professionalization and Resource Mobilization," (General Learning Press, 1973).
16. See Bruce Andrews, "Criticizing Economic Democracy," *Monthly Review* (May 1980), pp. 19-25.
17. I will consistently use conservative estimates since I have no intention to appear to be inflating the scope of events in question. At the anti-Haig demonstration, for example, it was estimated by some that at least 80,000 demonstrators were involved, probably a more accurate number than the police estimate of 50,000. German sources include the *Frankfurter Allgemeine* and *Die Tageszeitung*.
18. *Guardian*, April 28, 1982, p. 5 and November 10, 1982, p.7.
19. Radio Speech #2, April 18, 1982.
20. *Guardian*, February 16, 1983, p. 4.
21. See Paul Baran and Paul M. Sweezy, *Monopoly Capital* (Monthly

Review Press, 1968); Rosa Luxemburg, *The Accumulation of Capital* (Monthly Review Press, 1972); Seymour Melman, *Pentagon Capitalism* (McGraw-Hill, 1970).

22. Figures quoted from United Nations Secretary-General Javier Perez de Cuellar, speech to the UN Special Session on Disarmament, June 7, 1982.

23. See Daniel Ellsberg's Introduction to *Protest and Survive* (Monthly Review Press, 1982) and Steven Weissman and Herbert Krossney, *The Islamic Bomb* (New York Times Books, 1981). This latter book is somewhat inappropriately titled and focused, but nonetheless, it contains documentation of Israel's atomic armaments.

24. James and Grace Lee Boggs, *Revolution and Evolution in the Twentieth Century* (Monthly Review Press, 1976).

25. Sojourner Truth Organization, *Newsletter #2*, 1982, p. 37.

26. *Village Voice*, April 20, 1982; *Guardian*, June 23, 1982; and *Perspectiva Mundial*, June 14, 1982.

27. See Herbert Marcuse, *An Essay on Liberation* (Beacon Press, 1969), especially Part I.

28. Catherine Itzin, *Stages in the Revolution: Political Theatre in Britain Since 1968* (Eyre-Methuen, 1980).

29. *U.S. News and World Report*, January 25, 1982, p. 42.

30. Jim Campen (ed.) *Socialist Alternatives for America: A Bibliography* (Union of Radical Political Economists, 1974).

31. Michael John, *Cooperative Community Guide* (Rainbow Nation, 1980) and John Curl, *History of Work Cooperation in America* (Homeward Press, 1980).

32. Walter-Archeion Moritz, *Die Utopie Hat Begonnen* (Zero-Verlag, 1979); Paul Freundlich, Chris Collins, and Mikki Wenig (eds.), *A Guide to Cooperative Alternatives* (Community Publications Cooperative, 1979), p. 83.

33. Curl, *op. cit.*, p. 50; *Bay Area Directory of Collectives* (New Moon Press, 1980).

34. Curl, *op. cit.*, p. 53.

35. John Case and Rosemary C. R. Taylor, editors, *Co-ops, Communes and Collectives: Experiments in Social Change in the 1960s and 1970s* (Pantheon Books, 1979), pp. 20, 217.

36. William Ronco, *Food Co-ops* (Beacon Press, 1974).

37. *Akwesasne Notes* is reported to have over 100,000 readers, and *Off Our Backs* has a press run of 15,000 per month. Freundlich, et. al., *op. cit.*, pp. 73, 113.

38. Quoted in Alexander Cockburn, "Prisoners of Israel," *Village Voice*, July 13, 1982, p. 8.

39. See Herbert Marcuse, *The Aesthetic Dimension: Toward a Critique of Marxist Aesthetics* (Beacon Press, 1978).

40. See Herbert Marcuse, *Counterrevolution and Revolt, op. cit.*

41. Harold Cruse, *Rebellion or Revolution* (William Morrow and Co., 1968), p. 111.

42. Herbert Marcuse, "Marxismus und Feminismus," in *Zeit-Messungen* (Suhrkamp Verlag, 1975), p. 12.

43. Carnegie Commission on Higher Education, *Priorities for Action: Final Report* (1973), p. 84.

44. Lipset, "The Possible Effects of Student Activism on International Politics," in *Students in Revolt* (Beacon Press, 1970), p. 521.

45. There are important new works which do attempt such an analysis. See Serge Mallet, *The New Working Class* (Spokesman Books, 1975) and Stanley Aronowitz, *False Promises* (McGraw Hill, 1974). Although dealing with a different period, Meredith Tax has written an excellent history of *The Rising of the Women: Feminist Solidarity and Class Conflict, 1880-1917* (Monthly Review Press, 1981). For an indication of neo-conservatives' fear of the "new class," see Richard Goldstein, "The War for America's Mind," *Village Voice* (June 8, 1982), particularly pp. 19-20.

46. The National Advisory Commission on Civil Disorders, *Report* (U.S. Government, March 1, 1968), pp. 73-76; Nathan Caplan, "The New Ghetto Man: A Review of Recent Empirical Studies," in *Journal of Social Issues*, Vol. 26, No. 1 (Winter 1970), pp. 63-64.

47. Harry Braverman, *Labor Monopoly and Capital* (Monthly Review Press, 1974); Harry Boyte and Frank Ackerman, "Revolution and Democracy," *Socialist Revolution* 16 (July 1973), pp. 48-49.

48. Editors' Foreward to *The American Revolution* by James Boggs (Monthly Review Press, 1968).

49. James Boggs, "Thoughts on the Future," Address to the Martin Luther King Series, Purdue University, April 23, 1975, pp. 4-5.

50. See André Gorz, *Farewell to the Working Class* (South End Press, 1982).

51. *Dissent* (Summer 1965), p. 328.

52. *The Movement*, January 1966.

53. See James Boggs, "Citizens, Not Subjects; Individuality, Not Individualism," Lecture at the University of Michigan, December 2, 1975; and James and Grace Boggs, Freddy and Lyman Paine, *Conversations in Maine: Exploring Our Nation's Future* (South End Press, 1978).

54. See Oscar Negt, "Don't Go by Numbers, Organize According to Interest! Current Questions on Organization," in *New German Critique*, No. 1, pp. 42-51.

55. Marcuse, *Counterrevolution and Revolt*, *op.cit.*, p. 42.

56. Gorz, *Socialism and Revolution* (Anchor Books, 1973), p. 30.

57. It is the practice of these orthodox parties in the core in 1968, more than any other factor, which has led me to use the term "avant garde" rather than "vanguard" in this discussion.

58. See *Green Politics: The Global Promise* by Fritjof Capra and Charlene Spretnak (E. P. Dutton, 1984), p. 104. A North American Green who sees the need for the transformation of the existing system is Brian Tokar, *The Green Alternative: Creating an Ecological Future* (R. Miles, 1987).

59. Quotations are from *The Program of the Green Party of West Germany*, pp.

7-8. The official English translation is available from Die Grünen, Colmantstrasse 36, 5300 Bonn 1, West Germany.

60. The original Rainbow Coalition was organized in Chicago by Black Panther leader Fred Hampton in 1969. It helped radicalize black street gangs like the Blackstone Rangers and the Black Disciples and united them with groups like the Young Lords, a Puerto Rican revolutionary party which emerged among Latino street gangs. See Lawrence Lader, *Power on the Left* (W.W. Norton, 1979), pp. 269-70.

61. Sheila Collins, *The Rainbow Challenge: The Jackson Campaign and the Future of U.S. Politics* (Monthly Review Press, 1986), pp. 20, 142, 80, 296.

62. *Ibid.*, p. 247.

63. Ted Glick, "Rainbow Coalition on the Move," NCIPA Newsletter as quoted in Collins, *op. cit.*, p. 237.

64. Collins, *op.cit.*, pp. 328-9.

65. See Karl Marx, *Class Struggles in France, 1848-1850* (International Publishers, 1972), pp. 113-14.

66. Franklin Lamb (ed.), *Israel's War in Lebanon: Eyewitness Chronicles of the Invasion and Occupation* (South End Press, 1984).

67. Bruce Franklin, "Debt Peonage: The Highest Form of Imperialism?" *Monthly Review* (March 1982), pp. 15-31.

68. Gabriel García Márquez, "The Solitude of Latin America," excerpts from his acceptance speech when receiving the 1982 Nobel Prize for Literature.

69. L.S. Stavrianos, "A 10,000 Year Quest for Justice," *Los Angeles Times*, February 27, 1983, Book Section, p.1.

70. James E. Austin, *Nutrition Programs in the Third World* (Oegeschlager, Gunn, and Hain Publishers, 1981).

71. Joseph Skinner, "Big Mac and the Tropical Forests," *Monthly Review* (December 1985).

72. Seymour Martin Lipset, "The Possible Effects of Student Activism on International Politics," in *Students in Revolt, op. cit.*, pp. 520-21.

Chapter 6:
The Rationality of the New Left

1. Further discussion of the relationship between theory and practice can be found in Jürgen Habermas, *Theory and Practice* (Beacon Press, 1973), especially pp. 1-41 and 253-282; see also Herbert Marcuse, "The Relevance of Reality," in *The Owl of Minerva*, ed. by Charles Bontempo and S. Jack Odell (McGraw Hill, 1975), pp. 231-244.

2. See Max Horkheimer, *Critical Theory* (Herder and Herder, 1972).

3. Jürgen Habermas, *Legitimation Crisis* (Beacon Press, 1975), p. 28.

4. An excellent history of the Frankfurt School can be found in Martin Jay's *The Dialectical Imagination* (Little Brown and Co., 1973).

5. S. Huntington, *Political Order in Changing Societies* (Yale Unversity Press, 1968), pp. 369-71.

6. Immanuel Wallerstein and Paul Starr (eds.), *The University Crisis Reader*, 2 Vol. (Random House, 1971).
7. Lipset, *Rebellion in the University* (University of Chicago Press, 1971), p. 17.
8. Lipset (ed.), *The Berkeley Student Revolt* (Anchor Books, 1965), pp. 3-4.
9. H. Marcuse, *An Essay on Liberation* (Beacon Press, 1969), p. x.
10. Seale and McConville, *Red Flag, Black Flag* (Ballantine Books, 1968), p. 87.
11. Mandel as quoted in David Smith, *Who Rules the Universities?* (Monthly Review Press, 1974), p. 225.
12. *Naturwuchs* is a German word which does not have an exact English equivalent. The suffix comes from *wachsen* (to grow), and *Naturwuchs* refers to processes that have developed spontaneously, without human planning. It is used in contrast to processes that are the result of conscious human will and self-determination. See Jürgen Habermas's *Legitimation Crisis* for a fuller explanation.
13. Alan Blum, *Theorizing* (Heineman, 1974).
14. Aristotle, *Politics*, 1333a: 31-2; *The Basic Works of Aristotle*, McKeon (ed.), (Random House, 1941), p. 1298; also see Herbert Marcuse, *One Dimensional Man* (Beacon Press, 1964), p. 130; Blum, *op. cit.*, p. 108.
15. Blum, *op. cit.*, p. 4.
16. Marcuse, *One Dimensional Man*, *op. cit.*, p. 147; Herbert Marcuse, *Negations* (Beacon Press, 1969), pp. 88-9.
17. Herbert Marcuse, "Progress and Freud's Theory of Instincts," *Five Lectures* (Beacon Press, 1970), pp. 28-43.
18. In Thomas Kuhn's *The Structure of Scientific Revolutions* (Chicago, 1970), paradigms are defined as "some accepted examples of actual scientific practice—examples which include law, theory, application and instrumentation together—(which) provide models from which spring particular coherent traditions of scientific research" (p. 10). For an indirect critique of Kuhn's notion of paradigms as existing outside history, see Max Horkheimer, *Critical Theory*, *op. cit.*, pp. 195-96. The use of the word "paradigm" may presuppose a parallel structure to natural and social science (a presupposition I do not wish to encourage), but I will use it tentatively for explanatory purposes. Kuhn's notion of paradigms implies that scientific progress is achieved by disregarding prior paradigms rather than by a juxtaposition of the new onto the old. As such, Kuhn's model reflects the ideology of modern "throw-away" consumerism, and its application (particularly in the social sciences) has led to attempts to invalidate theories and experiences of the past rather than to build upon them through critique. See G.W.F. Hegel, *Lectures on the History of Philosophy* (Humanities Press, 1983), Vol. 1, pp. 10, 55, 265.
19. Ralf Dahrendorf, *Class and Class Conflict in Industrial Society* (Stanford, 1959), p. ix.
20. Kenneth Burke, "Dramatism," *Encyclopedia of the Social Sciences* (1968), p. 448.

21. See Max Weber, *The Methodology of the Social Sciences* (Free Press, 1949), especially pp. 164-188.
22. See William Leiss, *The Domination of Nature* (Beacon Press, 1974).
23. Max Horkheimer and T.W. Adorno, *The Dialectic of Enlightenment* (Herder and Herder, 1972), p. 54.
24. Jürgen Habermas, *Knowledge and Human Interests* (Beacon Press, 1971), pp. 32-3. (My emphasis.)
25. Jürgen Habermas, "On Systematically Distorted Communication," *Inquiry*, Vol. 13, p. 207.
26. Jürgen Habermas, "Towards a Theory of Communicative Competence," *Inquiry*, Vol 13, pp. 360-75.
27. Jürgen Habermas, *Toward A Rational Society* (Beacon Press, 1972), p. 88.
28. See Habermas, *Knowledge and Human Interests, op. cit.*, especially pp. 301-317; W. Ten Houten and C. Kaplan, *Science and Its Mirror Image* (Harper and Row, 1973).
29. Herbert Marcuse, *One Dimensional Man, op. cit.*, p. 236.
30. Herbert Marcuse, *An Essay on Liberation, op. cit.*, pp. 7-22.
31. Herbert Marcuse, *Eros and Civilization* (Beacon Press, 1974), p. 216.
32. Also see, Herbert Marcuse, "Obsolescence of the Freudian Concept of Man," in *Five Lectures, op. cit.*, p. 56.
33. Herbert Marcuse, *Reason and Revolution* (Beacon Press, 1960), p. 345.
34. Auguste Comte, *Cours de philosophie positive*, Vol. 4, (Paris, 1908), p. 132. There is still no full English translation of this work.
35. *Ibid.*, Vol. 6, p. 618. I have used the translation in Jürgen Habermas, *Knowlege and Human Interests, op. cit.*, p. 77.
36. *Ibid.*, p. 76.
37. *Ibid.*, p. 77.
38. Quoted from *Aspects of Sociology*, Frankfurt Institute for Social Research (Beacon Press, 1972), p. 4.
39. As defined by Bluntschli's *Deutsche Staats-Worterbuch* (1859), "society" is a "concept of the Third Estate."
40. G. Hegel, *Reason in History* (Liberal Arts Press, 1953), p. 68.
41. Marx and Engels, *The Holy Family* (Progress Publishers, 1975), p. 110. (Emphasis in the original.)
42. Marx, *Capital*, Vol. 1 (International Publishers, 1970), p. 75.
43. Marx, *The Poverty of Philosophy* (International Publishers, 1973), p. 135.
44. Marx, *The Eighteenth Brumaire of Louis Bonaparte* (International Publishers, 1972), p. 15.
45. Marx, *The Poverty of Philosophy, op. cit.*, p. 112.
46. Rosa Luxemburg, *The Accumulation of Capital* (Monthly Review Press, 1968).
47. Marx and Engels, *The German Ideology* (Progress Publishers, 1976), pp. 58-59.
48. Lyford Edwards, *The Natural History of Revolution* (Russell and Russell, 1965), p. 16.
49. Crane Brinton, *The Anatomy of Revolution* (Vintage Books, 1965), p. 16.

50. Talcott Parsons, *The Structure of Social Action* (Free Press, 1949). Also see "Talcott Parsons and the Phenomenological Tradition in Sociology: An Unresolved Debate," by Bennetta Jules-Rosette, *Human Studies*, 3 (1980), pp. 311-330.

51. Parsons, *op. cit.*, p. 43.

52. T. Parsons, *The Social System* (Free Press, 1951), p. 262.

53. C. Wright Mills, *The Sociological Imagination* (Oxford University Press, 1959), pp. 42-3.

54. Emile Durkheim, *The Division of Labor* (Free Press, 1964), p. 13; T. Parsons, "Society," in *Encyclopedia of the Social Sciences*, Vol. XLV, pp. 225, 231.

55. Herbert Blumer, "Collective Behavior," in *New Outline of the Principles of Sociology*, ed., A.M. Lee (Barnes and Noble, 1951), p. 171.

56. *Ibid.*, p. 181.

57. Alvin Gouldner, *The Coming Crisis of Western Sociology* (Basic Books, 1970), pp. 342-343.

58. *Ibid.*, p. 344.

59. T. Parsons and N. Smelser, *Economy and Society* (Free Press, 1956), p. 312.

60. T. Parsons, *Politics and Social Structure* (Free Press, 1969), p. xv and p. 395.

61. *Ibid.*, p. 312.

62. Leon Bramson, *The Political Context of Sociology* (Princeton University Press, 1961), p. 58. Actually there was at least one: Jerome Davis, *Contemporary Social Movements* (Century, 1930).

63. Ralph H. Turner and Lewis M. Killian, *Collective Behavior* (Prentice Hall, 1957).

64. Gary Marx and James Wood, "Strands of Theory and Research in Collective Behavior," *Annual Review of Sociology*, 1975.

65. Alvin Gouldner, *op. cit.*, p. 347.

66. N. Smelser, *Essays in Sociological Explanation* (Prentice Hall, 1968), p. 278.

67. N. Smelser, *Theory of Collective Behavior* (Free Press, 1962), p. 72.

68. *Ibid.*, p. 73.

69. *Ibid.*, p. 8.

70. Ralph H. Turner, "Collective Behavior," in *Handbook of Modern Sociology*, R.E.L. Faris (ed.), (Chicago, 1964), pp. 382-455.

71. Mayer N. Zald and Roberta Ash, "Social Movement Organizations: Growth, Decay, and Change," *Social Forces*, No. 44.

72. Joseph Gusfield, "The Study of Social Movements," *International Encyclopedia of the Social Sciences*, Vol. 14, (1968), p. 445.

73. L. Zurcher and R.G. Kirkpatrick, *Citizens for Decency* (Texas, 1976).

74. Roger Brown, *Social Psychology* (Free Press, 1965).

75. G. Lindzey and E. Aronson (eds.), *Handbook of Social Psychology* (Addison-Wesley, 1968).

76. R. Evans (ed.), *Readings in Collective Behavior* (Chicago, 1969).

77. James Wood, *The Sources of American Student Activism* (D.C. Heath, 1974).

78.   Chalmers Johnson, *Revolutionary Change* (Boston, 1966).

79.   Ted Gurr, *Why Men Rebel* (Princeton University Press, 1970).

80.   Anthony Oberschall, *Social Conflict and Social Movements* (Prentice Hall, 1973); Charles Tilly, *From Mobilization to Revolution* (Addison-Wesley, 1978).

81.   John D. McCarthy and Mayer N. Zald, "The Trend of Social Movements in America: Professionalization and Resource Mobilization," (General Learning Press, 1973).

82.   Joseph Gusfield, *Symbolic Crusade* (Illinois, 1966).

83.   William Kornhauser, *The Politics of Mass Society* (Free Press, 1959); Theda Skocpol, *States and Social Revolutions* (Cambridge University Press, 1979). "Mass society" theory differs from world systems theory, but in terms of social revolutions, each theory seems capable only of conceiving of the transfer of power between elites, not of the fundamental transformation of social structures. Skocpol hints at such a possibility at the very end of her book (p. 293), but, in general, her analysis is based on a statist model.

84.   Roberta Ash Garner, *Social Movements in America* (Rand McNally, 1977); Eric Hobsbawm, *Primitive Rebels* (Manchester, 1959) and *Revolutionaries* (New American Library, 1973); George Rudé, *Ideology and Popular Protest* (Pantheon, 1980).

85.   Antonio Gramsci, *Prison Notebooks* (International Publishers, 1975), pp. 428-9.

86.   Paul Lazarsfeld, "Remarks on Administrative and Critical Communications Research," *Studies in Philosophy and Social Science*, Vol. IX, New York, 1941.

87.   Emile Durkheim, *The Rules of Sociological Method* (Free Press, 1964), p. 14. The second chapter begins: "The first and most fundamental rule is: *"Consider social facts as things."*

88.   Niccolo Machiavelli, *The Prince* (Mentor Books, 1952), p. 84. (My emphasis.)

89.   See Weber, *The Methodology of the Social Sciences, op. cit.* For an intense and interesting exchange on Weber, see Otto Stammer (ed.), *Max Weber and Sociology Today* (Harper and Row, 1972). For discussion of the modern misinterpretation of Weber, see Herbert Gamberg, "Science and Scientism: The State of Sociology," *The American Sociologist* (May 1969), p. 115.

90.   Pitrim A. Sorokin, *The Sociology of Revolution* (J.P. Lippincott, 1925), p. 11.

91.   Gustav Le Bon, *The Crowd* (Viking Press, 1965), p. 3.

92.   *Max Weber and Sociology Today, op. cit.*, p. 138.

93.   The unity of theory and practice is clear here since Pool's theory must also obliterate the human construction of facticity. Methodologically, the positivistic construction of a fact based on numerical measure relies on the judgement of the human being who assigns the number to reality (the coders). This problematic is resolved by Ithiel De Sola Pool through the invention of the "human computer"—that is, by superimposing the qualities of a machine onto the researcher. The inter-

changeability of coders is assumed (in much the same way that instruments of mass production use spare parts), and the meaning of the numbers are assumed to be self-evident according to common sense. Ithiel De Sola Pool, *Trends in Content Analysis* (Illinois, 1959). For a further critique, see Aaron Cicourel, *Method and Measurement in Sociology* (Free Press, 1964).

94. Max Horkheimer, *Eclipse of Reason* (Herder and Herder, 1971), p. 91.
95. *Ibid.*, p. 75.
96. Jürgen Habermas, "Technology and Science as 'Ideology'," in *Toward a Rational Society, op. cit.*, pp. 81-122.
97. Herbert Marcuse, *One Dimensional Man, op. cit.*, p. 156.
98. Jay W. Forrester, *Industrial Dynamics* (M.I.T. Press, 1961), p. 5.
99. *Ibid.*, p. 1.
100. *Ibid.*, p. 17.
101. Hartmut Bossel, Salomon Klaczko, and Norbert Müller (eds.), *Systems Theory in the Social Sciences* (Birkhäuser Verlag, 1976), p. 14. Interestingly, during the 1950s without knowledge of each other, Bellman in the USA and Pontryagin in the USSR each developed versions of dynamic programming which have been important breakthroughs for the development of systems theory.
102. *Ibid.*
103. Forrester, *op. cit.*, p. 14.
104. See Hans Peter Dreitzel, "Social Science and the Problem of Rationality: Notes on the Sociology of Technocrats," *Politics and Society* (Winter 1972), p. 175.
105. Donella Meadows, Dennis Meadows, Jørgen Randers and William Behrens, *The Limits to Growth* (Signet, 1972), p. 175.
106. *Ibid.*, pp. 133, 144, 163.
107. *Ibid.*, pp. 173-4 and 178-9.
108. *Ibid.*, pp. 29, 179.
109. *Ibid.*, pp. 38, 148, 155-156, 159, 191, 195.
110. *Ibid.*, p. 28. (My emphasis.)
111. *Ibid.*, p. 55.
112. *Ibid.*, p. 61. That is a conservative and outdated estimate. In 1980 alone, 30 million children under the age of 5 died from malnutrition. See L.S. Starvrianos, "A 10,000 Year Quest for Justice," *Los Angeles Times* (Februrary 27, 1983), p. BR3.
113. *Ibid.*, pp. 50, 183.
114. *Ibid.*, p. 75.
115. *Ibid.*, p. 93.
116. *Ibid.*, p. 192.
117. Examples of such a vision can be found in L. S. Stavrianos's *The Promise of the Coming Dark Age* (W. H. Freeman and Co., 1967) and Paul and Percival Goodman, *Communitas: Ways of Livelihood and Means of Life* (Vintage, 1960).
118. T. R. Young, "A Critique of Systems Theory," Colorado State University, 1975.

119. Jürgen Habermas, *Legitimation Crisis, op. cit.*, p. 123.
120. C. Wright Mills, *The Sociological Imagination, op. cit.*, p. 171.
121. Herbert Marcuse, "On Science and Phenomenology," in *Positivism and Sociology*, A. Giddens (ed.), (Heinemann, 1974), p. 237.
122. N. Luhmann, "Komplexität und Democratie," p. 319 in *Politische Vierteljahreschrift* (1968); translation in Habermas, *Legitimation Crisis, op. cit.*, pp. 132-42.
123. Jürgen Habermas, *Knowledge and Human Interests, op. cit.*, especially pp. 301-317.
124. Jürgen Habermas, *Theory and Practice, op. cit.*, pp. 12-13. Habermas concerns himself with intersubjectivity in "Towards a Theory of Communicative Competence," *Inquiry* 13, pp. 360-75 and "On Systematically Distorted Communication," *Inquiry* 13, pp. 205-18.
125. T. W. Adorno, *Negative Dialectics* (Seabury, 1973), p. 24.
126. Kant's system was as abstract as Forrester's, as mathematically "elegant," but it was not one in which judgement was "mathematized." In his critique of Kant, Hegel conceived the role of dialectical thought as a way to "strip mathematics of this artificial finery, and to bring out its limitations, and thence show the necessity of another type of knowledge." *The Phenomenology of Mind* (Colophon Books, 1967), p. 104, as quoted in Rick Nadeau, "Critical Theory and the Critique of Instrumental Reason," (University of California, San Diego, unpublished essay, 1975).
127. Herbert Marcuse, *Reason and Revolution, op. cit.*, p. 144. Also see Jürgen Habermas, "The Analytical Theory of Science and Dialectics," in *The Positivist Dispute in German Sociology* (Heinemann, 1976), p. 132.
128. Jürgen Habermas, *Legitimation Crisis, op. cit.*, p. 42.
129. H. Lefebvre, *Dialectical Materialism* (Grossman Publishers, 1968).
130. Marx, *Critique of Political Economy* (Charles Kerr, 1904), pp. 10-13.
131. Marx, *Grundrisse* (Vintage Books, 1973), p. 272.
132. Herbert Marcuse, *Soviet Marxism* (Vintage Books, 1961), pp. 122-23.
133. Herbert Marcuse, *Negations, op. cit.*, p. 144.
134. Louis Althusser, *For Marx* (Vintage Books, 1970), p. 34.
135. *Ibid.*, p. 223.
136. Louis Althusser, *Lenin and Philosophy* (Monthly Review, 1971), p. 18.
137. Louis Althusser and G. Balibar, *Reading Capital* (New Left Books, 1972), p. 133.
138. Althusser, *For Marx, op. cit.*, pp. 231-2, my emphasis.
139. Althusser and Balibar, *Reading Capital, op. cit.*, p. 122.

BIBLIOGRAPHICAL ENDNOTE

Documentation of the material in this book is drawn from both primary and secondary sources in English, Spanish, French, and German. As often as possible, the sources are given in English to provide for further investigation of areas of interest. Although almost all of it is out-of-print, the literature on the New Left is so vast that a comprehensive bibliography would require an entire book. Those who would like to read only one or two other books on the New Left should consider:

* Herbert Marcuse, *Counterrevolution and Revolt* (Beacon Press, 1972). I consider this short book to be the best political analysis of the movement and the most philosophical—and hence, relevant—statement of its future prospects.
* Judith Clavir-Albert and Stewart Albert, *The Sixties Papers* (Praeger, 1984). More recently published, this anthology consists of well selected documents of the movement.
* Sohnya Sayres, Anders Stephanson, Stanley Aronowitz, Frederic Jameson, *60s Without Apology* (University of Minnesota Press, 1984). This anthology contains a number of insightful essays covering political and cultural questions related to the New Left.
* Nancy Zaroulis and Gerald Sullivan, *Who Spoke Up? American Protests Against the War in Vietnam 1963-1975* (Henry Holt, 1985). This book is a comprehensive history of the anti-Vietnam War movement in the United States.
* Greg Calvert and Carol Nieman, *The New Left: A Disrupted History* (Random House, 1971). Although long out-of-print, this book remains a readable and enjoyable synopsis of the movement's development and interruption.
* Clayborn Carson, *In Struggle: SNCC and the Black Awakening of the 1960s* (Harvard University Press, 1981). Extremely well written, this book offers a balanced discussion of the internal life of the student civil rights movement.

Among the many books dealing with revolutionary social movements and the prospects for fundamental change in the United States, I would especially recommend:

* James and Grace Lee Boggs, *Revolution and Evolution in the Twentieth Century* (Monthly Review Press, 1976).

Finally, there are two carefully crafted and current books on the Rainbow and Green visions for the United States:

* Sheila Collins, *The Rainbow Challenge* (Monthly Review Press, 1986).
* Brian Tokar, *The Green Alternative: Creating an Ecological Future* (R. Miles, 1987).

INDEX

312 IMAGINATION OF THE NEW LEFT

critical theory, 220-21, 228-30,
252-6
Crozier, Michel, 114
Cruse, Harold, 198
Cuba, 14, 20-21, 27, 35-7, 40, 47,
159, 161, 179, 183, 209, 212
Venceremos Brigades, 21, 159
cultural conformity, 19, 197-8
cultural imperialism, 24
cultural poverty, 98-102, 215
cultural revolution, 23-5, 35-7, 42-
3, 77, 140, 142-50, 181, 193-8
in Arab world, 35
as a global process, 82
Cultural Revolution (China), 57,
70-1
Czar, 14-16
Czechoslovakia, 24, 25, 41, 44, 59-
64, 67, 181

Dada, 100-1
Dahrendorf, Ralf, 226-7
Darwin, Charles, 251
Davis, Angela, 144
Debray, Régis, 36, 114
Debs, Eugene, 187
Declaration of Independence (United States), 29
de-industrialization, 165-9
Deir Yassin, 191
democracy, 23-5, 62, 67, 69, 70,
230-1
contraction of, 160, 164, 248
European and U.S. forms of,
186-8
extension of, 23-5, 70, 182, 193
increasing irrelevance of in U.S.
165-73
Democratic Party (U.S.), 4, 80,
125, 186-7, 190, 209-11
depoliticization, 161, 177, 185-93,
195-7
Detroit, 74-5, 138
"dictatorship of the proletariat," 18,
23
Diggers, 142, 146
direct actions, 27
limits of, 204

disarmament movement, 169-71,
183-5, 189-92
co-optation of, 190
Disneyland, ban on hippies, 148
divine right, 9, 230
division of labor, 17, 93, 95, 106,
234
dogmatism, 19, 198, 200, 204-6,
243
Double Helix, 17
draft resistance, 122
dual power, 102, 127-8, 181, 205
Dubček, Alexander, 60-1
Durkheim, Emile, 236-7, 241
Dutschke, Rudi, 51-2, 78, 180
Duvalier, Jean-Claude, 27, 217

Eastern Europe, 19, 29, 59-70
East Village, 42, 142
ecology, 108, 114, 132, 208-12,
214-5, 231, 245-7
economic determinism, 23, 197
Ecuador, 40, 45, 48
Edwards, Lyford, 234
Egypt, 14, 43
Eisenhower, Dwight, 40, 57, 166
El Salvador, 157, 161, 183, 212,
215
empiricism, 229, 239-41, 243-4,
250
"end of ideology," 5, 87, 230
Engels, Frederick, 23, 250-2, 255
enragés, 69-70
Environmental Protection Agency,
171-2
epistemology, 240, 249, 250
"epistemological rupture," 254,
255
Equal Rights Amendment, 150,
185, 189, 192-3, 209
Eritrea, 35, 212
Eros and Civilization, 229
eros effect, 3, 7, 10-11, 27, 33, 35,
42, 59, 64, 71, 73, 75, 117, 120,
123, 134, 139, 217, 220-1, 230,
240
Essay on Liberation, 223
Ethiopia, 40, 44, 157